PROMOTION

Persuasive communication
in marketing

PROMOTION

Persuasive communication in marketing

ROLLIE TILLMAN, D.B.A.

and

C. A. KIRKPATRICK, D.C.S.

Both of the
Graduate School of Business Administration
The University of North Carolina

1972 · Revised Edition
RICHARD D. IRWIN, INC., Homewood, Illinois 60430
Irwin-Dorsey Limited, Georgetown, Ontario.

© RICHARD D. IRWIN, INC., 1968 and 1972

Revised edition

First printing, February, 1972

Library of Congress Catalog No. 75–176052

Printed in the United States of America

Preface

Since the first edition of this book was published, forces in both the business and social sectors of the economy have moved to heighten interest in what has always been an intriguing and exciting sphere of communications: promotion. Cycles in the economy have brought managements face-to-face with problems of being more efficient in the promotion of their products to uncertain or unstable markets. The growth of consumer concern over products, promises, pollution, and practices of promoters has occurred at the same time.

In the preface to the first edition the authors acknowledged their most vexing problem as the choice of what to include and what to exclude in a one-volume treatment of promotion management. The choices for this edition were no less a chore. There is, at virtually every paragraph, the temptation to delve deeper, recite research, and explore illustrations of the point at hand. Yet we have to be constrained, because this is an introductory overview of these fields, and balanced treatment is our goal. The book presumes that to this overview the interested reader will add reading in depth on topics of his choosing.

This edition, like the first, opens with an introduction of the promotion topic as a component of the marketing strategy of a firm. For students who have had a beginning marketing course the first chapter is review, for those coming to the book from other backgrounds the chapter serves to set the stage for a realistic look at the role of promotion in the total marketing effort of the firm.

Part II attempts to provide a behavioral foundation for the promotion processes that are to be examined in succeeding parts of the book. In the three chapters of this part, we will explore some concepts from behavioral sciences as they relate to buyer behavior and to the communication process. This is an area of rapid growth in literature and development, and here the temptation to explore byways was particularly acute. We have kept the original thrust, however, believing that one approach well understood is better than a cafeteria of confusing and sometimes contradictory models to the buyer behavior process.

The next four parts of the book have to do with various elements of persuasion available to management. In this edition a whole new two-chapter element on public relations and publicity is added to the format of the first edition. Part III is the first of this major portion of the book, and focuses on personal selling as a persuasive force to be managed.

In Part IV we include three chapters on advertising. The first covers some of the types of advertising and the nature of the element. Chapter 8 examines major advertising media and contrasts features and benefits of each. Chapter 9 raises some questions about the management of advertising and the role of specialists and agencies.

Part V is a two-chapter sequence on sales promotion and is a part of this book for which there are no handy counterparts in other textual sources. We hope that it contributes to the reader's understanding by pulling together a wide assortment of stimulation alternatives into a two-chapter package that will itself stimulate further reading and study in the trade journals and business press.

Reflecting increased concern for the total communication mix of the firm, Part VI is new to this edition, and offers a two-chapter treatment of topics in public relations, publicity, and institutional advertising. Given the warnings in Chapter 4 of the multiple-channel communication process, these topics are a real and continuing challenge to promotion management.

The final part of the book has been expanded to give greater attention to the planning and management processes of these fields. Chapter 14 discusses the goal setting and strategy design phase of management, while Chapter 15 covers the planning of promotion programs. In Chapter 16 the plans are made both time- and dollar-specific through scheduling and budgeting. Finally, Chapter 17 reviews the problems and opportunities to evaluate and control the promotion programs of the firm.

Too many individuals and agencies, within both the business community and the academic community, have contributed to our work to mention individual names. We are nonetheless grateful to all of them for their gracious cooperation and thoughtful contributions to this revision.

January, 1972   ROLLIE TILLMAN, JR.
                                                        C. A. KIRKPATRICK

Contents

steps to a sale. Relation of appeals to motivation. Product features versus buyer benefits. Basic versus acquired wants. Emotional versus rational appeals. Positive versus negative appeals. How many benefits should an ad include? Suggestions about appeals. Layout: *Visualization versus layout. Weight. Optical center. Features of good layout.* Illustrations. Color. Copy: *Copy goals. Copy format or pattern. Headlines. Body copy or text. Copy length. Copy suggestions.* Typography: *Type faces. Type families. Type groups. Selection of type faces. Suggestions about typography.* Some social and economic considerations: *Some social questions. Some economic questions.*

PART V.   ELEMENTS OF PERSUASION: SALES PROMOTION

Institutional advertising: *What. Patronage advertising. Public relations advertising. Public service advertising.*

PART VII.   MANAGEMENT OF THE PROMOTION PROGRAM

PART **I**

INTRODUCTION TO PROMOTION

CHAPTER 1

The role of promotion
in marketing

ACCORDING TO the American Marketing Association's official definition, marketing is "the performance of business activities that direct the flow of goods and services from producer to consumer or user."[1] The critical items in this definition are "business activities" and "consumer or user." Since the authors believe that marketing—and indeed all management— must be consumer oriented, let us first consider the customers in the world of marketing.

TARGETS OF THE MARKETING EFFORT

Our marketing definition points *from producer to consumer or user.* Marketing effort is not spent recklessly in all directions; rather it is *aimed* at customers, at targets. All people are not suitable targets; age, sex, and social or economic status may keep some from being prospects for our product.

We can divide the total mass of consumers into three broad groups, as Figure 1–1 suggests. In the first, and often the largest, group are the nonusers of our product. Most of these people are not targets of any of our marketing effort. Some are too young; some are too old; some are too poor; some are too far away geographically. The use of the

---

[1] *Report of the Committee on Definitions* (Chicago, American Marketing Association, 1961).

FIGURE 1–1.   Defining target markets

GROUP I NONUSERS	GROUP II PROSPECTS	GROUP III USERS: (A) OUR BRAND (B) OTHER BRANDS

phrase *target customers* suggests that we have some criteria for defining who is and who is not likely to be a customer. The definition of these criteria by a marketing person is based on data from sales and market research which seeks to distinguish the differing characteristics of users and nonusers. The dividing line in Figure 1–1 between Nonusers and Prospects is based upon the application of those criteria.

For instance: A manufacturer of high-quality electric shavers might consider age, sex, and income as major criteria on which to evaluate people. Into Group I he would place preadolescent men, women, and lower-income families. His "prospect pool," or Group II, would consist of all males 14 or older in families of middle income or above.

The second group, Prospects, consists of those customers who meet the specifications of target customers. They qualify on the basis of whatever criteria we establish. They represent the *potential* customers. High on most lists of criteria is money; some disposable income is prerequisite to the purchase of most products. The other criteria must be established in the light of the particular product being marketed.

The third group, Users, represents the active current market for the product class. Some of the customers (III–A) buy our brand, others (III–B) do not. Both the buyers of our brand and those of competitors' brands are targets of marketing effort. We must encourage the first group to stay loyal to the brand and use more of it; we must persuade the others to switch to our brand.

The targets of marketing efforts are most likely to be the consumers in Group II (Prospects) and Group III (Users). Growth in sales for a firm can come from:

1. Increasing the size of the prospect pool.
2. Persuading prospects to become users of our brand.
3. Persuading users of other brands to switch to ours.
4. Persuading our users to use more of our product.

Marketing managers may decide to develop products with characteristics that will bring more people into the prospect pool. The design of a lower-cost "economy" model may allow many nonusers to be reclassified as prospects. The addition of a credit or installment plan might have a similar impact. A branch store location may overcome geographic barriers. A shaver manufacturer may bring out a light, stylish, "ladies model." A mail-order service may expand a retailer's prospect pool.

Just because customers meet the qualifications to become users of our type of product or our brand does not mean that they will do so. There are many other *kinds* of products competing for their scarce dollars. Thus new carpeting may compete with television sets or clothing or any of a number of other types of products. Marketing management is always alert for ways to persuade prospects to become users of its products. This is a particularly important role assigned to promotion.

Still another means of increasing sales is the active conversion of users of other brands to the purchase of, and continued loyalty to, our brand. Take chewing gum as an example. The only real criteria for classifying a consumer as a prospect rather than as a nonuser are: (*a*) teeth, (*b*) 10 cents, and (*c*) access to a store that sells it. The market battle here is on the two remaining fronts: making users out of prospects and converting competitors' customers to our brand. And because so many people are already in the user category, getting them to switch brands is an attractive strategy.

Finally, the firm may focus on the users of its brand with the aim of increasing their consumption of the product. The makers of Dr. Pepper soft drinks urge you to consume the product "at 10, 2, and 4" rather than just once a day. Persuading people to drink orange juice every day instead of occasionally is the goal of the Florida Citrus Commission's slogan "Make sure they get all the Vitamin C they need *every day*." The makers of Reynolds Wrap aluminum foil provide customers with a booklet describing decorating ideas as well as the usual kitchen uses of the wrap.

In using this last strategy, the firm focuses on heavy as opposed to light users of its products. Studies of users suggest that heavy users are a small proportion of customers but account for a majority of sales of many products.[2]

Three ingredients of a market

Another definition of marketing is "the creation and satisfaction of a market for a good or service." The word *market*, like so many English

---

[2] See Dik Warren Twedt, "How Important to Marketing Strategy Is the Heavy User?" *Journal of Marketing*, January, 1964, p. 72.

FIGURE 1–2a.   This ad is aimed at stimulating primary demand for picture taking

FIGURE 1–2b. This ad seeks to stimulate selective demand for a specific Kodak product

AUTO MATIC EST

If you appreciate a fine piece of equipment, you'll go for the new Kodak Instamatic® X-90 camera. It's the most automatic automatic of them all.

Just drop in the film cartridge. The X-90 automatically advances the film to frame #1, and to the next frame after each picture. Aim at a subject—the electric eye automatically computes and sets the exposure. Flash exposure is set automatically as you focus. Signals in the viewfinder light up automatically when you need to use flash, or when you need to change the magicube (the new flash that doesn't need flash batteries).

See the Kodak Instamatic X-90 camera at your photo dealer's. With fast f/2.8 Ektar lens, it's less than $145. You'll agree, it's the Automatic-est.

KODAK MAKES YOUR PICTURES COUNT.

Kodak

Price subject to change without notice.

words, has a variety of meanings. It may refer to a specific place, as the "Chicago Board of Trade," or the "Lincoln County Farmer's Market." Market can also mean a geographical area, like the "New York City market," or the "Common Market" of Western Europe. Still another denotation is that of the general price level for a product class, as "the used car market," or "the bond market." All three meanings are useful in their respective contexts. In the context of marketing management, and especially for promotion management, yet another definition is helpful. *A market consists of persons who have money and who are or can be motivated to buy our type of product.*

All three ingredients must be present: (1) individuals, (2) money, and (3) motivation. If people alone were enough, then we would expect to find the densely populated areas of Asia the chief markets of the world. Nor is the combination of people and money enough. While some might argue that people with money will always have motivation to spend it—and studies of consumption patterns would tend to bear this out—there are so many ways to spend money that we must persuade people to be motivated to spend it for *our type of product.* If we are concerned with industrial marketing, the same three ingredients are necessary. In that case *firms* (instead of persons) with money and motivation are essential to marketing success.

Primary and selective demand.   Both the "nonuser, prospect, user" approach to classifying buyers and the "persons, money, and motivation" approach suggest that there are two levels of demand. *Primary demand* is the demand for the products of *our* entire industry rather than *some other* industry—for clothing instead of carpets. *Selective demand* is directed toward a company or brand within one industry. If the consumer in the prospect pool decided on clothing instead of carpets, then selective demand refers to the customer's preference for clothing brand X over clothing brand Y. For instance:

When electric shavers first made their appearance, the whole concept of quick, dry shaving had to be sold. Once men started shifting away from blade-and-soap to the new electric shavers, specific brands had to be promoted. Deciding to shift from blade to electricity is a buildup in *primary demand*, while selecting Brand Z is the exercise of *selective demand.*

A combined view.   The two approaches to markets which we have been discussing are combined in Figure 1–3. Along the top of the figure we find our People-Money-Motivation trio. Now it is true that there

FIGURE 1–3. A combined view of markets

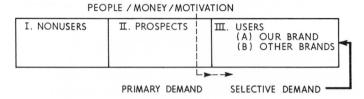

are often criteria other than money which move people from I (Nonuser) to II (Prospect). Just what these other factors are would vary with the product: age and sex for cosmetics, weddings for honeymoon cottages, education for books. But for *all* products money is a necessary qualifying condition to a greater or lesser degree.

Because prospects can spend their funds for other kinds of goods and services, motivation begins in sector II of the chart as primary demand is developed. With this developed they become classified as users, and they select either our brand or a competitor's.

Other customer classifications

There are other ways to examine the "market" portion of the phrase "marketing management." One of the more useful is the breakdown of all customers into two broad categories: ultimate consumers and intermediate consumers. *Ultimate consumers,* or final consumers as they are sometimes labeled, are those buyers who buy for their own personal consumption or for the consumption of their family or friends. This group is the great mass of buyers who purchase in retail stores, through mail-order services, or from salesmen calling door-to-door. Marketing managers often find it convenient to study these buyers in groups of *family purchasing units.* The reason for this grouping is that purchase patterns often vary according to the total *family* income, the number and ages of children in the *family*, the occupation of the head of the *household*, and the housing characteristics of the *family*. The housewife is considered a prime target for these units because of her role in many families as purchaser of food and clothing products.

Intermediate consumers, or business buyers, purchase products in order to carry on their respective businesses. They buy in order to produce, resell, or service ultimate consumers. There may be more than one intermediate consumer before the ultimate consumer is reached. For instance, steel may be sold as a raw material to a producer of electric motors.

The motor manufacturer may sell his motors to an air conditioner manufacturer who considers the motors as a component part. The finished air conditioners may be sold to wholesalers, who sell in turn to retailers. Thus before the ultimate consumer goes into the retail store, the steel that went into the motor has been sold and resold four times in various forms to intermediate buyers. Manufacturers, wholesalers, retailers, hospitals, prisons, schools, and other institutions (including all divisions of government) comprise this important category of the market.

Creative business activities

Until now we have considered only half of our definitions of "marketing." We have looked at markets and the target consumers who comprise them. This customer-first orientation was deliberate, because in marketing a study of consumers should always come first. But according to the first part of the definition with which we began this chapter, marketing is the *performance of business activities*. The second definition, the one with which we prefaced our discussion of market ingredients, suggested that these activities *create and satisfy* markets. What are these creative business activities?

Some of the business activities have been suggested in our previous discussion of target consumers and markets. For instance:

♦   We noted that a new version of a *product* can often bring people into the prospect pool from the nonuser category.

♦   A similar effect may result from a change in the *price* of the existing product or (in the case of an installment credit plan) in the manner in which the price is collected.

♦   In addition, if a product is made available at a more convenient *place*, new prospects may be attracted to it. While money often separates nonusers from prospects, geographical distance can have the same impact.

♦   Finally, any improvement in an offering to consumers must be communicated persuasively to them if motivation is to be built and sustained. *Promotion* is a pertinent business activity and of most value to a firm when it is persuasive communication.

These examples help illustrate the range of business activities that are associated with marketing management. They suggest that the marketing manager makes decisions about four major matters: about products, about prices, about the distribution of the products, and about the proper promotion of those products. To make decisions in these areas, the marketing manager must know who the targets of the marketing effort are, what characteristics separate nonusers from users, or users of our brand from users of competing brands. In short, he makes customer-oriented decisions based on a thorough knowledge of his markets.

THE MARKETING MIX: DECISIONS

Taken together, the sum of the decisions a firm makes in these areas has been called its *marketing mix*. What every marketing manager tries to do is create the most effective marketing mix he can. An effective mix is one that satisfies customers at a profit to the firm. A review of the marketing mix, with a look at some of the ingredients, will provide a useful background to our study of one of the major areas of marketing mix decisions.

Decisions about products

If marketing is to direct the flow of goods from producer to consumer, then marketing management must be intensely involved in all decisions as to *what* goods are produced. The old, production-oriented companies may have viewed the role of marketing as that of merely selling whatever the workers produced. Modern, marketing-oriented companies know that only the customer oriented survive and thrive. Recent experience with the consumerism movement to police the quality of products and the integrity of marketing claims has brought this fact vividly to the attention of business executives. The critical questions today lie not in the "Can we make it?" sphere, but rather in the "Should we make it?" and "Will customers buy it?" sphere. Four of the major types of decisions about products will be mentioned briefly.

Product design. Although the basic idea or concept of a product may begin in the research laboratory or on an engineering drawing board, the design of the specific product to be offered requires advice and direction from the marketing staff. Often marketing management discovers the basic idea or concept. The marketing research department of a firm may uncover needed products, or it may test out ideas on consumers to see how acceptable proposed new products are. Analysis of customer complaints about present products may lead to design modification on subsequent models.

In the area of product design are decisions related to the number of models and sizes of products, the matching of product design and quality to market needs for luxury or economy products, and the expected useful life to be built into the product.

Pressure from organized groups of consumers to modify product design or function may stimulate change.

Packaging. As more products are distributed through self-service outlets to consumers, the marketing implications of package decisions increase. Customers like packages which are convenient to open and use and easy to close and store if the contents of the package are not consumed at one time. Retailers and other middlemen like packages which are easy to stack in the warehouse or store. Above all other considerations, of course, the package must protect the product. The design of the package must take into account its need to be attractive, eye-catching, distinctive, yet economical.

Branding. Associated with decisions about product design and packaging are the choices management makes about brand names for its products. The need for a name to apply to several products must often be considered. A good brand name is an important asset to the firm and a cornerstone of the promotional programs. We have noted that in many areas of the market the battle is for *selective demand*, and a powerful weapon in that battle is an attractive, easy-to-remember brand name that is both pleasing and suggestive of product benefits.

Product services. A final example of product decisions is the whole matter of services to be offered customers. Many products require expert installation and repair services. Others require the availability of accessory equipment to modify the major product. An example of this is interchangeable type keys for typewriters to adapt the machine to the special needs of foreign language or mathematical typing. Delivery, credit, and education and training in the product's use, are other possible service ingredients in a marketing mix.

Decisions about distribution and place

The second major category of business activities in marketing is the management of the physical distribution of products from producers to consumers. Decisions in this area must take into account consumer buying habits, shifts in population that change the face of the market, and the institutional facilities available to carry out the distribution plan. The *manufacturer* of a product must create a channel of distribution to transfer efficiently his wares from the place of production to the place where customers need them. The *retailer* must make two major kinds of place

FIGURE 1–4. The idea of product development in one division is turned to institutional advantage for the parent corporation

When a product is this good...

you can't keep it a secret

A new concept in hair care—Breck Basic® Texturizer —was introduced with women in mind. But now men across the country are finding it works wonders for the male side of the family, too—improving hair texture, giving it more body and manageability.

And why not? John H. Breck, Inc.—a Cyanamid subsidiary—makes a science out of hair care. To develop Breck Basic they called upon the expertise of their own and other scientists in the Cyanamid family.

One of the things we do well at Cyanamid is to trade ideas and scientific advances throughout our twelve research and development laboratories.

It helps keep Cyanamid growing in many directions to meet human needs in food production, health, building materials, fibers, consumer goods and in chemicals used by other industries.

CYANAMID
AMERICAN CYANAMID COMPANY
WAYNE, NEW JERSEY

decisions, one related to the location of his store or stores, the other related to the placement or arrangement of products within the store. Our discussion of this second area of marketing decisions will consider briefly some issues and decisions each of these two marketing organizations, manufacturers and retailers, must consider.

Manufacturer distribution management. The producer of goods faces several alternative solutions to his distribution problem. He can sell direct to consumers, as the makers of Fuller brushes and Avon cosmetics choose to do. He can sell direct to retailers, as many clothing and furniture manufacturers typically do. He may even operate his own retail stores, as the Singer Sewing Machine Company or the Firestone Tire Company do. He may make and sell his goods to wholesalers, who in turn will sell to retailers. Finally, he may employ an agent such as a broker to sell to wholesalers and retailers. Quite probably he will decide to use more than one of these alternatives, as market conditions indicate. For large chain stores, he may arrange to sell direct, while reaching smaller stores through wholesalers. The goal of distribution management is to have the products available *where* they are wanted and *when* they are wanted and to accomplish this in the most efficient manner.

Coupled with these decisions about distribution channels are the choices related to the degree of market exposure a product needs. Some products are purchased frequently, are relatively low in price, and are not worth much shopping effort by customers. These goods, called *convenience* goods, will have to have widespread and intensive exposure or distribution. Other products cost more, are purchased less frequently, involve more risk to the buyer, and are thus able to command a greater shopping effort. These *shopping* goods may need less intensive exposure and can be distributed selectively or even exclusively. A general rule is this: the less willing customers are to shop for a product, the more willing manufacturers must be to make it conveniently available; conversely, the more willing buyers are to spend shopping time and effort for the product, the less market exposure is needed.

What other factors affect the manufacturer's choice? One is the nature of the market for his product. If his target market is large and concentrated in a geographic area, he may deal directly with customers; if it is widely dispersed, he may need to employ middlemen to help achieve the distribution his customers require. The nature of the product is another factor in his decisions about place and distribution. Expensive and complex machinery which requires technical service and advice may dictate direct sales to customers. Perishable commodities such as flowers, bread, or milk may need to be sold either to customers or at least direct to retailers to cut down the time from producer to consumer. Availability of middlemen to do the job is another consideration. They may not be available in the areas he wishes to market, or the middlemen in the market may be committed to competing brands and cannot take on another brand in the same product category. The size of the manufacturer's company and its product lines is still another consideration. A small producer of one product with a nationwide pool of prospects will need the help of middlemen; a larger producer of a variety of products may be able to spread the costs of direct distribution over his many products. Finally, the preferences and traditions of customers may dictate distribution channels. Industrial buyers often prefer dealing directly with the manufacturer, as do large chain retailing organizations.

Indeed, the growth of large-scale buying power by chains at "super stores" means that for many products it is the *retailer* who controls the channel of distribution. Buyers for these chains can, and do, write their own product specifications and find sources of supply to manufacture the goods on a private label basis for the chain.

Retailer place decisions. If we shift our focus to a retailing firm, we find that it, too, has to make decisions in each of these areas of marketing management. The place or location of the retail store is an obvious and important decision. In large companies, decisions have to be made about the location of branch stores to serve outlying markets. Banks, advertising agencies, accounting firms, and other service organizations face similar decisions. Within the retail store unit, however, another order of distribution decisions must be made. Arrangement of store layout and merchandise is a problem to be resolved.

Decisions about promotion

In the light of his knowledge of customers and according to the goals he has defined for his marketing efforts, the marketing executive must make decisions about the promotion of his firm's products or services. No matter how good the mousetrap, the modern businessman knows that the world will not beat a path to his door without the stimulation that promotion provides. In this brief review of marketing management we need to recognize the major types of decisions to be made in the promotion sector of the marketing mix.

Promotion targets. We noted that it takes a knowledge of customer characteristics to divide the mass of the population into nonusers and

FIGURE 1–5. Retailers are concerned with brand loyalty, too

who cares

Today, when a product doesn't live up to its promise, who cares?

And when you take the trouble to express your disappointment, who cares?

Perhaps it's naive of us to expect everyone to care *all* the time. (We know how common it is to hear people say, "I couldn't care less.")

But we'd like to make one thing clear:

We care.

At A&P.

When you buy anything at A&P that doesn't meet your expectations, tell us. We'll do more than refund your money promptly. We'll turn around and go to work on the problem—and pursue the matter right to the source.

When a product doesn't keep its promise, we care.

And—when you take the time and trouble to tell us about it, we care. All the way to the top.

In fact, if you have *any* comments on *any* product we sell—we welcome you to write the top. We mean it. Write to:

Mr. O. Philip Nyquist
President
Central Western Div.
The Great Atlantic and Pacific Tea Co., Inc.
6200 West Warren Ave.
Detroit, Mich. 48210

That way you can help *all* of us at A&P to serve you better.

we care

prospects. That same knowledge is helpful in selecting the targets of promotional efforts. In addition to identifying target customers, decisions must be made about promotion to middlemen in the channel of distribution. There are three alternatives:

1. Management may decide to *push* its products through the channel of distribution by aiming the promotional efforts mainly at the middlemen, who in turn will sell to final customers.
2. Another approach is to *pull* the product through the channel by aiming the promotion at final customers and creating demand for the product at the retail level. Retailers will seek and stock the product in response to customer requests.
3. Many firms, indeed most firms, use a *combination of push and pull* tactics. So, some promotional efforts are aimed at channel members, some at customers.

Some firms even decide that a useful promotion target is their customer's customers. Thus a steel producer who sells to other manufacturers may advertise to consumers the benefits of furniture, or appliances, or other products made of steel. By helping *his* customers sell to *their* customers, he is helping long run sales of steel.

When to promote? Decisions about the timing of promotional efforts must take into account such considerations as seasonal sales patterns, company plans regarding new models or products, and competitors' promotion programs. There is little sense in advertising in the North snow tires in July or suntan oil in January. If our marketing strategy includes introducing an annual model, promotion timing must be tailored to the production schedules for the new lines. Some questions of timing the promotion effort are decided by competitors' plans. If other sellers in our industry sponsor a traditional promotion, our firm may have to follow suit. Retailers, for example, traditionally hold White Sales in January.

How to promote? This question actually involves decisions on three levels. First, the firm must select an appropriate blend of promotional forces. The elements of the "promotion mix" are the face-to-face presentation of sales messages to buyers through *personal selling;* the mass communication of sales messages through *advertising;* and the supporting promotional activities of *sales promotion.*

The second level of decisions involves the actual selling message each of these forces is to employ. The choice of appeal or appeals is important at this stage of promotion management. These decisions, like the others of marketing management, must rest upon a thorough knowledge of customers.

At the third level of decisions are those related to the management of the promotion mix selected. If personal selling is important, sales management decisions about the recruiting, hiring, training, compensation, and supervision of the sales force must be made. If advertising and sales promotion are to play a role in the marketing strategy, the manner in which these functions are carried out must be selected. Either company

FIGURE 1–6. The promotion target for this campaign is the retailer who helps to sell the product

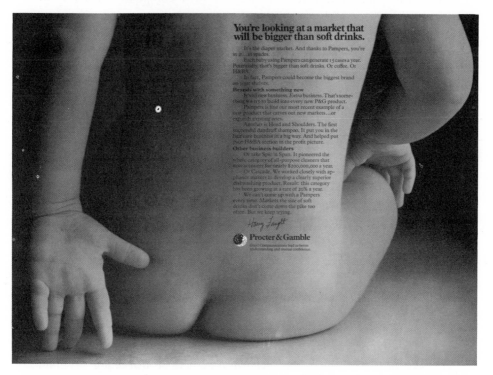

resources, advertising agency talent, media, market research firms, or a combination of all these must be organized and coordinated.

Where to promote? Again, only a clear definition of target customers can provide a meaningful basis for making decisions. The firm must seek to spend its promotion funds where they will accomplish the most. The choices of where to promote relate both to the geography of the firm's sales and to its capacity to produce and distribute its products. If the resources for production, promotion, or distribution are limited, the company may have to select a regional market across the country for its brand of products; if it is not large enough to serve the market well, better service in a more limited area would be preferred. The long-range plans may include gradual expansion to the national market as resources and capacity permit.

Decisions about price

The marketing manager must be concerned not only with the price final buyers pay but also with the whole structure of prices to middlemen within the planned distribution channel. In a competitive market the price must be set with an eye to the prices of competing products, to the nature of the demand for the whole product class, and to the costs the firm incurs in producing and distributing the products. A price plan which offers final buyers an acceptable price but does not adequately or competitively compensate middlemen will not be successful. A price plan which is attractive to middlemen but results in too high a price to final buyers will similarly fail to stimulate sales. A system of discounts may have to be decided upon to spur quantity purchases, to encourage prompt payment of accounts, and to recognize the differences in the amount of effort different middlemen put into the total marketing task.

Retailers must decide on the specific price customers will be charged for the product or else must agree to charge a price established by the manufacturer and required of all dealers. A variety of credit plans or alternatives must be considered. They range from sales on a cash basis only, to 30-day charge accounts, to more complex revolving credit plans or installment purchase contracts.

Stirring the mix

The phrase *marketing mix* suggests that the various decision areas we have been reviewing are *blended* together. A marketing program is not the sum of a collection of *independent* decisions. The various ingredients of product, distribution, promotion, and price decisions must be carefully selected so as to yield a balanced blend or mixture of marketing effort. Decisions in one area affect, and are themselves affected by, decisions in other areas of marketing. The interrelated nature of these marketing decisions must always be kept firmly in mind. A few examples will help illustrate this meshing and interaction.

1. A firm which creates a truly unique product that offers greater customer satisfaction than competing products may expect to earn a higher price. If customers are aware of these benefits and are willing

to put extra effort into shopping for the product, the distribution decisions of the firm take this into account and the result will be in fewer retail outlets.

2. A decision to bring out a high-quality product to satisfy high-income customers affects the *price policy* of the firm, the type of *retail outlet* in which the product will be distributed, and the character of its *promotional messages*. The brand name, the package, the whole marketing mix must reflect top quality.

3. A firm which offers a standard product but which is located in an out-of-the-way spot may have to lower prices and increase promotion to offset its place deficiency. The gasoline station on the edge of town faces such a problem. The station at the busy downtown location, selling the same brand of gasoline, may charge a higher price because of the location or place advantage. If the station is both on the edge of town and selling an unknown brand of gasoline, it has to compensate for weaknesses in two areas of the marketing mix. Prices may have to be cut even further; premiums or trading stamps may have to be offered to attract customers.

4. The company breaking into an established market where price and distribution are fairly standard will have to increase the promotion portion of the marketing mix to offset the unknown status of the new brand. A new soft drink or 5-cent candy bar would be examples where such a blend might be appropriate.

THE MARKETING MIX: LIMITATIONS

Marketing managers, we have seen, make a number of decisions that blend together to form a marketing mix aimed at satisfying target customers at a profit to the firm. In making these decisions they must be aware of the forces that restrict or restrain the freedom of the firm in its marketing activities. While most of these restraints are external to the business firm, some of them function within the firm but beyond the immediate control of the marketing manager himself.

Economic and market limits

The business firm operates in a broader economy which influences the firm and its component parts. Decisions about new products or pricing strategy or promotional tactics need to take into account the overall economic health of the markets to which the firm hopes to sell. These external economic influences are even more pronounced for the multinational firm selling its products in a variety of countries ranging from fully developed economies such as that of the United States to emerging and developing economies such as those of the new African nations or the nations of Latin America.

The economic environment may vary *within* a single country as well as *between* countries. The marketing decisions of retailers must be especially sensitive to local economic conditions. A prolonged strike or layoff may depress local spending power and call for a revision of product lines carried or price policies. On the other hand, industrial development may be bringing new families with higher incomes into the area; this increase in purchasing power must be considered.

Market saturation. The degree to which a market is saturated is another external factor which influences marketing mixes. Here we refer to the primary demand for the product class and the extent to which it can be expanded. If 98 percent of the households have some type of product A and only 28 percent have some type of product B, it is easy to see that the marketing problems of firms in these two industries differ. The firm selling product A must somehow make users want a new and improved version of product A, or create variations on the product suitable for special uses. The firm selling product B, on the other hand, needs to focus on prospects and nonusers. Primary demand still requires stimulation by firms in this industry—their market mixes must reflect this reality.

We have just used *percent of households* as a measure of saturation. We must recognize, however, that the correct basis for computing saturation is comparison of *actual* units with the number of *potential* units. If products A and B are suitable for any family, then the total number of households is the appropriate base. If the product appeals to a narrower market, then the base must be adjusted. The market saturation for hearing aids must be computed as a percent of the hard of hearing, not of the total population.

Market competition. Whatever the degree of market saturation, the marketing manager must also consider the nature of competition within the total industry. Are there many small competitors? Is there one large, dominant firm? Are there several leading firms which control most of the market? Answers to these questions are important determinants of the freedom a given manager has in constructing his marketing mix. Changes in the marketing mixes of competitors must be taken into account also. If a major competitor changes his guarantee from one year to five years, others may have to follow. If the industry leader lowers his prices, it may be necessary for others to fall in line.

As it was with economic conditions, so it is with market competition—local competitive situations must be considered. It is not uncommon to find a manufacturer with large national sales volume but still with low market shares in some areas and markets. Strong regional competition may occur in virtually every industry. The marketing manager must consider very carefully both the overall and the specific local competitive environment in which his firm must operate. Decisions about product, about distribution, about promotion, and about price must be made with full awareness of the nature of market competition.

Social and cultural limits

Target consumers do not exist in little isolated units. They are parts of a society or culture which influences what they buy and how they buy. Our discussion of consumer buying behavior in Chapter 3 will consider this problem in greater detail. In this review of marketing management, however, we can recognize that social and cultural forces do affect the decisions the marketing manager makes. In a society or culture that does not permit its members to drink alcoholic beverages in any form, a new product containing spirits would be unacceptable. Social and cultural forces also affect the promotion activities of the firm. Advertising illustrations or appeals considered "in bad taste" by prospects would be most unfortunate.

A society or culture concerned about pollution, about ecology, about discrimination, about standards of living for the disadvantaged, or about protection of scenic beauty can influence all segments of the marketing mix. Critics of marketing and advertising have become more vocal, and more organized in their policing of commercial activities. Alert sellers must be sensitive to the *collective* as well as *individual* concerns of its target customers.

These outside influences affect retailers as well as manufacturers. The product lines carried by a retail food store in an area heavily populated by first-generation Italians might differ markedly from a store in an area populated by persons of Norwegian extraction. Even within the store the product mixes of meat, bread, and dairy departments may shift periodically to reflect religious holidays or food practices. Fashions in clothing are another area subject to strong cultural reactions of approval or disapproval. Extremes in design that are accepted by sophisticated, urban societies may be totally rejected by more conservative rural consumers.

The plot thickens, of course, for the firm doing business in several countries. Both the broad culture and smaller subcultures in each country must be studied carefully by such firms. In the area of promotion management, for example, decisions must take into account differences in literacy rates. In countries like Denmark and Ireland where 98 percent of the adult population can read and write, the promotion mix may include printed communications that would be unfeasible in countries like Haiti and Iran, where the literacy rate is only 15 percent. In India, where some 51 dialects are spoken and only about 15 percent of the adult population is literate, mass persuasion is even more difficult and complex. A package design which sells well in one country where the color purple suggests quality and prestige may do poorly in another where purple is the traditional color of mourning and death.

Legal limits

The business firm must operate within the framework of the laws established by the national, state, and local governments of areas in which it does business. Decisions about elements of the marketing mix cannot be made without reference to the legal climate. The laws affect decisions in virtually every area of the marketing mix, whether the firm be a small manufacturer or industry giant, a roadside vegetable stand, or a 600-store chain of supermarkets.

Price regulations.   Most conspicuous perhaps of all the regulatory activities of government are those affecting pricing decisions. In its efforts to protect competition, the Congress has enacted several laws which dictate pricing practices to manufacturers in their dealings with retailers. Most of these have to do with spelling out what is meant by *price discrimination,* the charging of different prices to the same type of buyers of the same quantity of the same product. Other laws in the pricing fields prohibit unfair trade practices of selling below cost to injure competition. These laws are state legislations and not federal, and apply at the retail level as well as to sales to retailers. Still another group of laws, known as fair-trade laws, are more permissive than regulatory; they *allow* manufacturers to set and maintain retail prices for their products.

Promotion regulations.   In another area of marketing mix, both statutory and persuasive government limits are imposed upon the promotion choices. Municipalities may regulate door-to-door selling, outdoor advertising is subject to a variety of regulations at several levels of government, the content of selling messages must not mislead nor deceive, the plans for cooperative advertising allowances must not discriminate—these are a few of the kinds of limits that must be reckoned with.

Broadcast advertising is subject to regulation as to time available for messages and the number of messages per hour that can be handled. Some classes of products are not permitted to be advertised at all, either in broadcast or in printed media. Although these restrictions on time and availability of messages broadcast may not directly affect a particular marketing manager, the effect of these limitations may be to restrict the supply and drive media prices up in the face of growing demands for message time. Finally, in many countries of the world the broadcast media are owned and operated by the government, accepting no advertising whatsoever.

Product regulations. The most obvious regulatory activity in the product sphere of the marketing mix has to do with products consumed by human beings, either food, drugs, or cosmetics. In agricultural marketing, standards for product grading may be set by a government agency. Patent and copyright laws may protect or restrict marketing, depending on the position of the firm. Product features covered by patents may not be copied. A brand name which might confuse consumers by its similarity to an established brand would not be allowed.

Distribution regulation. In planning the distribution policies of the firm designed to have the product in the right places, some limits are encountered. For the retailer, local zoning laws may prohibit establishing a brand in a residential area. In international marketing, tariffs or outright import bans may preclude or impair distribution for some products. Manufacturers who wish to establish exclusive agency arrangements with dealers or wholesalers must be aware of the legal restrictions on such contracts if the effect is to lessen competition in an area of trade.

Internal limits

The economic, market, social, cultural, and legal limitations on marketing mix decisions are all external to the firm. There are also some *internal* limits to the marketing mix that need to be recognized. These are forces or conditions within the company that restrict the freedom of the marketing manager to make decisions about the various areas of the marketing mix.

Financial limits. Marketing decisions must take into account the ability of a firm to pay for its marketing programs. Large-scale advertising, selling, and distribution may be too costly for the smaller firm. Although target customers may be found all across the country, the firm may have to restrict its efforts to a smaller geographical area because the firm lacks the funds to support a nationwide distribution program. Success in a limited area may generate funds for gradual expansion into other areas of the country. In the short run, however, a lack of financial resources must often be considered a restraint on marketing decisions.

Nor is this condition exclusively the problem of a smaller firm. Some estimates of the cost of bringing a new consumer product to the market on a national scale run into tens of millions of dollars. Thus, even large firms may elect to begin on a regional basis before expanding to other parts of the market. This is especially true when a new sales force must be hired and trained, although this latter restriction is one of manpower as well as dollars.

Production limits.   The lack of financial resources may restrict the firm's ability to increase its productive capacity to meet the needs of a national market overnight. Only the very well-financed corporation can afford the capital outlays required. Shortages of skilled labor, raw materials, or component parts may similarly hamper production. Marketing managers need to take into account these limitations in planning the marketing strategy of the firm. Creating demand that cannot be satisfied is neither efficient nor wise; customers may turn to competitors' products even though *our* marketing program aroused their demand.

The technology of production may impose some limits to the marketing mix. Optimum or even feasible levels of production efficiency may require long mass production runs of a particular product. Marketing strategy may suggest that a large variety of colors and models is needed to satisfy the market. A compromise must be arranged. When all the possible combinations of body, motor, color, and optional features are considered, a modern car manufacturer may be offering as many as 5 *million* product combinations. This can be done only at a sacrifice of productive efficiency.

Policy limits.   The set of marketing decisions must be customer oriented; the decisions must also be *company oriented*. The goals and policies of the owners or directors must be fulfilled. While the marketing manager may desire the largest market share of his industry, his decisions must be tempered by the profit goals of the firm. His pricing decisions are especially affected by these goals. Profit maximization may require higher prices and a lower share of the market. If the goal of the firm *is* market share with a lower profit objective, then prices and promotion decisions must be adjusted accordingly.

Human limits. A final internal limitation may be described as a "managerial limitation." The firm may simply lack sufficient management talents or resources to accomplish a proposed marketing program. The decisions about the mix components must take this into account. These managerial limitations may take the form of *inadequate numbers* of qualified people in the organization. The company may not have enough trained salesmen, sales managers, marketing research staff members, or top marketing management personnel to carry out some programs.

The limitation may also take the form of *inadequate knowledge.* The number may be sufficient for the task, but their abilities may not. Management may be skilled in one area but not another. For example, a firm that has been selling technical instruments to the government or research institutions may not have the know-how to market a consumer product such as toothpaste or soap.

Finally, the limitation may be one of *inertia*—an unwillingness to change ways of doing things. Many imaginative marketing programs have been altered in the face of resistance to change within the organization.

These internal limitations may be overcome in the long run; people can be hired, funds amassed, production facilities acquired. But to do these things takes time and money, and in the absence of these factors, the marketing mix must be adjusted to take account of the limitations. Some of the limitations, especially the production-marketing conflict, are a constant internal limitation that must be accommodated if the firm is to move ahead in the marketplace.

The making of a set of marketing decisions known as the marketing mix is a complex process that operates within a framework of both external and internal limits or restrictions. Just as the decisions in one area of the marketing mix must interrelate with those in other areas, so must all of them be made in constant and keen awareness of these components of the decision-making environment. The successful marketing mix is one which is made with this threefold orientation: toward customers, toward external limitations, and towards internal limitations.

PROMOTION MANAGEMENT

A marketing mix, as we have seen, consists of a number of submixes of decision variables. Promotion is one of these component mixes. While the remainder of this book is concerned with the promotion mix, we must never lose sight of the fact that all decisions in the marketing mix must be mutually supporting. We dare not design any promotion strategy without careful consideration of the total marketing strategy of the firm.

Our study of promotion management began with a review of the total marketing management function of a firm. If we are to be concerned with persuasive communication in marketing, we must seek to understand something about the nature of human behavior and more particularly, *buyer* behavior. Chapters 2 and 3 deal with these topics and seek to give us a working model of buyer behavior that will help us to understand the role of various promotion alternatives. Chapter 4, building on our understanding of behavior, looks at communication systems and processes.

The nine chapters following Chapter 4 are divided into four parts and focus on the elements of persuasion: personal selling, advertising, sales promotion, and indirect promotion—public relations and publicity. Shelves of books have been written about each element and, indeed, about the subject matter of each chapter. We must therefore be brief and focus our discussion on the major dimensions of these persuasive elements. Our goal is to provide you with an understanding of the main features and problems in each area of promotion management.

Part VII, the final section of this book, consists of four chapters on the management of total promotion programs and activities where the various persuasive elements are blended into a promotion mix. The plan, then, is to move from the general discussion of marketing and human behavior to the specific details of personal selling, advertising, sales promotion, and indirect promotion, and finally to return to a broader look at the management of all three elements in a coordinated, strategic blend.

QUESTIONS AND PROBLEMS

1–1. For many products the task of stimulating primary demand is endless. Why?

1–2. Do the concepts of the marketing mix hold for a charitable drive like the United Fund?

1–3. What marketing strategy might be appropriate for a firm that designs a new 12-volt vacuum cleaner suitable for automobiles which would sell for a factory price of $8.00?

1–4. Discuss the demand creation tasks facing a manufacturer of small business jets.

1–5. How do decisions in the price and product area of the marketing mix affect decisions in the promotion area?

1-6. An inventor has devised a unit which detects smoke and activates an alarm bell. He asks your advice in marketing his product, which can be assembled by a local firm for $20.00 each.

1-7. How does the degree of market saturation affect the promotion decisions of the firm?

1-8. What are some signs that indicate that a firm does not distinguish between marketing and selling?

1-9. What are some characteristics that would separate nonusers from prospects for: (*a*) golf clubs (*b*) diet soft drinks (*c*) portable typewriters?

1-10. What marketing strategy would be appropriate for a small manufacturer of industrial parts that patents a new electronic oven which cooks food in a few minutes or even seconds? The two models tested could sell for $400 and $3,000 respectively. The firm has no sales force.

PART II

BEHAVIOR AND COMMUNICATION

CHAPTER 2

Individual behavior

Tʜᴇ ɢᴏᴀʟ of persuasive communication in marketing is to influence buying behavior. A sharper focus on the consumer behavior process can lead to a better idea of what customers want; it can also lead to knowledge of how the good news of a product's availability and benefits can be told in terms more likely to trigger that behavior most meaningful to marketing: *buying*.

Because we are about to plunge into this complicated matter of why customers buy, perhaps we should start with a quick, overall look at the road ahead. This road map analogy is not a bad one; a number of maps of this behavior terrain have been attempted. One of the early perspectives was that of the French sociologist and criminologist, Gabriel Tarde, whose *Laws of Imitation* was published in 1890. With this concept of imitation he sought to explain a wide variety of behavior in statements such as "weaker individuals tend to imitate the traits of stronger ones, and not the reverse." Other behavioral map makers have focused on instinct, perception theory, learning theory, psychoanalysis, and field theory. We must keep in mind that all these were ways of looking at the same phenomenon; the subject, individual behavior, is the same, but the maps differ.

Maps of the same territory also differ according to the purposes for which they are intended. If you wanted to reach a friend's house in a strange city, you would be most unhappy if your only guide was a topological map with detailed features but no streets, roads, or man-made features indicated. On the other hand, you would have a difficult time locating the highest point in town with only a street map to guide you. As students of promotion management, then, we need a map of *buying behavior* and not just human behavior. Thus we are not interested in such phenomena as the abnormal behavior associated with neurotics or psychotics; the behavior we are most concerned with is that of *a consumer contemplating the purchase of a product.* But, as buying behavior is just a special kind of human behavior, we need to understand some aspects of *general* behavior before constructing a map of the buying process.

Drawing such a map requires heavy reliance on the behavioral sciences of psychology, social psychology, sociology, and anthropology. This chapter will first take up some basic concepts of perception and learning. In doing so we will use elements of several theories of behavior, but essentially we will take a *field* or *Gestalt* approach. Building on our concepts of perception and learning from this chapter, Chapter 3 will develop a model (or map) of *buying* behavior which will help us understand the role of promotion in helping buyers satisfy their needs.

THE PERCEPTUAL FIELD

At the outset we must agree to a basic proposition: *consumer behavior is organized and meaningful.* That is, an individual doesn't respond in a random or meaningless way to the world around him. For his or her every act, there is an underlying explanation which is wholly consistent and meaningful from the viewpoint of the person doing the behaving. Consumers, in short, do not behave according to the "facts" of a situation as you or I see them, but according to the situation *as it appears to them.* The consumer's "facts" are not the physical or objective reality, but the *perceived* situation as it appears to him at that moment. Moreover, because an individual perceives every situation according to his own personal needs, values, expectations, and training, individual consumers see any object or event in different terms. Beauty, truly, lies in the eye of the beholder. Let us repeat this most basic proposition: an individual's behavior is an organized and meaningful response to the world around him *as he sees it.*

Each consumer has what is called a *perceptual field.* It is that individual's personal and unique field of awareness. It is the world around him as he sees it. It is his reality. The perceptual field includes the person's physical self; his surroundings; his awareness of family, class, and culture;

and the concepts he has acquired about all these *over the course of his lifetime* up to the given instant of behaving. By his perceptual field, we mean the consumer's entire universe, past and present, *as it exists for him* at the moment he is living and behaving.

Combs and Snygg present a clear illustration of the influence of different perceptual fields on behavior:

Several years ago a friend of mine was driving a car along a Western road at dusk. A globular mass, about two feet in diameter, suddenly appeared directly in the path of the car. A passenger screamed and grasped the wheel, attempting to steer the car around the object. The driver, however, tightened his grip on the wheel and drove directly into the object. The behavior of both the driver and the passenger was determined by his own perceptual field. The passenger, an Easterner, saw the object as a boulder and fought desperately to steer the car around it. The driver, a Westerner, saw it as a tumbleweed and devoted his efforts to keeping his passenger from overturning the car.

In understanding this behavior, it is not necessary to know what the object "really" was. Each individual in the car behaved towards it according to its nature in his own perceptual field.[1]

How the field shapes perception can also be illustrated by imagining four people looking at the same brick wall. One is an artist, who sees the wall in terms of texture, color, shadow, and form; another is a skilled brickmason who sees some uneven courses and rough corners; one is a demolition expert skilled in demolishing such walls, and he sees the weak spots in the brickwork; another is a prisoner who sees only a barrier to freedom. Each individual brings his own perceptual field, with its special needs, feelings, and values to focus on the same brick wall. And each "sees" what is important to *him*.

Limits to perception

Although the perceptual field is as limitless as the individual's universe, at any given moment he can focus on only a small part of his field. This limitation of focus is described by two terms: *figure* and *ground*. The portion of the perceptual field which is in focus at a given instant is said to be in *figure*. The *ground* contains the background or not-in-focus portions of the perceptual field. This process of selecting portions of the field to bring into figure is better experienced than described.

[1] A. W. Combs and Donald Snygg, *Individual Behavior* (New York: Harper & Row, Publishers, 1959), p. 10.

Take the simple case of the silhouette of a goblet or vase (see Figure 2–1). With a casual glance you can see the whole goblet but few details. When your eye looks for details in the base of the goblet, the base is in *figure* and the top fades to *ground*. Now shift your eyes to the top of the goblet; the details of the base fade to ground, and the top lip of the cup is in figure.

FIGURE 2–1. The Peter-Paul goblet

This drawing proves that perception depends on the perceiver.

But while you have been bringing various parts of the goblet into figure and letting others slip away to ground, along comes someone with the disarming observation: "Why are you wasting time on all that empty space when the interesting features are *those two gray faces looking at one another?*" What a difference that suggestion makes! Now *all* the goblet fades to ground as you focus, or bring into figure, the two faces. (In this case your perceptual field has been influenced by the suggestion that the illustration was of a goblet, and the caption below the illustration was designed to reinforce this perception.) One thing more: you can "see" the illustration as either goblet *or* faces, but not at once. Try it.

Levels of figure. An individual can focus on only one portion of his perceptual field at a time, bringing that one portion into clear focus while the rest of the perceptual field fades to ground. Another example may help illustrate this important concept. When you enter a darkened movie theater, you are "aware" of the bright screen but you are focusing on the seats, trying to find an empty spot. The seats are in figure, the screen is in ground. As you get settled into your seat, you may look around to see who is sitting nearby that you know, but gradually you bring the screen into figure and—if the movie is a good one—focus so intently on the screen that you are unaware of persons coming and going around you (unless they block the screen, of course!). When the action on the screen begins to seem familiar and you realize that this is where you came in, you let the screen fade to ground and gather your coat and prepare to leave. Now the row of seats is in figure and the screen is in ground. You stand up, with the row ahead in figure as you start to exit, and . . . ouch! your foot is asleep. Suddenly, from some obscure location far in the ground of your perceptual field—because your physical self is a part of that field—your right foot comes into sharp, clear figure as you are intensely aware of the numbness and pain.

Perhaps Figure 2–2 will help. In circle A, the moviegoer is just leaving, with the row of seats in figure, the screen in near-figure (conscious

FIGURE 2–2. Shifting from figure to ground

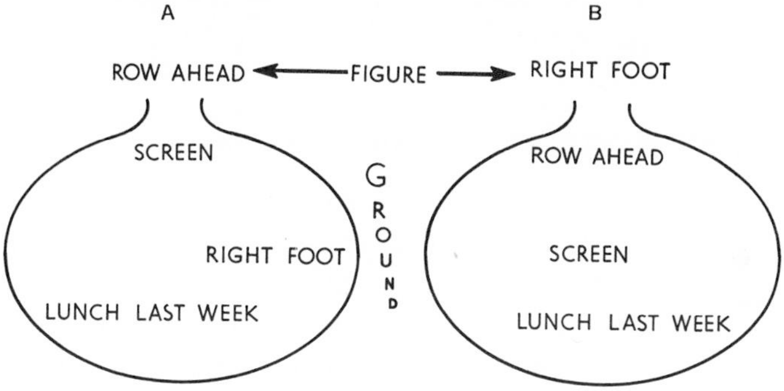

of it, but not focusing on it), and the concept "right foot" far into ground. In circle B, as weight is put on the right foot, the perceptual field shifts to focus on the foot; the row ahead is in near-focus, and the screen fades farther into ground. Meanwhile, all the rest of the perceptual field, including "lunch last week," remains in ground for this individual at this moment of his behaving.

Finally, as you read this, you certainly have as a part of your perceptual field the furniture in your room or study place. You know it is there, but it has probably been at a low level of awareness until now. Having had your attention drawn to it, you can call the "furniture" concept into clearer figure, and may even call it into full figure as you glance away from your reading for the moment or shift your weight on the chair. You cannot read this sentence and look at furniture simultaneously, but the furniture concept rose from deep in the ground of your field and into the fringes of figure as you read this paragraph.

Behavioral consequences. The meaning of any perceived event or object is always a relation of that which is in figure and that which is in the ground of an individual's field. So it was that the automobile passengers reacted differently to the sight of the "object" in the road. In the ground of the Easterner's field were memories of "Falling Rock" signs along highways and boulders by the roadside. Because he had never in his life "seen" a tumbleweed, his ground contained no concept "tumbleweed" with which to identify the object. Thus the meaning of the object in figure depended on the ground of the perceiver's field.

In terms of buying behavior, if we are to persuade a consumer to buy our product, the product concept and brand name must become a part of his perceptual field. Once our name is in figure for him, it may slip away to ground to be recalled by later exposure to our product or its promotion. He "remembers" by recalling the name to figure from the ground of his perceptual field.

DIFFERENTIATION, PERCEPTION, AND LEARNING

In the process of describing the perceptual field of an individual, we have noted that only a small part of the field can be in figure at any given moment. All the rest of his perceptual field is at varying levels of ground, ranging from conscious awareness to unconscious, "forgotten" dimensions of the field. The process of bringing parts of the field into figure is so important that we need to look at it in greater detail.

Differentiation

This emergence of figure from ground that we have been describing is known as *differentiation*. The more intensely or clearly the figure is differentiated, the clearer the stimulus is perceived. If, for example, you run across a telephone number such as 942–5068, you may differentiate the set of digits for a second or two as you read this sentence. Ten minutes from now, however, you probably could not recall the number from ground because it was not intensely differentiated. Let us give you another number, but preface it by telling you that if you call this number and identify yourself, you will receive one million dollars, tax free, as a prize. Here is the number—933–2186. Now if you believed the promise, the chances are that you differentiated this number with much more intensity than the number mentioned earlier in this paragraph. Let your eye run back over the paragraph and "find" the first number again. In the process, you were practicing different levels of differentiation. As you searched for the number, you had the whole mass of print in figure, but as your eye caught the number and brought just that small portion into clear figure, the rest of the paragraph faded to ground.

Learning theory in psychology offers three useful concepts to explain how material differentiated in the past is retrieved with varying ease. The concepts are: *frequency, recency,* and *intensity.* You can probably recall what you had for lunch yesterday (recency). If you *always* eat the same thing, you can tell me what you had for lunch a year ago (frequency). You may be able to tell me what you had to eat last Christmas, or on your wedding day, because those are special days of intense differentiation. For the marketer, frequency and recency are important scheduling issues, while intensity is a creative challenge.

Perception

The process of *perception* consists of taking cues from the field and organizing them into meaningful ideas or *concepts.* Concepts are what we think with; concepts are what we learn; concepts are what we communicate with. Take this set of cues:

lautpecrep dleif

If you have previously differentiated a concept which you labeled "lautpecrep dleif," then you will associate the cues in figure with the concept in the ground of your field and you will *perceive* or understand. You probably haven't differentiated this before, so we shall reverse the order of the cues like this:

perceptual field

Now you "see" it; now you *perceive* because you have differentiated this combination several times in this chapter and, if you have done so carefully, the sight of the cues brings the concept into figure.

The perceptual field, then, is a "sensory storehouse" and a present field of awareness all at the same time. Stored away in the ground of the field are past differentiations and perceptions which entered the field through the sensory processes of the individual: sight, hearing, taste, smell, and touch. In addition, the perceptual field is a "cognitive store-house" where perceptions formed independent of external sensory stimulation are stored. For example, alone in a dark, quiet room the individual may bring differentiations from his field back into figure, "think about them," and form some new concepts or perceptions. As a result of this thinking or *cognition*, to use a technical term, new perceptions are added to the perceptual field of the individual.

For the manager of promotion, this process of differentiation and perception is important because it sets some conditions for successful communication with prospective buyers. While we will explore this in more detail in Chapter 4, let us note, now, that the firm's advertising and personal sales messages must become a part of the prospect's perceptual field, must attract his attention and be brought into figure and differentiated, and must be *perceived* or understood by that individual. Let's take an example from the packaging field:

The makers of Soapy brand washing powder decide to add bleach to their product and redesign the package to include a bright yellow band with red letters proclaiming "New Improved Formula—With Bleach." The package is displayed on the shelf of a supermarket along with other washing products. Three housewives pass by the soap section the first morning, and different experiences result.

Mrs. Jones has used Soapy in the past, comes by the display, notices (brings into figure) the new package, compares the differentiation with her past perception of Soapy packages, perceives that it is different, brings the yellow band into specific figure, and *modifies* her concept "Soapy" to include the fact that it is a washing powder that contains bleach.

Mrs. Yatsumura is new to this country and is making her first visit to the supermarket. As she stops in front of the soap section she looks at (brings into figure) several brands of soap. The third brand that catches her eye is "Soapy," and she perceives that this brand includes bleach whereas the others did not. At this instant in time Mrs. Yatsumura has *added* a concept to her perceptual field that was not in her field a moment before when the competitor's brand was in figure.

Mrs. Harried has shopped in this store many times and has purchased Soapy on several occasions. She is late for an appointment and is shopping for only a few items. As she comes down the aisle with Soapy's new package she fleetingly differentiates the mass of soap containers, glances down at her shopping list (bringing that into focus at the moment she passes Soapy), concludes that she doesn't need soap, and leaves the store with the Soapy concept in her perceptual field unchanged. Even though the new package was for a moment a part of her perceptual field, she did not clearly differentiate it, hence could not modify her concept of Soapy brand washing powder.

Learning

The vast and endless process of *learning*, which begins in infancy and continues all our days, is just this process of combining cues into concepts and of using concepts to form new concepts. Some concepts we form correctly, some incorrectly. Thus earlier observers perceived ships dropping from sight over the horizon of the sea and formed a "flat world" concept. Much of our education, growth, and learning consists of reforming our erroneous or inadequate concepts.

Once an individual learns to communicate with others, the differentiation and learning process speeds up enormously. He can then *form* concepts through conversation and reading. Listen to a two- or three-year-old asking "What?" "How?" "Why?" for hours on end. He is endlessly acquiring concepts—there is so much to explore and perceive. If you hear a strange knocking sound out in the hall, you can go out and look and *form* a concept of "water cooler motor rattling," or you can ask someone walking by what that noise is and *acquire* the same concept.

Levels of concept attainment. There are, of course, levels of concept attainment. A child may hear a sound and be able to perceive it as "music" rather than "noise." An older child, whose perceptual field contains many more concepts which he has differentiated over the years, may be able to perceive the sound as "classical music" rather than "jazz." Still another individual may be able to differentiate the same sound and perceive "clarinet, oboe, French horn, and flute" and even "Sonata Number 38 by Zilch."

In Chapter 1 we discussed the concepts of primary demand and selective demand. In marketing terms, then, concept attainment must include the general product class concept as well as the brand name concept the individual seller is seeking to promote. Until you recognize the cues "air conditioner" as signifying a mechanical device for chilling the air, you won't be shopping for an air conditioner. Moreover, various manufacturers seek to provide you with enough cues to form the concept "brand name," and to remind you of it often enough to keep the differentiation from fading too far into ground to be recalled.

Concept varieties and valences. The concepts we have already differentiated, and hence are a part of our perceptual field, may be classified into several categories. Here are a few:

Physical objects, both animate and inanimate, persons and things.
Sensations, such as pain, hunger, and heat.
Events, which combine object concepts like "chair" with action concepts like "fall down."
Relationships, both physical (near, far) and social (member, brother).
Abstractions, such as roughness, triangularity.
Feelings, like lonely, happy, gay, angry.

We are forever adding to our store of differentiated concepts as we learn new words, combine them to form other concepts, and see and hear all that goes on about us.

We also attach different values to concepts. We attach *valences* to them. A valence is a value attached to cues and concepts ranging from very strongly positive to very strongly negative. For some cues and concepts, of course, we are neutral or *ambivalent*. Think, for a moment, of your own valences for concepts like "getting an A," "term paper," "beer," "draft board," or "surfing." The valences an individual attaches to concepts are subject to influence from a variety of areas in his perceptual field. A consumer's family, friends, work associates, social class, culture . . . all may help influence the valences he attaches to concepts.

For promotion management this factor of concept valences is most important. If we are to communicate persuasively with groups of individuals, we must take care to see that the words or concepts we use to describe a product or service have a positive valence for the prospective customers. For example, we would not use concepts like "shoddy," "flimsy," "inferior," or "uneconomical" to sell a product, because these concepts have negative valences attached to them by consumers.

CHARACTERISTICS OF THE PERCEPTION PROCESS

Before noting some characteristics of the perception process, let us review briefly the process itself. The emergence of cues from the ground into focus or figure is called *differentiation. Perception* consists of taking the differentiated cues and organizing them into meaningful *concepts*.

Individuals can form concepts; they can also acquire concepts from others. In the process they attach *valences* to many concepts which are probably similar to the valences their family, friends, and others attribute to the concepts. Now we need to consider four aspects of the perception process: its permanence, its organization, its selectivity, and its responsiveness to psychological influences.

Differentiation is permanent

Once we have assembled cues from our perceptual fields to form a concept, these concepts tend to remain with us. Indeed, the differentiation does remain with us. You may differentiate a sound but not be able to make any sense of it (hence, not form a concept) at the time. Later on, the same set of cues may be differentiated at a time when you *can* attribute the sound to its source, and you think "so that's what that noise was." Thus our ground keeps building up a greater and greater store of differentiated events and concepts. (Do you recall l a u t p e c r e p   d l e i f?) It is quite true that some of our past differentiations have sunk so far into ground that they cannot be consciously recalled to figure. We say we have "forgotten." But *they are there* and are a part of the perceptual field as we have defined it. Under hypnosis, or in the course of brain surgery, individuals are able to recall with supreme detail (sound, sight, color, smell) events from earliest childhood. This evidence suggests that once something is differentiated, it is a permanent part of the perceptual field. This is why we defined the field itself, earlier, as the individual's *personal, total,* and *unique* field of awareness.

An individual may, of course, have to "unlearn" some of the concepts he forms. While he can never truly "forget" his first differentiation and perception, he can modify or change his perception. An infant, for example, responds in the only way he can to hunger or discomfort—he cries. He soon learns that this act ("crying") brings food or dry clothing. Thus crying becomes a positive-valenced concept for him because "cry" = "comfort." As the child grows older, he must come to realize that crying is not an acceptable form of behavior for getting what one wants. The biblical quotation "When I was a child, I thought as a child . . ." speaks to this point that old concepts must be discarded in favor of new ones.

For marketing, the permanence of differentiation suggests that the product or service must deliver satisfaction every time. If, for instance, a consumer purchases brand X and the product is spoiled or broken or otherwise fails to satisfy, he has formed a concept that is difficult to change. "Brand X" = "bad deal," or "Brand X does not live up to claims made for it." He may, through later trials, come to modify his first perception, but if alternative brands are available he may never try again.

Perception is meaningfully organized

Almost by definition, because a concept is formed by combining cues, this combination is in an organized state. The phenomenon of closure illustrates this idea. Thes book iz about pe suasive comnumication. If you read that sentence rapidly, you probably made all the necessary corrections and additions to it to make it intelligible. You were organizing the visual cues into a meaningful pattern, seeing more order, in fact, than was there to be seen.

Perception is selective

We noted earlier that one's perceptual field is vast in that it includes the individual's universe of concepts and differentiations, yet limited in that one can bring into figure only a small bit at a time. As a result, the individual must pick and choose among cues from many parts of the field. This is why consumers differentiate *what they need to at a given time*. They differentiate not what you or I think is most important but what *they* select as important *for them*. You may be only vaguely attentive in class some day, letting the voice of your lecturer fade almost to ground as you bring into figure happy thoughts about the coming weekend party. But let the word *quiz* be spoken from the front of the room and you suddenly focus, full-figure, on the lecturer and what you need to hear about "quiz." A consumer may walk through the same parking lot every day and be only vaguely aware of the various makes of cars. But let him start thinking about trading cars and he will perceive far more details about the various new models as he walks through the lots.

An interesting psychological experiment reveals the influence of physiological needs on selective perception. If you put a blob of color behind a fogged glass, tell individuals it is a picture, and ask them to tell you what they "see," hungry persons will "see" it as a picture of food far more often than will persons who have just eaten. The hungry man needs to see food; he organizes the cues (in this case blurred masses of color) accordingly. The just-fed observer may report "seeing" flowers, a landscape, or any number of "things." The experiment proves two of our observations, however: (1) individuals try to organize meaningfully—they "see" *something;* and (2) they perceive in a selective fashion according to their needs or the state of their perceptual field at the moment.

Perception is influenced by psychological state

Our example of the hungry man seeing food suggests that *physiological* conditions influence perception. The *mental* set or mood of the individual also affects his perception. Leuba and Lucas report an interesting experiment in which selected subjects, made to feel either happy, anxious, or critical through posthypnotic suggestion, were then shown a picture of four college students sitting outside on the grass reading books. When asked to describe the scene, the descriptions varied according to the induced mental set. For instance, one "happy" observer saw a group of persons enjoying reading out in the sunshine on a warm spring day. He noticed the happy expressions of the students. Shown the same picture, a "critical" observer described the scene as consisting of four lazy louts who ought to be doing something more useful than lolling around pretending to study. He commented that the sloppy dressers with silly grins would probably flunk out before the year was over.[2]

You have probably experienced the influence of your mental mood on your perception. On days when you feel well and happy a minor mishap may be laughed off. But on one of those days when nothing seems to go right, the very same situation may be perceived as far more infuriating. And, of course, when someone comes along on such an occasion and says "Cheer up, it's not as bad as all that," *you* know that he cannot possibly understand what it is like. After all, it's *your* perceptual field!

We began this chapter with some comments about maps. At this point it might be well to ask, "Where are we?" Our study of perception suggests that individuals perceive by differentiating or bringing into figure parts of the perceptual field which is their universe of awareness . . . both present and past. They organize the differentiated cues into meaningful concepts to the best of their ability. Their perceptions are permanent, selective, and appropriate to their mental state at that

[2] *Journal of Experimental Psychology*, Vol. 35 (1945), pp. 513–34.

time. In other words, the perceptual field is at one and the same time both a product of the individual's perceptions and a force in shaping that which he differentiates and perceives. We now need to take a closer look at the perceptual field and try to map out some of the major areas or dimensions of awareness that shape human behavior.

DIMENSIONS OF AN INDIVIDUAL'S FIELD

As we attempt to map out some major dimensions of the perceptual field, we cannot fail to sympathize with those early explorers. Our map will be somewhat crude and limited for two reasons: (1) much remains to be learned about some of these areas, and (2) we must compress into a portion of one chapter some of the broad findings of extensive research by a host of students of human behavior. Let us hope that we can come to understand some of the broad dimensions of the field, develop an appreciation for the interaction of these dimensions, and achieve a fuller awareness of the complexity of human behavior. As most maps are drawn by proceeding from the general to the specific, by sketching the broad outlines and then filling in the details, so our map of the perceptual field will start with the broadest dimensions of awareness. Then we can progressively narrow our view until we end with the individual himself. For each dimension we shall explore a little of its influence on the individual's behavior.

Humanity

Perhaps the broadest awareness shared by all human beings is their membership in the family of man. How much of an individual's behavior can we attribute to "human nature"? Very little indeed. Behavior associated with *survival* seems to be the only wholly instinctive perception in man. So we are on shaky ground when we try to describe most behavior as "just natural" or "just human nature."

Cultural anthropology can cite examples to destroy virtually every notion we have about "human nature," including even the survival instinct. Kindness, compassion, loyalty . . . all seem to be learned or acquired and not "built-in" traits of human behavior. Food esteemed by one culture is loathed by another (they attach different valences to the same food concept). Maternal love may be instinctive as a means of insuring the survival of the species, but routine infanticide is practiced by some tribes. Hence the behavior, mother love, is more responsive

2—Individual behavior   47

to cultural pressures than to instinct. Marital jealousy is unknown in other cultures; Eskimos, for example, traditionally loan their wives to house guests. In still other cultures, those who love one another do not kiss; they spit in each other's faces because saliva is believed to have magical qualities.

Even the basic survival instinct can be overcome by cultural pressures. The sacrificial suicides of Oriental cultures is one example of this. The Eskimos provide another; when Eskimos become old and unproductive, they are expected to leave the group for an isolated ice floe to die in solitude from exposure and starvation.

Speaking to the "human nature" concept as a means of explaining behavior, Kuhn notes that "the weight of current evidence from psychology, anthropology, or elsewhere is overwhelmingly to the contrary."[3] While this concept is a recognized dimension of one's perceptual field, it is not too helpful in explaining individual behavior.

Culture

Our discussion of the humanity dimension was filled with examples from "this culture" and "that culture." Obviously, then, the cultural dimension of the perceptual field does begin to offer an understanding of individual behavior. When a large group of individuals share a common set of dominant goal concepts, we may say they form a culture. The culture of ancient Athens, for example, was characterized by the high value placed on intellectual and political acumen. In nearby Sparta the ability to make war was a dominant goal. A culture, then, is defined by a set of concepts to which a common valence is attached by large numbers of individuals.

An American's perceptual field is likely to include the goal concepts and valences of his culture. We seem to attach a positive valence to such concepts as "success," "efficiency," "competition," "freedom," and "material wealth" . . . to name just a few. One of the authors had occasion to purchase 10 postcards in Pittsburgh, Pennsylvania, and noticed that the descriptions of 7 of them mentioned the "cost" of the structure shown; 5 used descriptive competitive words like "best," "biggest," or "most complete"; and 4 of the 10 cards mentioned age-type adjectives like "first," "oldest," or "original." These are simple examples of values our culture holds dear.

---

[3] Alfred Kuhn, *The Study of Society: A Unified Approach* (Homewood, Ill.: Richard D. Irwin, Inc., 1963).

Cultural values can be extremely complex and cover a great range of concepts. Four examples, from different cultures, illustrate just some of the intricacies of the cultural influence on behavior.[4]

Time concepts.   To give a person a deadline in the United States conveys a sense of urgency and importance to the task but to do so in the Middle East is considered rude and demanding. To say, "I am going to Damascus tomorrow morning and will have to have my car by tonight," is a sure way to get the mechanic to stop work. With the Japanese a delay of years does not mean that they have lost interest in a proposal being considered. Time clearly has different meanings in different cultures.

Space concepts.   In the United States, men generally converse and conduct business physically separated at distances of 5 to 8 feet—not the 2 to 3 *inches* of other cultures. What we consider crowded may be considered spacious in the Spanish culture. Seventeen desks and employees in a room 18 by 20 feet may be "a nice spacious office with lots of room for everybody." The top floor of Japanese department stores houses the bargain department, not the executive suite, which is crowded into some less desirable (by our standards) space.

Possession concepts.   The American culture's emphasis on "things" and material possessions as symbols of status and position is not universally shared. Some cultures are family centered, while others emphasize the durability of things, not their newness or style. The counter-culture among young people explicitly rejects materialism.

Friendship concepts.   As a general rule, friendships are not formed as quickly in foreign countries, but they go much deeper, last longer, and involve real obligation. The American's tendency to become "First-Name Charlie" after a casual meeting is repugnant to members of other cultures. One is reminded of a subculture in the United States, however. A death notice of a 79-year-old man who had lived in Charleston, South Carolina, for 45 years is reported to have been headed: "Newcomer Passes."

Marketing managers need to recognize the impact of culture on consumer behavior. Products and promotions must be attuned to the culture of the target customers. In this age of expanding international trade, the cultural dimension of buyers' perceptual fields is of increasing importance to astute communicators. But this dimension of the field, rich as it is in meaning, is by no means enough for an understanding of

---

[4] These examples and illustrations are from Edward T. Hall, "The Silent Language in Overseas Business," *Harvard Business Review*, May–June, 1960, pp. 87–96.

individual behavior. There are other dimensions of the perceptual field to be mapped, as we shall see.

Social class

While much is sometimes made of the great American dream of a classless society, the fact remains that there is a class structure in America (as in all other cultures). In a survey of 1,337 people, Centers found that only 3 percent said they *did not know* in which social class they belonged.[5] His findings suggest that individuals who identify themselves with a particular social class tend to vote alike, behave alike, and hold similar social concepts and attitudes. In short, their behavior is shaped by their social class perceptions.

We defined a culture as a large group of individuals sharing a set of dominant goal concepts. Let us define *social class*, then, according to attainment of those goals. The more closely and completely a group has attained the cultural goals, the higher its social class or rank within the culture. Thus, in ancient Athens, the intellectual and the politician were of high status, while in Sparta the warriors were the preferred social class.

Sociological studies of towns in the United States have used a variety of social class categories. Perhaps the most widely known is the six-class system defined by Warner and Lunt. In brief, here are their six suggested classifications:[6]

1. Upper-upper—old families, with wealth and power.
2. Lower-upper—the newly arrived; "new wealth."
3. Upper-middle—mostly professionals and successful businessmen.
4. Lower-middle—white-collar, salaried workers.
5. Upper-lower—wage earner, skilled worker group.
6. Lower-lower—unskilled labor, unemployed.

Persons of the same social class are likely to live in close proximity. Nearly all towns and cities have their elite neighborhoods—and their slums or lower-class areas. Since we have defined perceptual field as the individual's personal, total, unique field of awareness, it follows that

---

[5] Reuben Centers, *The Psychology of Social Classes* (Princeton, N.J.: Princeton University Press, 1949).

[6] W. Lloyd Warner and Paul Lunt, *The Social Life of a Modern Community* (New Haven, Conn.: Yale University Press, 1950).

his social class is an important determinant of that awareness. His neighbors and friends are a very large part of his universe, and the valences they attach to concepts are likely to influence him as he acquires new concepts.

Because an individual's values are conditioned by the social class structure he perceives, consumer buying behavior reflects class differences. The socially stable individual will share the values of his social class; the socially mobile individual will likely appropriate values from the next higher social class as he attempts to move upward. At any rate, buying behavior should reflect class differences. Pierre Martineau's study of the Chicago market was concerned with this idea. In his conclusion he said:

> It is important to realize that there are far-reaching psychological differences between the various classes. They do not handle the word in the same way. . . . Income-wise they (two families of different classes) may be in the same category. But their buying behavior, their tastes, their spending-saving aspirations can be poles apart.

In commenting on reactions to advertising by members of different social classes, Martineau observed that "the kind of super-sophisticated and clever advertising which appears in the *New Yorker* and *Esquire* is almost meaningless to lower-status people. They have a different symbol system—their communication skills have been pressed into different molds." In other words, their perceptual fields contain vastly different grounds with which to perceive differentiated messages.

Thus the buying behavior of an individual *is* influenced by the social class dimension of his perceptual field. The family of a $15,000-a-year truck driver buys a different product assortment than does the family of a $15,000-a-year junior business executive. Though income is the same, the two families are by background, education, neighborhoods, occupation, and social associates in different social classes. Not only does *what* assortments of products they buy vary but *where* they shop differs too. As Martineau observed:

> The most important function of retail advertising today, when prices and quality have become so standard, is to permit the shopper to make social class identification. This she can do from the tone and physical character of the advertising. Of course, there is also the factor of psychological identification. Two people in the same social class may want different stores. One

---

[7] Pierre Martineau, "Social Classes and Spending Behavior," *Journal of Marketing*, Vol. 23, No. 2, pp. 121–30.

FIGURE 2–3. An ad with visual and headline appeal to many classes and
reference groups

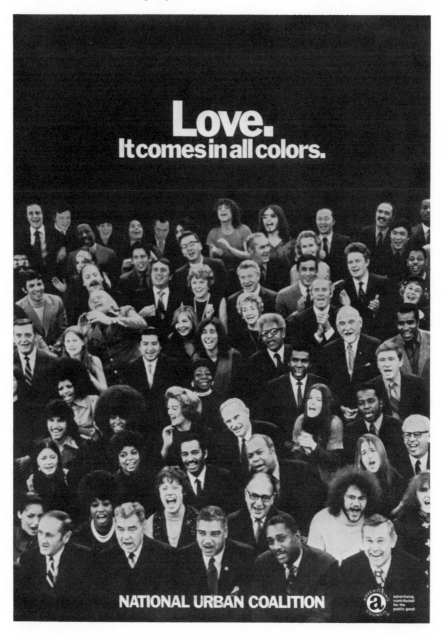

may prefer a conservative store, one may want the most advanced styling. But neither will go to stores where they do not "fit," in a social-class sense.[8]

While humanity and culture may set the general framework of values an individual holds, this third dimension of the perceptual field, social class, would seem to be far more important in helping us understand individual behavior.

Reference groups

Another important dimension is the concept of reference groups with which the individual associates. A consumer's earliest social contact is with his family. But later, play groups, classmates, sports teammates, work groups, club associates, church groups—all kinds of groups become a part of his perceptual field. He begins to understand himself and his world in reference to these groups and associations. These associations are both a part of *what* he perceives and experiences, and they also exert an influence on *how* he perceives cues from the field. More particularly, reference groups influence the valences he attaches to concepts. For example: Parents who attach positive valences to concepts such as "reading," "literature," "art," and "education" are most likely to influence positively their child's attitudes toward these concepts.

Of greatest importance to most consumers are those groups in which they hold membership. Just as social class depends upon attainment of a set of cultural values, so the member's position within the reference group depends upon his attainment of group-held values and goals. If you want to become a respected member and leader of a teen-age gang, do not try to become known as the most "gentle," "compassionate," "sensitive," or "cultured" member of the group! Better try for "tough," "clever," "strong," or "loyal." It is quite possible, however, for a consumer's field to include awareness of groups to which he *aspires to belong,* as we noted in the case of social mobility. Thus the values of the reference group to which admission is sought may dictate behavior in imitation of those already accepted members of the group.

Reference groups, then, are groups whose outlooks are used by an individual as frames of reference in the organization of his perceptual field. These groups may influence either (*a*) the primary demand for the product itself, (*b*) the demand for a particular brand, or (*c*) both.[9]

---

[8] *Ibid.*

[9] See Francis Bourne, "Group Influence in Marketing and Public Relations," in Rensis Likert and Samuel P. Hayes, Jr. (eds.), *Some Applications of Behavioral Science Research* (Paris: UNESCO, 1947), pp. 217–24.

a cold draft intrudes on our study. And like other dimensions of the field, this one is a blend of present differentiations and past perceptions stored in the ground of the individual's field. Americans who spend a year in England, for instance, are likely to find the winters uncomfortable. The Britisher will keep his house at a "cozy" 60–65 degrees; to the American visitor whose field includes many perceptions of a "cozy" 75–80 degrees, the change is startling. At any rate, the physical environment is so clearly a part of the perceptual field that we need spend no more time on it.

The individual himself

Next, there are the individual's perceptions about himself. We will be concerned with some aspects of this awareness in greater detail later on. Now, however, we must recognize that our awareness of self is a part of our perceptual field. The sudden leap into figure of the foot asleep that was mentioned earlier is reminder enough. We also have awarenesses of our psychological state—whether we feel happy or sad, brave or fearful. Generally, our awareness of this dimension of the field is a part of the ground, unless the individual differentiates signs to the contrary—such as a headache or fear and anxiety.

Specific stimulus

Finally, there is the specific stimulus that may be in figure for an individual. This may be a person with whom he is conversing, or it may be an advertisement in his favorite magazine. It may be the feeling of a cold draft or any of the other sensory stimuli which we mentioned earlier. What we must recognize is that the specific situation or object of attention is viewed *as a part* of the individual's unique field of awareness. Hence our object "brick wall" had varying meanings depending on the perceptual field of the individual viewer. The salesman's pitch, the television commercial, the outdoor sign—all specific stimuli which the individual may differentiate—are perceived in the light of his unique storehouse of perceptions.

Summary of perceptual field map

Our view is that human behavior is a function of an individual's perceptual field at the instant of behaving. The field is his total awareness

Where neither product nor brand is strongly influenced by refer
groups, promotion should stress the product's attributes and ben
Where reference group influence is likely to be felt, the promotion sh
stress the kinds of people who buy the product so as to reinforce
broaden the acceptability of the product. Products susceptible to re
ence group influence are those which are visible and conspicuous. He
cars, clothing, furniture (to name a few) are subject to group influe
while goods like canned foods, soap, and radios are not. The except
of course, is the influence of family as a reference group. Here the in
ence may extend even to baking flour "because mother always used
and to products not generally thought of as conspicuous in any se
of the word.

Sociologists have noticed that some members in a group are m
effective as "opinion leaders" than others. Their valences (and *purchas*
are more likely to be imitated than the values of others in the gro
Opinion leadership tends to be related to *who one is* (in the sense
discussed earlier of leaders tending to personify the group's values),
what one knows (where special competence is deemed important), a
to *whom one knows*.

Young, unmarried girls may be opinion leaders on matters of fashi
because they *are* youthful; older women, by virtue of experience, te
to be looked to for advice on food products because of *what* they *kno*
Finally, an individual may be looked to for advice because of *who*
he *knows*—he may "belong" to other groups.[10] Because opinion leade
in groups tend to be exposed to a wider range of information (the
read more, subscribe to more publications, come into contact with mo
people), they are of particular concern to the marketing communicato
Studies of new-product adoption testify to the power of opinion leade
as an important word-of-mouth route to influencing buyer behavior.[11]

Physical environment

Moving to an even narrower dimension, the individual's perceptua
field includes his physical surroundings. Changes in temperature or hu
midity are perceived. We behave in response to perceptions from thi
part of the field, just as from any other. For instance, we may take
off an extra sweater as a day warms up or close our windows when

[10] Elihu Katz, "Two-Step Flow of Communication: An Up-to-Date Report on
an Hypothesis," *Public Opinion Quarterly*, Spring, 1957, 61–78.
[11] William H. Whyte, "The Web of the Word of Mouth," *Fortune*, November,
1954.

of himself and his world. We divided the perceptual field into seven dimensions which would seem to contribute to individual behavior. Figure 2–4 illustrates the map we have drawn thus far in our exploration of behavior.

FIGURE 2–4. An individual's perceptual field

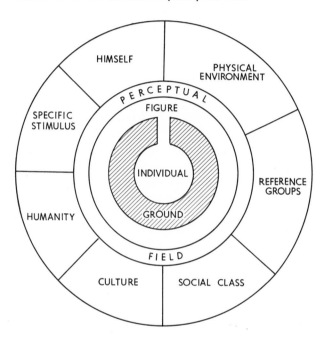

The individual selects from the field and differentiates or brings into figure a small portion at any given instant. He *perceives* by organizing the differentiated cues into meaningful concepts, to which valences may be attached. Much of the perceptual field is contained in ground—the past perceptions and differentiations of the individual, both of which result from his perception and influence the perceiving process.

The seven dimensions or categories we have sketched out in our map are not exclusive. They interact with one another to make the perceptual process even more complex. The individual may have as a part of his personal awareness the concept "strong" or "tall" or "smart" or "dumb" only in relation to other parts of the field. The "strong" concept may have been formed through observation of his ability to manipulate the physical dimension, but it is even more likely to be formed as a result of contact with others in reference groups.

Mention of reference groups brings us to a more troublesome kind of interaction, that of conflict in field dimensions. We have noted that the individual will most likely develop valences similar to those held by associates or reference groups. These can sometimes conflict. Consider, for a moment, the situation of a college student under an honor system which requires both a pledge of personal honesty and recognition of a duty to turn in observed violators for trial and possible punishment. "Honesty" is a culturally approved general concept. The student comes from a social class that at least gives lip service to "honesty," and two important reference groups—his family and the faculty—support the concept with positive valences. "Duty" is similarly positively valenced in the culture and society. At the same time, concepts like "informant," "tattletale," and "squealer" have a negative valence. Now the student is caught between reference groups. One group, the faculty, argues that "turning in violators" is a "duty" that is "honorable"; another group, fellow students, may view the same behavior as "informing." In the end, the student must cast his lot with one reference group or another.

THE SELF-CONCEPT

In Figure 2–4 the center circle, labeled "individual," is of crucial importance and deserves fuller treatment. In expanding our treatment, we will combine some of the field we labeled "the individual himself" with this circle to obtain a richer concept, which will be called the "*self-concept.*" Whereas the perceptual field embraces both the individual *and* his universe, the *self-concept* is concerned with the individual *in his field.*

Dimensions of self-concept

The self-concept refers to all perceptions of self a person has at a give instant. It is himself *as he sees himself* and not as he appears to others. Some people really do think of themselves as "great joke tellers" or "ladies' men" or "good singers" or "important," although you may have a very different opinion of them. What is important for us, as students of individual behavior, is the fact that each person tends to behave in accordance with his self-concept. Thus, the fellow who fancies himself a wit goes on and on telling jokes, sometimes not too well. Because the self-concept is so important in understanding behavior, we need to explore some of its dimensions.

Physical dimensions. Your self-concept has its physical components. You see yourself as tall or short, lean or fat, healthy or sick, weak or strong, handy or "all thumbs." These perceptions of self have an influence on behavior. A study of consumers of diet foods, for example, turned up a fairly sizable group of persons who, by all objective medical criteria of height-weight-age relationships, were not and had not been overweight. But the interviews revealed that these people *thought they were over-weight,* and they were therefore purchasing and consuming diet foods.

Social dimensions. Your self-concept also includes a variety of social dimensions. You see yourself as liked or disliked, accepted or rejected, loved or unwanted, a leader or a follower, a member of this or that social class, successful or a failure, married or single.

Moral dimensions. A part of your self-concept is your awareness that you are straightforward or devious, honest or dishonest, religious or atheistic, loyal or disloyal.

In short, the self-concept is the individual's unique and personal appraisal of himself at a given moment in time. While we have mentioned a very few of the facets of this concept, we can recognize that it is a most complex and vital part of an individual's awareness. We need to understand how it is formed, and what role this self-concept has in our mapping out and understanding buyer behavior.

Self-concept formation

Like any other concept, the self-concept is shaped by all segments of the perceptual field. Family, environment, friends, class, culture—each helps to form this most crucial of concepts. The individual begins to form his self-concept early in life and does so largely through contact with others around him. If his family repeatedly tells him that he is clumsy or unattractive, then he will "be" clumsy or unattractive. We say he will "be," because he will come to have these concepts as a part of his self-concept, and how he views himself is the only reality he has. A person comes to feel "accepted" or "a leader" or "loved" only in relation to other people as he forms his self-concept.

Once formed, the self-concept is essentially stable and resistant to change. While the individual may change his self-concept slowly over time, he will resist outside pressures which work to force a change. Quite normally, the individual replaces his "single" or "bachelor" concept with a "married" concept and later a "parent" concept. But he must effect these changes voluntarily if they are to become a fully functioning dimension of his self-concept. Teaching an old dog (or person) new tricks involves changing his self-concept, and this is why it is difficult.

The self-concept may include dimensions that are technically not self but which are so closely associated or identified with self as to have the same behavioral consequences. Parents may be wholly indifferent to their children, may even abuse them, but those same parents will rise up in righteous wrath if someone presumes to criticize their "little darlings." We routinely speak of "my school" or "my company," and our reaction to someone else's criticizing these extensions of self is like an attack on the self. Thus, the phrase "treading on thin ice" often means "getting too close to someone's self-concept."

Importance of self-concept to human behavior

If survival is the basic human instinct, *maintenance and enhancement of the self-concept is next most fundamental.* Combs and Snygg state the proposition well: "From birth to death the maintenance and enhancement of the self-concept is the most crucial, *if not the only* task of existence."[12] It follows, then, that the more an event is perceived to affect the self-concept, the more intensely it will be viewed by the individual. The sight of a lion 5 feet away may not provoke much reaction if he is perceived behind bars in a strong cage. Take away the bars, and the perception changes markedly. A lion 5 feet away without bars looks much closer because it is more threatening to the self. Do you remember how, in our example of the daydreaming student, the word *quiz* triggered his instant attention? Gone were the happy thoughts of weekend parties which were a part of his "social" self; in full figure were the instructor's remarks about "quiz" because "quiz" was uncomfortably close to his "student" self. If, with a sigh, he discovers the old drone is just talking about the dullness of quiz shows on television, the student will probably let the lecture drop quietly back to ground. The point is clear, however: the closer an event is perceived as affecting self, and more intently it is differentiated and the greater the behavioral consequences.

Even diverse behaviors like "conformity" and "nonconformity" can be explained by the self-concept notion. If a person sees himself as belonging to a group, if he has "group member" as part of his self-concept, he will probably behave in ways similar to those of his associates. He will probably even buy similar products. Fads and fashions of dress are notable examples of such conforming behavior. But all persons do not

---

[12] Combs and Snygg, *op. cit.* Italics added.

"conform." If an individual has, as a part of his self-concept, "not ruled by the establishment," then his behavior is shaped accordingly—the long-haired hippie may result. Whether an individual conforms or rebels, his basic need is to be comfortable with his self-concept, and his behavior is aimed at satisfying that need.

FIGURE 2–5. This ad asks the reader to consider the multiple dimensions of his self-concept

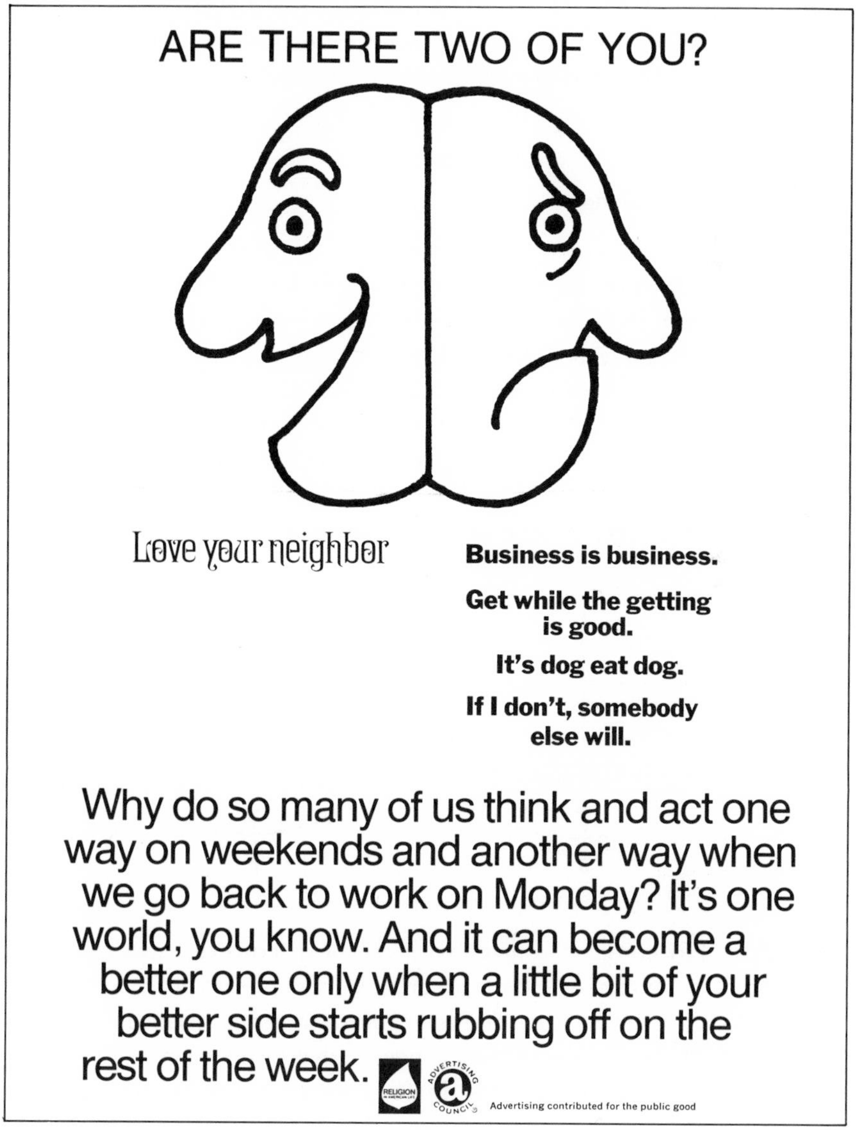
ARE THERE TWO OF YOU?
Love your neighbor
Business is business.
Get while the getting is good.
It's dog eat dog.
If I don't, somebody else will.
Why do so many of us think and act one way on weekends and another way when we go back to work on Monday? It's one world, you know. And it can become a better one only when a little bit of your better side starts rubbing off on the rest of the week.
RELIGION
ADVERTISING COUNCIL
Advertising contributed for the public good

This is, to be sure, a self-centered view of man, yet it seems to be a most realistic one. But how does this view of behavior take into account the unselfish acts we know take place? Such self-denial is entirely consistent with our map of human behavior *if* the individual has, as a part of his self-concept, concern for others. Then, by acting "unselfishly" he is in reality protecting a dimension of his self-concept. Sacrifice for children can therefore be a meaningful form of behavior for an individual who thinks of himself as a "good parent." Moreover, the fact that he *wants* to think of himself as a good parent can be traced to the cultural, social class, and reference group dimensions of his perceptual field. He knows that unselfish acts are rewarded by approval from these significant groups.

Marketing implications

The consumer has one basic motivation: to protect and enhance his self-concept. Because he is constantly bringing parts of his field into figure, selecting those cues which seem to have relevance for him, he is constantly being exposed to new opportunities for protection or enhancement. In other words, the consumer would like to maintain a state of self-concept satisfaction similar to a pendulum at rest as in Figure 2–6. When all is well with *his world*, the individual is like part A of

FIGURE 2–6.   Self-concept at equilibrium and threatened

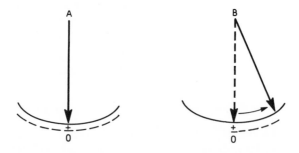

the figure. His constant contact with the field, however, will push him off center to a state of potential dissatisfaction. He will then seek to behave in such a way as to restore the concept to happy balance.

New experiences, new products, new advertising claims are always put to the test: What will this do for me? If the ad suggests that all is not well and proposes a remedy for the problem, the individual may follow the advice. For instance, a life insurance ad may threaten his "good provider" concept and suggest how he can achieve "peace of mind" (translation: satisfied self-concept) by the purchase of insurance. Until he read the ad, he might have been at equilibrium as in part A of Figure 2–6; after reading the ad, perceiving that he is not doing all he should as a good provider, he may move as in part B. The insurance company would be most happy to help him behave in such a way as to return to equilibrium!

SUMMARY

We began this chapter with a basic proposition: all behavior is organized and meaningful to the individual. We end the chapter noting that behavior which is meaningful is behavior which will enhance or protect the self-concept. The individual exists in a unique world of awareness we called the perceptual field. Our study of the perception process showed us how he selects from the field, differentiates, and learns. In the process, the ground of the field continues to build as new concepts are stored away, new experiences differentiated. Our study of the self-concept suggests that the individual will select and differentiate more intensely those events or cues in his field which seem to affect his self-concept. Indeed, the more closely the self is affected, the more intense the differentiation and perception.

In the next chapter we need to build on these views of individual behavior and seek to develop a map of the buying process which will be helpful to us as students of promotion management. We are concerned with persuasive communication in marketing. From this chapter we can begin to appreciate both the enormity of the problem (because each prospect can bring into figure only a part of his field at a time, and our television commercial may not be in figure) *and* the possibilities of using these concepts (knowing that our product must be sold in terms of how the prospect's self-concept will be benefited).

QUESTIONS AND PROBLEMS

2–1. Use the theory that concept's have valences attached to them to discuss "the generation gap."

2–2. Which might be more subject to reference group influence, brand of automobile or brand of toothpaste? Why?

2-3. How can a magazine ad achieve better differentiation of brand name and trademark? How can this be done on radio?

2-4. In the light of this chapter's discussion of individual behavior, comment on the often-voiced criticism that advertising causes people to buy things they do not need.

2-5. Use the self concept and perceptual field dimensions to explain the purchase of a wig by a 40-year-old balding bank executive.

2-6. If perception is selective, how does reference group influence a prospect's subjectivity of ad messages?

2-7. How can a salesman of vacation houses use the self concept and perceptual field dimensions in his sales presentation?

2-8. Bring to class examples of ads that use positive-valenced concepts, negative-valenced concepts, reference group identification, and social class appeals.

2-9. What implications for marketing communications do you see in the figure-ground concepts? Comment.

2-10. What marketing implications are there in the fact that differentiation is permanent?

CHAPTER 3

Buyer behavior

IN CHAPTER 2 we observed that an individual does not act in a random or meaningless way. His is an organized response to the world *as he sees it;* his behavior is *goal directed.* As we continue our map of buying behavior in this chapter, we need to begin with a look at the way in which goals are established by individuals. Our treatment in the first part of the chapter will be general, as has all our discussion of human behavior thus far. In the last part of the chapter we will develop a model of the buying process and use the model to suggest some appropriate strategies for promotion management.

NEEDS, WANTS, AND GOALS

The individual (with his unique self-concept) exists in a world of awareness (both present and past), equally unique and personal: his perceptual field. We have noted that he strives to protect and enhance his self-concept and that when he differentiates and perceives either an inadequacy of self, a chance to enhance self, or a threat to self, he will seek to restore his sense of well-being much as a pendulum, when pushed off center, seeks to return to equilibrium. If what he perceives is seen as having no relation to himself (or to anything he *identifies* with self), it is differentiated by unmotivating. For example, suppose a man is turning the pages of a magazine, and perceives the following headline in an ad: "Dad, can I have $20,000 for college?" If that reader is unmarried or childless or his children are beyond college age, the message may have no consequences for his self-concept. But if he has young children, the question is one that may be facing *him* one of these days; it involves his self-concept; it is likely to disturb his equilibrium unless he has no money worries. The message reveals an inadequacy of the self-concept "good provider" or a potential threat to that dimension of his self-concept. His response to the ad will depend upon how threatened his self-concept seems to be by the message. This brings us to the matter of varying levels of needs.

Levels of needs

Needs result from the contact of the self-concept with the perceptual field when those contacts reveal either threat, inadequacy, or a chance to enhance the self. There is but one fundamental, underlying need: *to protect or enhance the self-concept.* But just as there are varying levels of ground, ranging from near-awareness to complete forgetfulness, so there are varying levels of need intensity.

The *first* level, and lowest, consists of vague feelings not well differentiated and hence not clearly perceived. "I can't put my finger on what bothers me," is an expression of such a feeling. What may be happening, in such a case, is that the individual has in figure something unrelated to his self-concept but is aware of something in the field at a near-conscious level of ground that, if focused on, would indeed be need generating. He knows something is bothering him, but he hasn't brought that "something" into figure and perceived it as yet.

The *second* level of need is more clearly differentiated and directed toward a specific part of the perceptual field or self-concept. The second-level need may not be acted upon at once because it is not viewed as threatening enough to justify action. "One of these days I must do so-and-so" is a typical expression of this level of need. The individual knows that he can enhance or protect his self-concept, but the need is at a low enough level to justify postponement. In the following example, the individual moves from the first level to the second level of need.

Suppose someone is intently reading a book one evening near an open window. He is so intent on his reading that at first he doesn't realize that the wind has shifted and a cold breeze is making him uncomfortable. While he is still reading the book, he begins to shift around restlessly in his chair, in response to the first-level need. Finally, he realizes what is nudging into figure: "It's cold in here," he thinks. Now he is at the second level of need, for his attention is directly focused on the physical environment–physiological self-concept conflict. He *knows* what he needs: a warm self-concept. He may think, however, "I should close that window, but I have only a few pages more to read so I will wait until I finish before getting up."

The *third* level of need is an intensely figured perception requiring immediate response. Here the self-concept is perceived to be so threatened that nothing but action will suffice. The reading student, for example, may sneeze violently before he finishes reading the paragraph and decide that to avoid a cold he must act at once. (Note, however, that "catching a cold" may not necessarily threaten his *physical* self so much as his *social* self if he is counting on attending a party or dance tomorrow night. We can only infer from immediate action that *some* dimensions of his self-concept are involved.)

The promotion manager, of course, hopes to generate third-level needs by communicating so persuasively with prospects that nothing short of purchasing the advertised brand of product will satisfy the consumer. He realizes the consumers must be brought from a state of unawareness, through the second-level admission of need, to the third-level state of purchase insistence.

Wants

We have, in a sense, already defined *wants* in our discussion of needs. But we should make this definition explicit before moving on to a consideration of goals. A *want* is the conscious recognition of a need. The need, you recall, is the tension-producing contact between an individual's self-concept and his field. A want, which occurs at the second level of need, is the conscious realization that an opportunity exists to protect or enhance the self. In many, if not most, cases the need and want stages are simultaneously reached. A consumer perceives he has a flat tire, that the flat will prevent him from reaching a business appointment, and instantly *wants* to restore the car to operating condition. We may even go so far as to say that a want can exist in first-level need to the extent that the individual *wants* to know what it is he needs. This difference between need and want will be made clearer later in this chapter as we draw a map of the buying process and put it to use explaining some selected purchases.

Goals

Behavior, we maintain, is goal directed. A *goal* is a need-satisfying concept, as perceived by the individual. Here are some commonly accepted combinations of needs and goals which may help illustrate the definition: If the need is defined as "loneliness," the goal would be "companionship"; if "hunger," then "food"; if "thirst," then "drink." In terms of individual behavior, *a goal is an act which the individual has learned, or believes, will satisfy his need and restore his self-concept to equilibrium.* For example:

> Suppose you experience a toothache which, unknown to you, comes from an abscessed molar. With pain like that in figure, you have a third-level need and clearly want relief. You have a concept "aspirin," and you know from past experience that the act "taking an aspirin" helps relieve aches and pains. From your experience with aspirin in the past it has become a *reinforcer*. You take it; pain goes away. Thus the act "taking aspirin" is reinforced by the results obtained. This time, however, the pain persists. You have also learned that "heat" is often applied to sore muscles, and you try some warm water or a heating pad. With an abscessed tooth, heat will only intensify the pain, and thus the act "apply heat" is *not reinforced*. Finally, you try cold water, and the pain is eased. "Apply cold" is an act that is reinforced because it helps relieve the pain. But when you take away the cold water, the pain returns, so the goal "visit dentist" must be tried. But "visit dentist" as a goal concept depends upon the existence of this concept within your perceptual field. For another individual, with his own perceptual field, the goal may be "visit witch doctor."

Before we look at three types of goals, let's pause for a moment to return to our basic premise: the individual's behavior is organized and meaningful to him. To someone who knows the anatomy of teeth and the characteristics of abscesses, the behavior "drinking warm water" to relieve the pain caused by an abscessed tooth would appear almost insane. Yet to the poor soul seeking relief and without this knowledge in his perceptual field, the behavior is entirely consistent and understandable. He is searching his field for reinforcing concepts or goals for this need and systematically trying one after another.

Primary goals. These are goals which are closely related to the self-concept. Some are *physically* oriented—we want to be fed, comfortable, free from pain, and smoothly functioning. Some primary goals are *socially* oriented—we want to be accepted, loved, superior. Some are *psychologically* oriented—we want to be happy, relaxed, and at peace. And, not to ignore our fragment of human nature, we want to *survive*. In a sense, then, these primary goals might be considered *goals of being*, because they are reflections of desired states for the self-concept in its many dimensions.

Secondary goals. Secondary goals consist of goal concepts which we have learned satisfy primary goals. An individual may construct elaborate chains of secondary goals which ultimately lead to a primary goal and hence to the satisfaction of the self-concept. For example:

> You may want to have a *summer job* (secondary) so you can have *money* (secondary) in order to have a *college education*, so you can obtain a *graduate degree*, so you can have a *profession*, in order to acquire *material wealth* (secondary) so that you can *be* an upper-class professional man (primary goal).

All of these secondary goals are simply means of achieving the primary goal at the end of the chain.

Generalized goals. Some goal concepts appear in so many goal chains of most people that they can be considered *generalized goals*. The concept "money" is probably the most obvious generalized goal, because attainment of the goal "money" leads to attainment of a whole range of other secondary and primary goals. Other goal concepts which are typically considered generalized reinforcers are "power" and "love."

Goal hierarchies

As individuals perceive needs and experiment with goals for the satisfaction of these needs, they tend to establish an ordering or hierarchy of goal preferences. A simple case: "I'd rather have chocolate, but will take vanilla if you're out of chocolate." Experiments in psychology have shown that the more intense the need, the broader the range of acceptable goal alternatives. In severe cases of third-level need, for instance, people may include behavior which is otherwise unthinkable for them. For people near starvation, weeds or shoe leather may become substitutes for food. Interestingly, though, most civilized Westerners will even sacrifice the survival goal and starve before changing the self-concept to embrace cannibalism.

Goal hierarchies are actually the result of varying valences attached

FIGURE 3–1.   These two ads are from a campaign which appeals to a variety of secondary goals as well as a basic primary goal: fitness

FIGURE 3–1. *(Continued)*

to the concepts. At the top of the list would be the most positively valenced concept, followed by the next most positively valenced concept, and so on. Because these valences are subject to influence from social class and reference groups, it is not uncommon to find groups of individuals with fairly similar goal hierarchies.

Goal conflict and bivalent feedback

Since goals must be consistent with a multidimensional self-concept, there may arise conflicting situations. That is, the satisfaction of one dimension of the self-concept may be at the expense of a threat to another dimension. For example, you may satisfy your "good member" concept by going bowling with the group, but if you do so you may not satisfy your "good student" concept by being prepared for tomorrow's assignment. The goal or act "going bowling" thus has *two valences* for you, one positive and one negative. This dilemma is called *bivalent feedback* or, less elegantly, *mixed emotions.*

Bivalent feedback can occur in a variety of forms. Three of the most common situations will be described briefly:

♦ Goals which are equally attractive (+ +) are troublesome. Watch a child in front of the candy counter! With only 5 cents to spend, if he buys the chocolate, he can't have the licorice. If a consumer takes a vacation, he can't afford to redecorate the living room. Both are positively valenced concepts. The conflict lies in choosing one over the other. The choice will ultimately go to the alternative which the individual feels, at that time, will best satisfy his self-concept.

♦ Goals with opposite valences (+ —) for different dimensions of the self-concept make up the second group. Does the student bowl or study? A purchasing agent for a company may have both "likable" and "tough, hard-boiled buyer" as parts of his self-concept. Buying from a salesman will satisfy the likable dimension, but raising objections, asking tough questions, and being cold and abrupt will help the "hard-boiled" dimension.

♦ Alternate goals both of which are unpleasant (— —) must sometimes be faced. Do I cut the grass when the hammock beckons or let it go and have the neighbors think me a lazy sloth? Do I jump from the burning building and risk multiple fractures or stay where I am and risk burning? Again, the choice will be made either in favor of the more threatened dimension of the self-concept or for the less negatively valenced choice.

In marketing, bivalent feedback is a common problem for buyers. Because "money" is a generalized reinforcer, the buyer has a positive valence towards "saving" or keeping scarce dollars. Any purchase which involves a substantial outlay of dollars, therefore, falls into the first category described above. The buyer must choose between hanging onto dollars (+) and having the product (+).

Frustration of goal achievement

So far we have been considering what is going on when a consumer says "I want"; we have seen that consumers say it endlessly as a result of the constant interaction of the self-concept and the perceptual field. But what happens when the consumer can't achieve his goal—when the answer is *no?*

There are several main sources of goal frustration which keep persons from achieving their goals. The *physical environment* is the most obvious. There just isn't water in the desert, nor snow for skiing in Florida. *Biological limitations* are a source of goal frustration. All men just *aren't* created equal in strength and athletic coordination, and there really *are* 97-pound weaklings, both physically and intellectually. *Psychological limitations* may be the source of frustration. The individual may feel insecure and unsure of his need hierarchies and can't make up his mind. He *wants*, but cannot bring himself to resolve the bivalent feedback of the choice situation. Finally, *social limitations* play their part, too. The culture, class, or social group may not sanction certain goals or behaviors. Caste, race, and sex barriers may frustrate need satisfaction simply because of the race or sex of the individual. As a socioeconomic creation, the lack of money can be considered a social frustration. (The individual knows he wants, but also knows he cannot afford.)

But if the goal cannot be achieved, something has to give. And as we have seen, the self-concept is usually the last to change. How do we describe the adjustment to this conflict? There are two categories of responses to frustration according to psychologists: *adaptive* and *maladaptive.*[1]

Adaptive techniques. One very common approach is to *intensify effort* to achieve the goal. If a doorknob sticks, the first response is to pull harder. The man who cannot afford a secondary goal may respond by working longer hours or even take a second job in order to achieve

---

[1] See David Krech and Richard S. Cruchfield, *Theory and Problems of Social Psychology* (New York: McGraw-Hill Book Co., 1958), pp. 50–62.

his goal. Students who attain medium-range scores on college entrance tests often intensify their efforts and outperform students who score significantly higher on the tests.

A second adaptive technique is to *reorganize one's perception of the problem*. The result of initial frustration may be that the individual examines his need more carefully and discovers that it is not what he first perceived it to be.

In the process he may discover that he really doesn't have a need, or he may find other goals and come to the third adaptive technique: *goal substitution*. After a second look, he may perceive other behavior that will satisfy him, and he decides to seek the substitute goal.

The particular adaptive mechanism the consumer takes is of most important concern to the marketing manager. Faced with the physical frustration of a store's being out of stock of her favorite brand of a product (we classify this as physical because the objects are physically not available), the consumer may:

a)   Go to another store to get the brand (intensification of effort) or

b)   Decide she really doesn't need the item this week (reorganize her perception of the problem) or

c)   Reach for our competitor's brand (goal substitution).

The danger, of course, is that she will *like* the new brand, break her habit of perceiving our brand as the goal for that need, and be lost to us for future purchases. This is why many advertisers urge consumers to "insist on our brand, don't take substitutes."

Maladaptive techniques.   Certain approaches to frustration are labeled "maladaptive" by psychologists because they really don't get to the root of the problem of the unsatisfied self-concept. While more generally of concern to clinical psychology, some of these techniques bear mentioning; several of them, indeed, may be quite useful in promotion strategies. *Suppression* is one in which the individual pushes the need to ground. "I don't really need that," he tells himself. But once differentiated, the need is susceptible to recall to figure, and hence might be termed a "latent" need. *Avoidance* refers to the attempts to avoid exposure to perceptions that remind one of the need. A person whose desire for a product has been frustrated by conflicting goals or plain lack of money may react by avoiding ads for the product, ads which are constant reminders of the frustrated self-concept. Or, for the same reason, a person may even avoid contact with friends who have the product. *Rationalization* is a means of reducing the frustration caused by a message or ad;

the consumer may assume, for example, "that is just a pack of lies and propaganda." Rationalization also may be used to resolve goal conflicts and bivalent feedback. For example:

> A man who doesn't want to admit (to himself, let alone to others) that the purchase of a flashy automobile is the result of "striving" or "superiority" goals, may resort to rationalization and insist that there are long-run economy, safety, and comfort in such a car which attracts him. All of these, of course, are concepts to which society attaches positive valences.

Good persuasive communication may make subtle use of the more emotional appeals and, at the same time, provide some good, sound "reasons" to help the consumer rationalize and reduce the frustrations of the bivalent feedback.

A MODEL OF CONSUMER BUYING BEHAVIOR

We are now ready to use these concepts of individual behavior that we have been discussing in Chapters 2 and 3 to attempt to draw a map of consumer buying behavior. We need to try to specify what occurs between the emergence of a *need* and marketing-oriented behavior: *buying*. Just as a model airplane nowhere near approaches the complexity of the real machine, so our model or map of the buying process must necessarily be simplified. But, if the major components are present, then the study of the model can be useful in understanding the more complex reality.[2]

Steps in the model

We suggest a seven-step sequence in the basic model, with an eighth, "after-effect" stage, known technically as *cognitive dissonance*. After explaining the basic model and using it to explain certain illustrative purchases, some variations on the basic model will be explored. Here are the steps to be treated:

1. Need	5. Screening
2. Want	6. Selection (and possible frustrations)
3. Goal definition	7. Purchase
4. Listing	8. Postpurchase dissonance

---

[2] Readers interested in more elaborate models of buying behavior are referred to John Howard and Jagdish N. Sheth, *The Theory of Buyer Behavior* (New York: John Wiley & Sons, Inc., 1969).

Need. Our map of individual behavior led us to conclude that needs result from the contact of the self-concept with the perceptual field. When the consumer perceives an opportunity to protect or enhance the self-concept, a tension or disequilibrium is produced, and he will act in such a way as, to reduce the tension. The important fact about this concept of need is its reality to the consumer. There are no imaginary needs; according to this view, individuals just don't buy voluntarily anything they don't need. Purchase behavior results from the pressures of contact with the only reality the consumer knows: his perceptual field.

Want. This is the stage where the consumer recognizes that tensions exist and actively, consciously, begins wanting to do something about them. When a need has been differentiated by the consumer, we say a want has been established. For example, after a large Thanksgiving meal an individual may say, "I won't be able to eat again for a week." Yet during the afternoon, while he watches a ball game, perhaps, he digests the meal and, even though the game is in figure, hunger pangs begin to develop (a need) and push closer and closer into figure. As the game ends, the individual brings these pangs into figure, stretches, and says, "I think I might fix a bite to eat." At the moment he differentiates the hunger pangs, he has a *want*.

Goal definition. At this stage in the buying model, the consumer begins to select the goal or reinforcer which will, he believes, satisfy the need. In the marketing terminology of Chapter 1, this goal definition amounts to a *primary demand decision* on the part of the consumer. For instance, if a husband comes home from work and gradually perceives a certain coolness on the part of his wife, he may want to do something for her—especially if, in the process of differentiating the need he "recalls" (from ground to figure) the fact that today is their wedding anniversary! As he slips out of the house for the nearby shopping center, he is frantically involved in step three goal definition. Should it be clothing, candy, flowers, jewelry, or some combination of these goals? These are all, note, *types* or categories of products. Hence the decision at this stage of the model is a primary demand choice. The goal alternatives depend upon the concepts stored in his perceptual field. These, in turn, depend upon his culture, social class, family, reference groups, and so on.

Listing. The selective demand process begins with this stage of the buying model. If our forgetful husband decides on candy in the goal definition stage, he must next select a specific *brand* of candy. Thus, if *our* brand name does not exist in his perceptual field, or if it hasn't been differentiated for so long that it is too far in ground to be recalled,

FIGURE 3–2. Buyers' perceptual fields include awareness of noise

In the last 5 years, the noise level in American cities has risen over 20%.

In the last 5 years, sales of the very quiet Ford LTD have risen over 160%.

FORD

Take a
Quiet Break...
'71 Ford.

The noisier it gets out there, the more people seem to want to be in here. In a strong, solid Ford LTD. Where quiet is built in to stay. Where rough roads are unheard of. And bumps get a silent treatment that's a specialty of ours.

Consider the frame. We use a computer to locate vibration-free body mounts. We use heavy gauge steel in the body. We use double-action shocks. Rugged suspensions. Even acoustically tuned mufflers. And to make all that smooth-running

quiet even sweeter we add such luxury features as a 351-cubic-inch V-8. Power front disc brakes. And provide options like air conditioning with automatic temperature control, Tilt steering wheel, and four V-8's including our new 400-cubic-inch regular fuel V-8.

The Ford LTD for 1971. Very strong. Very luxurious. Very quiet. What we're saying is . . . Ford gives you better ideas.

Better idea for safety: Buckle up.

our brand cannot hope to survive the buying process. In the listing stage, then, the consumer mentally lists the specific alternatives of the goal category he has selected.

This step in the model may be performed purely on the basis of concepts already differentiated; or, it may require some active information seeking on the part of the buyer. In our study of perception, we noted that individuals are selective; we illustrated the point by observing that a man who is about to purchase a car is far more alert to new cars as he walks through the parking lot every day. In building his list of alternatives, he may actively look for automobile ads in magazines or newspapers; he is building his list of alternatives.

Screening. Because the individual will usually purchase only *one* of the alternatives, he must evaluate them and screen out all but the one he intends to buy. The screening process is an active attempt to assign valences to the alternatives—to test each against his goal preferences, self-concept, and against the rest of his field. Some products will be eliminated quickly (too expensive; too cheap; too big; too something-or-other), and others will move up in the hierarchy as certain claims, appeals, or product attributes are perceived to have more positive valence for the consumer. He may seek opinions and advice from other owners of products he is evaluating.

Selection (and possible frustration). This is the stage where the specific goal is selected. The consumer selects the goal (in our case, the specific brand, type, and size of the product category) which, in his eyes, at that time, best satisfies the need he perceives. The product selected will be the one which, in his opinion, has the highest valence value.

There may or may not be frustration of goal attainment. If the goal attainment *is* frustrated, we know the customer must take some course of action. This may be postponement of the purchase until sufficient funds are earned through more intense effort; the action may be a cancellation of the need perception through reexamination of the problem; it may be that the consumer goes back to step five (screening) and examines substitute goals.

Purchase. This is the behavior that attains the need-relieving goal. The step is listed separately from the selection step because a significant time interval may elapse and because of possible frustration. There are people who have already made up their minds about products and are overcoming economic or other frustrations before purchasing. If it is *our* brand, we need to *keep them sold* on their selection while buying is temporarily delayed.

Postpurchase dissonance. There is always a degree of bivalent feedback involved in any purchase decision because of (*a*) other ways to *spend* a scarce resource, and (*b*) alternative ways of *saving* the money. Postpurchase dissonance is the anxiety which follows a purchase, when the consumer wonders, "Did I do the right thing?" This is, to be sure, far more common when the purchase involves a major expenditure than when it involves a low-cost "convenience" item. What is dissonant is the nagging thought that the decision may not have been correct (in which case such self-concepts like "shrewd" and "intelligent" are threatened).

The buyer may seek to reduce the postact dissonance by reassurance, whether from friends, from advertising, or simply from observing how many other people have bought brand X. Some research suggests that persons who have just bought a car are more likely to read ads for that brand of car than are consumers as a group. Why? Because advertising claims help reassure them.

> We have often observed a very amusing illustration of postact dissonance in the behavior of students taking examinations. Student A finishes the examination and leaves the room, but waits around outside the door. If the test included a major decision on which much of his grade will hinge, the fact that he has just made such a decision is reason enough for dissonance. Then it dawns on him that he is the *only one through*. Did others see something in the question that he overlooked? Did he miss a vital point? (Of course, if his self-concept includes the notion "smartest member of class," the perception that he is the only one though need not be disturbing.)
>
> Finally, student B comes out, and A hurries over to find out if B said yes to the question, too. If it turns out that B did *not* say yes, then we find *two* dissonant students waiting around in the hall, and they often seem to pounce on the third student. If A and C agree, they go off relieved, while student B paces the hall to find out what the next student did.

This aspect of postpurchase dissonance is included in our buying model for two reasons: (1) it is a fairly normal occurrence for large-scale purchases and needs to be recognized if our model of the buying process is to be complete; and (2) the phenomenon suggests the need for continued promotion to both prospects *and purchasers*.

Testing the buying model

We have drawn at long last a map of the behavior most meaningful to students of promotion management: *buying*. Our model of the buying process should help us understand what is going on when a consumer buys something. Let's now put the model to work and see if we can explore some buying situations in the light of the concepts of these last two chapters on behavior.

Test one. The first example is a simple one, but if our map of buying behavior cannot explain even a simple purchase, there is little need to try it out on more complex buying decisions. In the example, the left-hand column will contain a description of the buying situation, while the right-hand column will comment on the situation in terms of our buying model and our concepts of human behavior.

Situation	*Comment*
While reading in the library, student X's throat begins to dry out in the close, overheated atmosphere of the reading room. He is involved in his book, but we can observe him licking his lips and attempting an occasional swallow.	The *need* has resulted from the physiological part of his field—his throat needs moistening.
Gradually this perception of a dry throat comes up from ground into clearer and clearer figure, and he suddenly realizes: "My throat is dry."	*Want* now exists because he has clearly differentiated the need. What he wants, of course, is to relieve the need.
Having realized the need, the student can search through the concepts he has differentiated as reinforcers or goals which would satisfy this need. His goals might be candy mints or chewing gum which will produce salivation and moisten his throat, or any of a variety of "drink" concepts. He eliminates all that are intoxicating because he has a class in 20 minutes and, besides, it's before lunch. He favors a drink over candy or gum.	He is now at stage three of the buying model: goal definition. Some of the categories of goals, such as "intoxicating beverages" are eliminated because they conflict with: (*a*) his student self-concept, and (*b*) his reference group drinking customs or concepts (not "before lunch"). His decision, a primary demand one, is for the category: nonalcoholic drinks.
Having selected a goal, the student must now list the alternatives available. He does this on the basis of the concepts he has stored away	This, of course, is the listing stage of our model. If our brand of soft drink is not among the seven he "lists," there is little hope of

Situation (Continued)

in his perceptual field. The list could be extensive, for he "knows" water, coffee, tea, milk, and seven brands of soft drinks. He also "knows" that water is trapped in the base of cactus plants and available to persons marooned on the desert but probably doesn't list this at this time because his need and present situation are not that intense.

He screens out all those not immediately available because it is not worth too much effort for such a little thirst. There is a coffee machine in the basement, but he remembers that the last cup tasted like used battery acid and wasn't very hot either.

But he recalls (from ground to figure) a cola machine down there, and he decides to get a cola drink. Down to the basement he goes.

As luck would have it, the machine has a little sign lighted which says "Use Nickels Only," and our student has only a quarter.

He goes over to a change-making machine near the door . . .

. . . and finds a familiar phrase written on paper stuck to the machine: Out of Order.

"What's the use," he thinks, "I'll just get a drink of water at the fountain in the lobby."

On his way back to the reading room, the student stops and takes a drink from the cooler.

Comment (Continued)

our making a sale to this consumer at this time.

The student first screens on the basis of "convenience"; then rejects the coffee alternative because of the negative valencies attached to the "library coffee" concept in his field.

Selection has occurred.

Frustration occurs here, because of the physical limitations of the machine and the student's supply of money.

Intensification of effort, an adaptive technique for frustration resolution.

More *frustration*.

Twice frustrated, he returns to his list of alternatives and uses *goal substitution* to solve his problem.

(*Purchase*) of at least need-satisfying behavior, as the water was free.

In this simple, everyday illustration, we can identify every major segment of the buying model except the postpurchase stage. A decision of this minor nature is not likely to produce any dissonance.

The steps between need and purchase may take place over days or even months of time, or they may take place in fractions of minutes. Impulse buying is of this latter category. A product attractively displayed may suggest to the consumer that he "needs" it, and the listing and screening steps are bypassed as the product is placed in the shopping basket. But wait—are the steps really bypassed? In that instant of perception, the brain is perfectly capable of testing the product notion against relevant areas of the purchaser's perceptual field and certifying the product as "acceptable" to the self-concept. Physiologists estimate that the eyes alone send signals to the brain at the rate of 100 *billion* bits per second. Thus, no matter how attractive the decanter or display, a nondrinker will not be stimulated to buy brandy on impulse.

There may, however, be shortcuts in the sequence. If consumers are not willing to search for alternatives, if they have built in a need-want-goal pattern which specifies the brand, then we say the consumer has a *habit* of buying brand X.

Test two. Let's test the buying model once more, this time using a situation involving a purchase of importance in terms of the dollars involved. Because this purchase involves more "risk" to the self-concept, we shall expect to find some postact dissonance in the example and here it is:

> Over the course of several months of visiting in friends' houses, a housewife begins to perceive new carpets in their living rooms instead of scatter rugs. As these perceptions occur, time after time, they begin to create a tension. The housewife's self-concept "member of this social group" or "member of this class" does not jibe with the perceptions of her friend's living rooms and her own. The *need* step has been slowly evolving as these cues or bits of information begin to take on a pattern and be differentiated. At first she may not know exactly what is wrong, but she begins to perceive that she is "out of step" with group norms or patterns of living. She now has a *want*, to restore her self-concept to a comfortable sense of belonging to her social group, a most important reference group in her perceptual field.
>
> One night, seemingly out of the blue to him, she says to her husband, "I want a carpet for the living room." She has now defined her goal. *Goal definition*, in this case, involves wanting a secondary

goal, a new carpet, in order to satisfy a primary goal, *being* accepted in her social circle. "Everyone is getting carpets," she tells her husband.

She begins to notice the carpet ads in home furnishing magazines and to question her friends about their carpets. Thus, the *listing* stage of the buying model begins. In the course of all this, she acquires many new concepts such as "broadloom," "pile," "Axminster," and so on. These concepts have valences which may come from her friends ("Of course, I think Axminsters are a little too gaudy, don't you, dear?") or from the way she perceives the new concepts in the ads.

As the valences are attached, the *screening* actually begins. Screening continues as she decides against wall-to-wall (costs too much) in favor of room-size carpeting. Many of the steps may have thus been taken before she ever sets foot in a store. But shopping she goes, adding some items to her list and eliminating some items for reasons of price, color, pattern, or whatever. This screening may take several weeks or months.

Finally, she finds just what she has been looking for and *selects* a specific brand and style of carpet as the answer to her "decorating problem." (Isn't that a clever bit of rationalizing? What started out as simply a group status problem has somehow become a decorating problem. And why not? Anyone can have a "decorating problem" without threat to her self-concept, but continued admission that one is blatantly "keeping up with the Joneses" *is* threatening.)

If her husband is willing to pay for it, our housewife *purchases* the rug. We might note in passing that the husband's willingness to buy may be the result of another whole need-to-purchase sequence where the "need" is to satisfy his "good provider" concept, or even to get the nagging wife off his back.

As soon as the new carpet is down, barely after the truck drives away, in fact, the housewife is on the telephone inviting friends to drop by. To each she will probably put questions designed to reassure her of her impeccable taste and relieve the *postpurchase dissonance* occasioned by such a major purchase.

Refining the buying model

The basic seven- or eight-step sequence which we have traced seems a useful way to explore a variety of consumer buying decisions. There are possibilities for improving on this model, however, and some of these need to be explored. These improvements or modifications consist of "loops" which must be built in at several stages of major purchase decisions.

Goal screening. In our example of the thirsty student, we noticed that he approached the goal definition problem by listing, screening, and selecting. In Figure 3–3 these modifications are built into the basic

FIGURE 3–3. Expansion of basic buying model to include goal definition loop

map. What is happening, of course, is a sequence of listing primary demand concepts (like alcoholic beverages, nonalcoholic drinks, candy mints, etc.) and testing these for general valences. The goal selection step then defines the goal, and the model proceeds to the listing of those selection list and from there goes to the next-base store on her list, and so on.

Store selection. Conventional textbook treatments of buyer motivation include discussions of *patronage motivation,* which is defined as the inclination or motivation to buy from a particular store. Stores may be chosen because of their convenience, their low prices, the fact that they are owned by friends, or for a variety of other reasons. Our buying model has not included any references to this concept, but we should see how store selection is accomplished. Let's take a simple situation first, and then build a general store selection loop for the basic model.

> Do you remember our forgetful husband, who dashed out to buy an anniversary present for his wife? Suppose he recalled immediately that she wanted a brand X electric hair dryer and selected that without further listing or screening. As it was late afternoon, you recall, he must find a store that sells the item and is still open.
>
> He *lists* the stores he knows which sell it (or takes a quick look in the Yellow Pages to help his listing), screens out A, (too far across town, though prices are lower), and heads for store B (nearby, stays open until nine, though prices are somewhat higher).

In other words, we should add a list-screen-select loop to our model to accommodate store choice. But where should it come?

For many heavily advertised, widely distributed products we might wish to place the store selection loop after the product selection step of the general model, as in Figure 3–4. The assumption in placing store selection after product selection is that, for these goods, the store is essentially offering availability and little else. Hence, goods classified as "convenience" goods might well use this version of the model.

FIGURE 3–4.   Expansion to include store selection loop

In the case of our carpet-buying housewife, however, we could argue that the store selection loop comes after goal definition and that listing will occur within the confines of the lines carried by the stores chosen. This is even more likely in the purchase of gifts or fashion items where the name or label of the store is an important part of the total product concept. What we are saying is that for some purchases the store is nearly as important a part of the purchase decision as the product itself. A wife setting out to buy her husband a Christmas gift of clothing may, for example, list several stores, screen, select the store from which she will buy, and then proceed to product listing when she gets to the store. If she finds nothing at the first store, she returns to the store selection list and from there goes to the next-best store on her list, and so on.

Next, we need to note a special case where the buyer is caught in *frustration* (after step six, Selection) for a long period of time. The cause of the frustration may be economic, or self-concept conflict, or whatever. If he does not move from *select* to *purchase* within a reasonable length of time, he may wish to review his decision to buy brand X. If, for example, he had selected a Loud-n-Clear Piano but could not afford the $900 price at the time, he may intensify his efforts and build up his savings account. But this may take months, or even years. When he has saved the right amount, he may return to the listing and screening steps to make sure he is still satisfied with the choice. As a result, though he originally selected a Loud-n-Clear, he may eventually purchase a Sweet-n-Soft because this new brand survives the screening with a higher valence than the brand he chose originally.

Finally we need to recognize the force of *habit* and its marketing response: *brand loyalty*. Since active shopping is tiresome, for many purchases the consumer skips from *want* to *selection* based on previous shopping experience. Moreover, she may select not only *good* but *brand* as well. For routine, frequently purchased goods, the normal inclination may be to select the brand bought last. Breaking brand loyalty habits means persuading the customer to think through the decision sequence again and evaluate present brands against potential substitutes. A bad experience with a prior purchase, an eye-catching appeal from a new brand, or a simple desire to experience variety may lend to brand switching. The point is that habitual buying routines can *and do* get built into buyer behavior patterns and can be a source of strength or challenge to the seller, depending upon whose brand commands the shopper's loyalty.

Implications for promotion

We are now in a position to make some comments about the buying model and its implications for promotional strategy. First, of course, is the possibility of working on the *need* and *want* steps. We have suggested that perceptions which motivate are those which relate to the self-concept of the buyer and that the closer an event (or product) is seen to self, the greater the behavioral consequences. Promotion must use concepts and values which are consistent with the target customer's field if that promotion is to stimulate needs.

The *listing* step is critical. If the consumer has not learned (differentiated) a brand name, that name cannot become a part of the purchase process. Unless the name is differentiated regularly, it may fade so far into ground that it is "forgotten," hence useless as an alternative. In major purchases, listing may be a more active process, as consumers *seek* information about purchase alternatives. Advertising, salesmen's presentations, the personal influence of friends and associates are all potential sources of product definition. In the process, however, valences will likely be attached to the concepts being learned. Naturally promotion seeks to create a positive brand image (or valence).

Screening also is crucial for sellers. *Our* job in promotion is to persuade consumers that *our* product best satisfies their needs. In the screening step, then, we aim to incline them toward our product and away from competitors' products. Thus:

"Acts twice as fast as aspirin."

"Cleaner than any other leading washday detergent."

"The only product that . . . ."

Frustration of goal achievement presents challenges to promotion, too. If goods are out of stock, this physical frustration may result in a loss of sales. We may urge them to intensify their efforts:

"If your grocer doesn't have X, ask him to get it for you."

"Don't settle for anything but brand Y."

Frustration resulting from conflicting feelings about the purchase may require some solid "rational" support for the more powerful need goal being appealed to. Suppression, as we have noted, creates a sort of latent demand or need perception which may respond to stimulation and return to figure. Postponement because of economic frustration may respond to promotion of credit terms and easy payment plans. Goal substitution may be *fought*, if ours is the established brand; it may also be *used* if we are trying to invade a market. "Isn't it about time you tried————?"

Purchase, as we have seen, does not automatically follow *selection.* A customer may actually get all the way to the selection stage of the model *and then forget.* People may postpone the purchase without too much anxiety if the level of the need is not very intense; they must be stimulated to "do it now." Quite often, however, the promotion message is perceived at home, but the decision to buy is pushed to ground in the confusion of the shopping trip. In-store point-of-purchase promotion can help overcome this problem as well as (in the case of impulse buying) trigger the whole sequence. Having made the purchase decision, customers may still balk at the dissonance of parting with scarce dollars, but they may be persuaded by being reminded of the many rewards and benefits the product brings them.

Postpurchase dissonance, especially for more expensive products, creates an opportunity for persuasion. Continuity of advertising and special, reassuring direct-mail pieces congratulating them on their wise choice are but examples of how this dissonance phenomenon can be turned into a promotional advantage.

A reminder about the buying model

We began our study of consumer behavior in Chapter 2 with the observation that maps are but representations (and sometimes crude ones at that) of reality. Let's conclude Chapter 3 with the reminder that what we have done is set forth *a* way of looking at consumer behavior. It is not necessarily the *only* way, but it offers, we feel, a useful means of fitting a terribly complicated process into a marketing-oriented model.

You are urged to make changes or additions to the model according to your knowledge and experience, for in the process you will be *forming* concepts which will probably long outlast the ones merely *attained* by passive reading.

QUESTIONS AND PROBLEMS

3–1.   What marketing implications are there in the concept of goal frustration?

3–2.   Relate bivalent feedback to the dimensions of an individual's perceptual field. Which areas are likely to be the prime sources of bivalent feedback?

3–3.   Use the buying model described in this chapter to explain the purchase behavior of the balding bank executive you confronted in question 2–5 at the end of the last chapter.

3–4.   Does the buying model vary for convenience goods as opposed to shopping goods? Which steps take longer for which product?

3–5.   How can advertisers help intensify needs among prospects?

3–6.   Bring to class some ads that seem to focus on the need-want stages of the model, some that aim at the list-select stages, and some that seek to move the prospect to the purchase or action stage.

3–7.   Why does bivalent feedback or goal conflict almost always accompany a large purchase?

3–8.   How does an advertiser insure success in the screening stage for his product?

3–9.   Under what conditions might the store selection loop precede the product selection sequence in the buying model?

3–10. How could a salesman for a computer manufacturer use the buying model to advantage in planning a sales presentation for a new, small, desk-model computer designed for the small business firm?

CHAPTER 4

Communication

THE PAST TWO CHAPTERS have given us some ideas about individual behavior and the buying behavior process both of which are of special concern to marketing. We now turn to the matter of communication. By understanding what communication is, how it is accomplished, and how it can become more effective, we will be better prepared to manage promotion—marketing's persuasive communication.

ELEMENTS OF COMMUNICATION

The word *communication* comes from the Latin *communis* or "common." When we communicate, we are establishing a oneness or commonness with some one or some group of individuals.[1] We communicate when our message is a part of (or in common with) someone's perceptual field. Unless there is this conjunction of message and perceptual field, communication cannot take place. If a buyer does not see magazine X, an advertisement in X cannot hope to communicate with him; so long as a salesman is in the waiting room, he cannot communicate with buyer Y because he is not in Y's perceptual field.

Our knowledge of perception and differentiation suggests an even more stringent requirement: effective communication takes place *only when a message is in figure.* Unless buyer Y *listens* to the salesman, his getting out of the waiting room and into the office will not assure

---

[1] Wilbur Schramm, *The Process and Effects of Mass Communication* (Urbana: University of Illinois Press, 1955), p. 3.

communication. To be effective, then, a marketing communication must get into a prospective buyer's perceptual field *and into focus*. And we know that he can focus only on one portion of his field at any moment.

The building blocks

Let's back up two chapters and repeat something that was said about perception: "The process of *perception* consists of taking cues or bits of information from the field and organizing them into meaningful ideas or 'concepts.' Concepts are what we think with; they are what we *communicate* with." If I am to communicate with you, I must somehow manage to get you to perceive what concepts or ideas I have in mind.

Signs and referents. We communicate by using meaningful *signs* in a system or *code* which is understood by both sender and receiver. A sign is an organized collection of cues sufficient to represent a concept or referent. A *referent* is a concept that you have differentiated. It is not the reality itself, but the concept you have in mind that *refers* to the real thing. Here is an example:

> In written communication the letters h r c a i are cues. If you organize them meaningfully, they can become a sign—chair.

Now if you have previously differentiated a collection of legs, seat, and back into a concept you labeled "chair," the sign has a referent in your perceptual field. You cannot sit on the sign, for it is merely ink and paper; you cannot sit on the mental image or referent. The sign evokes the image or mental referent to the reality we both label "chair."

By taking away one little cue, "c," what is left is "hair," and the sign changes because h a i r is another meaningful collection of cues which has a referent in your perceptual field. If we restore the "c" and add an "s" to the collection of cues, we have "chairs," and a slightly different mental picture is formed. Now you perceive more than one of the referents.

The mental image you form when the sign "chair" is communicated may not exactly match the mental picture I have in mind. If it does not, we have not established perfect commonness; our communication is imperfect. You may think of a desk chair, an easy chair, or even an electric chair, depending on your perceptual field.

Code form. We communicate by using meaningful signs *in a system or code which is understood by both sender and receiver*. In written

FIGURE 4–1. In family branding and package similarity a familiar referent can be extended to a variety of products

communication the code consists of spelling (ordering of cues), grammar (ordering of signs), and punctuation. In oral communication pronunciation and grammar are essentials.

If meaningful signs are strung together without regard to code form, no communication can take place. Try these:

"messages swiftly students a Which to Sharpens a cellophane"

In this instance the cues are ordered into meaningful and familiar signs, but the signs are in a hopeless jumble of nonsense.

On the other hand, if the sign order and punctuation is in proper form but the signs have no referents (and are therefore meaningless), no communication occurs:

"An axflat sarked a fluteling droomscal."

Our code form suggests that "axflat" and "droomscal" are probably nouns, "sarked" is a verb, and "fluteling" is an adjective modifying "droomscal." But since these signs have no referents, there is no commonness.

The signs l a u t p e c r e p   d l e i f may have meaning for you or they may not. If you remember differentiating them in Chapter 2 or recall that these cues were presented backwards (that is, you recall the code), then you may see the signs as meaningful. And if they have no meaning whatsoever to you, then what was intended as one message—"perceptual field spelled backwards"—has probably been received as: "Better study Chapter 2 again."

The building blocks of communication are meaningful signs communicated by sufficient cues in an understandable code to create a commonness of image or referent in both sender's and receiver's minds.

ELEMENTS OF COMMUNICATION SYSTEMS

Three essential elements of a communication system have already been suggested: a sender, a message, and a receiver. These three elements are familiar in a variety of situations: boy whistles at girl, salesman talks to buyer, retailer advertises to housewives, teacher lectures to class. It is even more helpful to visualize a five-step process to understand marketing communication. The steps are: (1) a source, (2) encoding, (3) transmission channel, (4) reception, (5) decoding. The process can be depicted as in Figure 4-2, where the overlapping circles represent the conjunction of perceptual fields of the source and receiver.

FIGURE 4–2. Five-step communication process

Let's examine each link in this chain:

1. The *source* or origin of the message may be an individual, as when A talks to B; it may be an organization, as when a manufacturer advertises his products.
2. *Encoding* involves putting the thoughts of the source into message form, assembling the cues into meaningful signs according to the rules of the code. In conversation the source encodes his own messages. In mass communication, encoding may involve an advertising agency writing the message and a professional announcer reading it.
3. *Transmission* is the actual carrying of the message from one to another. The channel of transmission may be direct voice, radio waves, or the printed page.
4. *Reception* occurs when the message is detected by the receiver *and* comes into figure in his perceptual field. Note that both access to the field and differentiation are required.
5. *Decoding* takes place in the receiver's mind as the signs are recognized and matched with referent concepts and perception occurs. A message may be received (detected) without being perceived or understood. If you send me a message in Russian, it may come through loud and clear *and meaningless,* since I cannot decode Russian.

Some variations in these five elements are shown in Figure 4–3.

Multiple channels

In step three, transmission may involve more than one channel of communication. A conversation, for instance, uses the spoken word as the primary channel of transmission. But facial expression, word intonation, and gestures are powerful secondary channels. The good salesman knows that distracting gestures or a bored tone of voice can impede or even destroy the effectiveness of his primary channel: the sales talk. He supplements his oral transmission with visual demonstrations which utilize the sight channel.

FIGURE 4–3. Some examples of communication systems

Elements	*Magazine advertisement*	*Radio commercial*	*Personal sales call*
1. Source	Manufacturer X	Manufacturer X	Salesman X
2. Encoding	By advertising agency	By both agency and announcer	Sales talk
3. Transmission	Magazine Y	Station Y	Speaks directly to buyer
4. Reception	Buyer Z sees X's ad in magazine Y, reads	Buyer Z has station Y tuned in and is listening	Buyer Z listens to what salesman X is saying
5. Decoding	Z understands X's message	Z understands X's message	Z understands X's message

Nor is this concept of multiple channels limited only to oral communication. Even in printed communications, where one might expect only the primary channel to operate, a host of secondary channels exist. The design of an advertisement, its placement on a page, its size, its illustrations, the kind of type used—all these elements communicate. Paper manufacturers advertise to remind business executives that their stationary and letterheads are important secondary communicators. Here are some examples of how the message transmitted in the primary channel can be torpedoed by secondary channels:

Primary channel	*Secondary channel(s)*
1. "This semester we are going to explore together the exciting and dynamic field of promotion management."	1. Mumbled dully in a monotone by a professor staring glassy-eyed out the window.
2. "With us, Mr. Buyer, dependability is a watchword and habit."	2. Spoken by a salesman who was 15 minutes late, and who just mispronounced the buyer's name.
3. "Welcome to Blotch's . . . the Store for Discriminating Shoppers of Impeccable Taste."	3. Flyspecked sign in a finger-smeared window displaying a dusty jumble of merchandise.

Persuasive communicators need to be alert to these secondary channels and to be sure that all communication channels are working together for maximum effectiveness.

Feedback

In face-to-face communication each person in the system (sender and receiver) is both encoding and decoding at the same time. The salesman is *encoding* a sales message and transmitting it to the prospect, and he is constantly *decoding* both secondary transmissions (puzzled looks, yawns, nods of agreement) and primary transmissions (questions, objections) from his customer. The salesman, in other words, is alert to *feedback* he is getting from his customer. He alters his encoding in response to that feedback in the hopes of improving his communication. We get feedback from our own messages and can correct misspellings and pronunciation; sometimes we try to say things and "they don't come out quite right" as we hear ourselves talk.

FIGURE 4–4.   Feedback is a part of the complete communication system

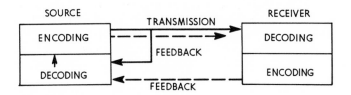

The advertiser, who is communicating to a mass audience far removed, faces a more difficult communication task simply because he is cut off from feedback. He cannot see puzzled looks, sneers, or frowns of disapproval. He can only test his messages on samples of consumers and infer from surveys of readers or listeners whether or not he has succeeded. Thus he may be weeks, months, or even forever removed from feedback from his intended receivers. Good promotion management recognizes the need for feedback and tries to create flows of information back from the marketplace in order to evaluate and improve communication.

Receivers

Special attention needs to be paid the receiver, because the message must be tailored to his communication needs. Receivers of marketing messages can fall into one of several categories: The user group was identified in Chapter 1, and divided into users of our brands and users of competitor's brands. Figure 4–5 divides these two groups further into satisfied and dissatisfied users, with differences in communication goals and problems noted.

Receivers may, of course, lie in the prospect pool or in the group of nonusers of the product. Some of these may have felt needs for the product and should be encouraged to try it now. Others may have not felt a need, either because they haven't heard of the product or do not perceive of it as a means to self-concept fulfillment. In either instance the message must be altered to the state of the receiver.

FIGURE 4–5. Selected message goals for receivers in different brand usage states

	Satisfied	*Dissatisfied*
Users of		
Our brand.......	Seek to increase use and purchase frequently	Seek to overcome negative valence
Other brands.....	Seek to force comparison on points where our brand has advantages	Seek to take advantage of receiver's state and promote switch to our brand

A most useful classification of communication audiences is offered by Crane in the following six-stage measure of advancement towards the advertiser's goal:

1. Some do not know the product exists.
2. Some know of the brand, but not what it claims to do.
3. Some know the claims, but do not accept them.
4. Some accept the claims, but prefer another brand.
5. Some prefer the brand, but have not yet purchased it.
6. And some, oh happy day, have actually bought the advertiser's brand.[2]

All of this is to suggest that persuasive communication must pay the strictest attention to the state of the intended message receiver in order to maximize the effect of the communication process.

PURPOSES OF COMMUNICATION

All communication can be divided into two broad categories: (1) that which seeks to inform, and (2) that which seeks to motivate or

[2] See Edgar Crane, *Marketing Communications* (New York, John Wiley & Sons, Inc., 1965), p. 32.

persuade. They are not, as we shall see, mutually exclusive in marketing. It is helpful to study each type separately, however, to understand the minimum conditions or rules for success.

Informing

Marketing communications may take the form of telling people that a product or service exists, of informing them about the product. The goal of such messages is either to help the receiver attain a new concept or to help him alter a concept he now holds. In the early stages of a product's life cycle, much of the communication is informational, as the seller seeks to build primary demand by informing customers of a product and of the functions it performs.

Take the concept "electroluminescence"; here is an informing message:

> Electroluminescence is the property of an entire surface to emit light when an electric current is applied. Normal light sources such as incandescent bulbs and fluorescent tubes emit light from a single source, then diffuse it through ground glass. Electroluminescent materials emit light from their entire surface; thus whole ceilings and walls may become light sources if built of these materials.

You have just been sent (transmitted by means of this printed page) a message designed to inform you about the sign: electroluminescence. Have we communicated? Do you understand what this new sign stands for? Have you *attained a referent concept?* If the answer to these questions is yes, it is because the message has met the following conditions:

1. We both agree on the rules of the code.
2. The message used concepts that both of us have previously differentiated.
3. We have the *same referents* (or very nearly the same) for these signs.

Condition one. The message must be encoded in a manner agreeable to both sender and receiver. They must agree on the rules of the code—that is, the spelling, grammar, and punctuation system used to encode the message. If a sender encodes a message in Morse Code or shorthand symbols, for instance, and the receiver is not able to decode Morse or shorthand, no communication can occur. A second aspect of code agreement is the relative abilities of sender and receiver to use the agreed-upon code. They may agree on English as a code form, yet differ widely in ability to decode English messages. Here we are talking about the complexity of the coding, not the signs that make up the message. One fairly common guide to message complexity is the length of each sentence. College graduates can decode messages of far longer length than, say, grade-school dropouts. The following two messages say the same thing, yet one is encoded in a far simpler form than the other:

Jack is a boy. He is tall. He has red hair. He is bouncing a ball. It is a basketball. The ball is red, too. Jack is bouncing the ball on the sidewalk. The sidewalk is made of stones. They are cobblestones.	Jack is the tall, red-haired boy bouncing the red basketball on the cobblestone sidewalk.

If we are to communicate with prospective customers, we must make sure these marketing communications meet condition one: The message must be encoded in a form appropriate or agreeable to both sender *and* *receiver*.

Condition two. The second requirement or condition is that the message use concepts that both sender and receiver have previously differentiated. In the message on electroluminescence, for example, signs such as "incandescent," "fluorescent," "emit," and "diffuse" must have referents in your perceptual field as well as mine if we are to communicate. What makes good communication readily understandable is the fact that the messages contain familiar signs and concepts. An advertiser of vitamins, therefore, will not use the same messages in selling to mothers that he uses in communication with medical doctors. If the intended receiver is a middle-class teen-ager, the message is cast differently from when the prospective receiver is a graduate physicist.

Condition three. Both sender and receiver must have the same (or very nearly same) referents for the signs used in the message. Again, to return to our example of the new light form, we communicated if you had previously differentiated the concept "incandescent bulbs" (thereby meeting condition two) *and* if you do not think of incandescent bulbs as belonging to the same category of concepts as "tulip bulbs" or "iris bulbs." In marketing, where identical messages must often be sent to great masses of prospective customers through magazines or television, the sender must take care to use words that have a common referent for all his prospects.

The essence of communication to inform is encoding in a form appropriate for the intended receiver, messages composed of signs familiar to the receiver.

Motivating and persuading

The second category of messages is the group designed to persuade the receiver. An effective persuasive message must first of all follow every rule of good informative communication. In addition, the persuasive message pays special attention to the valences of the signs it uses. Product X may be described by the words "fun," "youthful," "dependable," or by the use of other positive-valenced signs. Another approach is to suggest that product X helps the buyer avoid or overcome negative-valenced concepts. "Banish tattle-tale gray"; "Stop embarassing odor"; "No traffic jams with our doorstop parking" are examples.

Preparing persuasive messages requires a thorough knowledge of what valences the intended message receiver attaches to concepts. We know from our study of consumer behavior that what is ultimately important to buyers is their self-concept. Concepts perceived as enhancing or protecting the receiver's self-concept will have a positive valence attached. Since the valences customers attach to concepts are also subject to influence for culture, social class, and reference groups, it is apparent that great care must be taken to specify the intended receiver of persuasive communication. Similar care must attend the choice of transmission media. If newspaper A reaches one income group and newspaper B another, the messages may have to be constructed to suit the audiences.

Returning now to our concept of electroluminescence, let us examine a message intended to persuade. Our intended receiver is a business executive who is likely to attach positive valences to some signs and negative valences to others:

"Eyestrain, caused by inadequate light, increases worker fatigue, product rejects, and grievances. As a result, efficiency drops and morale suffers.

"A wholly new light source has been developed to bring you efficient, glare-free light which banishes shadows and eyestrain. Employees are happier and more productive; maintenance and operating costs are cut.

"Sparks Electric Company calls this new light . . . ."

As with the communication to inform, this persuasive message must be encoded in an acceptable form; the signs and referents must be mutually understood. But this message begins with some signs chosen for their probably negative valence in the intended receivers' minds. Words such as "eyestrain," "fatigue," "inefficiency," and "grievances" are a potential threat to the self-concept of a businessman who wants *to be* efficient, economical, and free from employee troubles.

The message then offers a promise of something *new* which offers a string of positive-valenced benefits. "Efficient," "economical," "happy," "productive," and "low operating costs" are just what the threatened self-concept needs. The third paragraph begins with the company name (which the advertiser *hopes* carries a positive valence both from past advertising and from receivers' own experiences with the company's products). The message will continue with some information about electroluminescence. But it will relate the product features to buyer benefits, for it is benefits that sell products.

Inform and persuade

This last illustration suggests that a single marketing communication may be designed to both inform and persuade the receiver. Our study of the buying process suggests that prospective buyers may be at one of several stages in the buying model. Some may need information to help them in their goal definition and listing stages, others may be at the point of evaluating and screening alternatives and require persuasion that ours is best. Still others may require both information and persuasion to overcome frustration and bivalent feedback.

The division of messages into "informing" and "persuading" was for the purposes of examining the rules or conditions that must be met for effective communication to occur. This division was helpful to bring out the special requirements of persuasive communication above and beyond the normal rules of informational communications. It is true, as we noted, that the *emphasis* may shift from informational to persuasive as a product advances through its life cycle, but most marketing communications must contain both types of messages.

THE IMPACT OF SOURCE ON COMMUNICATION

The plot begins to thicken when we realize that the meaning of a message depends not only upon what is said, but *who says it*. Considerable research exists to show that identical messages can have varied meaning to receivers when the perceived source of the message is changed. The message, "Where are you going to be working next week?" sounds like a jest from a fellow worker, but if the source is your employer, a different meaning is imparted. The first question we often ask, upon hearing something new, is "Who says so?" The phrase "chains and slavery" from the mouth of Patrick Henry does not mean the same thing to Americans as the same phrase would coming from Marx or Lenin.

In our description of the five elements of a communication system we labeled step one the "source" or origin of the process. Communication researchers point out, however, that receivers often confuse channel of transmission and source. "I read it in the newspaper," or "according to the radio," are phrases which point to this problem. A company may think of its salesmen as a channel of transmission, but customers may regard the salesman as the source.

Because the salesman can become the "source" so far as buyers are concerned, he becomes terribly important to the whole communication process. Just how important can be seen from the discussion which follows in source-message interaction.

Source and message attitudes

Buyers have attitudes toward both the content of a message and about its source. These attitudes, moreover, interact, as Osgood's congruity model suggests.[3] This theory provides us with a very helpful way of examining how attitudes toward source, products, and messages affect one another.

Let us suppose that I could rank seven sources from most liked to least liked and that I could rank seven products along a similar scale. Now a source can say something positive or negative about a product. Under some conditions, according to Osgood, my attitude toward both product and source will shift. Here is a simple example:

	Product	Source
Like most	+3 steak	+3 best friend
	+2 cake	+2 classmate
	+1 soft drink	+1 advertisement
Neutral	0 potatoes	0 stranger
	−1 pickles	−1 bus driver
	−2 cabbage	−2 neighbor
Like least	−3 cottage cheese	−3 professor

If my best friend says he likes steak very much, there is perfect congruence according to Osgood's theory, and my attitudes about source and product are merely reinforced. Similarly, if my professor says he

---

[3] C. E. Osgood and P. H. Tannenbaum, "The Principle of Congruity in the Prediction of Attitude Change," *Psychological Review*, Vol. 62, pp. 42–55.

FIGURE 4–6.   Recipes are a form of information and persuasion

*H*arvest time—a time to be thankful. A time to celebrate with good food and good friends. Kraft is proud to be included at times like this—to provide the dependable food ideas and quality products you always insist on. Your confidence is our good fortune, too. So naturally we'll continue to do everything we can to deserve it. We want to be invited to your next Thanksgiving dinner, too.

GREEN BEANS FORESTER
Made with Kraft Thousand Island Dressing...the different kind that pours, brimming with crisp little islands of pickle relish.

2 cups diagonally sliced celery
½ cup chopped onion
2 tablespoons Parkay Margarine
4 cups (2 1-lb. cans) cut green beans, drained

1 cup (8-oz. bottle) Kraft Thousand Island Dressing
8 slices crisply cooked bacon, crumbled
4 hard-cooked eggs, sliced or cut into wedges

Creamy Thousand Island, crisp bacon and golden egg slices turn green beans into a richly rewarding dish. Cook celery and onion in margarine until crisp-tender. Add beans; heat thoroughly. Add dressing and half of bacon and eggs; heat. Place in serving dish; top with remaining bacon and eggs. 8 servings.

PHEASANTS WITH HUNTER'S DRESSING
Made with Soft Parkay Margarine...has the fresh margarine taste that you'd expect from Kraft.

½ lb. pork sausage
2 cups day-old bread cubes
1 cup chunky-style applesauce
⅓ cup chopped onion
¼ cup chopped parsley

Soft Parkay Margarine
¼ teaspoon sage
¼ teaspoon salt
Dash of pepper

2 2½- to 3-lb. dressed pheasants or chickens
Salt
¼ cup dry sherry

It's hard to tell who's luckier...the hunter who brings pheasants home or the cook he brings them home to! For the dressing, brown meat; drain. Combine with bread cubes, applesauce, onion, parsley, ¼ cup margarine and seasonings; mix well. Then, wash birds; dry. Sprinkle body and neck cavities lightly with salt. Fill with dressing; secure with skewers and string. Spread birds with margarine. Place on foil; pour sherry over birds. Wrap securely. Bake at 350°, 1½ hours. Fold back foil. Continue baking, basting frequently, ½ hour or until brown and tender. 6 servings.

HOT SPICED FRUIT

2 cups (1-lb. can) peach halves
2 cups (1-lb. can) pear halves
2 cups (1-lb. can) pineapple spears
½ cup Kraft Pure Orange Marmalade

2 tablespoons Parkay Margarine
1 stick cinnamon
⅛ teaspoon nutmeg
⅛ teaspoon ground cloves

Peach, pear and pineapple in cinnamony syrup laced with cloves, nutmeg and marmalade! This is almost too good to be true. Drain fruit, reserving 1½ cups syrup. Combine marmalade, margarine, spices and reserved syrup. Bring to boil; cook 2 to 3 minutes. Reduce heat; gently stir in fruit. Heat 20 minutes. 8 servings.

HARVEST SPINACH RING
Made with Cracker Barrel Brand Cheese from Kraft...made in small, precious batches.

4 10-oz. pkgs. chopped frozen spinach
4 eggs, separated
2 cups (8 ozs.) shredded Cracker Barrel Brand Sharp Natural Cheddar Cheese
3 tablespoons flour
3 tablespoons Parkay Margarine, melted

2 tablespoons grated onion
1 tablespoon lemon juice
½ teaspoon salt
¼ teaspoon pepper

A feast for the eye as well as the palate; this proves how really elegant vegetables can be. Cook spinach as directed on package; drain thoroughly. Beat egg yolks; combine with cheese, flour, margarine, onion, lemon juice and seasonings. Add spinach; mix well. Fold in stiffly beaten egg whites. Grease 6½-cup ring mold; line bottom with strip of foil. Grease foil; spoon spinach mixture into mold. Place in large pan on oven rack; pour in boiling water to ½-inch depth. Bake at 350°, 30 to 35 minutes or until knife inserted comes out clean. Loosen sides of mold with knife. Unmold on serving plate. Remove foil. If desired, fill ring with small whole carrots, cooked. Makes 8 to 10 glorious servings.

PARADISE PUMPKIN PIE
Made with Philadelphia Brand Cream Cheese from Kraft...freshest-tasting cream cheese you can buy.

1 8-oz. pkg. Philadelphia Brand Cream Cheese
¼ cup sugar
½ teaspoon vanilla
1 egg
1 9-inch unbaked pastry shell
•   •   •

1¼ cups canned or cooked pumpkin
½ cup sugar
1 teaspoon cinnamon
¼ teaspoon ginger
¼ teaspoon nutmeg
Dash of salt
1 cup evaporated milk

2 eggs, slightly beaten
•   •   •
Maple syrup
Pecan halves

Some people we know say this is the whole reason for having Thanksgiving. See what you think. Combine softened cream cheese, sugar and vanilla, mixing until well blended. Add egg; mix well. Pour onto bottom of pastry shell. Combine remaining ingredients; mix well. Carefully pour over cream cheese mixture. Bake at 350°, 65 to 70 minutes or until done. Cool. Brush with maple syrup; decorate with nuts.

KRAFT
Division of
Kraftco Corporation

thinks cottage cheese is the greatest food in the world, this is about what I would expect from someone like him.

Suppose that my best friend $(+3)$ says he agrees, cottage cheese (-3) is the greatest food. The theory suggests that in such an instance my attitude toward cottage cheese will improve, if only a little: "Cottage cheese can't be all bad, I guess, if my best friend likes it." But at the same time my attitude toward the source will also shift slightly: "Joe's a good guy, *even if he does like some peculiar foods.*" Another variation might be for the professor (-3) to say that he *dislikes* cottage cheese above all foods. Now then the message and my attitude toward the product are congruent, so the professor comes up a little on the scale: "Anyone who hates cottage cheese can't be all bad."

Consider now what happens with a new product about which I know nothing. The message is, "Product X is truly wonderful." I am neutral about product X until this message is received. If the source of the message is a classmate $(+2)$ I will probably begin to attach a positive valence to product X. If the source is my neighbor or professor, the same message will incline me toward a negative valence out of mistrust of the source.

Implications for promotion

This confusion of source, and the interaction of attitudes toward source, product, and message, is meaningful for personal selling, advertising, and publicity. On the first call the customer probably regards the salesman as a transmission channel and the company as the source. But as repeated contacts with the salesman allow the customer to know him and form opinions about him, the salesman will come to be viewed as the source.[4] On the first call the salesman enters the communication process either as a neutral source or bearing the valences the customer attaches to "salesman's company" or "salesmen in general" or both. What he must do is try to build up his position with the customer by finding subjects of mutual agreement or disagreement. As he does this, he will begin to build positive attitudes in the customer toward himself. Then he can begin to attempt to transfer some of his attitude points to the company products.

For example, suppose a salesman calls on me to try to sell me a new product about which I know nothing. Suppose further that we are still using my set of attitudes outlined a moment ago. The salesman enters

---

[4] Edgar Crane, *Marketing Communications* (New York, John Wiley & Sons, Inc., 1965).

as a stranger (± 0) or perhaps with a slightly negative valence, since I don't trust salesmen in general. Suppose he chats with me for a moment or so and in the course of the conversation notes his love of good steaks, ($+3$), mentions wanting the name of a restaurant that serves good cake ($+2$) because he likes to have a piece of cake and a soft drink ($+1$) in the middle of the afternoon. He has already begun to build up a positive valence in my eyes because he has sent some messages which are highly congruent with my own attitudes. He may mention favorably my favorite major league team, compliment me on the picture my wife painted for the office, and otherwise continue to build positive valences. If he can manage to say something nasty about cottage cheese (-3) and cabbage (-2), he should be on the way to becoming my best friend! At any rate, he is now in a position to introduce his new product. Since it is new to me, I am neutral (or slightly positive, since I like anything new) toward it. But as I hear about the new product from good old steak–cake-and-soft-drink-loving salesman X, the new product will probably come equipped with positive valences in my mind.

In mass selling, both the company, the advertising medium (newspaper X or television station Y), and "advertising in general" are source concepts influencing the messages. Although a consumer may suspect all advertisers of self-interest in their messages, his own experience with the company's product, his faith in the channel not to transmit anything completely fradulent, and the believability of the message may all operate to lend positive valences to the sources, however he defines "source." Testimonial advertising, for example, seek to hook the message to a well-known source, such as an actor or sports celebrity.

For publicity and public relations, where the company is often not identified as source, receiver attitudes toward the channel of transmission are of special importance. It is one thing to be voted a model company by *Fortune* and quite another to get the same expression from the *Daily Worker*. In all forms of communication with consumers, alert marketing management is sensitive to both the content of the messages and to their perceived sources.

GAINING ATTENTION TO THE MESSAGE

Communication operates in a buyer's market. The signs of communication have to compete for an audience. From the buyer's viewpoint, communication is but another part of that vast and varied universe of aware-

FIGURE 4–7.   The slogan "you can be sure . . ." is a help in building positive source attitudes

For Sale: Modest-priced homes.

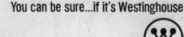

ness we called the perceptual field. In order for our marketing messages to establish a commonness with customers, they must be brought into figure; *they must get attention*. Of course, messages must be properly encoded, use signs the receiver has previously differentiated, and evoke mutual referents with a careful eye to the valences attached to the referents. But to do any of this the communication must be delivered and must attract attention.

Availability

The first step toward gaining attention is to make sure the message is available in the receiver's perceptual field. The communication must be readily accessible to him if he is to note it and bring it into figure. In the context of radio listening, you are more likely to tune in a program when the signal is loud and clear than listen to one which fades, blurs, and forces you to strain.

Making the message available in marketing communication requires a thorough knowledge of which media or transmission channels our intended receivers regularly scan and tap. In addition, for many of the channels we must know *when* they are used: what days of the week, what hours of the day? Advertisers try to schedule food ads on days when the heaviest grocery shopping occurs; cereal manufacturers and candymakers often aim television commercials at a juvenile audience in daytime hours; salesmen keep lists of prospects up to date and try to know when a company is going to need new equipment or supplies.

If the product has a seasonal demand, dependent upon weather or gift seasons, the message availability must take such a factor into effect. If a study of the buying model reveals that there is no special time for customers to reach the listing stage of the model, then the messages will need to be continuously available.

Relation to self-concepts

Given equal availability of messages, consumers will most likely be attracted by cues and messages which they perceive will protect, enhance, or threaten their self-concepts. Marketers of very special purpose products often take advantage of this with small space ads featuring large singleword headlines. They rely on their special receivers being attracted to the words *insomnia*, or *hay fever*, or *psoriasis* as they scan the page of the newspaper or magazine. As readers scan a page, deciding what to read and what to ignore, they will be drawn to items perceived as being "for them." A message about food will attract more housewives; a message about cars will attract more men.

Recall, too, that in many forms of marketing communication, multiple channels of transmission are operating. An illustration can appeal to the self-concept as readily as a headline. The whole tone or feel of a communication can help select intended receivers, too. Light, delicate-looking messages attract different receivers from bold, noisy-looking (or sounding) ones.

Since the whole of an advertisement or sales message cannot be in figure at once, often a few cues or signs, such as the headline, illustration, or opening sentence of a sales talk or commercial, must attract attention to the whole message. Communications research suggests that all cues should be relevant to the message. Tricky illustrations or scare headlines used only to gain attention for an unrelated sales message will quickly lose their effectiveness. They may also have an effect on the receivers' attitudes toward the message source and exert a long-run diminution of communication effectiveness.

We are entirely consistent with our view of buyer behavior when we assert that the relation of a message to the receiver's self-concept is a most important aid to getting his attention. Above all else, people are dedicated to the preservation and enhancement of that critical concept. The closer to self a message seems, the greater its attention-getting capacities.

Contrast

A third factor which helps call cues into figure from the background of the field is contrast. There are a variety of forms of contrast. It may be a difference of *intensity*, as when a loud noise forces itself into figure or a darker cue stands out from lighter toned surroundings. The reverse is equally contrasting; a sudden silence or a light-on-dark background cue may be brought into figure.

Contrast of *motion*, either physical or visual, is another approach. The moving display piece on a retailer's counter contrasts with the still surroundings. Visual motion may be achieved in printed communications through arrangements of the elements of the message, as the illustration shows. In oral communication, contrast is achieved through a varied pace of delivery, and a sudden slowing down, together with a slightly increased intensity or volume, suggests that these cues are of special importance.

FIGURE 4–8.   Relation of message to receiver's self-concept aids in
communication

**If you like to
camp,
hike,
contemplate,
picnic,
explore,
hunt,
meditate,
bird-watch,
breathe,
walk,
wade,
relax,
romp,
climb,
inhale,
swim,
fish,
ride or
dream,
don't burn
the woods down
doing it.**

Only you can prevent forest fires.

While the list of attention-getting techniques is endless, and far beyond the scope of this chapter, we must at least recognize these three: availability, relation to self-concept, and contrast. The importance of attention to messages cannot be overemphasized. Unless marketing communications are differentiated from the field of the receiver, all the careful planning of messages and their encoding and transmission are wasted. Without reception there can be no decoding, no perception, no communication.

QUESTIONS AND PROBLEMS

4-1. How does knowledge of the prospect's social class and reference group membership aid the persuasive communicator?

4-2. In the light of this chapter what advantages do you see for personal selling over advertising?

4-3. Find five ads which exhibit different levels of encoding complexity in their copy.

4-4. What are the advantages and disadvantages to the firm when the salesman becomes the message source in the mind of the buyer?

4-5. How does the notion of selective perception help communicators?

4-6. If an advertiser does not have access to feedback automatically, how can he create some feedback to improve his communication effectiveness?

4-7. What are the implications for the promotion manager in the fact that the source of the message influences the communication process?

4-8. The XYZ Company has just perfected a new dehydrated powder which, when mixed with water, becomes an effective antifreeze. Write a 50-word message to inform and another 50-word message to persuade, using this product as a subject.

4-9. What are the implications for the retailer in the concept of multiple channels of communication?

4-10. In your answer to question 2-1 regarding the "generation gap" did you use words which might be perceived differently by various age groups? Name five such words and define them in terms of their probable meaning to young and old audiences.

ELEMENTS OF
PERSUASION:
PERSONAL SELLING

CHAPTER 5

Personal selling as persuasive communication

THIS SECTION deals with *personal selling,* the most important of the four promotional forces. Next will come a section dealing with *advertising,* followed by a section on *sales promotion.* The final section deals with *public relations.*

BACKGROUND FOR SELLING

Salesmen's duties and activities

The salesman's major assignment is to bring about economic exchanges which benefit both buyer and seller. He informs as he communicates; he influences as he persuades; he motivates buyers to buy. The salesman translates. He transforms certain features of his product or service into benefits and satisfactions buyers will enjoy. If we choose to attempt a three-step sequence, step one can be the salesman's learning of a buyer's need, problem, or opportunity. Step two finds the buyer agreeing to the existence of that need, problem, or opportunity. In step three the salesman successfully recommends a product or service which will fill the need, solve the problem, or take advantage of the opportunity.

There are several activities common to most personal selling. The typical salesman hopes to spend more time in *face-to-face selling* than in any other one activity. In this activity he makes logical sales presentations and planned demonstrations, and he disposes of objections and "closes" sales. *Travel time* from buyer to buyer and *waiting time* to see and be seen by buyers are unavoidable and resented in most outside selling. *Customer service* is a common activity; this may be giving advice to customers, installing a product, adjusting a complaint—even collecting a past-due account. Then there is *reporting* to do, call reports, sales reports, expense reports, routing reports, and such. *Sales meetings* must be attended, meetings sales managers use mainly to inform, to announce, to stimulate. Salesmen must *plan;* routes, daily schedules, quotas, self-improvement, even each separate presentation must be planned. Finally, most salesmen must spend some time *prospecting;* they must locate new, fresh prospective customers, some of whom must be converted into active customers.

We would be remiss if we failed to recognize the basic, the productive, the essential role personal selling plays in our economy. A major responsibility of salesmen is to bring about change—to cause innovation—to replace certain habits with other habits. Salesmen and selling are necessary to launch new and improved products, and they continue to be necessary to keep those products on the market. No matter how revolutionary or dramatic, new products simply *will not* sell themselves; production *does not* generate demand on the part of ultimate consumers. Above the subsistence level, the consumers' freedom of choice operates. It forces sellers to create demand above that level for products and services. In the economy, mass production, high employment, and healthy capital investment are impossible without mass distribution and mass consumption; those two depend on salesmen and selling. In the individual firm, sales volume sets the ceilings for manufacturing schedules, personnel, and growth. Today's firms and those of the future must be oriented toward buyers and markets, not toward production or operations. Expressed tersely, without sales there are no jobs.

What does a career in personal selling offer? Because his contribution and productivity can be measured, the good salesman can expect higher than average earnings and faster than average advancement. Selling offers variety. The salesman meets and works with many types of buyers; he confronts and solves many kinds of problems; if he wants the variety of travel, he can have it. As for independence, the salesman can have whatever degree he prefers. Salesmen know the personal satisfaction of leading buyers to greater satisfaction. Salesmen cannot be made obsolete by automation or replaced by other forms of promotion. But, selling *is* hard work.

Do sound principles of personal selling offer anything to persons other than salesmen? Indeed they do. In a real sense, practically everyone "sells" himself, his ideas, his values, his tastes, his recommendations, and his decisions. And he sells those satisfactorily or unsatisfactorily to the extent that he uses effectively the same principles used by successful salesmen. Upon graduation, the individual "sells" himself to an employer. On the job, the accountant "sells" an internal control procedure to management, the production man "sells" a better work-flow sequence, the personnel man "sells" an athletic program for employees. Fathers and mothers, husbands and wives need to use and do use these principles. All leaders, too, use the same principles, because leadership is getting along with, it is influencing others to do what you want them to do.

Types of sales jobs

Salesmen and sales jobs can be grouped or classified on various bases. If one uses *type of buyer* as the basis, he finds salesmen selling to (1) merchants for resale, (2) purchasing agents, (3) professional persons, and (4) ultimate consumers. Some salesmen, of course, sell to more than one type of buyer.

The first group of salesmen—those who sell to merchants for resale—may include, for example, a manufacturer's salesman selling cases of canned peaches to wholesalers, or a wholesaler's salesman selling toothpaste to retailers. Two qualities or grades of salesmen are found here: regular and merchandising. The *regular* merchant-selling salesman does much *service* selling but little *creative* selling. Service selling involves little more than holding the account and seeing that the customer does not run out of stock; it is little more than order taking. Creative selling, by way of contrast, discovers needs or opportunities of which the buyer was unaware. It gets a buyer to make his first purchase of some item, it gets him to buy more than usual, or it takes a buyer away from a competitor. Creative selling is more often done by the higher grade of salesman who is known as a *merchandising* salesman. His major assignment is to give promotional advice and service to buyers and to buying influences. This service aspect has led to the salesman's being referred to sometimes as a *missionary* salesman. Some merchandising salesmen hold training sessions for wholesale and retail salespersons. Some travel with a wholesaler's salesmen, informing, coaching, and stimulating them. Some counsel and advise wholesalers and retailers about problems and policies of a managerial nature—about store layout, advertising, and display—about pricing, credit, and customer service. Such information and advice normally results in greater sales volume of the merchandising salesman's products.

A second group of salesmen sells to purchasing agents—the buyers in charge of procurement of products and services used by firms in their operations. Products include: installations (printing press); raw materials (lumber); fabricating parts (packages); operating supplies (light bulbs); accessory equipment (typewriters). Services include such items as insurance, transportation, and storage. Some purchasing agents buy for manufacturers, some buy for government, some buy for institutions. When a wholesaler buys a delivery truck or a retailer buys a cash register, each acts as a purchasing agent. Because he spends his *firm's* money and is held accountable for it, the purchasing agent must be a hard, rational buyer; he is much interested in quality, service, and price. In many purchases, particularly those involving large sums of money, the purchasing agent will be advised or even directed by one or more members of top management; these are known as *buying influences*. Many men selling to purchasing agents find they need to be well trained in their respective specialties (industrial lubrication, chemistry) *and* in the area of marketing. Some are engineers.

A third group of salesmen sells to professional persons. Various types of professional individuals are buying influences; a dentist may recommend a make of electric toothbrush, an architect may specify a make of bathtub. Probably the best known salesman who influences and sells to professional persons is the "detail" man who calls on medical doctors and dentists and on pharmacists. These salesmen "detail" doctors about drugs: they leave samples and literature. They hope doctors will specify certain drugs when writing prescriptions. In the drugstore, the detail man sells and helps the retailer to sell.

Our last group of salesmen sells direct to ultimate consumers. Some of these salespersons work in retail stores, some sell house-to-house. By and large, the quality of salesmanship in retail stores is low. Too often retail selling is done in an indifferent or routine manner. This is understandable when one considers the low earnings, high turnover, split shifts, ill-mannered shoppers, and hard work involved. But conversely, it suggests the opportunity retail selling in stores opens for an interested, competent, personable, and creative salesperson.

The range of house-to-house salespersons is wide in terms of honesty and ability. House-to-house selling is not for the timid, the sensitive, the self-conscious.

The salesman as a person

To be successful, one does not have to be a "born" salesman. Indeed, over time the trained salesman outsells the "born" salesman. Salesmanship can be taught—salesmanship can be learned. From the buyer's point of view, the outstanding salesman identifies and solves problems, he advises and counsels, he informs and instructs, he helps and satisfies buyers.

The social, mental, emotional, and human qualities needed to succeed in selling would permit success in many areas. The lists of characteristics desirable in salesmen include:

Aggressiveness	Ambition	Appearance	Confidence
Courage	Courtesy	Decisiveness	Dependability
Determination	Empathy	Energy	Enthusiasm
Ethics	Friendliness	Health	Honesty
Imagination	Initiative	Intelligence	Interest
Intuition	Judgment	Knowledge	Leadership
Loyalty	Maturity	Optimism	Perseverance
Personality	Persuasiveness	Poise	Rapport
Reliability	Resourcefulness	Responsibility	Sincerity
	Tact	Understanding	

The salesman and his firm

A salesman cannot do justice to his customers, to his employer, or to himself unless he has adequate information and knowledge of his firm. In many situations, the reputation and record of the selling firm are major considerations in a buyer's deliberations and decisions. Only if he knows his company can a salesman work in harmony and loyalty with it. Knowledge increases a salesman's productivity because it increases his confidence, his sincerity, his enthusiasm. Clearly, a salesman must be able to present, to represent, to defend, to explain, and to answer questions about his firm. To many buyers, he *is* his firm.

History is one area of this information. The origin of the firm may make interesting conversation. This may well include facts about who

FIGURE 5–1.   Johnson & Johnson check list for evaluating retail salespersons

---

EVALUATION CHECK LIST FOR IMPROVING YOUR SALESPEOPLE

SCORE salespeople numerically: *Good*, 3 points . . . *Average*, 2 points . . . *Poor*, 1 point.

WHAT ARE HIS PERSONAL CAPACITIES?

Score

1. How is his appearance?
Clothing..
Hair...
Hands..
Personal mannerisms..

2. What is his attitude on the job?
Is he enthusiastic and cheerful?.....................................
Does he cooperate with others?.......................................
Is he interested in his work?...

3. What are his personal attributes?
Is he trustworthy?...
Is he a self-starter?...
Is he well-mannered?..
Is he temperamental?..
Does he follow through?..
Is he resourceful?..

WHAT ARE HIS SALES CAPACITIES?

4. Does he know how to sell?
Does he express sales ideas clearly?................................
Does he try new demonstration angles?..........................
Does he know the merchandise facts?.............................
Does he give an impression of sincerity?........................
Does he really like his customers?..................................
Does he miss trade-up sales?...
Does he know how to keep stock?....................................
Can he handle difficult sales situations?........................
Can he make a window display sell?...............................
Can he make a store display sell?...................................

TOTAL.................................

---

55 or more means: GOOD (the good salespeople must be encouraged to help the average improve; in teaching others the GOOD ones will become BETTER)

Between 40 and 55 means: AVERAGE (An opportunity to improve his rating)

Less than 40 means: POOR (This man needs *your personal help*)

founded it, when, where, and why. The early period may be colorful in respect to operations and practices; growth and change may be impressive. Current features include the firm's industry; the firm's position in its industry; organization, production and service facilities and capacities; size and strengths; promotional activities; and plans.

Personnel constitute a second area. The salesman should know something of the firm's executives. He must know the individuals with whom he will be working, be they in production, credit, shipping, advertising, or sales promotion. Included here will be the persons through whose hands his customers' orders will flow and be handled.

Policies and procedures are the third and largest area of company information. Prominent here are these: channels of distribution, credit and collection, delivery, resale, pricing, advertising, complaints, returns and cancellations, and reciprocity.

What are major sources of information about his company? These are some: training program; company manuals, bulletins, or other literature; visits to and experience in the plant; fellow employees; buyers; and personal experience.

The salesman's products

Knowledge of his products is as necessary as is knowledge of his firm—and for essentially the same reasons. Product knowledge is a basis for a salesman's confidence in his product and in himself; it also encourages greater enthusiasm. Abundant product knowledge lets the salesman impress buyers favorably as a source of competent suggestions and sound recommendations. He is able to fit products more snugly to buyers' needs—to see and to explain how his products or line will meet the requirements and circumstances of different buyers. Product data are useful in convincing buyers of what products will do to and for them—of what they will get from the purchase. As products become more numerous and complex, as competitors become more wily, as some buyers become better informed while other buyers need more and more guidance, the salesman's need for product knowledge continues to increase.

There are several areas of product information. One consists of the history of the type of product (timepieces, writing instruments) and then the history of the salesman's brand. Another area involves the physical product itself. This may include raw materials and ingredients, manufacturing processes and construction features, quality control standards and research. Salesmen often need to know the "why" of product design, size, color, shape, or package. Product uses and applications can be essential information as can performance data and records. Salesmen of mechanical products must know how those products operate, what they do, how they should be used, and the service they require. There is the matter of competition. The salesman must know how his products compare with those of his strongest competitors; he must know the strengths and the weaknesses of the competing brands. This can be broadened to include the promotional efforts put behind each competing brand and the degree to which each competing seller stands behind his brand. Then there is the most basic difference between product features and buyer benefits. A product feature is a physical element or fact—a salt container which has a pour spout *and* a shaker screen in the top, or a watch which uses an electric unit in place of a mainspring. *But,* those features deliver certain benefits or satisfactions to consumers, and *they* are what buyers are really interested in and really buy. Finally, many salesmen must be familiar with products related to their own; a furniture salesman, for example, cannot afford to be ignorant about floor coverings, colors, and room accessories.

A salesman has to be informed about the prices of his products. List prices—the prices to the ultimate purchaser—are usually published. They are generally subject to discounts. Net price is list price minus discounts; it is what the merchant buyer actually pays. The more common discounts are: cash (for early payment), quantity (to encourage large orders), trade (functional discounts to types of middlemen), and promotional (often in the form of cooperative advertising undertaken jointly by a manufacturer and his retailers). Terms of sales are a basic element in a seller's price structure.

Sources of product information include: personal consumption, comparison, and experience; sales training instruction; manuals, house organs, catalogs, handbooks, and other literature; plant and factory experience; research findings; company employees; company advertising; and buyers, including both prospects and customers.

Because a salesman sells against competition, he needs information about his competition; such information does *not* endanger his selling. The salesman needs to know competing firms, their products and prices, their salesmen, and how they sell. Sources of information include: competitors' ads, personal examination and trial if practicable, other salesmen, buyers of competing products, and his own company. The smart salesman views and treats competition with respect and fairness; he does not "knock" it.

LOCATING AND LEARNING ABOUT PROSPECTS

Prospecting

Practically all salesmen must engage in prospecting throughout their entire selling careers. What is prospecting? It is identifying from a larger group of "suspects" those buyers who are genuine prospects for what the salesman is selling—prospects who deserve and will get some of the salesman's time, attention, and selling effort. The process of distinguishing prospects from suspects is known as *qualifying the prospect.* This must be a continuing activity because each year some of a salesman's customers die, some switch to other suppliers, some move away, some fail, some retire, and some no longer can use the salesman's product to advantage. Because it is essential for survival, prospecting must be planned and organized. This calls for a weekly or monthly quota of new prospects, for accurate and current records, for scheduling the activity and the procedure, for experimentation, and for making the plan work.

The salesman must ask questions about a *sus*pect and get affirmative answers if he is to recalssify the suspect as a *pro*spect. The minimum number of questions is two: (1) Does that person have (or can he be persuaded to have) a need or want my product will satisfy? Or, as it is sometimes phrased, is there a good chance that the person will be happy or at least satisfied if he buys? (2) Does that person have the money or credit with which to finance the purchase? Essentially, these questions ask: Can he benefit—can he pay? Sometimes, particularly in industrial selling, a third question asks whether the person involved has authority to make a purchase. On occasion, the salesman must ask if the suspect is entitled to buy or can qualify to buy. He does not try to sell alcoholic beverages to youngsters or life insurance to chronically ill persons; he does not include among prospects buyers wanting but not entitled to buy direct from some manufacturer. Sometimes the salesman must conclude that certain buyers are simply not appropriate for his time and efforts; few salesmen can approach the President of the United States *or* the president of General Motors.

Here are several of the more common prospecting techniques:

Observation. The salesman's own observation and hearing often identify prospects; sometimes a customer buying product A become a prospect for the salesman's product B.

Endless chain. The salesman gets one or more names of possible prospects during each interview. This is also known as the referral method.

Centers of influence. These are persons who have information about and influence over certain buyers. The buyers may be employees, borrowers, or associates. Bankers and office managers are examples.

Inquiries. Buyers may be "walk-ins," such as those who enter an automobile showroom. They may inquire in response to the advertising of the salesman's firm.

Sales associates. Policemen, waiters, and service station attendants may stay on the alert, submit names to a salesman, and get a reward for each purchase. Friends and acquaintances may do the same job without pay.

FIGURE 5–2.   Referral blank used in prospecting

Whom do you know who might be better off in his future planning for having seen this kind of plan – whether or not he buys?

Name	Address	Job	Age	Children

Suggestions: Co-workers, Neighbors, Relatives, Friends, Their Families, New Home, Just Married, Youths, New Baby, First Job, Recent Promotion.

I may ☐   may not ☐ mention your name as one of my clients.

S 457 (3-65)

Direct mail and telephone calls. These can be used with a list of buyers in the hopes of setting up appointments with prospects. Some salesmen follow up their mailings with telephone calls.

Cold canvass. The salesman tries to call on all members of some group (doctors, housewives in a certain area, offices in a certain building). Typically, the salesman has a minimum of information about each buyer.

The preapproach

Once a salesman has determined that a certain individual is a prospect, he then moves into the stage known as the *preapproach*. This phase is somewhat of an extension or continuation of qualifying the prospect. Preapproach work is the planning which precedes the presentation; it is the salesman's doing his prep before he calls; it is the collection of more information about the buyer. Most preapproach activity takes place before the salesman gets with the buyer, but some may be a feature of the first few moments of the interview.

The amount of personal information and the amount of business information salesmen will need vary; the quantity that can and should be collected varies. There is also variation as to which items of information are desired and significant.

Preapproach is a phase of selling which the salesman cannot afford to treat casually. The greater his fund of facts, the better he can plan his approach, the better he can select which benefits to promise, the better he can design his presentation. Thorough preapproach often identifies mistakes to avoid. It can help the salesman in respect to when and where to make his presentation. It can help by identifying the key buying influences in industrial selling. It permits the salesman to recommend with greater confidence. Indeed, it gets the salesman more interviews and more sales.

As was indicated, some of the information collected in the preapproach is *personal* information about the buyer as an individual. These are typical items:

Name	Age	Family status
Address	Education	Social group
Telephone number	Hobbies	Politics
Memberships	Job	Income bracket
Achievements	Problems	Opportunities
Goals	Buying habits	Interests
Buying motives	Quality of mind	Tastes
Beliefs	Religion	Nationality

Business information about the buyer's firm includes:

Trade name	Buying authority	Markets served
Address	Personnel	Credit rating
Sales-volume	Organization	Buying influences
Competition	Large customers	Buying procedures
Problems	Line of products sold	Policies

There are several common sources of buyer information used by salesmen before making the sales call. These include family, friends, and associates; noncompeting salesmen who sell to the buyer; and customers of that buyer. In the case of new salesmen, their companies' records can be most helpful. News stories sometimes contain valuable facts.

Even the buyer himself may supply data which is preapproach in character. This information could be secured by mail or by telephone, or it could result from a preliminary survey the buyer allows the salesman to make. Salesmen's observation produces certain information. Finally, in the opening moments of the sales call, the salesman may observe, listen, and even ask a few questions to acquire additional facts.

THE SALES PRESENTATION

Planning the presentation

A salesman's presentation should be planned rather than extemporaneous; it should be well thought out in advance rather than played by ear from moment to moment. The presentation is what makes the sale—or fails to make it. Among its virtues, the planned presentation saves time for salesman *and* buyer and contributes to the salesman's confidence. It results in his making a better impression on the buyer. It can be made complete and clear, and its tailored and individualized character produces bigger and better sales volume.

Certainly the salesman will plan presentations which are *buyer* directed and oriented, presentations which focus on the buyer. In an effort to do this, some salesmen intentionally and consciously think of themselves as problem solvers—solvers of buyers' problems. In this role, the salesman adopts the "you" point of view and plans to let the buyer be a "king." In so doing, the salesman recognizes and respects the fact that no product, indeed, no person, is of as much interest to the buyer as is the buyer to himself. The salesman, his company, even his product mean nothing *unless* they can mean something to the buyer personally.

Because the salesman must find points of common interest with buyers, because he must learn buyers' views and beliefs so as to accommodate himself to them, there should be provision for two-way communication during the sales interview. Such communication is conducive to buyer-salesman identification, rapport, and understanding between the two. It reflects the salesman's respect and good manners. Quite importantly, what the buyer says and asks is often very revealing. The more that salesmen practice and the better they develop their skill of questioning buyers, the more information they get, the more agreements they get. Better salesmen also work to perfect the art of listening, knowing full well that silence on their part can play a constructive and creative role in their selling.

The five buying decisions[1]

A sales presentation is planned to do a single job—to get affirmative answers from the buyer on the five buying decisions. Until the salesman gets all five affirmative answers, there can be no purchase, no sale; when he obtains all five, a purchase and a sale take place. The five buying decisions are those of *need, product, source, price,* and *time.* Buyers do not make these decisions in the same sequence or order. When a student dashes frantically into a drugstore just before closing time on the day before Mother's Day, he has already said yes to *need,* to *source,* and to *time.* He may well be uncertain about *product* and *price.* By way of contrast, the salesman of life insurance typically calls on buyers who have not made any of the five decisions in the affirmative; he must start by working on the need decision. At this point we must note that a buyer's comments and statements about where he stands on one or more of the decisions may not be sincere and genuine. More about this when we examine *objections.*

Need. Back in Chapter 2 we recognized that during a person's life, all his voluntary behavior is controlled—even dictated—by his twin ambitions: (1) to maintain or protect his self-concept, and (2) to enhance or improve his self-concept. Viewed thus, a person has "needs" all the time. In a certain sense, then, the salesman does not have to try to implant, to create, to generate *need.* Of course, if the person does not see clearly a specific threat to his self-concept *or* a specific opportunity to upgrade his self-concept, the salesman must help sharpen that person's vision.

Product. The salesman recommends his product as the best answer to the buyer's need. In so doing, he must take pains to fit his product (or one specific item in his line) to that need. He translates such physical and objective matters as patented features which are unique, or delivery service which has no superior for speed and dependability, into buyer benefits and goals. Simplified to the extreme, ultimate consumers want personal satisfaction, business buyers want profit.

Source. Buyers obviously make voluntary and optional purchases only from sellers who are acceptable as vendors. From buyers' points of view, source can be retail salesperson, retailer, wholesaler, or manufacturer. A major hope of many salesmen is to get their firms accepted as *preferred* sources of supply.

Price. As was true of source, the buyer must accept price when

---

[1] Compare this concept of a purchase and sale with the buying model presented in Chapter 3. The two complement rather than contradict one another.

he buys, even though we all tend to think that every price is entirely too high. The buyer's main concern is to get maximum satisfaction for each dollar he spends. So, the salesman's hope is to build up the utility of his product in the buyer's mind and to enhance its value. The price decision is closely related to the need and product decisions; it is frequently one of the more difficult decisions to get.

Time.   No sale is made until the buyer decides to buy *now*—and follows through by doing just that. When a properly qualified buyer agrees that the time is at hand to make a purchase, he buys. This is one of the more difficult (often the *most* difficult) decisions for the salesman to secure. Most buyers are somewhat fearful and dubious about the wisdom of immediate purchase. Most want to buy *and* do not want to buy; they know that if they pay $10 for product A, they cannot have product B, also $10. More on this when we take up *closing* the sale.

Opening the presentation

Whether the salesman gets face to face with buyers through the use of appointments or not, his frame of mind at the first moment of each and every confrontation is significantly important. He should feel confident and optimistic, never apologetic or unsure. Indifference, anxiety, or arrogance are not to be tolerated. The salesman has every reason to expect to be welcome. He has qualified for some of the buyer's time, he is there to help the buyer make better buying decisions, and he is entitled to recommend how the buyer can get more satisfaction for his dollars. Incidentally, the salesman's last act before moving into the presence of the buyer is to do a last-minute check of his appearance and his equipment.

Once with the buyer, the salesman's first undertaking is to capture the buyer's attention. Unless the buyer attends, he will not hear, grasp, accept, or be influenced by the salesman's presentation. Analogies are numerous. Unless a minister gets the attention of his congregation, unless a parent gets the attention of a child, unless your instructor gets *your* attention, none of the three achieves communication; consequently, none influences or persuades. So, the salesman does all he can to encourage the buyer to tune the salesman in, to become receptive, to prepare himself to take in the salesman's message. Mechanical methods of inviting attention include the use of printed material, demonstrations, and visual aids employing color, isolation, size, intensity, contrast, and motion. Interest methods include comments, promises, and questions about the buyer's goals, problems, interests, and personal concerns. Openings which affect and relate to the buyer's self-concept usually have great attention-getting power.

Salesmen dare not underestimate how crucial the "first 10 seconds and his first 10 words" can be. In a matter of seconds, literally, the salesman attempts several jobs. He wants to make a good first impression, being courteous and deferential, agreeable and interested. He wants to establish a friendly, relaxed, and confident atmosphere. He wants to make the buyer feel important. If any information he collected in the pre-approach turns out to be inaccurate, the salesman hopes to identify the mistake and correct it as quickly as possible. During this early period, the salesman sizes up the situation; he is alert for indications of any buying decision already made in the affirmative.

As for actual, specific openers, a basic distinction is made between the standard, verbatim type and the tailored, personalized type. Almost every salesman needs a few tried, tested, and proved openers which, figuratively, he could execute perfectly in his sleep. In cold-canvass prospecting, salesmen are forced to rely heavily on these "canned" openers. But, whenever practicable, the better salesman prefers to tailor and individualize his techniques of opening. Buyers recognize and are flattered by openers which could not have been used on any other buyer. Standard or tailored, a great number of openers contain *news*, or *buyer benefits*, or both. These make for strength.

Here are 12 widely used opening methods or patterns:

Introduce self	Show the buyer something
Ask the buyer a question	Compliment the buyer
Give the buyer some information	Promise a benefit
Demonstrate the product	Make a personal comment
Report a case history	Offer some service
Make a provocative statement	Use curiosity or showmanship

Making the oral presentation

A sound pattern for a salesman to follow in telling his story is known as the Advantage-Proof-Action sequence. *Advantages* presented and promised to the buyer are the satisfactions and benefits he wants. Study of buyers and of his product should supply the salesman with enough advantages. He will try to make them specific and personal to each individual buyer. Because buyers are inclined to doubt or at least question salesmen's claims, *Proof* may be needed, proof that the product will live up to what the salesman promises about it. This proof is the salesman's bid for acceptance, belief, and conviction on the part of the buyer. Product demonstrations, research findings, testimonials, and case histories

FIGURE 5–3. Suggestions for improving salesmen's presentations*

Be familiar with each buyer's operation, needs, and problems.

Plan, organize, write out, and rehearse the presentation.

Make the presentation brief, factual, and specific.

Have complete product information, including competing products.

Present all facts about prices, terms, and delivery.

Know the details about the manufacturer's promotion program and allowances for retailers.

Get down to business promptly, stick to business, then leave.

Leave samples and a written summary of the presentation.

*These points summarize the recommendations of a group of large retailers buying merchandise from manufacturers' salesmen for resale.

are examples of proof. After making a promise of an advantage and proving it, the salesman asks for *Action.* The action the salesman wants from the buyer is agreement—agreement to the salesman's statements of fact, to his promises, to his recommendations. Enough of these agreements and the buyer makes all five buying decisions in the affirmative.

When telling his story, the salesman does his best to respect the buyer's preferences and personal tastes. Instead of correcting the buyer in an overbearing manner, instead of telling the buyer that he is wrong about some matter, the salesman displays tact and diplomacy—he solicits the buyer's views and opinions. Delivery of the story is important; variables here are speed, volume, variety, emphasis, sincerity, and enthusiasm. While telling his story, the salesman should not be guilty of any unfortunate and distracting mannerisms, either oral *or* physical. Rehearsal before a mirror is a most valuable habit for young salesmen. Choice of words is important because words are one of a salesman's most important tools. The salesman must always be braced for interruptions—telephone calls to the buyer or the intrusion of third parties can change completely the buyer's mood. Buyers themselves often interrupt sales presentations.

Demonstrating the product

There are several compelling reasons why salesmen must *show* as well as *tell*, why they must communicate through the buyer's sense of *sight* as well as his sense of *hearing*. A demonstration can be a good opener, and it can strengthen the body of the presentation. It can be a very appropriate method of handling an objection and represent a strong attempt to close the sale. It can capture attention and develop interest and desire. Some authorities rank the attention-getting power of the sense of sight at 87—that of the sense of hearing at 7. Product demonstrations are powerful proof of a salesman's claims and promises. Buyers much prefer observation, actual operation, and experience to salesmen's statements. Many buyers go along somewhat with the old admonition, "Don't believe *anything* you hear and only *half* of what you see." Demonstrations encourage buyers' grasp and understanding. They save time of both salesman and buyer. They can be impressive and convincing, because the buyer cannot argue with, he cannot deny, what an operating product is doing. Finally, demonstrations rank high as regards memory and retention. There is a claim that a buyer remembers 10 percent of what he hears, 35 percent of what he sees, but 65 percent of what he sees *and* hears.

FIGURE 5–4. Salesman uses a lighted match to demonstrate the properties of SUNSCREEN, the aluminum screen that "blocks the sun—not the view"

Some form of demonstration is available, appropriate, and beneficial to every salesman. Any salesman who does not use it is undeniably remiss. We know how handicapped a salesman of automobiles, television sets, or records would be if denied the use and power of physical product demonstrations. But, salesmen selling such intangibles as insurance, transportation, communications, and advertising agency service can also appeal to the buyer's sense of sight through the use of visual aids of many sorts. Examples of these aids include: displays, charts, graphs, drawings, photographs, sound-slide films, testimonial letters, diagrams, and pencil-and-paper computations. Certain salesmen, obviously, will appeal through the buyer's sense of taste, of smell, or of touch.

Demonstrations demand preparation and planning just as do the salesman's oral presentation. The purpose of the demonstration must be clear and specific. The salesman must know in advance just what he will demonstrate, where, when, and how. Often the buyer must be prepared or conditioned prior to the actual demonstration. This step can continue into the drafting of a sales story or commentary to accompany the demonstration. This can insure that the buyer "gets" the full impact of the message; it can also provide for requests for agreements from the buyer. Frequently, the salesman wants the buyer to participate in the operation; this can be very desirable and effective provided the salesman keeps control of the situation. The salesman should prepare himself by practicing and practicing until his demonstrations are perfect, just as actors rehearse and rehearse until they can give outstanding performances. Truly, salesmen must be good actors. Items to be used in the demonstration and the place of the demonstration need a last-minute check lest defective features or unsatisfactory circumstances jeopardize success. If indicated, demonstrations, like oral presentations, should be tailored to individual buyers.

Some salesmen benefit from injecting showmanship into their selling. Showmanship can make product demonstrations more impressive and effective, give them greater impact; it can make a demonstration dramatic, breathtaking, thrilling, theatrical. Showmen in selling have been known to make good use of blowtorches, white gloves, thermometers, and hourglasses. A second area for showmanship is that of the salesman's personal behavior or manner. He may drive a vintage or otherwise unusual automobile. He may always have a flower in his lapel.

Showmanship must be appropriate to the salesman. Unless it suits him and unless he carries it off, it does far more harm than good. Never must it be just show-off-manship.

Handling objections

Objections—what and why.   The resistance salesmen meet when trying to make a sale is thought of and referred to as buyers' *objections.* Actually, the word *objection* is used to describe two types of difficulty. One is really an *excuse* for not buying. When a properly qualified prospect claims that he cannot afford the salesman's product, he is obviously confronting the salesman with an excuse. The other difficulty, also called an objection, is a serious, genuine matter in that the buyer truly believes it is justification for not buying. Excuses and objections can be barriers between a salesman and a sale; they can keep qualified prospects from buying.

Objections, thus, are the pressures, the influences, the considerations which prevent a prospect from making all five buying decisions in the affirmative. Indeed, every objection which keeps a prospect from buying can be classified under, and can be tied to, *need, product, source, price,* or *time.* Here are examples of buyers' objections classified under the buying decisions:

Need	"My customers will not buy your product."
	"I have all the life insurance I should have."
Product	"But your product is too large."
	"Your line won't take hard usage."
Source	"I don't care for imported products."
	"Your company once gave me a raw deal."
Price	"Prices will be lower next month."
	"You'll have to raise your trade-in allowance."
Time	"I'm not ready to decide."
	"Let's talk about this on your next call."

Once the salesman understands exactly what is holding up the purchase, he at least has a good idea of the missing buying decision. This understanding is basic, because sometimes the voiced objection may not be the real objection. For example, the buyer may say that he is short of time when he actually thinks he is short of money—that he does not like the color of a product when actually what he does not like is the retail salesperson trying to sell the product.

Why do qualified prospects object to buying? Their ignorance, their misconceptions, their doubts, and their prejudices form one group of explanations. Ignorance can be of their circumstances and needs, or it can be ignorance of products. Habit and inertia are a pair of explanations. Uncertainty postpones decisions to buy. Fear of future disappointment and regret is a deterrent. Finally, weak presentations and inept demonstrations can cause objections intended to dismiss the salesman.

Salesmen's attitudes toward objections.   The salesman's proper attitude toward objections, the one characteristic of able and experienced salesmen, is that of welcome; the completely wrong attitude is that of fear. The buyer who talks, even if his talk consists of objections, is much easier to communicate with and to influence than is the silent buyer. Objections can mean that the buyer is paying attention to the salesman's story, they can reflect interest on the buyer's part, and they can indicate that the salesman is making some progress. Above all, an objection can point clearly and unmistakably to a missing buying decision, thus identifying the area in which the salesman must do more selling. The salesman can take comfort from the fact that a properly qualified prospect cannot voice an objection which cannot be handled, because if he can, then qualification was in error. As an alert salesman quickly learns how to handle most objections impressively and successfully, he enjoys and draws confidence from disposing of them. So, salesmen should welcome objections, viewing them and treating them as requests for additional information.

Dealing with objections.   The salesman may prefer not to handle a buyer's objection at the moment it is raised. For example, he seldom cares to come to instant grips with an early objection to *price* when voiced before he has had time to build up the utility and value of his product. Or, he may have a thorough, powerful explanation for the objection in a later part of his presentation. Or, he is often smart not to handle each of a large number of petty, harassing objections. One possibility in such cases is for the salesman to ignore the objection, to disregard it, to appear not to hear or not to grasp it. If the objection is a matter of real influence, the buyer will repeat it. A second tactic is to recognize the objection, ask permission to postpone handling it, promise to handle it later. If the salesman does not have a good answer and if he cannot think of one, a third tactic is to promise to bring the buyer an answer on the next call.

The safer and more common practice is to deal with each point of resistance when it is raised. On rare occasions, a flat, direct denial may be indicated; this, of course, is dangerous, since it may arouse resentment. On equally rare occasions, the salesman can "boomerang" the objection, converting the buyer's reason for *not* buying into a reason *for* buying.

Sometimes the salesman's best move is to demonstrate his product, showing that it does *not* operate as the buyer feared. Sometimes the salesman should compare his product with a competing product point by point. If the salesman's product has an undeniable competitive disadvantage (only one size or color, light or heavy in weight), he should admit this disadvantage but counterbalance it with all of his product's plus points. Sometimes a series of questions will clear away the buyer's difficulty. Finally and most usable of all, there is the indirect denial, the "Yes . . . but" technique. Here the salesman starts by understanding the objection and by reflecting partial or limited agreement—then he points out why the buyer's thought or view does not apply in this instance. The salesman agrees before he disagrees, he disagrees without being disagreeable. The "but" can be a new concept, a forgotten bit of information, a basic difference in circumstances, or a recent development.

Suggestions about objections. By observing several "do's" and "don't's" a salesman can reduce greatly his difficulties in handling buyers' objections. First of all, he should acquire the habit of listening to each objection, listening in a serious, interested, respectful manner. After having his full say and after being given a full hearing, many an objecting buyer talks himself out, gets his objection off his chest, and becomes much more docile. A second "do" is to determine exactly what the buyer is thinking—exactly what his objection really means. Sometimes a restatement of the buyer's words helps achieve a meeting of buyer's mind with seller's mind. Sometimes tactful questioning helps to clarify the buyer's thinking, with the word *why* being the most valuable word the salesman can use. Only if the objection is clarified dare the salesman try to infer which buying decision is missing. A third "do" is to spend an adequate—even a generous—amount of time handling each objection; buyers do not like to feel that they are getting rushed or hurried treatment. A fourth "do" is that the salesman's attitude and behavior reflect respect, sincerity, reassurance, and helpfulness.

On the "don't" side, the salesman must not, except on rare occasions, resort to bald contradictions; indeed, he must try to avoid arguments. He should neither magnify nor minimize an objection; each has an unfavorable effect on the buyer *and* can lead to an unwise budgeting of time. A third caution is not to make the buyer look bad, ignorant, or stupid; once he loses face, the buyer becomes more hostile and difficult.

Typically, the five or six most common objections account for as high as 90 percent of all the objections the salesman hears. This fact suggests that the salesman try to prevent or forestall those specific ones by anticipating them—by building strong answers to them into his regular presentation.

The salesman as a listener

We have just looked at opening and making the presentation, at demonstrating the product, and at handling objections. In each of these, the salesman must be as good at listening as he is at talking; two-way communication is essential, demanding that a salesman receive as well as send. Instruction has been and is common in speaking, in speed reading, and in writing skills. But, there is a fourth phase of communicating, *listening*, and it, too, must be mastered. Incidentally, how many (or few) really good listeners do *you* know?

Listening is an art that each salesman must *learn*, and to learn it, he must *practice* it; he must *want* to listen, and he must *work* at listening. Active rather than passive listening is much more than hearing; it requires much patience on the salesman's part.

When listening successfully, the salesman pays close attention to the buyer's tone, actions, and manner. He listens for what the buyer really means, not just to assess the buyer's moods; sometimes the buyer's main ideas are difficult to sense, sometimes his views or positions do not please. The salesman must not let himself be distracted by the personal features of the buyer or by his own personal concerns. He must not relax or fake attention while drafting his own next communication or while guessing what the buyer's next words will be. The salesman's behavior must imply that he is listening; this includes maintaining eye contact. He must not interrupt, either to offer *his* ideas, to correct, or to finish the *buyer's* sentences. The salesman must work at asking questions *and* at being silent. We are forced to conclude that the good salesmen are good listeners.

Closing the sale

Nature of the close.   The terminal stage or phase of the sales interview is featured by the salesman's attempt to complete the sale-purchase transaction. The salesman's ultimate goal is to make, to "close," profitable sales. His route toward that goal included planning and then making his sales presentation, demonstrating his product, and disposing of objections; now he wants to consummate the sale. The closing period of the sales interview is not a new or different type of conference between the salesman and the buyer. It is simply a logical development or continuation of what started when the interview started. We speak of the salesman's closing the sale. Actually, the *buyer* closes it by buying; otherwise the salesman failed on that particular call. Closing profitable sales which stay closed identify the outstanding salesmen. Weak closers are weak salesmen and low-income earners.

The nature of the close causes the buyer's feelings to reflect ambivalence. He wants the product's benefits and satisfactions, *but* he is reluctant to buy. Perhaps he hates to make decisions, perhaps he views buying as too risky, or perhaps he just resists doing what a salesman suggests. So, the salesman must be and appear to be confident, calm, and reassuring; he must not allow himself any feelings of fear, of nervousness, of anxiety. He dare not tolerate any sense of tension or pressure in the atmosphere. He must both assume and imply that the buyer is going to buy. He will speak of what the product *will* do for the buyer—not of what it *would* do *if* he bought. He will speak of *when* the buyer owns the product—not about *should* the buyer buy.

Closing clues.   Buyers often indicate their closeness to buying by giving ready-to-buy signals to the salesman. There may be several closing clues or buying signals during a single sales interview. The smart salesman works at perfecting his skill in spotting closing clues and at increasing the accuracy of his detection and inferences.

Here are buyers' *questions* which sound like closing clues:

"Is this available in walnut?"
"Is the guarantee for five years?"
"How much would I have to pay down?"
"What about installation?"

These *comments* from buyers sound like closing clues:

"Monthly payments *would* be convenient."
"I'd *have* to have it by next Tuesday."
"My sister *does* like hers."
"Space *will* be available next week."

Physical *actions* which look like closing clues include:

Buyer operates the product, demonstrating it to himself.
Buyer nods his head.
Buyer reexamines one certain product several times.
Buyer removes his glasses and reaches for his pipe.

Trial closes. Every time a salesman thinks he detects a closing clue, he should execute a trial close, because the buyer should be offered an opportunity to buy every time he is ready to buy. These trial closes are safe attempts to close the sale at that moment. They do not endanger salesman-buyer relations; even if unsuccessful, they do not bring the sales call to an end. One possible response to trial close is a purchase. Another result is that the salesman almost always learns something of what the buyer is thinking, and this helps the salesman chart his course from that point.

Here are two *oral* trial closes:

"All this waste must be eliminated at once. Don't you agree?"
"Is there anything else you want to know before going ahead?"

Here are two *physical* trial closes:

Salesman starts to write up an order.
Salesman starts to wrap some merchandise.

Developments other than closing clues may justify a trial close. For example, after making a most impressive product demonstration, the salesman may sense that the time is ripe to try to close. Or, after the skillful handling of an objection, or after the buyer's acceptance of a dramatic proof of one of the salesman's claims, the salesman may try to close. By executing a number of trial closes during each presentation, by closing as early as is feasible, the salesman avoids the unhappy experience of talking himself into a sale—then, by continuing, talking himself right out of the sale.

Closing techniques. Salesmen have developed various closing techniques. Several of the most widely used are now examined briefly. Obviously, this group of six is illustrative only and not complete.

Closing on a choice. This is the most popular and the most successful of all closing techniques; it is often a feature of other closing methods. The salesman constructs and presents to the buyer a choice involving a minor decision. He is careful not to give the buyer the choice of buying or not buying, and, whichever option the buyer elects, he buys.

These are examples of trial closes based on a choice:

"Will six be enough?"
"Do you prefer delivery Thursday—or Friday?"
"When do you want this to become effective?"
"Will this be cash or charge?"

Numerous agreements approach. This is more than a closing technique; it is an extremely desirable practice and habit to establish. Throughout his presentation, the salesman asks questions ("You'll like that, won't you?" "Isn't that right?" "You certainly don't want that to happen to you, do you?") for the purpose of nailing down agreements.

FIGURE 5–5. Report made after failure to close

```
                    BUSINESS PLACED ELSEWHERE
                              due to
                LOWER QUOTATIONS, BETTER DELIVERY,
                        OR OTHER REASONS


                                           Date:_____

Customer:_____  Material:_____



Size:_____      Pounds:_____
Business taken by:_____
Our price:_____ Date of Quote:_____ Base No.:_____
Competitive price:_____ Date of Quote:_____
Our Delivery:_____
Competitive Delivery:_____
REMARKS:




Mail to:  General Sales Dept., Room 110, General Office    Office: _____
Copy to:                                                   Signed:_____
99 071 REV 7/63
```

By so doing he erects barrier after barrier *behind* the buyer. This makes the last agreement, the agreement to buy, then and there, more easy to get.

Single-obstacle approach. Sometimes there is just one single barrier between the buyer and a purchase; for example, it might involve the *price* buying decision, or that of *source*. The salesman gets the buyer to agree that the *one* barrier is the *only* barrier—that the buyer will buy if that one difficulty could be resolved. Perhaps a clerical employee says truthfully that he will enroll for a correspondence course if his firm will pay one half the cost. The salesman goes to work on that one deterrent, disposes of it if he can, then closes the sale.

Summarize the satisfactions. In this technique, the salesman makes his presentation, then reviews briefly in summary form all the benefits the buyer will enjoy, asking for buyer agreement on each. He then assumes the buyer is ready to buy and moves to wind matters up, probably closing on a choice.

"Standing room only." Here the salesman puts pressure on the buyer. He may hint of an imminent rise in prices. He may warn of short supply, of inability to repurchase and replenish once present inventory is sold. He may threaten to make his offer to the buyer's keenest competitor unless the buyer accepts it. In extreme cases, he may question the buyer's ability to handle the product or to qualify for it. SRO closing must be handled with great care.

Special concessions. When unable to make the sale on the initial basis, the salesman may offer some special inducement or consideration to the buyer in order to get him to buy now. The salesman may cut his price or increase the trade-in allowance. He may offer to throw in something "free" as a premium for the order.

MANAGERIAL DUTIES OF SALESMEN

Customer development

Regardless of whether a sale was made, future customer development depends much on the final moments of *this* call. At this time, appreciation should be expressed for the purchase or for the buyer's time and consideration. By reassuring the buyer who bought, the salesman works to allay postpurchase dissonance. This is also the time to offer any appropriate favors. Above all, the salesman must get any information he will need in roughing out a plan for the next call on this specific buyer. Nothing is more mandatory in the handling of buyers than is the rule that *every* call should be a planned call—that not a single one should be a "drop-in" call.

As soon as practicable after leaving the buyer, the salesman should jot down all that should be recorded about his sales interview just completed. He may, for this purpose, set up a card or even a folder on each buyer so as to have all information in one place, information which includes ideas and plans for the next visit. Also, as soon as practicable, the salesman should review and evaluate his attempt to sell, noting what he did well and what could have been done better. A checklist may be helpful here, one made up of such items as adequacy of buyer information, quality of his sales story, impressiveness of his product demonstrations, skill in handling objections, and the number and wording of his trial closes. Such a review is particularly desirable when no sale was made. If he is honest as to the cause of failure, he will improve by selling *smarter*—not just selling *harder*.

Customer development will be maximized only if the salesman classifies his customers as to call frequency. Perhaps the "A" group should consist of big accounts deserving maximum attention and service; call frequency may be once a month. The "B" group could be the average accounts. Because the salesman must have their volume of purchases, he gives them considerable attention and calls on each every other month. "C" accounts may contribute so little to sales volume and profits as to be allotted only three calls a year.

A word or two may be in order here about two problems which plague most salesmen. These are (1) individual orders so small that they are unprofitable, and (2) individual customers each of whose annual purchase volume is so small as to be unprofitable. These are often related in that most of the orders placed by small, unprofitable customers are small, unprofitable orders. A common experience is for a salesman to discover that 20 percent of his customers account for 80 percent of his sales volume and that 80 percent of his customers account for only 20 percent of his sales volume. There may be some help from his firm in the form of establishing the minimum amounts the buyers must buy to quality for continued sales calls, quantity discounts, or service. Perhaps a better course of action is better selling. Salesmen have no option but to drop small, unprofitable accounts which seem to have a continuing dim future.

Time management

Time is the salesman's most precious possession. He can replace his employer, his territory, his product line, his customers—but he cannot replace one lost hour. Truly, control of a salesman's time is control of his earnings. In trying to maximize the productivity of his time, the salesman tries to log more hours each week in face-to-face selling to buyers in order to increase sales volume and to decrease selling costs.

The first step toward the control of his time is for the salesman to list the activities which constitute his job. Common activities include: planning, prospecting, travel, waiting to see buyers, service to customers, records and reports, attending sales meetings, public relations, credit and collection, market research, and, of course, face-to-face selling. Next is to set the quotas desired (sales volume, calls, new prospects, etc.) and then to budget time for achieving each quota. Every day should be a scheduled day, every week a scheduled week, if the salesman is truly to be the marketing manager of his territory and if he is to get the most possible out of that territory.

The difficult battle for face-to-face selling time can be inferred from this daily breakdown of one salesman's work day:

How 8.7 hours were spent:

Plans and records, 0.4	Travel, 2.4	Lunch, 1.0
Prospecting, 0.9	Waiting, 2.0	Selling to buyers, 2.0

Note that the time spent in traveling suggests strongly that great attention and study be spent in setting up the routing for each day.

Uses of telephone and mail

In maximizing his sales performance, a salesman usually finds that telephone calls and mailings to buyers can be most useful as auxiliary selling tools. A few salesmen do all their selling by telephone, and some sellers sell only through direct mailings. Most salesmen rely mainly on face-to-face selling and supplement this with the telephone and with mailings. One or both of these tools can be used to:

Presell	Keep in touch between calls
Make actual sales	Stimulate inquiries
Make appointments	Report or inform
Identify prospects	Get buyer information
Handle problems	Send personal messages

Both telephone and mail communications are personal and private. Cost may be no more than a very small fraction of the cost of a personal call. Communication is under the control of the salesman in that he can choose which buyers to reach, select day and sometimes even the hour, and can design whatever message he deems appropriate. Few buyers refuse to take long-distance calls. Telephone calls are very speedy, and mailings do not take much time. So, these two selling tools permit more

FIGURE 5–6. The telephone is a versatile tool for many salesmen

TELEPHONE APPOINTMENT PLANNING GIVES YOUR BUSINESS THESE ADVANTAGES

More sales at lower costs

☐ Visit customers and prospects on a planned schedule.
- achieve more complete sales coverage
- develop business potential
- see more customers each day

☐ Get more selling hours into each day.
- no lost time spent in the "outer office"
- gain access to the person you want to see
- reserve time to sell

☐ Personal visits are adjusted to meet needs of individual customers.
- qualifies prospects needs
- improves customer service
- stimulates buying
- avoids untimely visits

☐ Gain access to customers and prospects while competition must wait.
- meet competition more effectively
- maintain customer loyalty
- lessen "brand shifting"
- you're there when customer is ready to buy

☐ Reduce overall cost of sales visit.
- unnecessary traveling expenses are cut
- fewer "call backs" are necessary
- greater territory covered for sales dollar

☐ Increase frequency of orders.
- get more selling hours into each day
- produce more opportunities for selling
- gain more orders per sales visits
- sell by phone if personal visit cannot be arranged

contacts with more buyers; they help reduce travel time, waiting time, and expenses.

Plans, goals, and records

The most important element in well-managed selling is that of planning. Basically, planning involves how creative the salesman's selling is and how much of it he does. The better his planning, the more and

FIGURE 5–7. Typical report made after each call

CALL REPORT

Representative District Date

Concern

New Potential
(by major products)

Street and No.
City and State
Interviewed

Business

☒ Gen'l Sales, Rm. 208	☐ Ans.	☐ Det.	☐ L. A.	☐ Wat.	☐ AMH	☐ AAB, Ltd.
☒ Rep. File	☐ Buff.	☐ Ken.	☐	☐ Small Tube	☐ FMG	☐ Sales Prom.

cc:

99.08 REV. 6-64

the better presentations he makes. The need for planning is seen clearly when the salesman recognizes that he has a total of fixed expenses each week. Until his sales volume each week is enough to cover those expenses, he is working for *others;* once they are covered, he begins working for and paying *himself*. Obviously, he wants to start working for himself on Wednesday rather than Friday.

As was implied in the section on time management, each salesman must set up what for him is the most appropriate group of goals. All these goals have one feature in common—the dimension of *time* which relates the salesman's goals to his overall time budget. They include:

Sales	Sales-to-calls ratio	Product demonstrations
Calls	New prospects	
Expenses	New customers	Miles traveled

The salesman must keep a record for each goal, each objective, each quota he establishes. He does not have time to keep records which he does not find useful or used. Analysis of records permits a comparing of actual performance against planned performance. It facilitates the identification of elements of strength and those of weakness in his performance.

Building goodwill

What is 'good" will? What is "bad" will? Goodwill is an intangible asset which consists mainly of the warm, friendly, favorable feelings buyers have toward a salesman, his products, and his firm. It is a matter of buyer confidence and satisfaction. It is the buyer's inclination to buy from a particular salesman; it is the buyer's preference for the products of the salesman's firm. It is a source bias such as we discussed in the chapter on communication. The source (salesman) with goodwill has a positive valence in the buyer's mind which carries over to the messages the salesman brings and to the products he recommends.

How do salesmen build goodwill? Salesmen of goodwill are truthful, trustworthy, and dependable over time. They are considerate in their dealings with buyers, respecting and being guided by each buyer's preferences and tastes. They take a sincere interest in each buyer, always determined to be of service, always helping each buyer get what he wants, careful to see that each buyer buys what he should and uses it as he should. They are friendly and courteous; they handle complaints promptly and fairly; they offer helpful counsel and advice.

How does goodwill help? Goodwill is well worth cultivating on several counts. You know from your own experience as a consumer that buyers tend to buy from salesmen they like. So, the more goodwill he enjoys, the more sales and earnings for the salesman. These are not one-time sales, either. They represent repeat patronage. Another benefit is the favorable word-of-mouth publicity the salesman's customers give him. Such publicity enhances the salesman's reputation to a most delightful degree. Then, the salesman takes more pride in his work, he derives more satisfaction from it, he is touched by the friendship and the loyalty of his customers. Finally, he benefits from the assistance and cooperation of his customers. They refer him to new prospects, supply testimonials and case histories, recommend the salesman to their friends and associates, and aid in product demonstrations. Our conclusion must be that goodwill is worth cultivating even though success and achievement in this undertaking may take years.

QUESTIONS AND PROBLEMS

5–1. A salesman has just made his first sale to a certain buyer. What mistakes should the salesman avoid?

5–2. Why does the outstanding salesman combine *visual* proof of his promises and claims with *oral* proof?

5–3. Why do so many persons, including students, look on a career in personal selling as one of low social status and prestige?

5–4. List the major *product* features about which a salesman should be informed.

5–5. *a*) If you had to name the essential characteristics of successful salesmen what would they be?

 b) What are some traits of mature salesmen?

5–6. What do you think most salesmen could do to improve their sales presentations? Add to those in Figure 5-3.

5–7. Some salesmen are expected to memorize a standardized sales story and deliver it verbatim. What is *good*—what is *bad* about such "canned" stories?

5–8. Time is the most valuable possession of most salesmen. Make some helpful suggestions to a young sales trainee about his future handling of his time.

5–9. *a*) What good can a salesman accomplish by asking the buyer questions?

 b) How can the salesman make good use of buyers' questions during sales interviews?

5–10. Make some general suggestions to salesmen about the handling of buyers' objections.

CHAPTER 6

Sales management

A firm's most important budget is its sales budget or sales forecast. The sales figure budgeted represents revenue or income from the sale of the firm's products or services—the dollars counted on by the firm to cover expenses and profits. Sales produce the dollars needed to finance such other budgets as purchasing, production, advertising, and personnel. If the firm sets next year's sales forecast at 100 but, during that period, sells only 90, then there is trouble in paying expenses and in producing profits. The firm must revise its procurement plans, its production schedules, and its cost and profit estimates.

The executive most responsible for selling the budgeted figure, for "making forecast," is the sales manager. He heads the sales department, leads and directs his sales force, and administers a sales program which he believes will achieve the net sales figure budgeted and forecast for next year. Because sales management is so basic and important, the sales manager is usually the senior manager, enjoying more prestige and pay than the executives who manage personnel, credit, advertising, and even production.

For the typical vice president for marketing, the personal selling done by the firm's salesmen is his most serious concern and responsibility. This marketing vice president leans most heavily on personal selling to communicate, to inform, to persuade. He knows that his firm's sales volume is greatly influenced by the selling the salesmen do. The sales manager usually reports to this top marketing executive. The sales manager must work within the framework of company goals and policies, of marketing strategy, and of promotional objectives and procedures. He must establish selling goals or objectives which are in harmony with, and are actually part of, promotional goals and objectives. The two most common goals of the sales manager are (1) sales volume in dollars or units and (2) share of market expressed as a percentage of total market. The nature of the items to be sold, the nature of the buyers to whom they will be sold, and the nature of competition are three powerful influences on selling goals and objectives.

SALES TERRITORIES

What and why

An early and, indeed, continuing responsibility of the sales manager is that of deciding what to do about market coverage. Although there are some exceptions (automobile dealers, real estate firms, life insurance agencies), the common practice is for a salesman to be assigned a specific territory by his sales manager. The territory may be a geographical area—as small as a part of a city or as widespread as 15 states. Or it may consist of the individual buyer or buyers for whom the salesman is responsible.

Soundly constituted sales territories make sense in several ways. They permit responsibility and authority to be clearly fixed and established. They make less difficult the setting of sales quotas and other performance standards. They work for good relations with customers, because each customer gets the service he needs; this is possible because no salesman is given too much to do. Plans, budgets, and controls operate more effectively in terms of individual sales territories. There is less opportunity for duplication of effort and for the neglect of desired effort. Sales volume stands a better chance of being maximized and selling expense of being minimized.

Methods of establishing

The first step in establishing sales territories is to decide what the *basic unit* shall be. The basic unit is the smallest unit recognized; sales territories are composed of basic units.

The *city* is a possible basic unit. Legal city limits may be unrealistic in some instances. Too, some cities are entirely too large for one salesman. This poses the difficult questions of how the city should be subdivided and how to get needed marketing data for each subdivision.

The *county* is probably the basic unit most widely used by manufacturers. For most manufacturers, most counties are smaller than most sales territories. Only a few (such as those containing Los Angeles, Detroit, or Chicago) are too large for one salesman to handle. Much statistical information is available on a county basis.

The *Standard Metropolitan Statistical Area* can be used as a basic unit. A SMSA consists of one county or a group of contiguous counties. It must contain one city of at least 50,000—or two contiguous cities with a combined population of at least 50,000. Total population for the area must be at least 100,000. The key county of a group of counties must be metropolitan in character, and the contiguous counties must be tied closely to the central city socially and economically. These areas observe county lines but ignore state lines. There are about 225 SMSA's in the United States. They account for roughly two thirds of our population and two thirds of our retail sales.

The *wholesale trading area* for the product in question is a logical marketing unit to be considered as a basic unit. It respects trade and traffic lines while ignoring political boundaries, even county lines. Delineation of wholesale trading areas is a difficult undertaking, as is the collecting of marketing and other statistical data in terms of the areas.

Finally, there is the *state*. This unit is too large for many manufacturers.

Once the basic unit has been selected, the next step is to group basic units into appropriate territories. For example, a manufacturer of consumer products using counties might select as key counties those containing our 100 largest cities; he would then add to each those counties tributary to each. Or, for another example, a manufacturer might forecast sales for the coming year, assign a quota to each basic unit, then combine units into appropriate groupings; these would be sales territories. Or, he might decide on the average annual sales volume per salesman, divide this figure into his total sales forecast, then establish that number of logically constituted sales territories.

As one looks at the sales territory patterns of many manufacturers, one is aware of the wide ranges in number and size; this holds for individual sales territories, for sales districts, and for sales regions. Influences on numbers and sizes include:

Number of prospective customers	Potential purchases/customer
Desired frequency of contact	Sales and profit considerations
Seller's competitive position	Nature of product line
Travel facilities	Service customers need

Routing

Efficient coverage of a sales territory demands efficient routing of the salesman. Routing is a matter of the sequence and the scheduling of calls; it is a matter of how the salesman travels through his territory. His routing plan tells *where* the salesman will be, *when* he will be there, and on *whom* he will be calling. The routing patterns may be charted on a map of the territory.

The salesman himself may develop the pattern; or his sales manager may; or the two may develop it together. Both stay alert to the possibility of improving the routes for more effective coverage of the territory. Satisfactory routing demands: (1) well-designed sales territories; (2) identification of the buyers or accounts on whom the salesman will call; (3) predetermined frequencies of call on each account; (4) predetermined number of calls to be made each day; and (5) complete knowledge of travel facilities and conditions.

The well-routed salesman minimizes his travel time and expense. He maximizes his face-to-face selling time. He tailors the frequency and length of his calls to each buyer's needs and circumstances.

RECRUITING

The quality and productivity of a sales force reflect the quality of the recruiting and selecting which are responsible for the current composition of the force. Hiring the wrong salesmen can be extremely expensive. Sales volume will be lower than it should, and selling costs will be excessive. Unskilled salesmen lose some customers completely; they arouse irritation and hostility in other customers. Mistakes of omission and commission generate friction and complaints, jeopardizing company and brand reputations. Supervisory costs are higher than they should be, including the sales manager's coping with the ill will of fellow salesmen. Termination and replacement are expensive. So, recruiting should be a sound and systematic activity which gets the time, attention, thought, and budget it deserves. It should also be a continuing activity; salesmen will continue to retire, die, resign, get promoted, and get fired. The sales manager must recruit in the same manner and for the same reasons as his salesmen engage in prospecting. He hopes always to know whence the next salesman is coming, even though he cannot always know when.

A carefully developed *job analysis* is absolutely prerequisite to satisfactory recruiting. This analysis calls for the study and determination of just what the salesman will be expected to do during his working hours on the job. This involves the salesman's duties, activities, work responsibilities, and assignments. The sales manager cannot identify promising candidates for a selling job until and unless he knows what he wants and expects in that job.

Common assignments include: to make sales, to prospect, to sign up new customers, to render services to customers, and to report. But, there is such a wide range of differences among selling jobs that the concept of a single, generally appropriate job analysis is utterly unrealistic. What the sales manager must do, consequently, is to separate his basically different types of selling jobs and do a separate analysis of each type. Salesmen of a firm's industrial products draw different assignments from assignments given to those who sell its consumer products. Merchandising salesmen have different responsibilities and engage in different activities from those of regular dealer-selling salesmen.

Job analysis leads to a *job description*. This description reduces to writing the findings and decisions of the analysis phase. It is a formal, official description of what the salesman is to do. Common subheadings found in job descriptions include: specific job title, daily duties and activities, authority and responsibility, compensation plan, relation to other jobs, and the opportunity to advance. The fact that the description is in writing and official works to minimize misunderstanding and disagreement.

A listing of *job specifications* is a logical extension of the job description. Where the description spelled out the salesman's activities and assignments, the specification list catalogs the personal features, characteristics, and qualifications desired in and of a salesman if he is to perform satisfactorily. Specifications are usually grouped under subheadings, examples of which are:

Physical (height, weight)
Mental (education, IQ)
Environment (social stratum, composition of family)
Experience (sales, military)
Personality (maturity, enthusiasm)

As for experience, some sales managers hire only experienced salesmen, while others hire and train only individuals who have never sold.

Drafting workable, usable job specifications is not an easy job. To start with, the specifications wanted by sales managers differ greatly because selling jobs differ greatly. In addition, the applicants' ratings

FIGURE 6–1.   State Farm uses these bases in recruiting and selecting

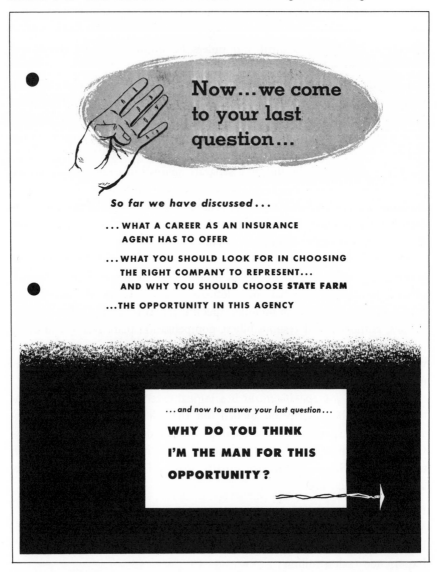

or scores on certain desirable characteristics can be most difficult of measurement. How, for example, can you measure honesty or courage, judgment or ambition? Which applicant will work hardest, which will have most confidence in his firm and its products? Finally, most sales managers take delight in supervising outstanding salesmen who rank low on certain features generally believed to be essential for outstanding selling perfor-

FIGURE 6–1. *(Continued)*

HERE'S HOW WE ANSWER THAT QUESTION

1. Aptitude Index
2. Inspection Report
3. References
4. Your Past Experience
5. Your Age
6. Your Credit Standing
7. Your Reputation
8. Your Social Contacts
9. Your Educational Background
10. Our Interviews
11. Your Wife's Attitude
12. Regional Office Interview

✓ Medical Examination
✓ Pre-Contract Orientation
✓ Examination For License
✓ Home Office Approval

THIS IS HOW WE MAKE UP OUR MIND . . .

56   Revised (9-63)

mance. Apparently a surplus of qualities or capabilities in certain areas can compensate for limitations or modest endowments in others.

Where do sales managers recruit for salesmen? Sometimes promising trainees are found within the firm, perhaps doing clerical, production, or engineering work. Recommendations from company personnel can include these inside persons as well as outsiders. Sales trainees or, indeed, qualified salesmen can be hired away from other firms such as suppliers, wholesale or retail customers, even competitors. Many companies recruit at colleges; the limited or nonexistent experience of graduates is typically matched by their willingness to sign up for lower pay than that demanded by experienced salesmen. Some persons walk in or write in voluntarily to apply for selling jobs. Employment agencies may put a sales manager in touch with the type of person he needs. Finally, in some situations the "want ad" seems to be worth running.

SELECTING

Applicants who qualify as to job specifications are normally given serious consideration for hiring. Thus, in a real sense, selection can be no better than the quality of the job analysis, the job description, and the job specifications. The penalties for improper, unfortunate selection and hiring are roughly the same as for inadequate recruiting: low share of market, low morale, unfavorable company and brand images, bad customer relations, and too many trainees dropped during the training program. The results are low sales volume, high selling costs, low profits. To repeat for emphasis, the achievements of the sales force reflect how well or poorly the recruiting and selecting jobs were done. In small companies, the president may do the hiring. In larger companies, the sales manager has the final responsibility and authority. In still larger firms, a group of executives may interview and grade applicants with the sales manager having the final say.

Now let's look at the selection tools in common use.

Application blank

When the sales manager asks an applicant to fill out and file an application blank, he is asking the applicant to submit a written, formal request for a selling job. This blank is one of the most widely used selection tools. It provides the sales manager with a relatively detailed personal history and background of the applicant. Information and data requested are related to the job of selling. Weights can be assigned as the sales manager deems appropriate, and scoring ranges can be provided. Frequently, the applicant is scored on each subheading, and these are added together to arrive at a single, total score. Recruiters at colleges may request a short, screening application blank or a brief, screening interview before the applicant is allowed to file a detailed application blank.

Here are subheadings found on many application blanks:

Personal (age, appearance)
Environmental (address, dependents)
Education (degree, major field)
Employment (firms, jobs)
Military (branch, rank)
Financial (insurance carried, credit report)
Activities (clubs, hobbies)
References (business, educational)

Physical examination

This selection screen should be scheduled early in the selection procedure. If the applicant cannot qualify physically, he should be dropped immediately from consideration so as to save time and money.

Personal interview

Because there is no substitute, very few salesmen are hired without going through one or more personal interviews. Indeed, the personal interview and the application blank make up the most widely used pair of selection tools. Certain personality traits and features important in selling simply cannot be detected except through interviews. How else, for example, can a sales manager evaluate an applicant's voice, delivery, vocabulary, or conversational ability? What is the nature and impact of his personality? The personal interview reveals this and also shows how the applicant goes about "selling" himself to the sales manager, including his answering of the sales manager's questions.

There are two basic types of interview. One is formal, structured, and uniform. In using it, each interviewer guides the applicant through the same experience, following word by word the patterned set of questions. The other is completely informal, unstructured, and nondirective; it encourages the applicant to talk freely much as is done in "depth" interviews. Many companies chart a course somewhat in between these two extremes. Interviewers may score the applicant on rating scales. Here are two examples:

(*Personality*, for example) A B C D E
(*Appearance*, for example) Fair   Satisfactory   Superior

FIGURE 6–2. Sales application blank

EMPLOYMENT APPLICATION
Saks Fifth Avenue

DATE OF APPLICATION	POSITION APPLIED FOR	ARE YOU NOW EMPLOYED?

PLEASE PRINT ALL INFORMATION

LAST NAME	FIRST NAME	MIDDLE INITIAL	SOCIAL SECURITY NO. — —
PRESENT ADDRESS (No., Street, City, Zone & State)		HOW LONG THERE?	PHONE
PREVIOUS ADDRESS		HOW LONG THERE?	SEX / NO. DEPENDENTS

LIVE WITH PARENTS	LIVE WITH RELATIVES	ROOM	BOARD	TENANT	HOME OWNER	SINGLE	MARRIED
☐	☐	☐	☐	☐	☐	☐	☐

DO YOU WEAR GLASSES? ☐ Yes ☐ No	HEIGHT ft. ins.	WEIGHT lbs.	HAIR	EYES	WIDOW(ER) ☐	DIVORCED ☐

IF YOU HAVE ANY PHYSICAL HANDICAP OR ARE UNDER A DOCTOR'S CARE, PLEASE EXPLAIN:

BIRTH DATE Mo. Day Yr.

WERE YOU EVER EMPLOYED BY S.F.A.?	HAVE YOU A RELATIVE NOW EMPLOYED BY S.F.A.?	IN CASE OF EMERGENCY, NOTIFY:	
PERIOD	NAME	NAME	
JOB	INDICATE IF SPOUSE OR PARENT	ADDRESS	
DEPT.	DEPT.	INDICATE IF SPOUSE OR PARENT	TEL. NO.

EDUCATION

PERIOD Mo. & Yr. to Mo. & Yr.		LEVEL	SCHOOL AND CITY	MAJOR SUBJECTS	GRADUATE Yes	GRADUATE No	DEGREE
		Elementary					
		High School					
		College					
		Business or Vocational					

WHAT PART OF YOUR COLLEGE EXPENSES DID YOU EARN? HOW?	LIST BUSINESS AND PROFESSIONAL MEMBERSHIPS	OTHER DETAILS, IF ANY (SPECIAL COURSES, SCHOLARSHIPS, ETC.)

WHAT ARE YOUR HOBBIES?	FOREIGN LANGUAGES SPOKEN

EMPLOYMENT HISTORY (List last job first and account for all unemployed time.)

Shaded Boxes Are For Use Of Personnel Dept.

PERIOD Mo. & Yr. to Mo. & Yr.		FIRM AND ADDRESS	JOB TITLE AND SUPERVISOR	SALARY AND REASON FOR LEAVING	Sent	App.
				$ per REASONS FOR LEAVING	Sent	App.
				$ per REASONS FOR LEAVING	Sent	App.
				$ per REASONS FOR LEAVING	Sent	App.
				$ per REASONS FOR LEAVING	Sent	App.
				$ per REASONS FOR LEAVING	Sent	App.
				$ per REASONS FOR LEAVING	Sent	App.

REFERRED BY

BM264R

THE NEW YORK LAW AGAINST DISCRIMINATION PROHIBITS DISCRIMINATION BECAUSE OF AGE

(OVER)

FIGURE 6–2. *(Continued)*

PERSONAL REFERENCES (Three persons, not relatives or former employers, who have known you over 2 years)

This Space For Use Of Personnel Dept.

NAME AND ADDRESS	OCCUPATION	HOW LONG KNOWN?	REFERENCE REQUEST Sent	App.

➤ **TO AID IN CLEARING YOUR REFERENCES:**
IF MARRIED WOMAN, GIVE PREVIOUS OR MAIDEN NAME.

EXPERIENCE CHECK-LIST (Indicate number of months or years experience.)

EXPERIENCE	YRS.	MOS.	EXPERIENCE	YRS.	MOS.	EXPERIENCE	YRS.	MOS.	EXPERIENCE	YRS.	MOS.
Accounting			Elliot Fisher			Section Manager			Unit Control		
Adjustment			Filing			Sewing			Wrapping		
Alterations			Key Punch			Shorthand (Words/Min.)			LIST ANY OTHER		
Bookkeeping			Marking			Statistics					
Cashier			NCR Operator			Stock					
Checking			Packing			Telephone Switchboard					
Comptometer			Personnel			Training					
Credit			Secretary			Typing (Words/Min.)					

MODELS ONLY		U. S. MILITARY SERVICE		
DRESS SIZE	BUST	BRANCH	LENGTH OF SERVICE	SPECIALTY
HIPS	WAIST	DATE OF DISCHARGE	TYPE OF DISCHARGE	ARE YOU NOW IN RESERVE?	ARE YOU IN NATIONAL GUARD?	WILL YOU TAKE SUMMER TRNG?

ENTER ADDITIONAL FACTS WHICH MAY HELP IN EVALUATING YOUR APPLICATION:
_____
_____
_____
_____
_____

APPLICANT'S AGREEMENT
(important - read carefully)

I understand that if I am accepted for Employment with SAKS FIFTH AVENUE I will be employed on a 90 days Probationary Status.

I hereby certify that the answers given by me to the foregoing questions are true and correct, without any consequential omissions whatsoever. I agree that SAKS FIFTH AVENUE shall not be liable in any respect if my application is rejected or my employment terminated because of the falsity of answers or omissions made by me in this application form. I agree to submit to physical examination if required. I also authorize SAKS FIFTH AVENUE to secure any information regarding myself, and I hereby release any person, firm or institution from all liability for any damage whatsoever for issuing such information. It is understood that if engaged, my employment may be terminated at any time, either by myself or SAKS FIFTH AVENUE.

DO NOT WRITE BELOW

FOR MEDICAL DEPARTMENT USE

Applicant's Signature

	CHECK-LIST	A	B	C	D	INTERVIEWER'S COMMENTS
	Appearance					
	Poise					
INTERVIEW	Speech					
	Attitude					
	Alertness					
	Personality					
	Potential					

INTERVIEWER _____ DATE _____

ENGAGEMENT	ENGAGED BY	DATE	POSITION	BUDGET NO.	WKLY. SALARY $
	DATE TO REPORT	DEPT.	STAFF NO.	REGULAR	CONTINGENT	PART TIME	HOURS	DAYS

Often the same applicant is interviewed by more than one company executive; often the same executive has more than one interview with the same applicant.

References

Many sales managers ask applicants for references and recommendations, all the while knowing that an applicant would hardly submit the name of anyone whose comments would be negative. Sometimes a person given as a reference *does* make a helpful comment or supply a bit of worthwhile information. Friends are usually called on for personal references; former employers and credit rating firms supply business references.

Psychological tests

The most controversial procedure or screen in the selection of salesmen is that of psychological testing. Some sales managers place entirely too much faith in and reliance on the accuracy and usefulness of these tests—and others have nothing but total scorn for them, have never used a single one, and have no intention of ever using one. The issue is essentially this: Can psychological tests detect the presence or the absence of personal traits which will affect an applicant's selling career—either positively or negatively?

Of the four most common tests, one is used to measure *mental ability* or *intelligence*. It purports to determine how well an applicant can learn and think, reason and solve problems. Although this is the most valid and reliable of the psychological tests, one must still wonder if a high IQ guarantees success in selling.

Personality tests undertake to measure personal characteristics and features which bear on and help determine successful selling. Here one must wonder how precisely a test can measure drive or ambition, honesty, loyalty, or durability.

Other tests try to determine an applicant's *interests* and then compare them against those of outstanding salesmen. Two questions here: Do or should all top salesmen have the same interests? Can an applicant lie and fake when answering these?

Finally there are the *sales aptitude* tests; these attempt to measure such variables as tact, memory, and verbal facility. The trouble here is that sales managers do not agree on what traits are sales aptitude traits.

What can we conclude about psychological testing as a selection tool?

First, it should not be the *only* selection tool. Second, it should be viewed as an *aid* to the sales manager's judgment and common sense, not as a *substitute* for them. Third, most of the tests are standardized tests (IQ, for example), but there are great differences among selling jobs. Finally, let's hope that as more experience is logged with the tests, their contribution to sounder selection will increase.

TRAINING

Once the sales manager has selected the individuals who will be his salesmen, the question of training then arises. The amount and kind of sales training vary from company to company; the program itself may require several hours—or several years. The newly hired trainees need to be taught what to do and what not to do as they look forward to working with buyers and making sales.

What about training for the firm's salesmen who have been selling for some time? Many firms schedule periodic training programs for their experienced salesmen, perhaps once a year, sometimes several times a year. The major goal of such refresher training is to keep the men from drifting into ruts and to encourage them to commit themselves to a never-ending program of self-improvement. Sales meetings are one vehicle used in this training. Special courses in selling are another. In both, heavy emphasis is put on product information, buyer information, and how-to-sell information. Many of the topics in Chapter 6 are the subjects of training sessions.

As for the benefits to be derived from proper training programs, they turn out to be essentially those of proper recruiting and proper selection: larger sales, lower selling expenses, greater profits; salesmen achieve their selling potential more quickly, and their supervising needs are lower than they otherwise would be; salesmen's turnover drops as morale rises; more of his customers become "fans" of the salesman and his firm. These benefits are to be had because principles of personal selling can be taught and learned—because salesmen can be trained.

Organizing for training

Who should train the firm's salesmen? Even though this varies, *one* specific person should be given the responsibility and the authority in the firm for this sales management activity. One possibility, suitable for large companies only, is to set up a staff position occupied by a sales training director whose only duties are to plan, to organize, to instruct, and to supervise within the training area. A second possibility is to charge some line official with the responsibility for training; he could be the sales manager, each regional or district sales manager, or each sales supervisor. A third possibility, that of turning training over to an outside, commercial training company, can be used alone or along with either of the other two possibilities.

As to *where* the training should be done, there are two common sites, but they permit several combinations. Training may take place at the home (or regional or district) office—or out in the field in the salesmen's territories. Some companies give their young trainees a brief training course in the field, have them do actual selling for a short time, then bring them into the home office for a thorough training program.

Where, as you see, also involves *when*. One pattern different from the split just mentioned finds the company scheduling full training at the home office (for up to three years, incidentally) before the salesman is assigned and sent to his sales territory. Periodic refreshers may be available to a salesman until he retires.

The matter of *how* salesmen are trained involves procedures or techniques, and it involves training aids. Classroom procedures include lectures, panels, conferences, and discussions, as well as sales demonstrations and role play. In sales demonstrations, two expert salesmen, one of whom might well be a sales manager, execute an outstanding, difficult, but successful sales presentation; explanation may follow. In role playing, typically a sales trainer plays the role of the buyer and a trainee or an actual salesman attempts to make a sale; analysis usually follows. Techniques other than those executed in classrooms usually are thought of as "on-the-job" training out in the field. The probability is strong that on-the-job training is greater in volume than is training in the classroom. In this training, the trainer (sales manager, regional sales manager, district sales manager, sales supervisor, or even a senior salesman who can teach) accompanies the salesman, observes what and how the salesman does on selling calls, then gives the salesman critiques on his selling.

We said that *how* involves training aids in addition to procedures or techniques. Among the more widely used aids are these:

Instruction manuals	Samples	Bulletins
Texts	Models	Portfolios
Presentation manuals	Charts	Teaching machines
Movie films	Product	Closed-circuit
Sound-slide films	demonstrations	television

FIGURE 6–3. Retailers have a sales training responsibility just as do manufacturers

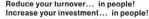

Training program content

What should be taught to sales trainees must obviously reflect their activities, duties, and assignments as determined in the job analysis and detailed in the job description. The training program should show the trainee how to do what he is expected to do. Reference to the previous chapter on personal selling will indicate what most salesmen do; consequently, it points to what salesmen should be taught—to locate prospects, to build sales presentations, to demonstrate, to deal with objections, to close sales, to maximize sales performances, and to help buyers make more satisfactory purchases.

Here are five topics included in most training programs with examples of subheads:

Company: History, personnel, policies, procedures, practices

Product or service: Features, competing items, uses, benefits, prices

Buyers: Prospecting, motives, habits, problems, attitudes

Selling Techniques: Getting and opening sales interviews, constructing sales stories, demonstrating the product, coping with objections, how to close

Self-management: Planning, budgets, scheduling, routing, records and reports

COMPENSATION

A major responsibility of the sales manager is to design and administer a satisfactory compensation plan for his salesmen. Most plans contain three elements. The *direct financial* part consists of the salesman's basic earnings, income, or pay. The most popular plan is salary plus some incentive, next is straight salary, and third is straight commission. The *indirect financial* part consists of such fringe benefits as insurance, paid vacations, and retirement income. The *nonfinancial* part is made up of such goodwill builders as a good climate to work in, interest, recognition, compliments, concern, and empathy on the part of the sales manager.

Sales managers want a plan that is competitive enough to attract and hold good salesmen—the caliber of salesmen the firm requires. Managers want the plan to help and not handicap the firm in its determination to operate profitably. Sales compensation must not be too great as a selling expense, nor must the plan be too costly to administer. Sales managers hope the plan will aid in their efforts to control and direct their salesmen in chosen activities and toward chosen objectives. At the same time, they expect it to work as an incentive, stimulating and motivating the sales force. Finally, sales managers want the plan to be adequately flexible.

As for the *salesmen*, they want to be able to afford an acceptable standard of living and even to raise it over time. Most salesmen want two types of income, one that is regular and stable enough to provide some security, the other an incentive element that provides extra rewards for extra accomplishment. Hopefully, his income will reflect only those variables over which the salesman has control. The compensation plan should be fair to each salesman in comparison with his fellow salesmen, and it should be closely related to the job he does. Salesmen want the plan to be simple and understandable; they want its operation to be prompt. Many salesmen want to have a voice in the construction and design of the compensation plan.

Compensation level

Compensation *level* is a "how much" matter; compensation *methods* involve "how." Level is the total dollar amount a salesman receives over a period of time; pay and fringe benefits have been referred to as *direct financial* and *indirect financial* elements of compensation. Compensation level is what the sales manager must offer if he is to hire and hold the kind of man he wants and needs for the selling job involved. Compensation level, thus, is the going market wage or price for the type and quality of salesman the sales manager expects to hire. Level reflects the job description and the job specifications. It must approximate what other firms pay similar salesmen, and it denotes the worth of the salesman to his company.

We now examine three compensation methods.

Straight commission

When salesmen are on straight commission, the sales manager is paying for performance. He is buying accomplishment, and he pays off when the salesman makes a sale. The commission rate can be fixed or sliding; its most common base is dollar sales volume. The commission is a variable expense to the company. It is variable compensation to the salesman, and it is fixed as a percent of sales volume.

On the plus side, straight commission acts as a powerful incentive. The salesman is encouraged to sell aggressively because his production determines his income. Salesmen enjoy the amount of freedom inherent in the plan. Sales managers like to be able to budget selling costs per unit. Some managers believe that this compensation method attracts the better salesmen.

On the minus side, straight commission gives the sales manager a minimum of control over his men. Each salesman tends to be quite independent, feeling that he is in business for himself. He may neglect his non-selling duties, may resort to high-pressure selling, and may for the most part sell only those items easy to sell. As his income can fluctuate wildly because of factors outside his control (strikes, price changes, the business cycle), the salesman suffers from some feeling of insecurity. If the firm uses several rates, its compensation plan may become entirely too complex.

Straight salary

Under this plan the sales manager buys some of his salesmen's time. He might pay one man $250 a week, another $1,500 a month regardless of sales volume. This is fixed compensation to the salesman and fixed expense to the firm; the amount of the salary varies as a percent of sales volume.

The great advantage of straight salary is the potential control it gives the sales manager; salesmen are paid to do what the sales manager tells them to do. The method is clear and simple, easy and economical to administer. The regularity of his income gives the salesman a sense of security. Straight salary is often the only practicable compensation plan for young salesmen, for new products, or for new territories. It is appropriate if the selling job is complicated, if customers must be given much service, or if buyers buy infrequently.

The straight salary arrangement is weak in providing incentive; it forces the sales manager to stimulate and motivate his men and to control closely their activities. The fluctuation of selling costs to sales volume is unfortunate. The typical sales manager can hardly avoid underpaying certain salesmen and overpaying others. Because of this possibility, the salary structure requires frequent review to determine if revision is needed.

Salary plus incentive

Paying salesmen salaries and also providing them with some sort of added incentive is the most popular way of compensating them. This technique represents an attempt to enjoy the strengths and advantages of straight commission *and* straight salary yet avoid or minimize the defects of both. Some sales managers see the *fixed* portion (salary) as the salesman's reward for servicing his customers and the *variable* portion (incentive) his reward for making sales.

We now look at four salary-plus-incentive plans.

Salary plus commission. This is probably the most common of the four. The salary portion may be as low as 30 percent or as high as 90 percent of the salesman's total compensation; 50 percent is not an uncommon proportion. Often the salary approximates the basic living expenses of the salesman's family. The commission may be paid on *all* sales ($500 a month plus 1 percent on all sales) or only on sales volume *above some minimum quota* ($500 a month plus 5 percent on sales volume above $50,000).

Drawing account plus commission. A drawing account is an advance of money to the salesman from his company to be repaid from commissions the salesman will earn. It is a fixed amount, such as $100 a week or $500 a month. *Guaranteed* draws do not have to be repaid if the salesman's commissions for the drawing period are less than the draw; instead, the difference is written off periodically, making the draw the same as a base salary. *Nonguaranteed* drawing accounts are the same as short-term loans against future commissions; the salesman owes his firm the amount by which the draw is greater than the commissions earned.

Salary plus bonus. A bonus is a lump-sum payment or gift. A firm may distribute a general bonus to all employees at Christmas or after a very profitable year. Such a bonus is not related to specific personal achievement. A *sales* bonus, however, can be used to reward a specific salesman for exceptional performance. Bases for the sales bonus are not always statistical and objective, and it is often difficult to make them completely so. Any apparent lack of an objective basis can lead to resentment and disatisfaction among those salesmen who do not receive a bonus or whose bonuses are smaller than they think fair.

Point plan. In this technique the sales manager awards points for various types of accomplishments. Maybe he credits each salesman with 10 points for every $100 of sales volume; then he awards a set number of points for each call made, for every product demonstration, for every point-of-purchase display installed, for each new customer, and such. He may build in a system of negative or penalty points. Points are given a monetary value, and the salesman's compensation each month is determined by multiplying this value times the number of net points the salesman earns.

SALESMEN'S EXPENSES

Keeping a salesman out in his territory is expensive. Because of the large amount of money involved and because both *over*spending and *under*spending by salesmen must be avoided, the sales manager must be in control of this selling cost. Most sales managers classify these ex-

FIGURE 6–4. Salesman's expense record

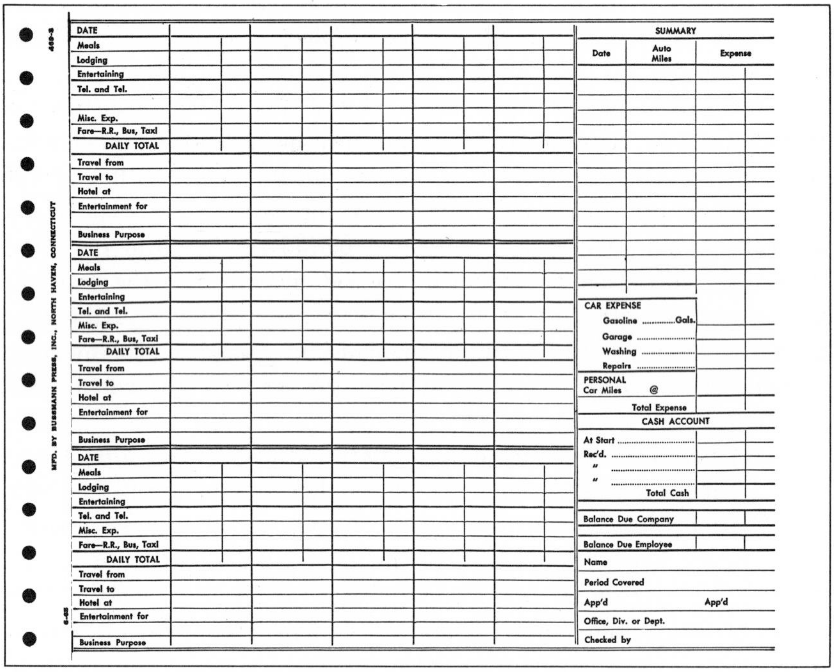
DATE
Meals
Lodging
Entertaining
Tel. and Tel.
Misc. Exp.
Fare—R.R., Bus, Taxi
DAILY TOTAL
Travel from
Travel to
Hotel at
Entertainment for
Business Purpose

SUMMARY
Date | Auto Miles | Expense

CAR EXPENSE
Gasoline ....Gals.
Garage
Washing
Repairs
PERSONAL Car Miles @
Total Expense
CASH ACCOUNT
At Start
Rec'd.
"
"
Total Cash
Balance Due Company
Balance Due Employee
Name
Period Covered
App'd
App'd
Office, Div. or Dept.
Checked by

MFD. BY BUSSMANN PRESS, INC., NORTH HAVEN, CONNECTICUT

penses as legitimate: out-of-town lodging and meals, transportation (including taxis), telephone and telegraph for business purposes, and tips. Many sales managers add laundry and valet expenses to this approved list. Gifts and entertainment are handled differently by different firms; they often are the subjects of disagreement and the causes of friction.

Agreement is probably unanimous that his company should pay all legitimate expenses the salesman incurs. Which are legitimate expenses? Those which would not have occurred had the salesman not been out selling for his company. Another agreement probably unanimous is that earnings dollars must be kept separate from expense account dollars. The salesman is not to view his expense allowance as a source of income; he should neither make money nor lose money on his expense account.

Here are the four most common expense plans.

Salesman pays

Under this simple arrangement, the salesman pays his own expenses and does not submit an expense report for reimbursement. This plan may encourage some salesmen to skimp, to spend less than they really should spend; it gives the sales manager little control.

Unlimited reimbursement

There are two versions of this method. Under the so-called "honor system" the salesman reports a lump-sum figure for his expenses for the week or month and gets reimbursed. Because there are neither limits nor itemization, padding and extravagance are possible. The sales manager has no or only little control over expenses. The nature of this method makes it more suitable for top managers than for salesmen.

In the second version, itemization replaces the lump sum. Typically, the salesman would draw an advance for expenses, spend, then submit an itemized expense report and be reimbursed.

Per diem allowance

Once again there are two versions. The first puts a maximum ceiling on the expense total—$25 per day or $125 per week, for example. The salesman itemizes his expenses, submits his report, and gets reimbursement. There is no ceiling on any one expense item; he can spend $13 on meals and $12 on lodging—or just the reverse.

The second version does impose ceilings on items. Meals, for example, must not exceed $10 a day, or lodging must be not more than $12 a night.

Flat allowance

Here the salesman is given a predetermined sum of money, perhaps $150 a week. He spends it as he pleases; there are no reports, no disputes about what is and is not legitimate, no administration chores in the home office. There is some danger that the salesman may try to make money on this type of expense allowance, that he may curtail desirable activities the moment he has spent the entire allowance.

SALESMEN'S QUOTAS

Sales quotas are assignments made to marketing units by the sales manager; quotas are what he expects from those units. The most common quota by far is the dollar sales quota assigned to a salesman and his sales territory. Salesman S, for example, may be asked to produce net sales of $700,000 in his territory next year. On rare occasions, the figure assigned refers to physical units, 5,000, perhaps, rather than to dollars. The sum of the dollar sales quotas assigned to the salesmen is the firm's sales forecast for the coming period, usually one year. If salesman S is to make his year's quota of $700,000, he must break this figure down, assigning subquotas to each buyer, to each basic unit of his territory, over his product line, by week and by month.

Two less common types of quotas deserve mention. Because some sales and salesmen are more profitable than others and because the firm's most basic objective is to generate profits, sometimes quotas are assigned for gross margin, expenses, and net profit. The other type is the activity quota, reminiscent of the point plan in the salary-plus-incentive compensation methods. Activity quotas are expressed and assigned in points rather than in dollars or units of sales volume. Assigned activities are rated in points (each call 5 points, every $100 of sales 25 points) and the salesman's quota for the week or month is the number of points he must earn during that period.

Quotas are essential in planning and controlling. They reflect the performance standard expected of the salesman; they are the goal he is to achieve. If his commission or bonus is affected by his percentage of quota attainment, and of course it usually is, the relation of performance to quota directly affects the salesman's income. Over the long run, the salesman on straight salary, too, finds that his income fluctuates according to how he produces in relation to his quota.

The sales manager must assign realistic sales quotas which are attainable if each salesman works reasonably hard. If the quotas are too high or too low, then that most basic budget figure, the sales forecast, will not be as accurate as it should be. The sales manager hopes that each salesman will accept and approve of his quota; this will not be possible unless the quota is clear and understandable. In some cases, the salesmen themselves participate in budget setting. Budgets need some flexibility; they need periodic reviews and, on occasion, some revision.

DIRECTING AND EVALUATING SALESMEN'S PERFORMANCE

Directing salesmen

Direction is supervision. It is the sales manager's telling each salesman what to do and how to do it, then checking, verifying, and taking any action indicated. Directing is seeing that salesmen carry out their assignments, function within company policies, work their territories as expected, grow up to their respective personal potentials, achieve maximum productivity. Directing is endless because training and encouraging, controlling and enforcing, stimulating and motivating can never end. But, there can be *over*directing just as there can be *under*directing.

Who directs the sales force? Managers direct—general sales managers, divisional or regional managers, district or branch sales managers. Supervisors direct. They are often called sales supervisors or field supervisors, and they often sell as well as supervise. Finally, some senior salesmen are asked to do some directing. Whoever does the directing must be capable in both activities, selling and supervising.

The overall goal of direction is to maximize sales and profits. This calls for continuous training and supervision and for morale building. It calls for two-way communication—face to face, by telephone, by such written communications as correspondence, bulletins, and reports. Salesmen are asked to budget their time most carefully, to study each buyer and his problems before the sales call, to make only planned presentations, and to execute thorough postcall analyses whether or not a sale was made.

Those who direct salesmen use various tools of directing, the most valuable of which is the personal contact between the salesman and the person doing the directing. When a sales manager travels with one of his salesmen, he is in an excellent position to give critiques and counsel, supervision and aid. A second useful tool in directing salesmen is made up of three elements: the salesman's territorial assignment, his quota, and his compensation plan. Communication, listed as a goal, is also a supervisory tool. Reports, too, are a "how" item, even though they were listed earlier as a "what" item. Common matters reported on include calls, sales, expenses, and competitors' activities. Conventions and sales meetings are used by supervisors for purposes of conveying information, creating enthusiasm, and stimulating. Recognition, awards, praise, and publicity are nonfinancial directional and supervisory tools.

Sales contests

The nature and role of contests for salesmen demand our attention for a moment. The common, overall purpose of sales contests is to increase sales volume. More selective and more specific subpurposes include: to increase the number of customers or accounts; to push certain products, sometimes new products; to enter new markets successfully; to raise sales volume in seasons traditionally low or slow. These subpurposes, of course, lead back to the common purpose of increasing sales volume.

Those who favor contests for salesmen advance various arguments. Contests can lead to greater prestige and recognition for individual salesmen. They can be designed to channel selling effort toward something management wants; better balanced selling of the full line and more service to customers are examples. Some contests have transformed what was just work into friendly competition and rivalry. Salesmen see the possibility of extra pay for extra performance. Contests can reduce selling costs. Finally, contests have been shown to work successfully.

But, there are arguments against sales contests. Some salesmen feel in advance that they cannot win, some think contests kid stuff and childish, some feel pressured rather than stimulated, and others believe contests imply that the salesmen are loafing. Sometimes the "wrong" salesmen win, sometimes past winners keep on winning. Overselling and underservicing are encouraged. Extreme, intense competition can breed hostility and damage *esprit de corps*. A contest can be followed by a slump or letdown. Contests are difficult to discontinue.

Contests for salesmen, thus, are controversial tools. They are, however, a tool used widely by sales managers.

Evaluating salesmen's performance

Direction and evaluation constitute a continuing cycle. The sales manager directs by telling and showing the salesman what to do and how to do it. Then he follows up by determining how well the salesman carried out his instructions; this is evaluation. What the sales manager learned in his evaluation influences and serves as a basis for subsequent direction, and so it goes on and on.

The sales manager's purpose in evaluating is to determine how well the salesman performed on the assignments he was given. These assignments refer us back to the first section of this chapter where we saw the sales manager setting up his selling goals within the framework of the firm's promotional and marketing goals. So, the first step in the evaluation process was taken when the sales manager assigned realistic quotas to the salesmen. We have already noted the next step—the determination of each salesman's actual performance. In the third step, the sales manager compares performance against quota; sales volume is checked against sales quota, and cost of selling (earnings of the salesman plus his expenses) is checked against the gross margin in dollars.

Evaluation is essential if the firm is to maximize sales and profits, if each salesman is to develop himself and his territory to the fullest, if each salesman is to be paid what he deserves.

In the first of three approaches to evaluating salesmen's performance, the sales manager uses *accomplishment* data. He gets figures on such reflections of accomplishment as sales volume, expenses, gross margin, number and sizes of orders, account sizes, and new customers.

His second approach bases on *activity* data. Examples are number of days worked, number of calls made, product demonstrations put on, reports sent in on time, displays installed, and sales meetings attended or conducted.

His third and last approach is to make *qualitative judgments* of each salesman. Examples of these are customer goodwill, self-improvement and development, loyalty to company, attitude toward and interest in his work, ambition and motivation, and reputation with other salesmen.

QUESTIONS AND PROBLEMS

6–1. List some faults manufacturers' salesmen may find with their firms and with their sales managers.

6–2. Suggest some activity quotas a sales manager might assign to his salesmen.

6–3. Why do most sales managers break their markets down into salesmen's territories?

6–4. Will an outstanding salesman become an outstanding sales manager?

6–5. What can you say about the policy of recruiting and hiring only *experienced* salesmen?

6–6. What qualities do *you* think a sales manager should look for when recruiting sales trainees?

6-7. If you could gaze into a crystal ball, what might you see in the future for sales managers?

6-8. What are some of the influences which determine the size and nature of a salesman's territory?

6-9. In the selection process, what are some factors the sales manager finds difficult to measure or determine?

6-10. Consider yourself to be a good salesman for a manufacturer of industrial products. Describe the sales manager you would want to work under.

PART **IV**

ELEMENTS OF
PERSUASION:
ADVERTISING

CHAPTER **7**

Advertising as
persuasive
communication

CONTINUING our discussion of the promotional activities or forces a
seller may use, we turn in Part IV to advertising. Three chapters will
be devoted to this subject, and we begin by inquiring into the nature
of advertising and ads.

This text is about *promotion*, about the presenting and the recommending of products and services to buyers for purchase. Advertising basically
is a form of commercial promotion of products, services, institutions,
ideas, and, indeed, of persons who want something, perhaps election to
office. Stated simply, advertising is expected to make a buyer *aware*
of a brand, then to *like* that brand, and, eventually, to *buy* that brand.

WHAT ADVERTISING IS

Mass communication

Advertising is the mass communication of a promise. It promises the
satisfaction or gratification of some want—a satisfaction to be experienced
from the purchase and consumption or use of the advertised item. The
essence of the advertising message, thus, is the interpretation or the trans-

lation of a product or service into the capacity to satisfy buyers' wants.

We recognize six types of advertising media which transmit ads to buyers: newspapers, magazines, television, radio, outdoor (posters, for example), and transit (card cards, for example). These media reach and communicate to many rather than single buyers; consequently, the advertising they carry is mass communication rather than individual, person-to-person communication.

Advertising is *commercial* communication in that media charge the advertiser for transmitting his ads. Advertisting is *speedy* communication; advertisers can reach large numbers of buyers in a very short time. Advertising is identified by buyers as *promotional* communication in the sense that the buyers to whom it is directed know immediately that a seller wants to influence buyers' buying actions. Finally, advertising is *sponsored* communication because the seller signs his name (company name, brand name, or both) to his advertising messages.

Information

The typical advertising message is informative. Its content reflects the seller's interest in helping buyers make their buying decisions, his recommendations about better solutions to buyers' problems, his attempt to guide buyers to greater satisfaction.

The advertiser himself decides what his ads shall say. The advertising message is in final form when turned over to media for transmittal, and its content cannot be changed by media without the advertiser's permission. Advertising, thus, is under the tight control of the advertiser, whose control, of course, is matched by his responsibility. Politicians can claim to have been misquoted—advertisers cannot.

Persuasion

Unless an ad causes reaction or response favorable to the seller, it was a waste of time and money and a failure. The sole purpose of all advertising of interest to us is to influence and to persuade. Persuade to do what? Eventually *to buy*.

Persuasion involves the attitudes and actions of buyers and of those who influence buyers. Most advertising is designed to affect attitudes—to correct hostile or inaccurate attitudes, to implant sound attitudes, to reinforce favorable attitudes. If successful in these endeavors, the advertiser is entitled to hope that action, a purchase, will ultimately result. Only a minor volume of advertising tries to persuade a buyer to take overt, physical action immediately.

If a seller's advertising does communicate successfully, if it is informative and persuasive, then this promotion will contribute to the maximizing of profits. Sales revenue minus costs equals profits. Most advertisting is built to increase sales revenue. Advertising is a cost, but a promotional cost which is expected to more than pay its own way.

GROUPS INVOLVED IN ADVERTISING

Advertisers

Sellers who advertise constitute one group involved in the advertising process. Sellers at the manufacturing level who market consumer products are a prominent segment of this group of advertisers. Soap, food, automobiles, and beverages instantly come to mind as examples of the products sold. Retailers are a second prominent segment; these stock the products of many manufacturers and sell to ultimate consumers who buy for personal and for household use. Food stores and department stores are well-known advertisers at the retail level. A final segment consists of sellers of services. Life insurance companies, banks, theaters, and piano instructors sell and advertise services.

Buyers

One type of buyer an advertiser may try to influence is the individual who does not use the seller's *type* of product or service—but should. These buyers are prospects for sellers of air transportation, home organs, and correspondence courses. The advertiser's undertaking is to convert these persons into users of the *type* of item involved and, of course, the advertiser's brand.

Another type of buyer now uses the type of product or service, but he uses a competitor's brand. These buyers, too, are prospects. Here the advertiser engages in brand competition and in an encroachment attempt. If his wooing succeeds, he generates selective demand and wins patronage away from competitors.

Present customers are still another and quite important type of buyer. Here the advertiser wants (1) to hold their patronage and (2) to increase the volume of their buying. There are several approaches to enlarging a customer's purchases. He can be encouraged to consume the item more

FIGURE 7–1. The appeal of this white-on-black ad is based on an improved product

often; or, to consume *and replace* it more quickly. He can be urged to use the item for additional purposes; or, he can be urged to own two or three units, not just one. He can be advised to buy and to use in larger quantities.

A final group included under Buyers is a bit different from the others, but it still demands recognition. Its members are *buying influences.* They are of interest to advertisers because they do just what that phrase implies—they influence buyers and buying decisions. In an industrial firm, for example, certain engineers may have a voice in deciding what lubricants the purchasing agent will buy. Certain professionals are important buying influences. Dentists recommend brands of toothpaste, and architects recommend brands of appliances.

Media

The advertising media we treat were identified earlier as newspapers, magazines, television, radio, outdoor, and transit. These are hired by advertisers to carry ads to those persons the advertiser wants to persuade. Four media sell space and are primarily *print* transmitters; two sell time and are *broadcast.*

Advertising agencies

Completing the groups involved are the advertising agencies. The two big jobs of these firms are (1) to build effective ads for their clients, the most typical of which are manufacturers of consumer products, and (2) then to contract with media to carry those ads. More will be said about agencies in Chapter 9.

CLASSIFICATION OF ADVERTISING

There are several bases on which advertising can be classified. We look at two: by type of buyer and by type of seller.

By type of buyer

Ultimate consumers are the most important buyer group in the advertising area. They make individual purchases, family purchases, and household purchases. More dollars are spent for consumer advertising than for any other classification. *Middlemen* are usually thought of as being either wholesalers or retailers. Trade advertising is used in an effort to influence middlemen when they are buying merchandise for resale. *Purchasing agents* buy for industry, for institutions, and for government. Advertising addressed to purchasing agents is known as industrial advertising. Incidentally, when middlemen buy goods and services to use in the operation of their firms, they buy as purchasing agents. *Agricultural buyers* are both farmers *and* ultimate consumers. This explains why such a publication as *The Progressive Farmer* carries both agricultural advertising and consumer advertising. *Professionals* have been mentioned earlier. Like farmers, professionals play two roles—they are advisors or buying influences, and they are ultimate consumers. It is only natural, then, for professional journals to contain two kinds of advertising as do the agricultural publications.

By type of seller

The advertising done by *manufacturers of consumer products* is usually referred to as general or national. This is true even though the manufacturer does not have national distribution and even though his advertising is less than nationwide. Many *manufacturers of industrial products* use advertising in their promotional mixes; typically, advertising's role here is much less significant than in the promotion of consumer products. *Retailers* as a group buy much advertising; it is usually called retail or local advertising. Local advertising, interestingly, represents about 40 percent of our total advertising—national about 60 percent. *Sellers of services* are often substantial advertisers. *Groups of competing sellers* may band together to promote, with advertising, the interests of the group. Wood, glass, leather, and sugar are examples of generic products which have been advertised by thier respective industries. The term for this kind of advertising is *horizontal cooperative*. *Nonprofit organizations* such as churches and labor unions advertise sometimes. Finally, individuals advertise, often using what we commonly call "want ads."

ADVERTISING'S OBJECTIVES

We have observed that practically all advertising is bought on the assumption and in the hope that it will increase the advertiser's profits by increasing his sales volume. Even so, three pairs of goals are worth noting. (1) Advertising can be asked to stimulate either *primary* demand or *selective* demand. (2) It may promote either the *brand* or the *firm*

FIGURE 7–2. Technical copy such as this is appropriate in such a publication as *Science*

We want to be useful
...and even interesting

Kodak

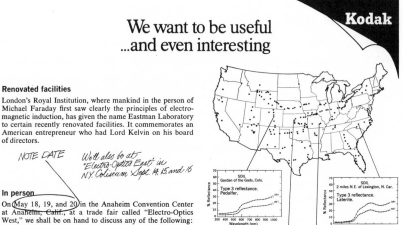

Renovated facilities

London's Royal Institution, where mankind in the person of Michael Faraday first saw clearly the principles of electromagnetic induction, has given the name Eastman Laboratory to certain recently renovated facilities. It commemorates an American entrepreneur who had Lord Kelvin on his board of directors.

NOTE DATE *We'll also be at "Electro-Optics East" in N.Y. Coliseum Sept. 14, 15, and 16*

In person

On May 18, 19, and 20 in the Anaheim Convention Center at Anaheim, Calif., at a trade fair called "Electro-Optics West," we shall be on hand to discuss any of the following:

Photographic problems in laboratory or field biology, including photomicrography and direct infrared photography.

Photographic materials for astronomy and physics

EASTMAN Organic Chemicals, including reagents and supplies for all manner of laboratory techniques and procedures in the bio-medical field, in organic synthesis, and in analytical chemistry

Counseling on photomaterials for advanced technologies still in the planning stages

Look-up service from largest commercially accessible bank of published and unpublished infrared spectra, from which, no later than next working day after receipt of submitted spectrum, we send names of closest matching compounds in decreasing order of match.

KODAK WRATTEN Filters to modify spectral distribution in and near the visible; also neutral density wedges, step tablets, and other gelatin light attenuators of high precision

KODAK IRTRAN Infrared-transmitting Materials and Optics: 6 materials to cover out to $30\,\mu m$, polycrystalline, with a broad choice of index, immune to cold flow, retaining strength and clarity despite heat, without cleavage planes, insoluble, grindable, polishable

Infrared Interference Filters on substrates of KODAK IRTRAN Material

IR Phosphor for seeing and photographing beam structure from GaAs diodes or other infrared lasers, 0.7 to $1.3\,\mu m$, on paper or transparent base, in sizes up to 20×24 in.

Q-Switch Solutions and Cells for neodymium and ruby lasers: stabilized saturable dyes and antireflection-coated, cement-free, high-precision cells to contain them

Laser Dyes: Rhodamine 6G and many others; production lots tested in actual dye laser systems and supplied as solutions for dilution

Photochromic Compounds

White Reflectance Paint and Standard of unsurpassed nonselective diffuse reflectance from 200 nm to 2500 nm; purified $BaSO_4$ that stays white longer than MgO smoke

Neutral Density Circular Wedges (Inconel alloy-Coated) on glass from stock, glass or quartz to order, nonselective over long spectral range covering UV, visible, IR

Liquid Crystal Mixtures from a constantly expanding list

Optical Cements, six different formulations for optical parts, three for instrument assembly

MgF_2, ZnS, CaF_2, MgO, ZnSe, or CdTe in chunks for well-controlled evaporation

Mail inquiries on any of the above can be directed to the same address as given at end of adjacent column.

The colors of America

Both standardized wet and standardized dry, we have measured spectral reflectance of soils, sands, and silts predominant at each of 160 places in the U.S.A. We have then tried some taxonomy on the curves. They seem to fall into three types, one of which splits again.

Our work suggests that a spectrophotometer may not always be needed. Our study of the curves indicates that a good-to-excellent match of most of them can be calculated from reflectances measured at just five wavelengths. This can be done from aloft with readily available Kodak aerial film, narrow-band interference filters, and targets of known spectral reflectance. There are places where one click of the shutter provides more data than a thousand hand-collected samples like ours. The camera is mightier than the trowel.

Talk of collecting data from aloft has been leading to arguments. How far aloft? How much data. How much is it worth? Who decides? On what grounds?

While awaiting reasonable answers we felt that a study of the photographically accessible spectrophotometric variability of soil was something we ought to do, so H. R. Condit of the Kodak Research Laboratories did it.

In Photogrammetric Engineering *for September, 1970 Condit gives a table of the constants which, when substituted in*

$$R_\lambda = a_{0.\lambda} + a_{1.\lambda}R_{440} + a_{2.\lambda}R_{540} + a_{3.\lambda}R_{640} + a_{4.\lambda}R_{740} + a_{5.\lambda}R_{860}$$

$$R_{440} = \text{reflectance at 440 nm, etc,}$$

yields quite a decent fit to actual spectral reflectance, as seen from the dots along the above sample curves. The paper presents curves for 30 locations. Reprint on request from Eastman Kodak Company, Dept. 55W, Rochester, N.Y. 14650.

selling that brand. (3) It may try to cause *indirect* action or *direct* action.

Primary versus selective demand

Advertising can be used to stimulate *primary* demand. This is the demand for a generic product or service—for a type of product or service; it is not for a particular brand. It is for tea, wine, or wool; it is for life insurance, transportation, or full-service banks. Primary demand can be increased (1) by getting present users to buy and use more; (2) by getting nonusers to begin buying and using the type of product or service; and (3) by promoting new uses of the type of product or service.

Primary advertising is sponsored most often by a group of sellers, usually competitive, who have organized into an association to promote the product or service sold by members of the group. The group may consist of manufacturers of some consumer product; the American Dairy Association is an example. The group may consist of firms who sell a service; the Institute of Life Insurance is an example. Sometimes a geographic area sponsors primary advertising; Colorado, Montana, and Oregon are examples of states which promote their respective attractions to tourists. Sometimes the numerous small growers of some agricultural product come together to promote primary demand—for almonds, rice, prunes, or cotton.

Seldom does a single manufacturer of a branded product resort to primary advertising. Of course, the maker of the first electric razor had to sell an idea, an innovation, a change, before he could sell his first unit. Campbell Soup may have such a dominant share of the canned liquid soup market that Campbell could justify sponsoring some primary advertising.

Most advertising is used to stimulate *selective* demand, the demand for a particular brand or make of product or service. Whereas primary advertising pits commodity against commodity (tea versus coffee) selective advertising pits brand against brand (Lipton tea against Tender Leaf tea). Prudential sells life insurance; the company wants much life insurance to be bought, a primary matter. But, Prudential wants more *Prudential* life insurance to be bought than any other brand. Sugar Information advertises sugar; Domino wants its brand to be the favorite.

Primary demand determines total market, selective demand determines each competing seller's share of market. To each seller, the selective demand for his brand is a segment or part of primary demand. Assume an aluminum industry consisting of three firms, Alcoa, Reynolds, and Kaiser. If you sum their respective market shares (a selective demand figure) you get the industry total of 100 percent (a primary demand figures). If that 100 percent is thought of as a pie chart, Alcoa wants the Alcoa slice to be the biggest.

Brand image versus corporate image

When a seller designs advertising to promote the item he sells, his concern is with his brand's image in the market; this is a product concept. When he builds advertising to promote his company, firm, or organization, his interest is in his institution's image; this is a patronage concept.

Advertisers hope and strive for favorable, attractive images, both brand and corporate, for understandable reasons. Probably the greatest contribution of attractive images is their preselling influence. The job of selling is easier when buyers are favorably inclined toward the seller and his brand. Buyers see salesmen more often, more cordially, more confidently. Relations with media, vendors, suppliers of capital, and residents of plant cities are more satisfactory. Attractive images help attract and hold desirable employees as well as desirabe customers. Finally, the seller can add products to his line more successfully.

Imagery is a matter of personality. In respect to their basic nature, the image or concept you have of Ivory soap and the image you have of your instructor have much in common. Brand image is what buyers "see" and "feel" when the brand name Ivory is called to their attention. It is Ivory's mental representation, Ivory's meaning to buyers; it is Ivory's impression on buyers *and* buyers' impressions of Ivory. It is the sum of the concepts and their valences which come to mind when the word *Ivory* is perceived. When buyers think of Ivory, most reactions probably are pleasant and favorable; the reaction of some persons, however, may be unfavorable. Buyers like and dislike, they are attracted to or repelled by certain brand names, just as you feel, act, and react toward certain instructors. Similarly, the ideas and attitudes buyers associate with Procter & Gamble determine corporate image.

Brand image is the buyer's picture of how that specific brand differs from others. Among the determinants of brand image are corporate image, consumers of the brand, retailers who stock it, the product's physical features, the satisfaction the brand provides, the product's price, and the ads promoting the brand. In his efforts to achieve the brand image he wants, the seller is trying to make his brand into the *specialty* type of product mentioned in the basic marketing texts. Brand image is usually stronger than corporate image because buyers know more about brands than about the firms back of the brands.

Corporate image is the buyer's picture of the character and personality of the firm. Advertising to establish and maintain a corporate image is often called institutional advertising—sometimes strategic advertising. Typical purposes of this kind of advertising are to make friends, to build goodwill for and confidence in the firm, to raise the firm's prestige, to publicize the firm's strengths such as research, policies, personnel, engineering, or production facilities. The great bulk of corporate advertising makes a bid for patronage; it tells why the seller is entitled to buyers' dollars. Most of the rest of corporate advertising bids for better public relations; examples of influential "publics" are customers, middlemen, employees, and residents of plant cities.

Direct action versus indirect action

A small amount of advertising tries to cause *direct*, immediate response. Mail-order sellers want buyers to order, at once, by mail. Advertisers who include coupons in their ads want the coupons filled in and mailed, at once. Retailers want increased floor traffic (and increased sales) within a matter of hours. The goals of direct advertising are obviously short range in nature. Direct advertising is often used to encourage buyers to act on needs of which buyers are aware.

Indirect action advertising, the bulk of all advertising, has long-range goals. Its immediate concern is with attitudes rather than with action. It cultivates respect, approval, confidence, pleasant associations, and kindly feelings. Eventually, to be sure, the advertiser hopes for action—buying action—brought about because of the influence attitudes have on action. This type of advertising is often used to make buyers aware of needs they do not feel.

ADVERTISING IN THE PROMOTIONAL MIX

In some manner or other, every seller must "buy" the patronage of buyers—he must "buy" customers. The retailer who locates on one corner of the town square buys customers with the high rent he pays. The manufacturer with a larger-than-average sales force pays for orders in the form of salesmen's compensation. The seller who supplies extraordinary services to those who buy from him pays for and with those services. The seller who offers the lowest prices pays in the form of a below-average markup. Finally, a seller can buy patronage with heavy, effective advertising.

Advertising, then, is an item in the seller's promotional mix or program, and promotion is an item in his marketing program and budget. A glance at a hypothetical operating statement would show the location of the advertising item and its relationship to marketing. In such a statement, net sales might be expressed as 100 percent, cost of goods sold as 45 percent, gross margin as 55 percent. This 55 percent would be available for three items: profit, general administration, and marketing. If marketing got 40 percent of the 55 percent, marketing management might get 5 percent, market stimulation might get 35 percent—perhaps four units of personal selling, two units of advertising, and one unit of sales promotion.

WHY SELLERS USE ADVERTISING

All the advertising of interest to us is bought and run for just one purpose—to realize greater profit than would have been realized without the advertising. Because profit reflects the relationship between sales revenue and costs, then advertising must be done on the assumption that it will increase revenue and/or reduce costs. The great majority of all advertising is intended to increase sales volume and sales revenue. It is used to inform buyers and buying influences and to influence them; it is asked to presell, to work toward the creation of customers, to stimulate demand, to develop and expand markets. Advertising can help firms operate at higher capacities. It can help them smooth out the ups and downs in a sales curve. Even when the advertiser is promoting his corporate image, even when he seems to be concerned with nothing more than goodwill or prestige, he expects his sales volume to reflect the persuasiveness of his advertising.

Some small amount of advertising is run for the purpose of reducing costs, particularly the relatively high costs of personal selling.

Finally, an interesting but unmeasurable volume of advertising is defensive in nature. Seller A feels forced to advertise because competing sellers B, C, and D advertise. Seller A assumes that his profit showing would be worse if he did no advertising.

HOW BUYERS USE ADVERTISING

To buyers, advertising can be a worthwhile source of helpful, useful information. A large mass of this information relates to products. Adver-

FIGURE 7–3.   Note large size coupon

Need technicians?
Help yourself.

If you're like most businessmen, you're probably all too aware of the technician shortage. If current projections are right, one out of three new technical jobs won't have any applicants.

The National Industrial Conference Board and The Advertising Council are concerned about the shortage, too. As a public service, they've prepared a full-scale advertising campaign to get young people to take up technical careers.

You can help. You can distribute a new guide to technical careers to schools, church groups, youth clubs—wherever young people gather in your town. And you can put up a "Be-a-Technician" poster wherever young people can see it.

For samples of the guide and the poster and information on quantity reprints, use the coupon below. Samples are free. Reprints are cheap. Only $4.00 per hundred for the poster. $5.00 per hundred for the guide. For a small additional charge, we can even imprint your company's name.

A small price to pay today for a good supply of technicians tomorrow.

For samples of poster and guide send this coupon:

How to have a college man's career without four years of college.

Men and women are badly needed for high-paying technical jobs. This guide from the U.S. Office of Education tells you how to get them.

For your free copy write Careers, Washington, D.C. 20202

25 technical careers you can learn in 2 years or less.

To: Technicians, P.O. Box 313, Radio City Station, New York, N.Y. 10019

Gentlemen: Please send me free samples of "Technician" material and information on getting quantity reprints.

Name_____ Title_____

Firm_____ Business Address_____

City_____ State_____ Zip_____

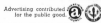

Advertising contributed for the public good.

tising can tell of new or improved products or services, of new uses for present products or services. Product information includes basic facts of interest to buyers, facts about performance and operation, capabilities and limitations; facts about how best to use and to care for products.

Ads can report price information, a very basic consideration for practically all buyers when approaching the buying decision. We immediately think of ads promoting annual or semiannual sales, and of end-of-the week ads for supermarkets. Those food store ads may save a housewife time in building a shopping list and in routing her shopping trip in addition to saving her money.

Buyers use advertising in their efforts to protect or enhance self-concept. Advertising can enable an individual to buy more intelligently, to come closer to maximizing personal satisfaction with whatever amount of purchasing power he has to spend. Many get psychic satisfaction from buying, owning, and consuming advertised brands whose brand images are attractive, whose quality may be more uniform than that of unadvertised brands. Some buyers, after making certain purchases, rely on ads to help minimize the possibility of postpurchase dissonance.

Business buyers read ads in their ceaseless search for greater sales, lower costs, greater profits.

CONDITIONS FAVORABLE TO ADVERTISING

If advertising is to be effective, the goods or services promoted must have basic utility; they must provide benefit and satisfaction to those who buy and use. Brand names, packages, and prices must be appropriate. The more differentiated brand A is from competing brands, the better the opportunity for brand A's advertising to succeed. The stronger the primary demand is for brand A's type of product, the more effective the advertising can be.

Big markets and expanding markets are more friendly to advertising than are small or contracting markets. Manufacturers selling to the ultimate consumer need adequate distribution through retailers and good relations with them. If buyers feel strong emotional motivation toward the product, they are more responsive to its advertising. Perfume and investment counsel, for example, are easier to advertise satisfactorily than are ink and fuel oil.

If a firm's management is informed and understanding about the nature of advertising, then that firm's advertising manager is fortunate. Such management will insist that policies and operations be sound, that public relations be healthy; it will insist on proper promotion programs, well designed and well administered. If used, personal selling and sales promotion will be coordinated with advertising. Adequate marketing research will be done by such a firm. Advertising will be viewed as a sales- and profit-increasing expense, as commercial and mass communication intended to influence buyers. It will not be considered a worker of miracles, nor will it be asked to compensate for defects or weaknesses in product, in channels, in pricing, or in promotion.

ADVERTISING APPEALS

An ad is a promise—a promise of satisfaction to prospects who buy and consume the advertised product or service. An ad is built on and presents this satisfaction, this appeal, which is the heart or core of the communication. We start our probe into the nature and role of advertising appeals by reviewing the psychological steps through which a seller takes a buyer when making a sale to that buyer. We are to think of them as possible goals of an ad.

Psychological steps to a sale

Attention.   The first goal of an ad is to capture the attention of as many prospects as possible. Who qualifies as a prospect? Any buyer who (1) thinks he stands a good chance of benefiting, of being happy, if he buys, (2) has the money or credit to buy with, and (3) makes his own buying decisions. No ad tries to get the attention of all buyers—but each ad does want the attention of all prospects. Even this smaller job is a most difficult undertaking because there are so many competing bids for each prospect's attention. Just as soon as a prospect notices an ad, he should know instantly the type of product being promoted and its brand name.

Interest.   The ad's next job is to develop initial or instant attention into mental or emotional attention. Our needs and wants determine largely what we give our attention to—what we perceive—what captures our interest. Buyers are interested when they are influenced by the ad to think specifically about needs, type of product advertised, brand name, and price. Natural interests of most men include sports, automobiles, homes, religion, and travel; for women these are clothes, religion, food, children, and housekeeping. *All* buyers are interested in what products and services will do for them.

Desire. The third job is to whet buyers' desire, to make them want the advertised item, to see it as "the" answer to some want. In stimulating desire, the advertiser stresses benefits and advantages which appeal strongly to, and are ranked high by, buyers.

Conviction. In the conviction stage, the buyer admits he should do something about his problem or want. He grasps and receives the advertiser's message. He finds acceptable the relationship between the amount of satisfaction he anticipates and the amount of money he will have to pay. He actually makes the buying decision—to buy at some future time.

Action. As was mentioned in the section on advertising goals, some ads do try for overt, specific, physical, and immediate response. Most, however, strive for emotional reaction, for pleasant and favorable associations, for friendly feelings toward the advertiser and his product.

Relation of appeals to motivation

Earlier, in our sections on behavior, we recognized the consumer as a complicated personality, one most difficult to understand satisfactorily. He wants to play a certain part, to have a certain image, to be a certain person in his various worlds such as family, social group, and business associates. His wants are as complex as they are numerous, and they are becoming more so. Instead of being permanent, they are ever changing. No seller knows just what consumers' wants are in any broad, comprehensive sense. Neither does the consumer himself know. Unsatisfied wants cause tensions, some of which can be relieved by the purchase and consumption of some product or service. Advertisers are interested in both (1) present wants of which consumers are aware (the "do" wants), and (2) wants unknown to consumers which can be established and stimulated by advertising (the "should" wants). The advertiser hopes to build his ad on an appeal, the specific satisfaction promised, which will stimulate buying motivation in the direction of a purchase. Advertisers, of course, are not omnipotent in this effort to stimulate; they may *persuade* consumers to buy, but they cannot *make* them buy.

The selection of an advertising appeal is complicated and made more difficult by the fact that motivation is an individual matter. Some of you pride yourself on your skill at golf, or bridge, or skiing; others of you will never spend one minute or one dollar on any of the three—and still be just as happy. Suppose you and your instructor were each offered free any record album in the shop but were required to listen to the other's choice. The instructor might writhe on the floor in agony and revulsion at what delighted you, whereas *his* taste and choice might inflict violent nausea on you. Clearly, each individual, selfish and self-centered, determines his own aspirations, adopts his own scale of values, ranks his goals according to desirability, and decides to which appeals he will react favorably. His questions to sellers are:

What will your product and you do *for me?*
What will *I* get out of the purchase?

Product features versus buyer benefits

The buyer benefit or appeal is the most important element in the ad. This benefit, this form of satisfaction, is possible only because of one or more product features. These product features are parts of the product itself *or* of the seller's offer which can provide buyer satisfaction. Price, package, sizes, and raw materials are examples of product elements. Guarantees, terms of sale, and delivery service are examples of offer elements.

Buyer benefits are what buyers actually buy. These include the satis-faction of human wants, gratification, moods, utilities, states of mind, and experiences. Benefits originate in product features; they are the results of product features. Because of this relationship and because of the basic differences between them, the advertiser must handle each group with care. He should never stress a product feature and then stop; this makes for weak advertising of low interest to buyers. He should, instead, trans-late features into benefits wanted by his prospects.

Basic versus acquired wants

Buyers' wants to which advertisers appeal may be *basic* or *acquired*. Every normal person is born with the actual or the future capacity to feel basic wants—those arising out of such physical and personal needs as food and drink, comfort, survival, safety, sex, and approval. Basic wants, thus, are universal. Some are constant and continuing, some recur frequently. Basic wants tend to get somewhat uniform treatment and handling by consumers.

Acquired wants are those a person learns to value and to satisfy; if basic wants are thought of as primary in nature, then acquired wants can be considered secondary. Examples are beauty, durability, economy, profit, convenience, and cleanliness.

Emotional versus rational appeals

The old view was that every voluntary purchase was unplanned, impulsive, and emotionally motivated (by fear, pride, revenge, and such) *or* weighed in advance, well thought out, and rational (by the buyer's desire for economy, accuracy, dependability, and such). The current, the sounder view, is that consumers make *few* voluntary purchases which are 100 percent emotional *or* 100 percent rational. Practically all if not completely all of their purchases fall within narrower limits—from quite emotional to quite sensible. A review of your purchases of the past week will probably show that there were feelings and sentiment *as well as* hardheadedness and objectivity in most of them. Perhaps our assumption should be that the typical consumer ponders, analyzes, weighs, compares, and shops more when making some purchases than when making certain other purchases.

Positive versus negative appeals

The advertiser can frame his promise either *positively* or *negatively*. Positive appeals promise the events and experiences consumers enjoy; they promise what the consumer wants to be or have or feel; they promise the pleasant, the desired. Negative appeals promise the consumer that he will avoid some experience or fate he fears, dreads, or wants to avoid. The negative versions of positive appeals are appeals to *fear* in some form. The advertiser can base his message on pleasure, or the fear of pain; on approval, or the fear of disapproval; on success, or the fear of failure; on safety, or the fear of danger.

Appeals based on fear can be memorable and powerful. Because they sometimes generate feelings of irritation, shame, or guilt, they may get less readership and acceptance, perhaps less reaction, than do positive appeals. Most ads are built on positive appeals, reflecting the consumer's preference to identify with the pleasant rather than the unpleasant.

How many benefits should an ad include?

Just how many benefits or satisfactions should an ad promise? Just how many appeals should it include? One can argue soundly that each ad should limit itself to the promise of one benefit, that it should be built on a single appeal. Such an ad can be strong because of its unity and simplicity. It is easy for the consumer to grasp and accept. And, remember that the establishing of *one* benefit is often quite an achievement.

There are arguments in favor of including two or more benefits. Different buyers find different satisfactions in the same product. They use it for different purposes, and they react favorably to different stimuli. Sometimes the advertiser will lead with a "human interest" appeal to get attention and readership, then follow with a rational appeal to encourage buying consideration.

Suggestions about appeals

The most important step in building an ad is the selection of what to promise the buyer. Two benefits of equal weight may be best; one major benefit and one or more minor ones may be best; a single benefit is often best. Twin mistakes are to include too many and to include any which is weak. The ad should try always to leave just one impression in the consumer's mind. It should try always to promise what the consumer really does want—not what the advertiser *thinks* the consumer wants—seldom what the advertiser thinks the consumer *should* want.

LAYOUT

Let's assume that we have decided to promise one benefit in a full-page magazine ad; let's settle on comfort. Now we come to grips with the job of actually starting to build the physical ad.

This section takes up *layout*. After distinguishing layout from visualization, we consider weight and the optical center. Next come the five requirements for good layout. The section ends with a discussion of illustrations.

Visualization versus layout

Visualization is creation. The visualizer, an artist, asks and then answers this question: What elements or units should be included in the ad? Incidentally, we use the terms *element*, *unit*, and *mass* interchangeably. The more common elements are headings (headlines and subheads), illustrations, body copy (also called text and copy blocks), and logotypes (also called signatures, nameplates, and display symbols). Typically, the logotype is the brand name or the advertiser's name. Other elements include trademark, trade character, prices, package, product, and coupon.

The visualizer thinks, he pictures, he wonders, he imagines. His goal is to settle on the combination of units which will communicate and persuade most effectively. He soon finds himself making rough lines and crude sketches on paper, converting his ideas into physical form and pictorial presentation. He may be joined by a copywriter in this process of visualizing.

Whereas visualization *creates*, layout *arranges;* visualization decides *which* units the ad will contain, layout decides *where* each of these units will be placed. Visualization, of course, cannot avoid some preliminary arranging. The artist literally cannot think very long about which elements to include without also and simultaneously thinking about their positions. When he begins to sketch, he cannot avoid some "laying out." But, even though visualization does shade into layout, indeed, even though both are done in the same session by the same person, the two are basically different.

In blueprinting, in composing, in arranging, the layout artist strives for construction which is sound and logical, clean and appropriate. He wants it to be pleasant and interesting. He hopes his layout will invite prospects to look, to understand, to identify, and to read; he does not want them to be aware of the layout as such. Simplicity is one of his objectives because the clear, direct, uncluttered layout helps the reader to get the message with little, or even better, with no, difficulty. Layout can give emphasis to the important elements and withhold it from the unimportant. After capturing the reader's observation, it can help direct and guide his looking and reading.

Weight

We now look at the "pull" each element or mass exerts for readers' attention. If element A captures the attention of 300 readers and element B only 100, A is thought and said to have three times as much weight as B. Weight, then, is the strength or power to attract the notice of readers.

Size, obviously, is one determinant of weight. We can generalize that large coupons and illustrations attract more attention, that they weigh more, than small ones. Shape influences weight. Circles weigh more than do squares or rectangles of the same area; irregular shapes weigh more

FIGURE 7–4. Ad in formal balance. Notice the weight of the command-type headline

than do circles of the same area. Color affects weight in that an element in color weighs more than it would in black and white.

Optical center

On a blank magazine page the spot of greatest attention value is called the optical center. Most readers can "see" the invisible vertical line which divides the space into left and right areas of exactly equal size. But, those readers are inclined to place the invisible horizontal line which separates the upper half from the lower half *somewhat above* the physical center of the space. The optical center is the point at which these two lines cross. Thus, the spot which readers designate as the center of the area, the first spot on which their eyes choose to fall, is slightly above the geometrical center of the space. If the advertiser wants to emphasize some element such as headline, price, or part of the illustration, he may place that element in a horizontal zone or band containing the optical center.

Features of good layout

Balance. The general rule is that ads should be in balance and that balance rests on or hangs from the optical center. Balance is a matter of the distribution of weights; so, it involves the placement of sizes, shapes, and color in relation to the optical center and in relation to each other. Of the two dimensions involved, left to right and top to bottom, the left to right is by far the more important. Readers are little bothered by a wide range of top-to-bottom ratios; they are, however, easily and quickly disturbed if the left half weighs more or less than the right half. Because imbalance distracts, it should be avoided by building stability and equilibrium into the layout, by placing the units so they appear settled and correctly located.

The simple way to do this is to employ *formal* or *symmetrical* balance. Here masses in the left half are duplicated in the right half in corresponding locations. Each mass centers and balances on the central vertical axis. Imbalance is impossible because each half contains exactly what the other half contains. Formal balance is associated with strength, quality, refinement, and dignity. On the other hand, it strikes some readers as forbidding, cold, dull, and too respectable.

Most ads employ *informal, asymmetrical* balance. Here the left and right halves are *not* identical in sizes, shapes, color, and the placement of units—but they *do* weigh the same. Informal balance is subtle and visual, not obvious and mechanical. Why do most advertisers prefer informal balance? It can be original, unusual, and dramatic. It can be lively, modern, and interesting. Its warmth is inviting, its equilibrium has charm.

Proportion. This prerequisite of good layout has two aspects. First, there is the shape of the ad itself. Having assumed a full-page magazine ad, we have no leeway or responsibility about this. For smaller ads, there is the height-to-width relationship. Readers' attention is called to and by unsatisfactory ratios; that is bad.

The other aspect of proportion involves the division of the space inside the ad. Here the layout artist is concerned with the dimensions of the ad's units—with the relationships of each mass to the other masses and of each mass to the ad as a whole. Basic forms are the circle, the square, and the triangle; each is subject to adaptation into more or less irregular forms.

White space, the area not occupied by any unit or mass, is a factor in proportion, even to the point of delineating the dimensions of the units. Judicious use of white space makes for uncrowded, more easily assimilated ads. It provides breathing space, isolation, and contrast; it suggests quality and prestige; it can help direct and control readers' attention.

The able layout artist avoids areas the relative dimensions of which are obvious. If the reader is instantly aware of one-to-one or one-to-two dimensions, proportion is not good; one-to-one is particularly flat and uninteresting. Two-to-five, three-to-five, and five-to-eight are good proportions.

Contrast. Contrast is difference. Size is a contrast possibility; large versus small, short versus tall, and wide versus narrow are examples. Shape is a contrast possibility; because the circle complements the square, those two shapes provide harmonious contrast. Color or tone permits contrast; at some time, most of us have experienced the powerful, even painful contrast between red and blue, and we all know the checkerboard pattern of dark squares and light squares. Direction affords contrast; vertical versus horizontal and left versus right are illustrations.

Contrast is lively and interesting because it is a type of variety. The tension inherent in contrast fights montony and helps to transform ordinary ads into distinctive ads. Contrast can make ads more emphatic and better read.

Unity. Ads well laid out are unified ads. Unity is one-ness, it is completeness, it is appearance which reflects logic, compactness, order. Unity

FIGURE 7–5. The generous use of white space is an outstanding feature of this ad

TRY SOMETHING BETTER.

There is only one J&B Rare Scotch. And only one reason for drinking it. The delightful rare taste you pour every time from every bottle. Isn't something like that worth a few cents more?

J&B Rare Scotch

From the house of Justerini & Brooks, founded 1749.

86 Proof Blended Scotch Whisky. The Paddington Corp., N.Y. 10020

makes an ad cohesive by tying its elements together, by combining several units into a single whole. It can increase attention to and comprehension of an ad.

The time to insure unity is when visualizing is being done. It is then that the number of units to be included and their respective weights can be controlled. When visualizing, the artist can discard irrelevant units and screen out unnecessary ones. He can avoid scatter and separation as well as clutter and conglomeration. In his determination to achieve unity through simplicity, he uses borders, overlapping groupings, and panels to hold units together. He works hard lest some element call unfortunate, *unintended* attention to itself.

Movement. This quality, movement, helps greatly in separating heavy, lifeless, static ads from active, dynamic, rhythmic ads. Actual movement is possible in television and some outdoor ads, and movement can be pictured in illustrations. At the moment, however, we are interested in the motion or movement built into layout, usually flowing in visual sequence from left to right and from top to bottom. Such movement encourages attention and interest because it contributes to the ad's attractiveness and gracefulness. It also provides a route for the reader's attention to follow, just as a marked road map serves a touring motorist.

Structural motion consists of lines of direction and movement built into layout by mechanical means. Useful devices include arrows, pointed fingers, lines of dots, spirals, and numbered flags or units.

Gaze motion is created when some person (sometimes some animal) looks directly out of the ad to capture attention. Readers tend to look back when stared at, just as students, engrossed in a crossword puzzle or a personal letter have been known to return the attention of an instructor once they feel fixed by his stern stare. Gaze motion also takes place when the person in an ad is looking at some element (product, perhaps) the advertiser wants the reader to notice. We all know our inclination to identify, to bring into *our* focus what others are looking at.

Conclusions. Good layout is characterized by what can be described as good feeling tone. Most readers are instantly aware of the defects, the omissions, the mistakes which make layouts bad or weak. Unfortunately, there is no formula which will guarantee outstanding layouts. Artists have to develop a feeling and a sense of what is best, what is in good taste. Sometimes an ad seems unbalanced to us although the artist saw it in balance.

ILLUSTRATIONS

Most ads contain illustrations because illustrated ads, in general, get better readership than nonillustrated ones. Magazine readers today are visual minded and picture conscious; they are used to illustrations, they expect them. Readers often need illustrations to enable them to understand the meaning of the advertiser's message.

The illustration can do *several* jobs for the advertiser. It can capture initial attention. It can make the advertiser's promise of benefit easier to understand; sometimes it contains proof which makes that promise easier to accept. Readers use illustrations to help identify the ads they should read and to help identify products and packages. Illustrations can communicate quickly and clearly, they permit less copy, and they can encourage reading. Because they can affect the tone or atmosphere of the ad, they are able to influence the mood of the reader. Illustrations can make ads more dramatic and, hence, more memorable; this is often true for a series of ads. Finally, words alone cannot do justice to such concepts as a baby, or a new automobile model, or a tourist attraction.

How many illustrations should an ad contain and *how large* should it or they be? A single dominant illustration, one which occupies two thirds or more of the space, seems to be a better choice than several of equal size with no center of attraction. Several small illustrations, of course, have their uses. They can break up a large amount of copy, making it less formidable and more inviting. They are effective in telling a sequence story and in showing a number of product features. They can inject a certain amount of movement into the layout. The advertiser's objective is a powerful influence on the number and size of the ad's illustrations.

Then there is the question of *what* to picture. Influences include the advertiser's aim, the job assigned to the illustration, the nature of the product, the buyer to whom the ad is addressed, and the medium. Pictures of just the product or a part of the product tend to rank low in interest value; the new automobile models are an exception, of course, to this generalization. Product plus persons is a better choice most of the time; the buyer, a person, is attracted more by other persons than by products. Ofter the illustration can show the product in use, giving obvious satisfaction to individuals using it.

Photographs—or drawings? There is some indication that, in general, photographs are superior to drawings. The accuracy of photographs encourages belief; their realism and authenticity bid for conviction and acceptance. Photographs are usually quick, easy, and economical to get. Drawings and other artwork communicate more vigor, style, and distinctiveness; so they are better in expressing certain atmospheres and in conveying certain impressions. Artwork is better both in glorifying products and in showing construction details. Another advantage is that the artist can draw whatever persons, expressions, and positions he prefers. What is past, what is in the future, and what is inaccessible or impracticable cannot, of course, be photographed here and now.

Here are a few suggestions about illustrations. The responsibility of the typical illustration is to do more than attract attention; it also includes

FIGURE 7–6.   Note the handling of illustrations in this ad

The big ones with the better ideas

Want more roadtime, less downtime?

Better check into Ford's better ideas for increased reliability, simplified maintenance, higher driver efficiency, lower operating costs.

Ford has one better idea...

Wide-open working space around engine cuts service time.

Color-coded air tubing speeds tracing, lasts longer.

and another...

after another...

Deep-dip Electrocoat primer resists rust, helps cabs last longer.

Four electrical junction blocks on L- and W-Series speed circuit tracing.

and another...

and another...

Movable L-Series steering column maintains ideal 20° wheel angle.

E-Z Read gauges on L-Series linehaul panels show normal at "3 o'clock," can be checked at a glance.

and another...

and another...

Wheel cuts as tight as 49° save maneuvering time.

Large windshields give drivers superior vision for easier, safer driving.

and another...

FORD HEAVY-DUTY TRUCKS
AT FORD AND MERCURY DEALERS ACROSS CANADA

FIGURE 7–7. Ad dominated by its illustration

This is the one that's
protected, cared for and given
all the time it needs to
become America's finest
cheddar.

Cracker Barrel Brand
from Kraft.

helping influence the attitudes or actions of buyers. For this reason, it
should be relevant and realistic instead of freakish, corny, repelling, or
too clever. Illustrations should be technically sound. Housewives working
in the kitchen should look like housewives working in the kitchen, not
like glamour girls going to a party. Athletes should look real, not like
models trying to look like athletes. Meaning should be instantly clear,
demanding no study on the part of the reader. This argues against illustra-

tions which are too involved and complex. Believability is encouraged by photographs which are normal, natural, seemingly unposed. Most illustrations should help tie the headline to the rest of the copy. All should be chosen for their functional value rather than because they are conveniently at hand; this argues against pictures of the factory and of the founder of the firm. Illustrations should be means, not ends.

COLOR

Color plays a larger and larger role in our economy and in our culture, in our living and in our buying. No one questions the influence of color on the emotions of individuals, be they buyers or workers. Many products are now available in color, and much advertising is in color. In our illustrative medium, the magazine, the advertiser can elect an ad in black and white, in black plus one color, in black plus two colors, or in full color, which can be had with black plus the three colors of red, yellow, and blue. These three are the primary colors; they can be combined so as to produce almost any other color, but none of the three can be produced by combining other colors. Although not a color in the technical sense, black joins red, yellow, and blue to constitute the colors in the four-color process. Much body copy is black because of its great legibility.

There are three attributes or qualities of color. *Hue* is the quality by which we distinguish one color from another. We "see" the difference between red and blue, between blue and yellow. *Value* is the degree of lightness or darkness of a color. This is a matter of depth; some reds and blues are dark—some light. Third is *chroma;* this is a matter of intensity which separates strong colors from weak colors.

Many colors have emotional associations. Even in our talking we describe ourselves as green with envy, as painting the town red, as in a black mood. Red, orange, and yellow are warm colors because they remind us of fire and the sun. Blue, violet, and green are cool, suggesting the sea and the sky. Here are certain color implications in our culture:

White: sickness, fear, purity
Green: youth, nature, cheapness
Blue: serenity, truth, restraint
Red: passion, bravery, action
Yellow: hate, optimism, joyousness

In advertising, color is put to various uses. It can capture attention and arouse interest. Its eye appeal can whet desire for food products.

The advertiser can choose certain colors for purposes of mood, prestige, and atmosphere, or to give life to his ad. The realism of color allows the consumer to identify products, packages, and labels. Emphasis can be achieved through color. Buyer benefits can be illustrated, interpreted, and proved with color. A series of ads can be tied together with color.

Typically, advertising in color costs more than in black and white. The challenging question: Is color worth its premium price?

COPY

Our undertaking is to treat the building of an ad within a single chapter, even though we know that entire books had been written on each of the major subheads of this chapter. The limitations imposed by space and time demand that we restrict ourselves to the typical, the normal, the current. So, our magazine ad, already laid out in conventional pattern, will contain the copy elements most ads do.

Copy is the reading matter, the words and figures, in an ad. Specifically, it consists of the words, sentences, paragraphs, subheads, headlines, figures, and the logotype—the firm's name or the brand name. Illustrations plus copy constitute practically all of our ad. Our hope is that prospects' reaction to these two elements will be "What a great product"—not, "What a great ad."

Copy goals

The copywriter writes what he believes will influence buyers, and those buyers have different feelings toward the brand being promoted, sometimes toward the advertiser himself. From the advertiser's point of view, the most unfortunate state in which to leave the reader is one of hostility. Many hostile buyers will never be changed into friends by advertising. Next most undesirable is a state of ignorance; but advertising can do something about this. The third least favorable state is that of awareness; these buyers know the brand but have not bought it. Fourth is acceptance; here the buyer becomes willing to try the brand for the first time—and does. Fifth is the happy state of preference; this results from a happy experience in stage four. Sixth and last is the wonderful, delightful state of insistence; this represents the top in brand loyalty, because the buyers will not accept substitutes.

Clearly, if the copywriter is to be successful in moving buyers up that six-rung ladder, he needs a clear picture of, and adequate information about, those buyers. He must know much about their values, hopes, ambitions, and motivation. He must know much about products, what those products represent, why they are bought—or not bought—what they do to and for consumers. Only with such information can the copywriter hope to build his ad on the Big Promise which will be most effective. That brings up the matters of *attitudes* and *actions*.

We have mentioned direct action advertising objectives and indirect. There are comparable copy goals. Some copy is written to cause immediate response. Sellers who use no promotion except advertising want their copy to produce purchases. Sellers who use ads containing coupons want coupons mailed. Retailers want visits to the store or phone calls. Most copy, however, is written to affect buyers' attitudes, to cause a psychological rather than a physical response. The copywriter strives for favorable impressions and pleasant associations. True, the advertiser's assumption is that favorable mental reaction today will help lead to favorable buying action tomorrow.

Copy format or pattern

Early in the building of an ad, the copywriter must decide *how* he will construct his message. Probably the most common format or slant is the conventional, straight technique which combines an illustration, a headline, some text or body copy, and a signature. Other possibilities include question and answer, verse, strips, cartoons, dialogue, first person, case histories, testimonials, and editorial style.

Headlines

We can say that all headlines have *two* basic jobs—that some undertake a *third*. First, the headline tries to make visual contact with all buyers the advertiser wants to reach, alerting them and capturing their attention. Second, the headline tries to induce the maximum number of those buyers to read the body copy, the smaller print. There is indication that ads with headlines *do* get more readership than ads without. The third job, one attempted by some headlines, is to deliver a complete, even though brief, selling message.

There are various classifications of headline *types*. One, distinguishing according to *content*, recognizes label or identification (brand name or advertiser's name), boast, news, and promise of benefit. As to *form*, there are these: question, command, selective ("Students," "Motorists"), and curiosity. This last type, also termed the *blind* headline, tries to be provocative enough to entice the reader to read the text so as to discover the meaning and relevance of the heading which, alone, does not make sense.

What comments and suggestions are in order about headlines? First of all, the headline demands respect because it is the most important, the most read copy element. It may be 50–75 percent responsible for an ad's effectiveness. It and the illustrations are almost 100 percent responsible for getting initial attention and readership. Second, *content* (what it says) is more important than *form* (how it says it). Headlines should be clear in implying, "Here is a product (or service) you will enjoy, here is satisfaction that will please you." Three to 12 words are an acceptable range in length; these should be in rather large letters, in a prominent spot, often just below the illustration and just above the text. There are headlines which certainly should contain price and brand name. Your authors take the position that curiosity or blind headlines should not be used; we favor headlines which promise big benefits, newsworthy if possible.

Body copy or text

The body copy or text, sometimes called the copy block, is the copy element which informs and persuades. It expands, clarifies, and explains the big promise which, basically, an ad is. The organization of the copy block should be governed by the reader's needs and interests; its sequence should be logical, its continuity and flow orderly.

The first, the *lead* paragraph, is the most important paragraph. It continues the thought expressed in the headline. It appeals to the self-interest of buyers by stressing satisfactions and benefits. It recognizes a buyer problem or want and recommends the advertised brand as the solution or answer. Most lead paragraphs are short and to the point. A range of 25 to 50 words can be good, as can three sentences of from 12 to 15 words each.

The interior paragraphs which separate the lead from the last paragraph should flow smoothly from the lead as they develop and amplify, expand and explain. They try to personalize the ad's promises and claims. The headline and illustration captured attention for the ad; the headline and the lead paragraph transferred this attention to the satisfaction promised; the interior paragraphs try to convert this attention into interest in and contemplation of buying. This interior copy is the most logical place for proof of promises and claims if such is to be included. Types of proof include share of market, guarantees, sample and trial offers, testimonials and case histories, product construction or features, and research findings.

The last paragraph is the closing one in both senses of the term. It closes the body copy, and, like a salesman's close, it bids for the response the advertiser wants. The close may be a single sentence, or it may be longer. Closes range from the very subtle and restrained to the bald imperative ones which even include a powerful reason for acting *now*. Closes must be clear and specific.

Copy length

When is an ad too long? Too short? There are no formulas, no rules for copy length. In the magazine medium, maybe body copy of fewer than 100 words can be considered *short*—of more than 200 words, *long*. The most significant comment about length is that length does not matter so long as the reader's interest is held. What is said and how it is said are far more important than how many words are used to say it. Sometimes the promise, the buyer, the product, the advertiser's purpose, and the medium call for long copy, sometimes for short.

Certain advantages are claimed for short copy, others for long copy. Short copy can be inviting, require less reading time, be read by more buyers, and may cost less. On the other hand, long copy can present more information, contain more persuasion, do a more complete job, offer more proof, and permit the inclusion of human interest material.

Copy suggestions

Copy cannot be effective unless readers find it interesting, both in substance and in style. The subject of greatest interest to the buyer is, of course, his own self. If the buyer's feelings and preferences are to be respected, copy will stress what the advertised item will do to and for him, for his problems, for his self-image.

Another "must" is that of believability. This is a matter of the reader's acceptance of the advertiser's promises and proof. Belief is personal and emotional, influenced by feeling as well as by reason. Each buyer tends to believe what he wants to believe, what his background and experience tell him to accept, what friends and authorities support. Truth is essential, but truth is not enough. Copy that is candid and factual, specific and clear is far more believable than exaggerated, extreme claims. Plausible promises backed up by proof make a strong bid for acceptance. Weasel words *and* overstatement hurt.

Unless copy persuades and influences, it fails in its assignment. To accomplish its purpose, copy must convince the buyer that the advertiser is interested in him. Helpful suggestions and sincere recommendations about how the product can make buyers happier and better satisfied contribute to persuasiveness.

What about the inclusion of prices? There *are* times when the omission of prices is indicated, perhaps even unavoidable. There is strong support, however, for the practice of including prices unless there is extremely good justification for omission. The buyer cannot seriously contemplate buying something so long as he does not know its price; in his thinking and deciding, price plays a most basic role. The odds are that there are many, many more ads which do not contain prices but should than ads which do contain prices but should not.

Good copy is readable copy. *Words* should be accurate and precise; the copywriter should not use the word *infer* if he really means *imply*, or *figuratively* if he means *literally*. Short words are usually but not always better than long ones; contrast *do* with *accomplish*, *ask* with *interrogate*. If 75 percent of the words are of one syllable, that is good rather than bad. Words that are tired from overuse are to be avoided. Personal words join familiar nouns and pleasant verbs in contributing to readability.

Sentences, too, should usually be short. Any sentence can be too long, but no one sentence can be too short. A range of 10 to 20 words is good; 12- to 15-word sentences can communicate particularly well. Each sentence should be limited to a single idea. Monotony can be reduced and attractiveness increased by varying the opening words, the lengths, and the types of sentences.

Paragraphs should each be limited to one basic idea. This should be expressed in the topic sentence, which is often the first sentence. The other sentences explain, develop, and expand the substance of the topic sentence. A paragraph can consist of one sentence—or of several. The flow from paragraph to paragraph must be smooth.

TYPOGRAPHY

The promise which is our magazine ad's message has been chosen, the ad illustrated, its copy has been written. The copy must now be set for printing, and this leads to a brief consideration of typography.

Type faces

Only a cursory glance at two or three magazine pages is needed to detect differences among type faces. The term *type face* refers to the shape, the proportion, the design of the letters and figures. Type faces differ as handwriting differs, as the faces of your friends differ; no two are identical. Just as you and your friends have names, so do type faces. Caslon, Bodoni, and Garamond are well-known type faces. Where do type faces come from? They are designed by typographical artists. If advertisers like and use new type faces, they will continue to be seen in print ads.

Type families

Bodoni type, just mentioned, is the name of a type face *and* of a type family. The Bodoni family consists of the alphabets, weights, and widths in which Bodoni faces are available. The five most common alphabets are these: lower case (small) and upper case (capital) regular letters, lower case and upper case italics, and small capitals.

abcdefghijklmnopqrstuvwxyz
ABCDEFGHIJKLMNOPQRSTUVWXYZ
abcdefghijklmnopqrstuvwxyz
ABCDEFGHIJKLMNOPQRSTUVWXYZ
ABCDEFGHIJKLMNOPQRSTUVWXYZ

Weight is a matter of thickness of line. Four well-known weights are lightface, medium, boldface, and extra bold.

This is lightface Bodoni.
This is Memphis Medium.
This is boldface Bodoni.
This is extra bold Bodoni.

Width has to do with how much lateral space is occupied by a type face. Three common widths are condensed, regular, and extended. The same line of type can contain more letters and words of the condensed version than of the extended version.

This is Cheltenham Bold.
This is Cheltenham Bold Condensed.
This is Cheltenham Bold Extended.

Type groups

Families which have the same general features and somewhat similar faces constitute type groups. Of these, the Roman group is the most important. Roman faces trace their origin to letters carved in stone in Rome when that city ruled the world. The lines or strokes of Roman letters are not of uniform width, some being thick, some thin. The letters are simple combinations of curves and angles. Serifs are a feature of Roman types; these are the small bars or lines that mark the ends of the main strokes by crossing them. The Roman group is the largest in number of type faces; most magazines, books, and newspapers are printed in Roman faces. Outstanding features of the Roman group include: superb legibility, the versatility and contrast which can be achieved within a single family, and general familiarity stemming from wide usage and long acquaintance.

Our second group, Gothic, consists of block type faces. Lines are of uniform width and thickness; there are no serifs. Angles are uniform, curves are arcs or segments of a circle. Many letters consist of straight lines plus circles or parts of a circle. Gothic type is modern and clean, less legible than Roman, better for headings than for body type.

Although not a type group, italics are best mentioned at this point. They are a version available in most Roman and in some Gothic faces. Italic letters are sloping adaptations of and slanting companions for their vertical counterparts. They are appropriate for headings addressed to women and for emphasis, contrast, and decoration.

Type other than Roman and Gothic can be placed into a third, a Miscellaneous group. Two examples are Script and Text. Script, a variant of the italic letter, simulates handwriting. Although delicate, personal, and graceful, Script is less legible than Roman and Gothic. In Script, all lower case letters in a word touch, forming a continuous line. If those letters do not quite touch, the type is called Cursive. Text, also called Old English, is ecclesiastical in origin, being the kinds of letters monks made when copying religious manuscripts with reed pens. Text connotes reverence and antiquity; it is quite difficult to read.

Selection of type faces

Several influences bear on the selection of the type face or faces to use. Nature of the product advertised, type of buyer addressed, benefit promised, nature of illustration, size of ad, amount of copy, medium, and faces currently favored by advertisers are such influences. Above all, our magazine ad must be readable. This argues for the selection of a familiar, highly legible, popular Roman face. Five such as Bodoni, Bookman, Caslon, Garamond, and Times Roman. A second desirable characteristic is appropriateness. Some faces are masculine, others feminine—some bespeak prestige, others shout bargain—some reflect antiquity, others modernity. Appropriate faces can help create the atmosphere most helpful to the advertiser's objective. If standard type cannot give the advertiser what he wants, he can get a commercial artist to handletter precisely what is needed. Many headlines are handlettered.

Suggestions about typography

Length of line and size of type must be watched closely to see that legibility is good. Long lines of many words each discourage readership and tire the reader; but, short lines can be choppy and difficult. As for size, the letters should be large enough for easy reading. Small letters in long lines and large letters in short lines are bad. Incidentally, the basic measurement of type size is the *point*. This is a vertical measurement reflecting height only. There are 72 points to an inch.

Any one ad can quickly and easily contain too many different faces. This number must be held down; often *one* type family is best. When two or more families are included, pains should be taken to see that the combination is compatible and complementary—that there is no clash.

Variety, a feature of good typography, can be incorporated through the handling of such variables as faces, sizes, weights, widths, and spacing. The typographer's aim is to make the copy lively and inviting, to employ contrast so as to avoid monotony.

Typography should be used to emphasize what needs emphasis. For this purpose these techniques are available: capitalization, italics, boldface, color, underlining, circles, boxes, panels, and decorations. The big caution here is that the tactic used *not* call attention to itself *as a tactic*. Good typography is such that the reader is not conscious of the fact that typography is involved.

Spacing is important, spacing between words, between lines, between paragraphs. Each of these three can be too close together—or too far apart. Incidentally, the amount of space between lines is measured in points and is referred to as leading, pronounced "leding."

A final suggestion is that headlines not be messy and "too too" in a typographical sense. When they are in a spiral, a curve, or even a

FIGURE 7–8. Typographical advice for outdoor ads

Common mistakes:

1. Crowding too many letters into a space tends to repel the eye and defeat the objective of getting type as large as possible.

OVERCROWDING

2. Too great a contrast between thick and thin elements leads to confusion, and loss of identity of basic shapes and letters.

CONFUSION

3. Minimizing differences between letters by uniform rounding at the top or lining up of all horizontal centers loses legibility.

ABREGHM

4. Strokes which are too fine do not utilize fully the basic shapes, and fade into the background and become invisible at a distance.

ANEMIA

5. Too-heavy letters become blobs at a distance, basic shapes cannot be distinguished, and letters are not recognizable.

OVERWEIGH

6. Script and similar styles sacrifice the basic shapes for the decorative aspect, and individual letters cannot be identified.

Illegibility

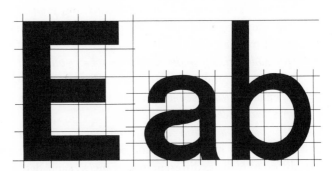

Legibility factors:

For easiest legibility at a distance, experience and research indicate that the width of a letter's vertical strokes should be about one-fifth its height. Horizontal strokes may be slightly thinner. These proportions apply equally to Capital and lower-case letters.

diagonal, legibility and readership suffer. If too many type sizes and faces are included, that hurts. If all or part of the headline is overprinted on some other unit or element of the ad, communication is reduced. Too much isolation, word to word *or* headline to text, must be avoided.

SOME SOCIAL AND ECONOMIC CONSIDERATIONS

Various individuals and groups are hostile to advertising. This is understandable partially because there is so much we do not know and cannot prove about advertising's effects. All we have space for here is to glance at a few examples of social and economic questions *and* at a few examples of germane comments on them. For more detailed treatment, see some of the basic advertising texts.

Some social questions

1. *Is advertising false, deceptive, and misleading?* Some small bit is, but none should be. The fact that most sellers must have repeat business from buyers puts pressure on them to run truthful ads. Self-regulation and legislation are two other curbs.
2. *Does advertising insult buyers by appealing to their emotions?* Emotion is present in practically all buying decisions ultimate consumers make—indeed, in practically *all* voluntary decisions. Offended "intellectuals" must remember that advertising is *mass* communication and that they are a minority group. Even "intellectuals" are much influenced by their emotions.
3. *Does advertising make you buy what you don't need?* Advertising can't make you buy a product. *You* buy only what will protect or enhance *your* self-concept. Only you and no one else can decide what *you* need.
4. *Are many ads and advertising media in poor taste?* Taste is a personal, an individual, a subjective matter. Ultimate consumers have different values, different preferences; each determines what is valuable and tasteful to him. Media do not survive unless a satisfactory number of individuals approve of and patronize them. What *is* your taste in music, in art, or in food?
5. *Has advertising made us a society of conformists?* Advertising cannot make you conform; you yourself decide to conform—or to be different. You have much choice as to your reference groups and the opinion leaders you will follow. Advertising encourages more products and more brands, widening your choices.

FIGURE 7–9.   As the copy says, advertising sells good works as well as goods and services

"What good does advertising do?"

Advertising Sells Good Works
(as well as goods and services)

Have you noticed how often, when an important public cause is at stake, people turn to a good salesman for leadership? Successful businessmen have given uncountable man-hours to America's schools, churches and charities, and have led in solving major national problems. For its part, advertising—good salesman that it is—has provided the means to communicate such causes to the American people.

For 25 years ads like these have been prepared by advertising agencies who volunteer their services. Radio and television give time on the air; space is donated by newspapers and magazines. Last year alone, for example, business publications like this one gave more than a million dollars' worth of space in the public interest through The Advertising Council of which the American business press is a part.

25 years of advertising contributed for the public good

6. *Is advertising responsible for our society's being materialistic?* Because our society is affluent, it can afford to be materialistic. We approve of striving for more and better possessions. We are not satisfied with minimal, functional utility. Advertising merely recognizes and reflects that fact.

FIGURE 7–10.   Creative code adopted by the American Association of Advertising Agencies

---

The following advertising practices are disapproved in a code adopted by the American Association of Advertising Agencies and endorsed by the Association of National Advertisers:

a. False or misleading statements or exaggerations, visual or verbal.
b. Testimonials which do not reflect the real choice of a competent witness.
c. Price claims which are misleading.
d. Comparisons which unfairly disparage a competitive product or service.
e. Claims insufficiently supported, or which distort the true meaning or practicable application of statements made by professional or scientfic authority.
f. Statements, suggestions, or pictures offensive to public decency.

We recognize that there are areas which are subject to honestly different interpretations and judgment. Taste is subjective and may even vary from time to time as well as from individual to individual. Frequency of seeing or hearing advertising messages will necessarily vary greatly from person to person.

However, we agree not to recommend and to discourage the use of advertising which is in poor or questionable taste or which is deliberately irritating through content, presentation, or excessive repetition.

Criticisms by advertisers or agencies are sent to the Secretary of the A.N.A.-A.A.A.A. Committee, c/o 200 Park Avenue, New York 10017.

Some economic questions

1. *Does advertising promote inferior, even worthless, products?* Advertising encourages sellers to compete on a product basis by constantly improving their products. No one buys a worthless product *a second time* no matter how much advertising is promoting it; advertisers know this. A product that does nothing for *your* self-concept may do wonders for *someone else's.*

2. *Do advertised products cost more than unadvertised products?* There is no proof of what advertising does to the costs of advertised products. Unit production costs *and* total promotion costs can be lower with heavy advertising than without it. Sellers would not use advertising if there were a lower-priced substitute. There are indications that some advertised brands deliver more satisfaction than unadvertised competing brands.

3. *Does advertising discourage price competition and encourage price rigidity?* In the short run, yes; but, over the long run, price rigidity is unknown. Promotion costs, an element in the prices buyers pay, are high because of our free enterprise economy, not because of advertising. There is no proof that advertising makes the ultimate consumer pay more for the same amount of satisfaction.

4. *Does advertising promote monopoly?* Advertising is believed to stimulate the proliferation of brands, and that works against monopolistic conditions. Every seller knows that if his prices are relatively high, they invite small firms to appear with competing products at lower prices. A small *local* seller can spend just as many advertising dollars in his small market area as can a large *national* seller in that same area.

5. *Is advertising responsible for the business cycle?* There were business cycles long before advertising. Because advertisers spend lavishly in good times and cut back in bad times, the distance between the peaks and the low points of cycles may be greater. Consumer purchasing power influences the business cycle far more than does advertising.

6. *Is advertising wasteful, contributing nothing to economic growth because of its competitive nature?* There is some waste in advertising, but advertisers are under constant pressure to reduce this waste. Mass promotion is essential if we are to have mass consumption and mass production. Advertising is part of our competitive economy. Abolish advertising because it is competitive? Then abolish competition. We have advertising; we have the world's highest standard of living; maybe there's a connection.

QUESTIONS AND PROBLEMS

7–1. Why is advertising *not* a science?

7–2. List types of products that do little or no advertising.

7–3. Most persons in advertising condemn the "addy" ads. What features make an ad look "addy"?

7-4. Suggest reasons why a manufacturer might be smart to omit prices from his ads.

7-5. Suggest some qualities or features of good advertising illustrations.

7-6. Compare the advertising promises made for expensive watches with those made for inexpensive watches.

7-7. "It pays to advertise." Does it? Whom does it pay?

7-8. List some significant differences between retail advertising and industrial advertising.

7-9. The last two chapters treated personal selling and sales management. Write a "want ad" that a sales manager might run in recruiting for his sales force.

7-10. a) What are some of the patronage motives of ultimate consumers?

b) What are some of the patronage motives of purchasing agents who buy for government, industry, and institutions?

CHAPTER 8

Advertising media

THE PRECEDING CHAPTER described the design and construction of an ad. That ad was viewed as a seller's promise of satisfaction, of buyer benefits. Now we are ready to communicate that promise to the individuals the advertiser wants to influence—we must transmit that message—we must get it seen or heard. Transmission is done by six advertising media, functioning as vehicles which carry ads to buyers and to buying influences. These include publication media, newspapers and magazines; broadcast media, television and radio; and, in addition, outdoor and transit advertising. This chapter points out the basic facts about these six media.

NEWSPAPERS

Classification

Daily. Of the 1,652 daily (Monday–Saturday) newspapers published in the English language in the United States in 1969, 311 were morning papers, 1,325 evening, and 16 "all day." Their combined daily circulation was about 62 million. Daily newspapers are thought to reach about 90 percent of U.S. families and to be read by about 80 percent of all consumers over the age of 21.

The morning paper is apt to be somewhat more masculine in appeal, featuring world news, sports, and business. Because of its hour of publication, it can circulate over a wide geographical area. Morning papers have a significant street sale; many are read on the way to work and

TABLE 8–1.   Ad volume in 1968 and 1969

Medium	1968 Millions	% of tot.	1969† Millions	% of tot.	% change '69 vs. '68
Newspapers					
Total	$5,265	29.1%	$ 5,753	29.5%	+ 9.3%
National	990	5.5	1,059	5.4	+ 7.0
Local	4,275	23.6	4,694	24.1	+ 9.8
Magazines					
Total	1,318	7.3	1,376	7.1	+ 4.4
Weeklies	657	3.6	662	3.4	+ 0.8
Women's	284	1.6	308	1.6	+ 8.5
Monthlies	342	1.9	374	1.9	+ 9.4
Farm, national	35	0.2	32	0.2	− 8.6
Television					
Total	3,231	17.8	3,585	18.4	+11.0
Network	1,523	8.4	1,678	8.6	+10.2
Spot	1,131	6.2	1,253	6.4	+10.8
Local	577	3.2	654	3.4	+13.4
Radio					
Total	1,190	6.6	1,273	6.5	+ 7.0
Network	63	0.4	58	0.3	− 8.0
Spot	360	2.0	380	1.9	+ 5.6
Local	767	4.2	835	4.3	+ 8.9
Farm publications					
(Regional)	33	0.2	33	0.2	0.0
‡Total farm pubs.	(68)	(0.4)	(65)	(0.4)	− 4.4
Direct mail	2,612	14.4	2,670	13.7	+ 2.2
Business papers	714	3.9	752	3.9	+ 5.3
Outdoor					
Total	208	1.1	213	1.1	+ 2.4
National	137	0.7	138	0.7	+ 1.0
Local	71	0.4	75	0.4	+ 5.6
Miscellaneous					
Total	3,556	19.6	3,827	19.6	+ 7.6
National	2,035	11.2	2,154	11.0	+ 5.8
Local	1,521	8.4	1,673	8.6	+10.0
Total					
National	10,883	60.0	11,518	59.1	+ 5.8
Local	7,244	40.0	7,964	40.9	+ 9.6
Grand total	**$18,127**	**100.0%**	**$19,482**	**100.0%**	**+ 7.5%**

†Revised. ‡Included in other media totals—not to be added.
Note: Estimates include all costs—time and talent, space and production.

Source: *Marketing/Communications*, Copyright © 1970 by Decker Communications Incorporated.

are not carried home. Buyers can respond to ads on the same day the ads are read.

Afternoon newspapers pay more attention to the interests of women readers and of the family; features include comics, puzzles, and syndicated columns. They cover a smaller geographical area than morning papers. Many are home delivered. The hour of publication is ill timed for the reporting of last-minute news, and fast-breaking stories frequently make necessary expensive alterations. These handicaps, added to greater competition in late afternoon from TV newscasts, have made the going hard

TABLE 8–2. U.S. daily and Sunday newspapers: 1945–1969

Year	Number of Newspapers			Total M&E			Number Sunday	Total Sunday		
	Morning	Evening	Total M&E	Circulation (000 omitted)	Daily Joint Min. Rate	Daily Milline Rate	Number Sunday	Circulation (000 omitted)	Sunday Joint Min. Rate	Sunday Milline Rate
1945	330	1,419	1,749	48,384	$140.57	$2.91	485	39,860	$81.59	$2.05
1946	334	1,429	1,763	50,928	154.21	3.03	497	43,665	90.09	2.08
1947	328	1,441	1,769	51,673	162.66	3.15	511	45,151	97.87	2.17
1948	328	1,453	1,781	52,285	173.85	3.33	530	46,308	111.56	2.41
1949	329	1,451	1,780	52,846	176.83	3.35	546	46,399	114.89	2.48
1950	322	1,450	1,772	53,829	188.38	3.50	549	46,582	123.54	2.65
1951	319	1,454	1,773	54,018	200.81	3.72	543	46,279	129.83	2.81
1952	327	1,459	1,786	53,951	209.40	3.88	545	46,210	136.67	2.96
1953	327	1,458	1,785	54,472	214.64	3.94	544	45,949	139.81	3.04
1954	317	1,448	1,765	55,072	219.63	3.99	544	46,176	140.56	3.04
1955	316	1,454	1,760	56,147	229.79	4.09	541	46,448	147.72	3.18
1956	314	1,454	1,761	57,102	236.78	4.15	546	47,162	148.93	3.16
1957	309	1,453	1,755	57,805	253.62	4.39	544	47,044	161.18	3.43
1958	307	1,456	1,751	57,418	264.70	4.61	556	46,955	167.60	3.57
1959	306	1,455	1,755	58,300	271.44	4.66	564	47,848	167.79	3.51
1960	312	1,459	1,763	58,882	279.60	4.75	563	47,699	170.00	3.54
1961	312	1,458	1,761	59,261	288.06	4.86	558	48,216	174.93	3.63
1962	318	1,451	1,760	59,849	300.42	5.02	558	48,888	180.13	3.68
1963	311	1,453	1,754	58,905	299.21	5.08	550	46,830	177.47	3.79
1964	323	1,452	1,763	60,412	308.06	5.10	561	48,383	182.39	3.77
1965	320	1,444	1,751	60,358	312.11	5.17	562	48,600	182.56	3.76
1966	324	1,444	1,754	61,397	334.40	5.45	578	49,282	190.24	3.86
1967	327	1,438	1,749	61,561	337.99	5.49	573	49,224	198.21	4.03
1968	328	1,443	1,752	62,535	352.39	5.63	578	49,693	207.39	4.17
1969	333	1,443	1,758	62,060	370.20	5.97	585	49,675	219.07	4.41

"All day" newspapers counted only once in total M&E.

Source: Editor & Publisher Yearbook. Prepared by Research Department, Bureau of Advertising, ANPA.

for these papers, and many have folded in recent years or are operating at a loss.

Sunday. About 580 newspapers are published on Sunday; they have a circulation close to 50 million. Obviously, many of the 1,652 dailies do not publish on Sunday, forcing their readers to turn to some other newspaper on that day. The typical Sunday paper is sectionalized. This (1) facilitates editorial support for various types of advertising (business, sports, books) and (2) permits several readers to consume the paper at the same time. The large size of the issue demands much reading time, but, much time is available. Readers are relatively relaxed, and family discussions and decisions are relatively easy to achieve.

Nondaily. Many nondaily newspapers publish once a week, others twice a week. These publications are quite local in editorial content and in circulation. They are thought to get thorough readership and to enjoy longer life than dailies. The cost per reader is higher than for dailies.

Sunday newspaper magazines. Some Sunday newspapers include as one of their sections a magazine supplement. The syndicated type (*Parade, Family Weekly*) is sold to noncompeting Sunday newspapers. It is edited and produced by its own staff. Its flavor is more national than local, and its advertising is national or regional. The local or individual type (*New York Times Magazine; Chicago Tribune Magazine*) is published and distributed by its parent newspaper only. Advertising is local, regional, and national, and editorial flavor is more local than is true of the syndicated type.

Each type is an integral section of the newspaper distributing it; each is a magazine sent to the mass newspaper audience. The supplement's life is longer than that of the newspaper but shorter than that of the typical consumer magazine. It benefits from reader confidence in the newspaper and from its physical distribution facilities.

Size. As to size, most newspapers are either *standard* or *tabloid*. Dimensions of standard size papers are 21–22 inches deep and 15–16 inches wide; eight columns, each about 2 inches in width, contain a total of approximately 2,400 agate lines. (An agate line is one column wide and $\frac{1}{14}$ inch deep.) The typical tabloid page is 10 by 14 inches; its five columns contain a total of about 1,000 lines.

Features

The newspaper has great reach in that it covers its market intensively, yet there is market selectivity in a geographical sense. The newspaper's job is to deliver news, to communicate in detail and depth. Its flavor is usually local, and its appeal is broad enough to include just about everybody. The daily papers make satisfactory frequency possible to advertisers. Insertion of ads can be arranged or copy changes made almost overnight. Reading easily becomes a daily habit as does dependence on the ads as a shopping guide. Incidentally, advertising occupies about 60 percent of newspaper space, editorial material the other 40 percent.

As for limitations, the medium provides little or no qualitative selectivity in its market, because it tends to be edited for and read by all consumers. Exceptions are found in some large metropolitan areas where a tabloid may appeal to an income and education group different from that or those appealed to by the other morning paper(s). The physical life of each issue of any newspaper is short, and the reading it gets is often brief and hurried. When contrasted with magazines, particularly on such bases as color and appearance, the newspaper occupies second place.

Advertising carried

The major portion of newspaper advertising is *display* advertising; it starts on page 2 or 3 and runs on through most of the pages. *General* display is the advertising of national or sectional sellers, stressing product type and brand. *Retail* display is the advertising of local retail stores and hometown sellers of services, stressing where to buy. About 70 percent of advertising revenue comes from retail display. Classified ads represent about 23 percent of a newspaper's advertising, leaving 7 percent for "other" advertising. Classified ads are the so-called "want ads." When classified ads are dressed up a bit with borders, small illustrations, ornaments, or white space, they are called *classified display*.

In a recent year when newspaper advertising revenue totaled $5.6 billion, about $1 billion was for national advertising, $3 billion was for local, and $1.6 billion was for classified. Advertising revenue, incidentally, accounts for two thirds to three fourths of total newspaper revenue.

Position

Most advertisers buy space on an r.o.p. (run-of-paper) basis. Here the publisher puts the ad where he wants it. Special position can involve section, page, or position on page; it may cost a premium of 25 percent or more. Advertisers like "full" position. This is (1) top of column with reading matter along one side, or (2) reading matter on two sides. "Next-

FIGURE 8–1. Typical want ads

If he won't believe you about staying in school,

maybe he'll believe the want ads.

, uu Tremon.

resume in cc.

NATIONAL BUSINESS cc.
146 Oak St.

...ainees

Recent HS Grad

Learn all phases of credit-finance work.
Rapid advancement!
CARTER, INC.   7575 Front St.

TRAINEE HSG

Bright, able to make contact with
prospects. Some knol. Spanish
KNOCK AGENCY   420 Center

H

ies

Trainee Manager

TOP CO SEEKS BRIGHT HS GRAD
Multi-phase management training.
Fee paid.   CALL MISS LEE—785-4532
SHALEN AGENCY

TRAINEES   HS Grads C

Lrn textiles. F/Pd. ALL AGENCY. 956 B

State St.

) Sal

State St.

TRAINEE-CREDIT ASS

GOOD OPPTY FOR NITE STUD
Learn all phases of Credit. No
necessary. Good Bonus.
A-C-T-I-O-N AGENCY   85

TRAINEES TRAVEL CORP

Coll Grads

Excellent potential. Free travel.
J. V. Blair. ALLIANCE AGENCY. 673 Bway

DM
Fee pd.

Trainees-HSGs

w/wo Coll

Train personnel. Very good growth
B-O-S-S   156 Gre

1. Learn
s.
State St.

TRAINEES

INSURANCE

INVESTIGATORS

GOOD NEWS FOR RECENT GRADS!
This top National Co. Formerly Required

Trainee-Admin Assi

HSG preferr   Fee pa

ER

enefits.

They show people who quit high school average $45 a week less than people who finish.
Another fact: 7 out of 10 people looking for jobs are graduates. If your child isn't, he'll have that much more trouble getting a job in the first place.
So when he asks, "Why do I have to stay in school?" now you know what to answer.

Advertising contributed for the public good.

CONTINUE YOUR EDUCATION CAMPAIGN
Volunteer Agency: Ogilvy & Mather, Inc.   Volunteer Coordinator: Charles R. Corcoran, Commercial Communication Corporation

FIGURE 8–2. Newspaper advertising volume
(millions of dollars)

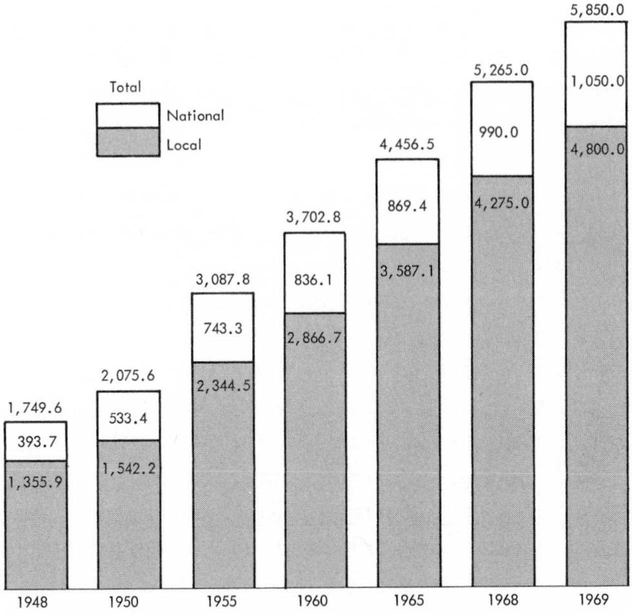

Source: *Advertising Age*, April 20, 1970. Data from Bureau of
Advertising, American Newspaper Publishers Assn.

to-reading" position also is desired; it provides reading material on one
side. Locations next to reading matter have higher visibility to readers.

Circulation

Newspaper circulation breaks down into three geographical areas.
"City Zone" is the corporate area plus continuing areas which overflow
the city limits and are similar to the city proper. "Trading Zone" sur-
rounds and extends farther out beyond the City Zone. These two zones
constitute the retail trading area of the market; consumers living within
this area normally buy shopping goods in the city where the newspaper
is published. "All Other" consists of those copies bought outside the
two zones.

Rate structure

Newspapers quote rates for (1) the agate line which, you remember,
is one column wide and $\frac{1}{14}$ inch deep, and (2) the column inch. If

the figure is "flat," no discounts can be earned by advertisers; if the newspaper observes a sliding scale, then discounts are offered. Such discounts may be based on the amount of space an advertiser buys or on the frequency of his ads. The discounts are applied to the "open" or "one-time" rate; this is the highest price quoted.

Typically, a newspaper quotes from a *general* rate card to manufacturers and regional advertisers of the nonretail type but from a *local* or *retail* rate card to local retailers. The general rate may be 60 percent higher than the local rate on weekdays—75 percent higher on Sunday. Why the differential? Most papers grant a 15 percent commission off the general rate to advertising agencies. Most pay a newspaper representative a commission for doing the space selling job in other markets, particularly the largest markets. Cash discounts are offered to general advertisers and to their advertising agencies. These three items may reduce the differential by as much as 25 percent. Market research and local merchandising (calls on retailers, installing store displays, etc.) may be demanded by general advertisers. Retail advertising, furthermore, is consistent and of large volume; it builds circulation and readership. Usually, the general advertiser feels that he is treated unfairly.

What about color advertising in newspapers? Advertisers can reach a large majority of ultimate consumers with color ads. Some advertisers use roll-fed preprinted ads (Hi-Fi, Spectacolor), some use the newspaper's

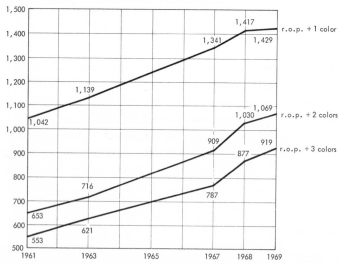

FIGURE 8–3. Papers offering r.o.p. color

Source: *Advertising Age*, April 20, 1970. Data from Research Department, Bureau of Advertising, ANPA.

r.o.p. color facilities. An r.o.p. page ad with full color costs about one third more than the same ad in black and white.

When comparing newspaper costs, advertisers usually use the *milline rate*. This figure is computed in this manner:

$$\frac{\text{Line rate} \times 1,000,000}{\text{Circulation}}$$

For example:

$$\frac{\$0.80 \times 1,000,000}{200,000} = \$4$$

A high milline rate may be explained by the newspaper's excellence, by the high incomes of its readers, or by the absence of competition.

MAGAZINES

Classification

Magazines, our second medium, can be classified on several bases, one which is *size*. The four most common sizes are:

Pocket—*Reader's Digest*   Flat—*New Yorker*
Standard—*National Geographic*   Large—*Life*

Frequency of publication is another basis; first is the monthly group, then come the weekly and biweekly groups.

Consumer magazines constitute a classification. Mass magazines such as *Reader's Digest* and *Life* contain articles, fiction, and features for the general public. Class magazines have smaller circulations because they are edited for homogeneous groups with more specialized interests; examples are: *Golf Digest, Modern Bride, Sports Illustrated, Playboy*.

Women, of course, are consumers, but even so, *women's* magazines are usually considered to be a group in their own right. Magazines such as *Ladies Home Journal, McCall's, Good Housekeeping, Glamour,* and *Seventeen* view women as (1) purchasing agents for their families and (2) individuals with personal problems and goals. Family, food, fashion, and fiction are typical of the types of editorial material included. *Woman's Day* and *Family Circle* are store distributed only; they have no subscription circulation, hence no subscription promotion expense and low distribution costs.

Business magazines are characterized by small, homogeneous circulations, very little waste circulation, rational and businesslike content, and low page rates. Each editor knows the readers he wants to reach; his editorial item is some variant of (1) how to increase sales or (2) how to cut costs. Some publications are vertical in character in that they are edited for various types of reader within a single industry; examples are: *National Petroleum News, Banking,* and *Power.* Horizontal business magazines appeal to one type of executive in many industries; examples

TABLE 8-3. Business press ad volume, 1945–1969

Year	Dollars	Pages
1969*	$811,800,000	1,213,000
1968	781,300,000	1,201,000
1967	760,000,000	1,219,000
1966	735,300,000	1,254,000
1965	682,400,000	1,205,000
1964	634,200,000	1,165,000
1963	593,700,000	1,160,000
1962	556,300,000	1,139,000
1961	538,600,000	1,160,000
1960	567,600,000	1,250,000
1955	416,000,000	1,177,000
1950	233,800,000	788,000
1945	178,400,000	1,101,000

*Estimated. Note: Dollar volume includes space costs only.

Source: American Business Press.

are: *Purchasing; Sales Management, The Marketing Magazine;* and *Advertising Age.* Some business magazine circulation is *controlled;* the copies are sent to a selected and controlled list of persons *free.*

Let's look briefly at some types of business magazines. *General* publications are horizontal and executive in character, edited for top management; *Business Week* and *Fortune* are examples. *Industrial* magazines are vertical, pointing out how to produce more and better products at lower costs; *Textile World* and *Coal Age* are typical. The *institutional* group is edited to help such institutions as hospitals, hotels, and schools toward better operaton; members of this group: *Hospital Management* and *American Hotel Journal.* The *merchandising* or *trade* group is concerned with the problems and practices of wholesalers and retailers. These middlemen buy as merchants when buying merchandise for resale, as purchasing agents when buying for business use. *Chain Store Age* and

Glass design by Donald Pollard • Engraving design by Alexander Seidel • Limited to an edition of ten • Height, including base, 15½ inches • $7,800.00

Spring Trilogy

Here, captured in crystal, is the spirit of spring. Three crystal leaves unfold, seeking the warmth of the sun.

Within each leaf is engraved a cluster of spring flowers.

On the center leaf, daffodils sway in the breeze, beckoning to a hovering bumble bee.

On the outer leaves are the other flowers of early spring, crocuses and snowdrops.

The crystal leaves are mounted on a curved base covered with spring-green silk.

STEUBEN GLASS

FIFTH AVENUE AT 56th STREET · NEW YORK · N.Y. 10022

FIGURE 8–4. Inclusion of price limits this ad to highly selective magazines

Progressive Grocer are examples. *Professional* magazines may seem out of place in a group of business publications. But, advertisers want to sell to and through such groups as architects and doctors; *Architectural Record* and the *American Journal of Medicine* are professional magazines. Finally, there is the *agricultural* group, publications which appeal to the farmer as a business man *and* as a consumer and family man; *The Poultryman* and *Nation's Agriculture* are examples.

Features

Magazines enjoy many characteristics of strength. One of the most outstanding of these is *selectivity*, achieved by the control of the nature of the editorial content. Each magazine is constructed to appeal to a similar group of readers. What about magazines with huge circulations such as *Reader's Digest* and *Life?* Their readers are above average in purchasing power and education. Magazines have *long life*, permitting leisurely reading, more than once, and by more readers than the original purchaser. Their paper, color, artwork, and typography add up to *impressive reproduction*. Many times, *retail enthusiasm* is generated by a manufacturer's advertising in magazines. Finally, readers respect and have *confidence* in magazines they read; they accept editorial content as authoritative and therefore believable. Editorial content, incidentally, occupies about 55 percent of a magazine's space. Readers are impressed by the authors who write for magazines, by the screening of ads magazines do, even by the cost per copy.

Infrequency of issue is one handicap of magazines; another is the inability of most editors to localize editorial content. Furthermore, any one magazine suffers from its quite limited reach or coverage within each geographical market; no magazine comes close to the newspaper coverage figure of 90 percent of U.S. families. Finally, there is a time disadvantage. Magazines have to "close" days and even weeks before publication date. Artwork and engravings may take even additional weeks. Because they cannot make changes after the closing date, advertisers feel some pressure to limit themselves to "safe" ads.

Advertising revenue is about 60 percent of total magazine revenue.

Position

The most expensive advertising page for most magazines is the outside back cover, the "fourth" cover. This page in four colors may cost twice

FIGURE 8–5. Why magazines sell

Authority	Magazine authority dates back to man's very acceptance of the printed word as dependable . . . to his own signature which is accepted as a binding pledge.
Color	Magazine color spreads before the reader a spectrum of exciting visual pleasure. Color stimulates interest . . . creates desire . . . enhances image . . . identifies the package. Color *sells*.
Believability	Magazine believability builds reader confidence. Its influence affects ideas . . . opinions . . . desires. People believe what magazines have to say.
Permanence	Magazines last. People save them . . . set them aside for future reference . . . return to them again and again. The permanence of magazines gives your advertising the time it needs for careful consideration . . . the time that it *deserves*.
Selectivity	Magazine selectivity targets places and people. It reaches your best prospects . . . wherever they are . . . while they are most receptive to ideas and information.
Flexibility	Magazines offer a full range of prospects . . . with divergent interests . . . in one or all of the nation's key markets. The degree to which an advertisement stimulates . . . dramatizes . . . *sells* products is entirely at the discretion of the advertiser.
Efficiency	The ability of magazines to offer the widest range of incomparable values which can be translated into dollar sales makes magazines the choice of leading advertisers.

Source: Magazine Advertising Bureau of Magazine Publishers, Inc., New York.

as much as an interior black-and-white page. The outside front cover is seldom offered to advertisers. The second and third covers, the inside front and the inside back covers, often cost more than interior pages and may be priced at approximately 80 percent of the fourth cover's rate. Many magazines demand that the three covers be done in four-color process. Desired pages not often premium priced are those facing the table of contents, facing the two inside covers, facing the pages in which letters to the editor or the lead editorial feature appear. The "Campbell

Soup" page, the first advertising page after the main editorial section, is another favorite; so named because Campbell Soup long ago recognized the desirability of this right-hand page and arranged to occupy it.

Circulation

A number of breakdowns of magazine circulation are worth our notice. One involves the difference between primary circulation and secondary. Primary circulation consists of the number of copies readers buy. This is a hard, specific, audited figure. Primary circulation is high in quality because the reader has the money to buy with and the willingness to exchange it for the magazine. A family may include two or more readers of high quality for the same copy. Secondary circulation is also called "readership" and "pass-along" circulation. Secondary circulation cannot be audited. Its quality is usually lower than that of primary circulation— the person involved either cannot afford the magazine, or his interest is not great enough to bring about a purchase. Reading magazines in waiting rooms, in a library, or in a friend's home are examples of secondary circulation.

Another circulation breakdown is that between the guaranteed figure and the delivered figure. A magazine guarantees to advertisers that it will sell a specific number of copies—200,000 or 2 million or 16 million. The 2 million, for example, is the figure that magazine feels safe to promise; normally the 2 million guarantee is *close to but under* the delivered figure, the number actually sold. If this magazine sold only 1,750,000, advertisers would get proportionate rebates. Should the actual sale be 2,150,000, advertisers get the 150,000 as a bonus. If the delivered quantity climbed to 2,400,000 and seemed likely to hold at about that level, the guaranteed figure might well be raised to 2,250,000 *and* advertising rates raised in proportion.

Still another breakdown depends on whether a magazine offers circulation only on a national, total basis or provides additional choices. The more common added option is regional circulation. Suppose a manufacturer has distribution in the South Atlantic states only. He is able to arrange with certain consumer magazines to have his ads included in those copies of the magazine which are distributed in the South Atlantic states. A regional issue, thus, is the national edition (editorial and advertising) plus regional ads. The region may be a metropolitan market, it may observe state lines, or it may be a marketing area which ignores state lines. Regional ads are 15 percent to 90 percent more expensive than nationally circulated ads. A second option is national circulation but at less than 100 percent intensity. A magazine with a circulation of 2 million, might allow a manufacturer to place his ad in every other copy; or, he might be allowed to place ad A in one half of the copies and ad B in the other half.

A final breakdown separates subscription circulation from single-copy circulation. Magazines with a high proportion of subscription circulation boast of their readers' purchasing power; of their willingness to buy a year's supply at one time; of rural as well as urban circulation. The other publications (movie, romance, television, etc.) point out that *their* readers can cast a negative vote every time a new issue appears on the newsstands by not buying it—but do not.

Rate structure

Magazines quote prices on covers, full pages, fractions of a page (half pages, quarter pages), and agate lines; all prices reflect the circulation guarantee mentioned earlier. Some offer "junior units," the only advertising space on an interior page but with editorial material above and along one side. For example, a full page ad in *McCall's* contains 680 lines, whereas the junior unit contains only 429 lines.

We have noted that covers usually cost extra. So does color; black plus three colors costs more than black plus one or black plus two colors. Bleed usually commands a premium, a bleed ad is one in which the illustration, type, or background continues in one or more directions through the margins to the binding or cut edge of the page. Inserts, too, cost the advertiser extra; these are ads or return mailing cards he has had printed on other than regular magazine paper stock. Inserts provide novelty, contrast, and impact; they can be used as mailings or for retail display.

Magazines do not have the general-local dual rate structure as do newspapers. Most *do* grant a 15 percent commission to recognized advertising agencies. Most offer two types of discounts. One, volume or quantity discounts, can be based on number of pages bought during a period of time, number of dollars spent, or size of individual ad in that a half page may cost 60 percent of what a full page costs. Another type of discount is based on frequency of insertion.

Cost comparison in the magazine medium is effected through the computation of *cost per black-and-white page per 1,000*. For example, *National Geographic*:

$$\frac{\$12,600}{3,000,000} = \$4.20 \text{ per } 1000$$

A high-cost/black-and-white page/1,000 figure may reflect large page size, high selectivity, outstanding prestige, or reader loyalty.

TELEVISION AND RADIO

Radio dominated the broadcasting world from 1925 to 1950; since 1950, radio has had to adapt its nature and role because of the growth of television. The two broadcast media have points of similarity as well as points of difference. Our pattern in this broadcast section will be to treat television first, then to follow with comments about radio when that seems indicated; these comments will point out how radio differs from television. Our first two media sold space, these two broadcast media sell time.

Classification

The great majority of our 800–900 television stations are VHF (very high frequency) and use channels 2–13. The small number of UHF (ultra

FIGURE 8–6. 1969 advertising volume of four major media (in millions)

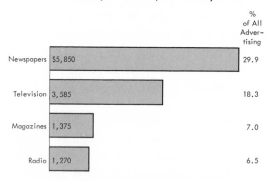

Newspaper figure includes $4,800 in local and $1,050 national. Television includes $1,675 network, $1,245 spot and $665 local. Magazines include $660 in weeklies, $310 in women's, $373 in monthlies and $32 farm. Radio includes $65 network, $370 spot and $835 local.

Source: *Advertising Age*, April 20, 1970. Data from McCann-Erickson; Bureau of Advertising, ANPA.

high frequency) stations use channels 14–83. Broadcast pictures are transmitted by AM (amplitude modulation) and broadcast sounds by FM
(frequency modulation). FM is clear and strong. Television sound usually
travels from the transmission tower to the horizon and no farther—about
50 or 60 miles. There are three prominent television networks, Columbia
Broadcasting System, National Broadcasting Company, and American
Broadcasting Company; each consists of over 200 stations. Over 95 percent of our homes have television receivers, a larger percent than have
telephones.

There are about 4,300 AM radio stations and about 2,100 FM stations.
Over 98 percent of all U.S. homes have at least one radio in working
order, and the typical household have five sets.

There are three types of AM stations. *Local* ones use up to 250 watts
of power. They reach the immediate vicinity up to about 25 miles, and
many broadcast during daytime hours only. *Regional* stations use up
to 5,000 watts and may reach as far as 65 miles away. They may cover
several states at night. *Clear channel* stations use up to 50,000 watts,
have the exclusive use of their respective frequencies during evening
hours, and cover large areas.

Cable antenna TV

Master antennas appeared in the early 1950's on mountains, high buildings, and high towers. Their jobs are to provide better reception and
wider choice to subscribers. Now urban as well as remote and rural,
cable antenna TV (CATV) carries signals (programs) by wire directly
into subscribers' homes.

Subscribers pay an initial hookup charge of about $10 plus a monthly
maintenance fee of about $6. One estimate is that there will be 28 million
CATV subscribers by 1980.

Large CATV companies originate live local programs. They create
and sell ads to local and regional sellers.

Cassette TV

At the time of this writing, there is much interest in video cassettes
or cartridges which can be inserted and "run" in home playback equipment. This frees the viewer from dependence on old TV and movie
programs. He can have, instead, control over what he watches; he can
have a communication center instead of just a TV set.

Rental films will present opera, sports events, and classic movies. They will provide entertainment, education, and instruction (cooking, sewing). Cassette TV seems to be a versatile tool for schools and for industry. Problems: the prices of playback equipment and the prices of the cassettes.

Features

Certain features are common to both radio and television. Stations are licensed by the Federal Communications Commission. Advertisers enjoy geographical selectivity and program selectivity. The programs or shows are the editorial part of the media. Both television and radio are intimate. Commercials do not compete directly with other commercials as do two or more ads on the same page of a newspaper or magazine. The entertainment and information consumers get from the media are

FIGURE 8–7. Radio's strength throughout the day (average quarter hour ratings Monday–Friday, 6:00 a.m.– midnight)

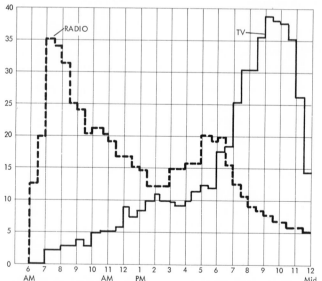

Recent all-media studies conducted by The Pulse, Inc., document that radio listening surpasses television viewing for two/thirds of the broadcast day. An illustration of radio's dominance is shown on the following chart based on persons 12+ from the Three-Stage All-Media Pulse Survey conducted in the New York area.

Source: Radio Advertising Bureau.

"free" in a way that the content of newspapers and of magazines are not free. Television and radio suffer from the fact that each day contains only 24 hours. Our four time zones and our institution of daylight saving time are common problems. Many persons accuse both media of over-commercialization. Broadcast advertising is neither physical nor lasting.

Certain features are peculiar to television only. Its sound, motion, color, and picture permit excellent product demonstration and oral persuasion. Television demands more of the consumer's attention than does radio. Because the nature of television makes it a medium for communicating to masses rather than to small groups, television must be classified as an expensive medium. On the average day television reaches 100 million U.S. consumers; the typical set is in use more than six hours a day. Product protection is a serious problem. The amount of protection provided to advertisers is determined by the length of the time period separating two competitive commercials—Coke from Pepsi, or Crest from Colgate. There is some resentment of the amount of clutter or "junk" at station breaks. Examples of clutter are commercials, credits, station identification, and promotions of other shows.

Radio, too, has some features of its own. Because it uses only the sense of hearing, radio is our sole nonvisual medium. Radio reaches a dispersed and fragmented audience, ranging from the transistorized teen-ager to the discriminating lover of FM music and drama. There are 325 million sets in homes, and 80 million in automobiles; over 90 percent of automobiles leave the factory radio-equipped. Most home radios are in bedrooms, kitchens, and living rooms, and often each member of the

FIGURE 8–8. Radio reaches women shoppers (special RAB retail survey)

Radio listening habits among women shoppers of major retail chain

Time spent with radio daily......................	3 hours: 38
Percent listening all seven days...................	59.0
Percent listening when traveling by car to shop at major retail chain........................	73.7

RAB sponsored a recent survey in two metropolitan markets to determine the radio listening habits among adult women shoppers of a major retail chain. Trendex, Inc., an independent research firm reported these results.

Source: Radio Advertising Bureau.

family owns one, making radio a personal, an individual medium. Because it can set up to communicate to small groups, radio permits specialization of stations, audiences, and even of commercials. Radio is more mobile and more modest in cost than is television. Above all, radio's words and sounds stimulate consumers' imagination and involvement; each consumer paints his own pictures, each "sees" what he wants to see.

Types of advertising

Three types of advertising are found in the broadcast media. *Local* is the same local as in newspapers; hometown retailers advertise over one of their broadcast stations. *Network* is carried on a program which originates in one station and is broadcast simultaneously by a number of stations; the advertiser sells over a large area. *Spot* advertising is sponsored by a national or a regional seller who buys time, market by market, from stations individually. The word *spot* in this context refers to a geographical concept in that the advertiser "spots" his advertising in the markets he chooses.

Sponsorship versus announcements

Advertisers in the broadcast media can sponsor programs which will carry their ads, or they can place those ads at station break time or on unsponsored programs. If the advertiser elects to be a sponsor, he has three options. Full sponsorship means just that—the one advertiser is the only seller using that show—*his* show. Or, he can join another advertiser in alternate week sponsorship; advertiser A alone sponsors the show this week, advertiser B is the sole sponsor next week. Or, third, A and B can be cosponsors, sharing the cost and the commercial time of each show. A variation of this third pattern sees four different advertisers each sponsoring a 15-minute segment of a one-hour show.

Sponsorship, particularly sole sponsorship, allows the advertiser some or complete selection and control of the vehicle, the show, which will carry his advertising. There can be tailoring and fitting of show to product. Prestige and sponsor identification can be built up in the minds of consumers *and* retailers. Popular programs are easily "sold" to a manufacturer's middleman and to his sales force as effective promotion. In television, many types of show are available: comedy, western, mystery, medical, quiz, sports, drama, news, and such. In radio, news, music, weather, and sports programs are prominent. The role of the program is to capture the audience to whom the advertiser wants to communicate. Audiences have two dimensions—*size* (how many) and *composition* (who are these viewers or listeners). Ideally, the audience would consist of every prospect for the advertised item. The "minus" feature of sponsorship, of course, is the high cost.

Since the appearance of commercial television, there has been a major move away from sponsorship and toward the "participation" type of program. The participation program is designed, controlled, and promoted by a station or a network. Its advertisers have no control over the nature of the show—and no responsibility for building its audience. Short commercial announcements are sold to advertisers, usually and largely noncompetitive advertisers, for broadcast during the show. Revenue from these sales is available to pay for the show's time and talent. Because this pattern is quite similar to that found in the magazine medium, it has been termed the *magazine concept* in broadcasting; the pattern is very common in radio. Announcements are flexible. They can be bought in substantial number even with a small advertising budget, and they are good for reminder use.

We have noted that the job of programs or shows is to capture the audiences advertisers want to influence. The responsibility of actually persuading and influencing, however, rests squarely on the commercial. As one advertising agency has observed, "The commercial is the payoff." In television, widely used time periods include: the 8-second I.D. (identification) which is part of station break time, 20-second, 30-second, and 60-second announcements. Some advertisers have experimented with television commercials shorter than 10 seconds and longer than 60 seconds. In radio, 30-second and 60-second announcements are the most popular.

Every broadcast commercial should be built on a big sales idea; its promise, as in newspaper and magazine ads, should be of some benefit or satisfaction buyers want. The commercial must get the immediate attention of those it hopes to influence and then follow through with a promise which is clear and instantly grasped. Commercials in both media can be quite entertaining.

Circulation

The broadcast media join the publication media in selling circulation—but with some basic differences. You may recall that newspapers and magazines sell *audited* circulation to advertisers. The implication is that newspapers and magazines can tell with precision how many copies they sell. This type of audited circulation is not possible in the two broadcast media.

Each television station, each radio station covers its own particular geographical area, and within each such area is a certain number of television sets or a certain number of radios. In a real sense, if a certain television station covers an area in which there are 500,000 television sets, that station's maximum *potential* circulation or audience consists of the viewing group owning and/or looking at those 500,000 sets. Note that the more basic figure refers to *television receivers*, not to individual

FIGURE 8–9. Hours or TV viewing per TV household per week (December, 1969)

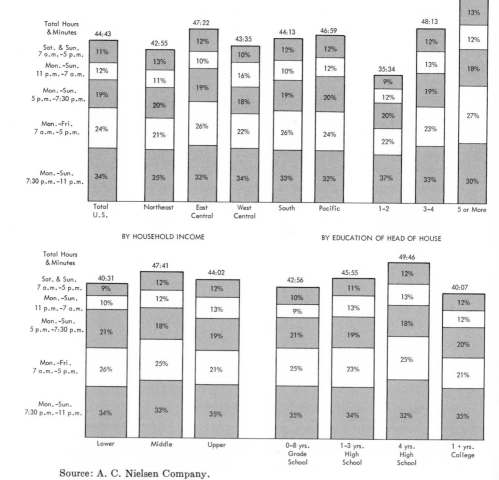

Source: A. C. Nielsen Company.

consumers. *Actual* circulation or audience consists of those persons who do view a show or a commercial announcement, and this is much under the influence of programming. From the point of view of a 30-minute show, for example, this influence involves the day of the week, what show preceded this one on the same station, what show will follow, the nature of the show we are interested in, and shows that compete simultaneously with it.

Because there is no practicable method of auditing the use of all of the 500,000 sets mentioned, measurement of circulation must depend on the use of a sample. Suppose a sound sample is established consisting of 100 sets. Once again, refer to our 30-minute show. There are approaches (to be described shortly) to the determination of how many sets were in use during that 30-minute period, the percent of the total sample viewing *all* shows during that time interval. The next refinement is to establish *our* program's rating, that is, the percent of the total sample viewing our program. The final step is to compute share of audience. This is done by dividing our show's rating by the percentage of sets in the sample tuned into any program. For example, assume that 60 (60 percent) of our 100 sets are in use. Then assume that 30 of the 100 sets comprising our sample are tuned to our show; 30 percent is our rating. Thirty percent divided by 60 percent gives us a 50 percent share of the audience—the percent of all operating sets tuned to our show. For the 500,000 total, 300,000 sets were in use, 150,000 of which were tuned to our show.

What methods are used to measure broadcast audience samples? One, the electronic recorder, takes two forms. One is a small gadget attached to the sample sets which makes a record on film of the minute-by-minute operation of the set; it reports when the set was on and to which channel it was tuned. It does not tell who *if anyone* was really watching; indeed, maybe no one was even in the house. This gadget is independent of the telephone and therefore rural as well as nontelephone houses can be included in the sample. The other type of electronic device gives instantaneous ratings. A central installation might be connected to a sample of sets in a market—Philadelphia, for example. At any moment, inspection of the central board can tell which of the sample sets is on and to what channel it is tuned.

A second technique relies on telephone interviews. Coincidental calls are made to a sample of telephone users who are asked if their set is on at the moment and, if so, what program is being seen or heard. This method is quick and modest in cost; it involves no memory factor.

Nontelephone homes are automatically excluded from the samples; calls are practicable only between 8 a.m. and 10 p.m.

A third possibility is the personal interview. Consumers making up the sample are shown this morning a list of programs broadcast locally last night and are asked to identify those programs viewed. The accuracy of the responses depends on respondent's memory and honesty. This is an urban-only technique.

Finally, there is the diary method, in which viewers and listeners log their viewing and listening and periodically mail in their diaries. Samples can be sound (nontelephone, rural, etc.), and the method is relatively inexpensive; there is, of course, the problem of the human factor.

Automobile radio listening is difficult to measure accurately. The extent of listening and viewing in public places is also difficult to determine. The portable transistor receiver poses still another problem in the attempt to measure broadcast circulation.

Rate structure

Broadcast stations start designing their rate structures by classifying the hours and days of the week into classes of equal quality and desirability. Here is the grouping made by one television station:

Viewing hours and days	Desirability (percent)	Class
7:30 to 10:30 p.m., Sunday through Saturday	100	A
6:00 to 7:30 p.m., Sunday through Saturday and 10:30 to 11:00 p.m., Sunday through Saturday	80	B
5:00 to 6:00 p.m., Monday through Saturday and 12 noon to 6:00 p.m., Sunday	60	C
9:00 a.m. to 5:00 p.m., Monday through Saturday 9:00 a.m. to 12 noon, Sunday and 11:00 p.m. to sign-off, Sunday through Saturday	45	D
Sign-on to 9:00 a.m., Sunday through Saturday	25	E

Because television siphons away from radio as the afternoon moves on toward evening, some radio stations quote only a single rate for their entire broadcast day.

There is a built-in type of quantity discount in this station's prices for time periods of different length regardless of class:

1 hour................	100%
½ hour................	60
¼ hour................	40
10 minutes.............	35
5 minutes.............	30

A similar differential pattern is common in radio for program time and for announcement time.

Most stations offer frequency discounts based on the number of programs or commercial announcements bought during a period of time. A 15 percent commission off the general rate to advertising agencies is common. Not all stations have a general-local rate differential. Because viewing is down approximately 30 percent in the summer, some television stations have summer season rates which are somewhat lower than winter season rates.

Although ratings are not as scientific as the broadcast industry and advertisers would like, they are essential if there is to be a "cost-per-1,000" figure, a figure wanted by all concerned. In television there is not a single cost per 1,000—there are two. One is cost per 1,000 homes reached. Often the "cost" figure selected for use here is the station's highest price for one hour of time. Suppose this figure is $1,000, total television homes in the station's coverage area number 500,000, and average number of homes reached is 30 percent or 150,000. Then:

$$\frac{\$1,000}{150,000} \times 1,000 \text{ homes} = \$6.66 \text{ per 1,000 homes}$$

The other cost computation is for cost per 1,000 homes per commercial minute. Suppose a 30-minute show contains three 60-second announcements, costs $120,000, and reaches 10 million homes; each commercial minute costs $40,000. Then:

$$\frac{\$40,000}{10,000,000} \times 1,000 \text{ homes} = \$4 \text{ per 1,000 homes}$$

As ratings rise, so does the total cost of the show. This is similar to a magazine's raising its page rate as circulation rises.

OUTDOOR

Classification

Important types of outdoor advertising are posters, painted displays, and spectaculars, sometimes referred to as the print, the paint, and the electric segments of the medium. An outdoor advertising *plant* consists almost entirely of the firm's physical properties. Its big asset? The sites on which it has outdoor advertising structures—panels for posters, bulletins and walls for painted ads, and the framework and illumination which at night become electric spectaculars.

Posters.   A poster results from the gluing of pieces of paper onto a panel or frame 12 feet high and 25 feet wide. Most important in size is the 24-sheet poster. Once upon a time, 24 separate sheets were glued on, but today that figure is 10 or 12. Other sizes frequently seen are the 30-, the 6-, and the 3-sheet poster. Panels are located on streets and roads with considerable traffic, in retail centers, and in downtown locations. Regular posters tell their story from about 6 A.M. to 6 P.M.; illuminated posters are those with enough 6 P.M. to 12 midnight traffic to justify their being equipped with lights. Manufacturers usually change their posters every 30 days; retailers change theirs less often.

Painted displays.   Some of these are on the walls of buildings. Others are painted bulletins made of wood or sheet metal. Bulletins range from 12 feet to 18 feet in height and from 40 feet to 72 feet in width. They are located in cities, in suburbs, on highways, along railroads. Some painted bulletins feature "embellishments" such as clocks, thermometers, irregular borders, and three dimensions. In some markets, a rotary pattern is available; a bulletin might be in the northeast quarter of the market for a period of time, then be moved physically to another frame or structure in the northwest quarter for a period of time, and so on. Ads on walls and bulletins are hand painted; some are illuminated.

Electric spectaculars.   These are the fabled and fabulous signs which have made Broadway and Times Square "The Great White Way." They are unique because of size, color, motion, animation, and bright lights. Spectaculars are custom built; their high costs demand locations where sidewalk and street traffic are heavy.

Features

Outdoor is truly a mass medium, posters alone reaching about 93 percent of the total population aged 15 or over of any metropolitan area. It is low in economic and social selectivity within a market, somewhat resembling newspapers in this regard. Essentially, outdoor is an immobile medium, communicating only to consumers who come to its fixed location. Copy must be brief, and there is no editorial matter to support those brief messages. Furthermore, the outdoor ad battles many distractions and much competition for consumers' attention. Its long life permits repeated exposures; posters in some markets reach 94 percent of automobile-owning households an average of 21 times a month. Outdoor can be used both nationally and locally; about 70 percent of the money spent annually for outdoor advertising is spent by national advertisers.

Circulation

The big concept in outdoor circulation is the total number of potential exposures as determined by a traffic count. *Gross* circulation is the total number of persons passing the ad. *Effective* circulation for posters is arrived at by refining gross circulation; pedestrian and automobile counts are reduced by 50 percent, bus and streetcar counts by 75 percent. The aim, obviously, is to include in effective circulation only those consumers moving toward the poster who can, without strain, see it. The quality of a poster panel location is determined by these visibility factors: length of approach in seconds, speed of travel, angle of panel, nearness of other panels, and distance of location off to the side of line of travel. The outdoor medium boasts of its almost complete coverage of all age, income, occupational, and educational groups.

Rate structure

Picture the owner of an advertising plant who goes into a market in which there is no outdoor advertising. He leases or buys the positions or sites he wants for poster panels which he is able to lease and buy. Suppose he ends up with 350 poster panels. His next job is to group these into "showings." Perhaps he establishes 15 No. 100 showings each consisting of 20 panels, 10 illuminated and 10 unilluminated. Then he designates 5 No. 50 showings, each consisting of 5 illuminated and 5 unilluminated. He now has 20 units to lease to advertisers. All 15 No. 100 showings are equal in circulation, effectiveness, and cost; the same holds for the five No. 50 showings. The No. 100 intensity provides thorough coverage of the market; it provides adequate representation and repetition in the market. The plant owner, in effect, assures advertisers that each of his No. 100 showings will reach all consumers moving about outside during the posting period; this is 30 days. No. 50 showings are about one half as intense as No. 100 showings. Here are three examples of No. 100 showings:

	Unilluminated	Illuminated	Cost/Month
Atlanta..........	36	44	$5,200
Syracuse.........	16	16	1,600
Gary............	10	6	852

Painted bulletins are bought unit by unit. Contracts can be for one year or more, and cost may run several hundred dollars per month per bulletin.

Electric spectaculars, too, are bought unit by unit. Contracts run three years or longer, and cost may be $10,000 per month or more.

There is no general/local rate differential in the outdoor medium. There is a 16⅔ percent commission to advertising agencies. Agencies use the extra 1⅔ percent to help finance the operation of a single organization through which an advertising agency can place advertising with the 800–1,000 individual outdoor advertising companies in the country.

Size of market has considerable influence on cost per 1,000 circulation. The range may be from a low of 15 cents per 1,000 in our largest markets to $1.50 per 1,000 in our smaller markets.

TRANSIT

Classification

The three main versions of transit advertising are located in and on the vehicles and stations of our public transportation systems. *Inside space* is dominated by the car card. *Outside space* is dominated by the bus poster. *Station posters* are available in and on some stations and terminals, including airports. Outside space accounts for well over one half of the money advertisers spend annually in the medium. The general/local split is close to 50–50.

Inside space. Busses and streetcars—elevated, subway, and suburban trains carry car cards. Popular sizes are 11 by 28 inches, 11 by 42 inches, and 11 by 56 inches. Three intensities are available: *full service* or *run* calls for one card in each vehicle. *Medium* service or run calls for one card in one half of the vehicles. *Low* service calls for one card in one fourth of the vehicles. Because New York subway cars are long and have three to six doors, the number of car cards is doubled in each intensity; two cards per subway car, one card per subway car, one card in every other car. An advertiser's cards are so placed in the vehicles as to equalize, to average out, position value; each advertiser gets locations above average, average, and below average.

Outside space. Bus posters are the large signs on the outside of busses and streetcars, on their fronts, sides, and rears. Perhaps bus posters can be considered cousins of outdoor posters. The King Size bus poster is 30 by 144 inches, the Queen Size is 30 by 88 inches, the Traveling Display is 21 by 44 inches, and Front End and Rear End Displays come in other sizes. Bus posters are sold on a unit basis *and* on a showing basis.

In some markets the buses have backlighted "busoramas" on the rooftops of vehicle extensions. Approximately 21×144 inches, these run the length of the bus over the windows.

Station posters. These ads are typically seen on the platforms of subway and elevated stations in four markets: New York, Chicago, Boston, and Philadelphia. They are sold by unit *or* by showing; their circulation is the same as for car cards.

Merchandising bus. The merchandising bus is a mobile promotional vehicle available to advertisers in transit markets for special merchandising programs. In conjunction with a major scheduled advertising campaign, a regular transit vehicle is chartered. The bus is carded completely, inside and out, with the advertiser's message. Special horizontal fittings placed over seats convert the bus interior into a traveling exhibit for product displays and promotion. The mobile showcase is brought directly to the door of the key retailer or wholesaler. Retailers, wholesalers, or consumers, depending on the promotional objectives, are invited aboard the bus. Sales presentations about products and services can be presented to audiences in a dramatic setting with maximum concentration, free of ordinary distractions.

Features

Transit advertising is a by-product of, and an activity unrelated to, public transportation. This is a mass medium, one low in qualitative selectivity of consumers; the breadth of its audience is indicated in that

TABLE 8–4. CPM impressions (300 king size bus posters, Boston market—4 counties)

Audience	Base	Reach 2 Weeks	Fre- quency 4 Weeks	Impressions (reach only)	Total impressions 4 Weeks	Cost 28 days	CPM impres- sions
Total men............	1,052,217	84%	16x	883,862	14,141,792	$10,200	$ .72
Total women.........	1,073,473	81%	12x	869,513	10,558,730	10,200	.97
Total adults.........	2,125,690	83%	14x	1,753,375*	24,700,522*	10,200	.41
Total teen boys.......	134,244	86%	16x	115,450	1,847,200		
+ Total men.........					14,141,792		
					15,988,992	10,200	.64
Total teen girls.......	142,548	85%	12x	121,165	1,446,662		
+ Total women.......					10,558,730		
					12,005,352	10,200	.85
Total teens..........	276,792	85%	14x	235,273	3,293,822		
+ Total adults.......					24,700,522		
					27,994,344	10,200	.36

*Total men and women added instead of fractionating percentages.
Source: Metro Transit Advertising, division of Metromedia.

it sells 10 billion rides a year. Even though available in almost 400 markets, transit still must be recognized to be an urban medium. Readership of car cards is encouraged by the length of the average ride—25 minutes; readership is also encouraged by the amount of repeat exposure. One study showed that the typical rider was exposed to subway advertising 40 times in a month; another finding was that 8.5 million persons ride public transportation vehicles to and from work regularly. Communication is "out of the house," and this can be quite an advantage.

Circulation

Who sees transit advertising? The great majority of our basic consumer population. For inside space and for station posters, each rider is one unit of circulation. The month is the circulation time unit, circulation being expressed as number of riders per month. Approximately 40 million persons ride transit vehicles each month. Quality of rider circulation ranges from medium to high. For outside space, circulation consists of just about everybody in transit system markets. A fairly recent approach to measuring the circulation of bus posters makes use of a camera mounted just over the King Size poster. This device records on a sample basis the consumers who were able to see the King Size poster.

Rate structure

We have noted that car cards are sold by service or run, that bus posters and station posters are sold by unit or by showing. Because the display period is one month, rates are quoted for the month. Usually the more months an advertiser buys, the lower the monthly cost. There is no general/local rate differential.

Here are two examples of cost computations. Full service in Atlanta calls for car cards in 450 busses. Spaces for 450 cards of 11 by 28 inch size costs $675 for 30 days. Riders per month totaled 5,581,759, working out to be 12 cents per 1,000. In another market, the bus poster researched was the King Size poster. Cost per 1,000 potential exposures was less than 6 cents.

QUESTIONS AND PROBLEMS

8-1. Is newsstand circulation of magazines more valuable to advertisers than subscription circulation? Explain.

8-2. Compare TV advertising with door-to-door selling.

8-3. If you were selling space in a consumer magazine what are some of the points you would stress and features you would emphasize to the prospective advertiser?

8-4. List some of the more common goals or objectives of ads in business magazines.

8-5. Argue that outdoor advertising is a supporting rather than a primary medium.

8-6. List some matters you think sellers should consider when deciding which of the six advertising media to use.

8-7. Suggest some of the strengths of Sunday newspaper magazine supplements.

8-8. Point out the basic differences between consumer magazines and business magazines.

8-9. Contrast the features of outdoor advertising with those of transit advertising.

8-10. Why do retailers put most of their ad dollars into the newspaper medium?

CHAPTER 9

Advertising management

C<small>HAPTERS</small> 7 <small>AND</small> 8 have looked at advertising as persuasive communication and at the media which carry ads to buyers and buying influences. This final chapter of Part IV deals with the management of advertising. The following sections take up (1) the advertising manager and his department, (2) the advertising campaign concept, (3) media strategy, (4) budgeting, (5) the role of advertising agencies, and (6) the relationship between clients and their agencies.

THE ADVERTISING DEPARTMENT

The title of the head of the advertising department is usually that of advertising manager. In some firms he is a top marketing executive; in others he is little more than a clerk or a stooge. In more and more of our larger firms he is being accepted as a member of the top executive echelon. In many small firms he reports to the sales manager; in larger companies he often joins the sales manager, the sales promotion manager, and the marketing research director in reporting to a vice president in charge of marketing. The competent advertising manager is able in both areas, the advertising area and the management area; he needs to be a promotion man—even a marketing man.

In the area of advertising, the advertising manager recommends policies and strategy. He drafts and submits an advertising budget and the program it will finance. He serves as the liaison between his own company and its advertising agency or agencies. He stays abreast of advertising developments. He contributes to the imaginative, the productive, use of advertising by his firm. He tries to measure just what his firm got for the advertising dollars it spent.

In the management area the advertising manager plans, staffs, organizes, and controls as must all managers. He administers his advertising department because he is its head and because he has line authority over it. He helps set the advertising goals and objectives of his firm. He "sells" his recommendations and the worthwhileness of his plans to top management, of which, hopefully, he is a member. He represents his firm in advertising circles and organizations.

Advertising departments range from one person to scores of persons. This wide range in personnel reflects a broad range in the responsibilities and functions assigned to advertising departments; it does *not* reflect range in the size of advertising budgets. The following types of internal organization are found within advertising departments: (1) The department may be organized by subfunction (copy, media, etc.). (2) It may be organized by media (consumer media, business publications, etc.). (3) The organization may be along product lines (paint, chemicals, etc.). (4) It may reflect the different types of buyer or end user (purchasing agents, consumers, etc.). (5) Finally, the organization may be geographical (domestic, foreign, etc.).

Where is the advertising department found in company organizations? In single-division firms the advertising manager reports to the top executive, to the top marketing executive, or to the top sales executive. In multidivision firms, three patterns are found. In one, the advertising department is a centralized unit in the home office. Or, there is complete decentralization—each division has its own advertising department. Finally, a firm can have divisional advertising departments *plus* a central advertising unit in the home office.

There is considerable variety among the job assignments made to advertising departments. This may be explained by the fact that some manufacturers have sales promotion departments—others do not; some have public relations departments—others do not; some use advertising agencies—some do not; some do for themselves what others buy from outside firms. For the manufacturing concern with a sales promotion department or a public relations department, the advertising department is usually asked to create some advertising or at least some ads, to do certain types of marketing research, to keep records, to check the appearance of ads and approve payment for them, and to keep in touch with such outside companies as media, customers, various types of suppliers, and advertising agencies.

What about *retail* advertisers? In small firms, the owner-manager is ad manager just as he is credit manager, personnel manager, and so on. Often this contributes to unplanned, weak advertising. In the large firms, there may be a complete department staffed by specialists in copy, art-work, layout, typography, and media. The head of this ad department and his counterpart, the display director, may report to the sales promotion manager.

ADVERTISING CAMPAIGN CONCEPT

Much national or general advertising, particularly that done by manu-facturers of consumer products, consists of campaigns. An advertising campaign is made up of a series of ads, a planned, organized, unified series. Although each ad is complete and independent, the group of ads is featured by psychological continuity and even physical and intended resemblance. The campaign has one theme, basic idea, or promise. Its short-run goal is usually to increase awareness and to affect attitudes, but the long-run goal is practically always a sales goal. Some campaigns run only a few days, some a few weeks, some extend throughout a season, some run for the entire year. A few campaigns make use of only one type of media, but most use more than one type.

We now look briefly at three types of advertising campaigns. The first and most common type is the *product campaign* which promotes some brand of product or service. The heart of such a campaign, indeed, the core of each ad in the series is the promise of some benefit or satisfac-tion which buyers want. Sometimes this promise is called the campaign's theme, sometimes its keynote idea. By concentrating on this theme, by respecting it as a track or guide, the advertiser unifies his campaign; in addition, communication to buyers is more successful. Here are exam-ples of campaign themes:

Breck promises Beautiful Hair
Ivory promises That Ivory Look
Longines promises the World's Most Honored Watch

Should each campaign have its own slogan? Not necessarily. If the advertiser chooses, he can express the campaign theme in slogan form. Once in a long while, a slogan catches on so well that the advertiser

Everybody's in bed and I'll be soon, but not yet, because
the bath is so soothing and I can relax and . . .

This...is the L&M moment.

The time to take things easy and
really enjoy the rich flavor of L&M.
See for yourself. When you're
ready to unwind, light up an L&M.
Any place.
RICH, RICH L&M

19 mg. "tar", 1.3 mg. nicotine
av. per cigarette by FTC method. (Jan. '71).

FIGURES 9–1 and 9–2. Only two ads are needed to sense the campaign theme
and to note ad similarity

Saturday morning is the supermarket and car
wash and laundry and noisy crowds and
finally, it's time to relax, and...

This...is the L&M moment.

A time for you to take it easy...
and enjoy a whole new cigarette.
New L&M. With a rich new blend
and rich new flavor. Share the
pleasure, share the moment... now.
NEW, RICH L&M

publicizes it campaign after campaign, year after year; "It floats" is such a slogan.

The good slogan is short, simple, clear, catchy, easy to remember, and easy to repeat. Its substance is some buyer benefit or satisfaction. Puns, plays on words, rhyming, rhythm, and balance can be built nicely into slogans. Always to be remembered is the fact that a slogan is a deftly turned phrase intended to be repeated verbatim.

A second type is the *institutional campaign*, sometimes called the corporate campaign, occasionally the strategic campaign. This type of campaign promotes the advertiser or the advertising firm—not its product or service. Institutional campaigns are quite appropriate for services (insurance, transportation) and for products the quality and value of which are difficult for buyers to determine.

The objective of most institutional campaigns is to cultivate and stimulate patronage. This may be attempted by highlighting the firm's policies, facilities, history, personnel, size, or reputation. A smaller number of institutional campaigns have public relations objectives. Here the institution hopes to build up goodwill with one or more of its "publics." Strikes, and the threat of hostile legislation may create circumstances in which public relations institutional campaigns might be effective.

A third type is the *horizontal cooperative campaign*. Most of these are sponsored by groups of competitors, often through their trade associations. The advertisers may be manufacturers (glass containers), sellers of services (banks), growers (oranges), or retailers (shopping center). Horizontal cooperative campaigns seek to stimulate primary demand for the product or service. They do not promote brands; indeed, brand names are seldom if ever mentioned. So, these efforts are closer kin to institutional than to brand-promoting campaigns. Typically, the horizontal cooperative campaign intends to inform, to educate, to justify, to explain—occasionally to deny.

Several serious problems are found in the area of horizontal cooperative campaigns. An early one is that of recognizing the presence and the nature of a problem, a need, or an opportunity confronting the group of competitors. Another big job is that of enlisting the support of all (or certainly *most*) of the members of the group, then of holding it. Still another problem is that of devising an acceptable basis for raising the advertising fund. Each firm tends to favor a levy which hits him light and others heavy. Getting group approval of advertising strategy and tactics is not always easy. The same is true of getting the group to stay together and support the effort as long as it should be extended.

Finally, unless there is strong and capable leadership within the group, the campaign will probably do less than hoped.

Manufacturers of industrial products can run ad campaigns for promotional purposes. Typical campaign objectives: to upgrade brand image; to reach buyers and buying influences who seldom or even never "see" salesmen; to launch a new product; to locate prospects by inviting inquiries from them; and, of course, to hold or increase share of market. The promises on which industrial campaigns are built are usually of a rational nature.

The campaign concept and actual campaigns are not common in retailers' advertising. Instead, the retailer tends to promote his store and his merchandise much the same month after month, making no clear breaks or drastic changes. The merchant needs store traffic, and he can use advertising to stimulate it. His ads may promote merchandise at regular prices, or at reduced prices, or at sharply reduced, clearance prices.

MEDIA STRATEGY

Campaigns must be scheduled to appear in one or more of the six advertising media mentioned in the preceding chapter. The scheduling we have in mind is done within the calendar year. Its strategy involves *to whom* the advertiser should communicate and *when* or *how often* he should communicate. First we look at the major considerations influencing media strategy—then we examine briefly the variables of scheduling, namely, *reach* and *frequency*.

Considerations in media strategy

The nature of the product or service to be advertised is a basic influence in the selection of those media which should be used to carry the advertiser's messages. For example, the need for excellent color reproduction may make magazines the best choice. If package identification is important, then outdoor and transit are appropriate. When a retailer advertises a high-priced product usually bought only after family consultation, the Sunday newspaper comes to mind. Feminine products of a personal, intimate nature are more at home in magazines than on television, though they are beginning to appear on TV too. Most retail assortments are too wide for the use of radio except as a supplementary, supporting medium.

254 Promotion: Persuasive communication in marketing

The nature of the message is an influence. The transit medium is good for messages that benefit from repeated exposure—that need strong memory impact—that can communicate mainly with color and illustrations instead of words. If the operation of a product is to be demonstrated, television is usually superior to radio. If the message is newsy, radio is more appropriate than magazines. Outdoor is fine for reminder copy and humorous treatment but not suitable for long copy.

The characteristics of the market are basic considerations. The advertiser properly asks, "Who are the buyers and buying influences I want to reach? Where are they?" Patently, each advertiser must make contact with *his* intended audience or group. Equipment and supplies bought by farmers are not advertised in the transit medium, an urban medium. Three-sheet posters are good for smaller retailers located in secondary shopping districts. If purchasing agents constitute the advertiser's market, then daily newspapers are hardly an ideal medium. Television can be used by retailers to reach schoolchildren on Saturday morning. Car cards are appropriate for items which have markets of wide, general consumption.

By now, one has already inferred that circulation is a most basic consideration in media strategy. In a real sense, what a medium sells, what an advertiser buys, is circulation. The advertiser's two interests are in *who* constitutes the circulation of a medium (this is essentially a matter of quality) and *how many* they number (obviously a matter of quantity). The advertiser starts by defining or describing the group he needs and intends to reach. Then, for each medium entitled to his consideration, he tries to determine how many members of his group it will reach. The more nearly a medium's circulation and the advertiser's group of buyers and buying influences are the same, the more attractive that medium is to that advertiser.

Editorial quality is a consideration. If its circulation was achieved through excellence of editorial or program content rather than through price cutting, and if reader confidence and loyalty are high, then the medium is even more attractive. The editorial images of certain media recommend that certain advertisers use those media, that other advertisers not use them.

Still another interest of the advertiser is in the identity of the advertisers who place their ads in the media under consideration. Editorial content influences a medium's image, *and* the advertising it carries also shapes that image. The typical advertiser is understandably curious about the media strategy and choices of his competitors.

Finally, there is the most basic consideration of cost. Because space and time costs take the lion's share of most advertising budgets, media decisions and budget decisions are closely related. Media decisions affect the budget—the size of the budget acts as a limitation on the range of media the advertiser can consider buying.

Now for the variables of reach and frequency.

Reach

Reach is coverage. Reach is the number of buyers and buying influences (or the number of households in the broadcast media) "reached" during a certain period of time. In many instances, reach is the total number of persons who saw or heard an ad at least once during a month.

Reach or coverage strategy involves two big decisions: (1) which *types* of media to use, and (2) which *individual* media to use within the types chosen. As to types, we looked in the preceding chapter at the features of the two publication media, the two broadcast media, at outdoor, and at transit. The only point to make here is that cost comparisons between any two types of media is a most unscientific undertaking. Which is worth more to a manufacturer of soap or food—(1) a housewife's seeing and reading a one-page magazine ad containing 150 words of copy, or (2) that same housewife's "receiving" completely a 60-second television commercial for the same brand? *How much more* is the better communication worth? How smart would the manufacturer be to schedule *both* ads for the same week? There are news stories and case histories of advertisers who drop out of one type of medium for an indefinite period of time; other advertisers return to one type after an absence of years. These patterns are disturbing because they imply that advertisers cannot prove that their media of the moment are the best for that moment. Related and equally disturbing is the advertiser's haunting uncertainty about just how many housewives really read his magazine ad—about just how many really saw and heard his television commercial.

Having decided which type or types of media to buy, the advertiser next must select the individual, the specific, media to buy within that type or those types. In this phase, for example, he compares the images, the circulations, the costs of *Time* versus *Newsweek*, of *The New York Times* versus the *New York News*. He wonders how many magazines are too large a group to buy, how many are too few. If he buys *many* magazines, some consumers will see the same ad in, say, both *Time* and *Life;* in addition, his advertising effort will be relatively thin, and/or his ads will be small, and/or his campaigns will be short, and/or his advertising fund will have to be huge. He instantly sees that a full-page newspaper ad has more reach than a quarter-page ad, that the back cover of a magazine has more reach than an interior page; *but*, he remembers that they cost considerably more, too. Which for him is the better buy? That is a difficult, often an impossible, question to answer.

Before selecting individual, specific media, the advertiser needs information about them, information for which there are various sources. One course of action is for the advertiser to inspect, examine, and analyze a copy of a newspaper or magazine—to listen to and view what is broadcast over stations under consideration. Each medium is a source of data about itself; its salesmen, its own ads, its rate cards, its promotional literature all can supply facts. The media representatives who sell space and time for their clients are another source. The Standard Rate and Data Service compiles much statistical information about newspapers, business publications, television, radio, transit, consumer magazines, and farm publications. Each of the six types of media has an active trade association which collects and disseminates information. Special reports can be secured from commercial research firms.

Frequency

The second scheduling variable, frequency, has a short-run dimension and a long-run dimension. Whereas reach asked how many buyers and buying influences—or how many households—were "reached" during a month, short-run frequency asks *how many times* on the average were they reached during the month. Within the campaign period, short-run frequency is basically a matter of how many ads the advertiser runs per day, per week, per month. As we noted, the fewer the media, the smaller the ads, the shorter the campaign, or the larger the advertising fund, the higher the frequency can be. Some scheduling is even—ads of the same size and the same interval. Some scheduling is alternating—big ad, small ad, big ad, small ad. Then there is the buildup pattern—ads increase in size and appear at shorter intervals. Finally, there is the step-down pattern, the reverse of the buildup pattern.

Long-run frequency is a matter of regularity, of continuity. For example, picture an advertiser using television for 39 weeks in the year but not using the medium during the 13 weeks of summer. How close together his ads are during the 39 weeks is a matter of short-run frequency; the fact that he disappears from the medium for one quarter of the year is a matter of longer-run frequency. Should he stay out of television for five years, that would be long run.

Conclusions

At some point in time, each advertiser must approve an advertising schedule. Its elements are:

List of publications, broadcast stations, markets

Dates of appearance of ads

Sizes and types of ads (space, time, color)

Cost

In a very real sense, every schedule is a compromise involving reach, frequency, and budget. The more reach the advertiser buys, the less frequent his ads; and the closer scheduled his ads, the less his reach. The only other option? More budget. Much more needs to be learned about what compromises are best.

BUDGETING

In taking up budgeting, we first need to clear up some terminology. An advertising *appropriation* is properly thought of as a lump sum, a total dollar figure for the year. In contrast, an advertising *budget* is a broken down, detailed schedule of advertising expenditures planned to be made during the year. As such, the budget is a managerial tool to be used in the future as a *plan* for company advertising and as a *control of* that advertising.

Normally, the advertising budget is drafted in the advertising department and presented to top management by the advertising manager. When the final program has been approved, it is turned over to the advertising manager for administration. As weeks and months pass, he checks the advertising done against the advertising planned as he controls and directs the advertising his firm does.

As to location, the budget is one item in the promotion budget or, as it is sometimes called, the market stimulation budget; the other items making up this promotion budget are the sales budget and the sales promotion budget. The marketing management budget plus the market stimulation budget make up the total marketing budget. Because advertising is a promotional force, the advertising budget is closely related to the firm's first and most basic budget, the net sales forecast.

Expense classification

Before any dollar figure can be considered to be the appropriate amount to be spent for advertising, each advertiser must classify his expenses and decide what are proper charges against his advertising budget. Each advertiser must do this for himself because the cost accounting of advertising has not become standardized. Nor are organization charts uniform; a firm with a sales promotion department which has its own budget may well charge fewer items against its advertising budget than it otherwise would.

What *are* proper charges against the advertising budget? Most advertisers agree that media costs, the costs of space and time, should be charged to advertising; these items often take 80 percent of the budget. Production costs are proper charges—photographs, drawings, engravings, typography. Five percent of the budget may go for production costs. Administrative overhead should be charged against the advertising budget. This includes such items as advertising department salaries, rent, and travel. A figure of 15 percent is not out of line for administrative overhead.

Research is a moot item. Some firms charge certain types of research against the advertising budget; others centralize all marketing research in a marketing research department, the head of which reports to a vice president in charge of marketing. An advertising reserve is another moot item. Some retailers determine what they expect to spend during the coming year, then add an arbitrary 10 percent as a reserve which will be available for unforeseen problems and opportunities.

Approaches

Ideally, the advertiser would set the size of his advertising fund at that point where the last dollar included in the amount would just equal the profit from the sales produced by that dollar. That last dollar is the "break-even" dollar in that it just replaces itself; it neither increases nor decreases profit. If the advertiser spent less, his net profit would be less than possible; if he spent more, the same would be true. This marginal concept is useful even though advertisers do not think or decide in terms of just one dollar.

Now we look at the percent-of-sales approach, the task approach, and at certain approach considerations.

Percent-of-sales approach. Here the advertiser starts with his sales forecast for the next year. Then he settles on a factor or a multiplier, maybe 2 percent, maybe 4 percent; he may use his industry percentage, or he may use the figure he has been using. He multiplies the sales forecast by the percent, and the result is the advertising fund for next year. Suppose he forecasts sales of $3 million and settles on 3 percent; $90,000 is the portion of next year's sales to be spent in advertising.

A variation on the percent-of-sales, called the fixed-sum-per-unit-of-product approach, uses a product unit base rather than a dollar base. A manufacturer forecasts the sale of 500,000 appliances next year; he asks each unit to contribute $5 to the advertising fund; his advertising fund amounts to $2.5 million.

Each type of multiplier (3 percent, $5) varies from industry to industry, from company to company within an industry. Each type can be changed at any time, even annually, but in actual operation, change is infrequent.

The approach is simple and speedy; it gives the appearance of control. Furthermore, every seller does or should reduce each expense item to a percent of net sales. Otherwise comparisons are more difficult.

There are, however, actual and potential weaknesses in this approach. The advertiser is tempted to take the multiplier from his best past year's operations and stay with it. Or, he could adopt the "common" figure of firms of similar size and type; often this is the industry figure. The approach encourages the spending of exactly that amount, although conditions may call for more *or* less. Normal development is for advertising cost per unit of output to decline; this approach works against such development. Its reasoning that advertising results from sales is backwards—the reverse is true. It has little to offer to new firms or new brands. Above all, it neither recognizes *need* as the proper determinant of the size of the fund nor does it adjust for *differences* among sellers and sales territories.

Task approach. The task approach, too, has as its first step the setting of next year's sales forecast. In step two the advertiser outlines advertising's role and responsibility—its task—in achieving that sales volume. Picture, for example, a manufacturer of consumer products whose promotional mix includes personal selling, advertising, and sales promotion. In step two he asks, "How much will I rely on advertising next year to help me 'make' forecast? *What amount* of advertising and of *what type* will I need."

Step two is most difficult because precision is impossible. There can be no specific, concise answer to the question which asks how much advertising should be done next year to help the firm sell next year's sales forecast. Perhaps two, three, or four tentative programs are roughed out, each of which *might* discharge advertising's responsibility, each of which *might* result in advertising's making its proper contribution to the firm's making its forecast.

In step three the advertiser prices the programs worth his consideration. He compares their costs against their respective promises of success. In a final move he selects the program which seems most desirable. Its cost is the ad budget for next year; it represents advertising's share of the firm's cost of capturing the sales volume adopted as next year's forecast.

The task approach attempts to match the advertising fund to the advertising job. It hopes by letting the advertiser's *needs* determine the amount to avoid spending too much or too little. There is no addiction to or worship of past ratios. There is encouragement of bold, creative thinking. There is the recognition that advertising causes sales.

The task approach, however, is as difficult as it is respectable. It demands research, analysis, and sound forecasting. In step two there is heavy reliance on judgment. Once again we are reminded of the most unsatisfactory, most challenging feature of all advertising—the advertiser's inability to measure what his ads do to his sales volume. Even so, the task approach is the logical, the potentially soundest approach.

Budget approach considerations

The first of four budget approach considerations relates to the least amount of advertising a seller should run. There is some volume, some tonnage, some magnitude which is the minimum an advertiser should do. Below the minimum level, advertising may be largely ineffective. Can you think of any advertiser who should buy one or two ads in *Life* during the year—or one who should buy one radio commercial a month?

The second consideration involves the firm's financial condition. No firm can spend dollars it does not have. True as this is, the approach that asks how much a company can afford to spend for advertising can easily lead to spending that is too conservative. For new companies, the advertising fund may be limited to the amount of money remaining after other expenses have been paid. For a new product entering an established market, the costs of launching the new product may actually result in losses during the first year or two. Thus the firm must be prepared to spend the number of promotion dollars necessary to accomplish the launching and plan its financial affairs to provide for the early losses which it hopes will be repaid in future profits once the product captures a satisfactory share of the market.

Then, third, there is the matter of competitors' advertising. Advertisers try to keep tab on what their competitors are doing, including what they are doing in advertising. A large portion of many advertising budgets is defensive in nature; advertiser A advertises in large part because competitors B, C, and D do so. Advertiser A may elect to match one of them *or* to spend more than one of them. If advertiser A has a 15 percent share of the market, he may try to spend in advertising 15 percent of what his industry (A plus his competitors) spends. One is entitled to question the logic of one firm's adopting the policy of matching the advertising fund of some other firm.

Fourth, management's attitude toward advertising ranges from hostile to friendly. Occasionally the top executive (*not* the advertising manager) looks on advertising as an unavoidable luxury to be tightly restrained. Sometimes he has little confidence in advertising but still is afraid to discontinue it. He may be *the* man in a one-man operation and make entirely too many decisions, including how much to spend for advertising. His whim is not a sound basis for setting the size of the advertising fund. In contrast are the executives who are convinced from experience that advertising can increase sales and profits.

Administering the budget

Most advertising budgets are set up to cover the calendar year. They should be compared month by month with the advertising the firm actually did. The monthly review makes for prompt revision when such must be made.

The budget poses fewer administrative problems if well allocated along the following bases. It must be earmarked by *sales territory* for reasons of control and suitability. It must be broken down by *media type and specific medium*. For manufacturers, the budget must be allocated by *product;* for retailers it must be allocated by *department*. The budget must be scheduled by *time period*—by month, by week, by day. It must be assigned among the approved advertising *expense items*. Finally, if the seller will be sponsoring different types of advertising next year (product promoting, institutional, horizontal cooperative) each *separate advertising effort* must have its own allocation.

What should be done about the business cycle? Most advertisers spend freely when times are good but retrench when times are bad. They will probably continue to follow this pattern. A reasonable assumption is that when times get bad, some sellers should increase their advertising, some should make no change, some should cut back. Every seller should always be striving toward *his* best promotional mix or program, whatever the stage of the business cycle.

NATURE AND ROLE OF ADVERTISING AGENCIES

What agencies are

An advertising agency is a business firm; its business is advertising, and advertising is a business. The agency is built around a group of specialists, advertising specialists in every case, other specialists (marketing, merchandising, communication, public relations, etc.) also in some cases. Employees may number one or two persons—one thousand or two thousand persons; customers served may total one or two advertisers—one hundred to two hundred advertisers. Most large agencies are in large cities; many have branches, both domestic and foreign.

The agency's customers are sellers who advertise, and they are referred to as *clients* and also as *accounts*. There is nothing unusual about an agency's having 10, 15, or 25 accounts. All of an agency's clients together may spend under $1 million during a year—or over $500 million. This dollar amount is the "billings" figure; it is the amount the advertising agency bills its accounts for—it is the amount they pay to their agency. Agency size is *not* based on number of employees or number of clients; it *is* based on billings.

What agencies do

In a short sentence, advertising agencies plan, prepare, and place advertising for clients. In several sentences, they create advertising plans for and recommend advertising programs to clients. Then they build and schedule the individual ads. Next they contract in their own names for space and time in the six advertising media. Remaining is the actual placement of the ads in the media bought.

The major job of an advertising agency by far is the creation of effective *general* or *national* advertising. Thus the agency works mainly for noncompeting manufacturers and for noncompeting sellers of services who market and advertise over a wide area, often all 50 states, even internationally. Most of that advertising is directed at ultimate consumers.

Most of it interprets the advantages, the benefits, the satisfactions of a client's product or service to consumers. To do this effectively, the agency must be informed on these matters: advertiser's product or service; prospective buyers of that product or service; advertiser's competition; distribution channels; and advertising media.

Origin and development

The earliest version of today's advertising agency appeared about 1840. The first firms were brokers and wholesalers of out-of-town newspaper space to makers of consumer products. Gradually the agency began to do more in its efforts to sign up advertising customers and soon found itself building ads. It abandoned space wholesaling and operated only as a selling agent for media.

The next development found agencies operating as *buyers* of space rather than *sellers*, identifying and aligning with the advertiser rather than with the medium. What did that do to the aggressive selling of space then, and of space and time today? A type of selling firm appeared usually called a media representative. One such firm may represent a group of noncompetitive newspapers or radio stations. Its salesmen call mainly on manufacturers and on their advertising agencies, recommending and "selling" the use of its group of media.

More recently we have seen the "marketing" agency appear. The narrow advertising agency builds and places ads for its advertising clients. The broader marketing agency performs a wide range of marketing and management services and offers marketing and management counsel to its advertising clients *and* to other companies. The appearance of the marketing agency coincided with the appearance and the adoption of the "marketing concept" which, essentially, sees the selling firm as being completely customer oriented. Marketing agencies engage in such activities as:

Public relations	Dealer promotional programs
Marketing research	Direct-mail promotion
Publicity	Point-of-purchase promotion
Product and package design	International marketing
Sales promotion	Promotional literature
Sales training	Brand name selection
Merchandising	

Departments and services

Certain departments, functions, and/or services are almost universal in that they are customarily found in any advertising agency. Here are brief comments on each.

Copy. The heart of an agency consists of its *copy, art,* and *media* departments. *Copy* and *art* build the ads, copy and art are the ads; *media* carry the ads to buyers and to buying influences. In the great majority of ads, copy is the element which does or fails to influence and persuade.

Art. Personnel in the *art* department visualize what elements an ad should contain, they arrange those elements in an effective, pleasing layout; they decide about illustration. *Art* and *copy* are thought of as the agency's *creative* departments.

Media. This department analyzes and evaluates, it selects and schedules, it negotiates and buys space and time. The *media* staff often works closely with the *research* department.

Television-radio. These broadcast media were the last of the six advertising media to appear. Because they are so different from the older media, they are often grouped together in a separate department. Broadcast personnel may buy time, may build commercials, may recommend shows to clients.

Mechanical production. Persons in this department are concerned with print media only. They deal with and buy from such firms as typesetters, printers, and photoengravers. Their job is to arrange for the printing of printed ads, to transform layout, copy, and illustrations into printed ads.

Traffic. Responsibility for seeing that work flows as it should, that deadlines are made, is assigned to the traffic department. It schedules and controls the preparation, the processing, and the progress of an ad through the agency.

Accounting. As do all firms, agencies too must have their *accounting* departments. These are similar to any accounting departments. They are staffed with accountants rather than with advertising men, and they check the appearance of clients' ads, pay the media, and bill clients.

Research. This department does exactly what its name implies. It is responsible for researching all facets of advertising, with particular emphasis on buyers, products, competition, markets, and ads. Sound research helps get, serve, hold, and expand the advertising of clients. Typically, the agency will do some research and will buy some from commercial research firms.

FIGURE 9–3.   Typical organization chart for large advertising agencies

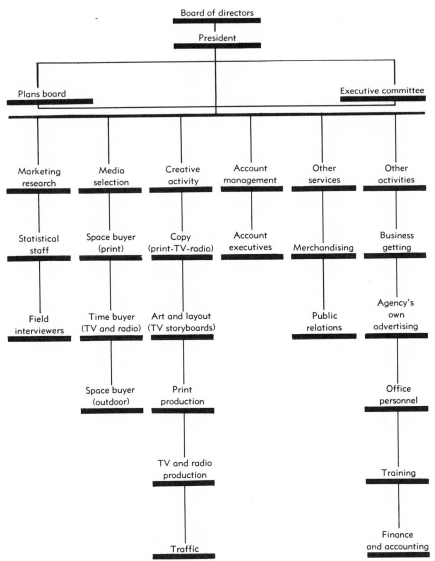

Source: American Association of Advertising Agencies

Account management. Here we have a service or a function rather than a department. When an agency acquires a new client, provision must be made for looking after, for serving, for working with that client. So, a person is assigned to that account and the account is assigned to him. This person is called an *account representative*, an *account executive*, or a *contact man.* He provides liaison between agency and client, representing each to the other. He is to see that the agency produces effective advertising for the client. He is determined to hold the account—he is hopeful of expanding it by getting its advertising budget increased. An account representative may have only one account, he may have more than one.

New business. Advertising agencies grow if they sign up new clients, if present clients spend more in advertising, or if the agency begins to offer additional services for a price. The *new business* activity (it may or may not be located in a separate *new business* department) is concerned with the first of those three—with capturing new clients. Thus the new business department in an advertising agency corresponds roughly to a client's *sales* department. It selects the prospects to woo, it tries to win them over into becoming clients. Even agencies which advertise lean much more heavily on personal, face-to-face solicitation to land new clients. When it has no new business department, the agency must depend on its top executives and on its account representatives to do the selling job.

Once in a while a manufacturer will insist that the advertising agencies he is considering make "speculative presentations" on which he will base his selection. Such a presentation consists of an advertising plan and schedule, sample ads, and sometimes the marketing research findings on which plan, schedule, and ads were based. Speculative presentations costing as much as $30,000 are rumored. Some agencies refuse to make these, arguing understandably that no outside agency has adequate information on which to build satisfactory plans and ads.

Other functions. Some agencies make special provision for such matters as *personnel, training, office management, finance, legal,* and *international.* The broad range of services found in marketing agencies has already been indicated.

Agency compensation

Recognition. Any treatment of how advertising agencies generate revenue or income from the sale of their services must start with a look at *agency recognition.* Each medium (newspaper, magazine, TV station, radio station, outdoor advertising plant owner, transit advertising firm) "recognizes" those agencies it judges to be entitled to recognition. Three features of considerable influence on the medium's decision are an agency's competence, its capital, and its clients. Each medium offers a functional discount, usually referred to as a commission, to the agencies it recognizes. The Curtis Publishing Company established its recognition policy back in 1901. It offered a 15 percent commission to recognized agencies only. From that time, most manufacturers advertising in Curtis magazines have felt that the only sensible course of action is to advertise through recognized agencies. Thus, recognized agencies get a commission on the advertising space and time they buy for their clients, a commission which cannot be earned by advertisers. The usual commission is 15 percent in the five other advertising media, 16⅔ percent in outdoor.

Types of agency revenue. For decades, ever since advertising agencies switched from buyers of space to sellers of space, the *media commission* just referred to has been the major type of revenue for practically all agencies. Here is how the commission arrangement works in the magazine medium: A page is listed at $10,000 on the magazine rate card. This is what a manufacturer would have to pay if he bought direct, because he is not offered the commission the magazine grants to recognized agencies. The magazine charges such agencies $10,000 less 15 percent; this amounts to $8,500. Usually the magazine offers a 2 percent cash discount for prompt payment—$170. So, the agency which pays promptly pays $8,500 less $170 or $8,330. The agency offers its clients $170 for prompt payment; it receives from the advertising manufacturer $10,000 less $170 or $9,830. When we subtract the $8,330 the agency pays the magazine from the $9,830 the agency gets from the client, the amount is $1,500 or 15 percent of $10,000. This $1,500 is gross revenue for the advertising agency.

A second type of agency revenue consists of fees charged to and paid by clients. One possibility is for the agency to operate 100 percent on a fee basis, performing all basic advertising agency services for each client in return for a predetermined fee. Here media commissions are credited to each client's account. This fee arrangement is common in industrial advertising. Because circulation is low in business publications, page rates, also, are low—too low to produce adequate revenue for the agency. Fifteen percent of $500 is only $75, and that is not enough revenue to the agency for building a full-page ad. In recent years the number of accounts handled completely on a fee basis has been growing; so, fee revenue, though still minor, has been growing as a percent of advertising agency revenue. A second possibility is for the agency to do some specific service for a client in return for a fee. Such a service might involve doing a client's direct-mail promotion, his point-of-purchase promotion, his publicity, or some market research job for him.

A third type of agency revenue consists of service charges paid by clients. Suppose the agency hires an artist to do an illustration for a client's ad and the artist charges $1,000. The agency commonly would bill the client $1,000 plus 15 percent or $1,000 plus 17⅔ percent. Why the 17⅔ percent? A thousand dollars plus $176.50 equals $1,176.50 and 15 percent of $1,176.50 approximates $176.50.

How agencies earn commissions. Why do advertising media pay advertising agencies to build ads for clients? For several sound reasons. The agency functions as a sales representative for media in that the agency "sells" sellers on the idea of advertising. The agency furnishes media complete and finished ads built by specialists; agency-built ads are presumed to be superior to media-built ads and to advertiser-built ads. Because agencies work up advertising schedules for and with their clients, media are relieved of that chore and expense. Because they can deal with advertising agencies, media deal with fewer firms, they have fewer accounts receivable, they incur lower production costs, they enjoy lower credit costs. Interestingly, each advertising agency and it alone is responsible for paying for the space and time its clients use. Should the agency not pay, the medium cannot look to the advertiser for payment. So, the medium keeps posted on the advertising agency's credit standing—the agency keeps posted on its clients' credit standing.

Trade associations

The American Association of Advertising Agencies was formed in 1917 and is national in membership. The AAAA includes most agencies of medium and large size; its members place about 75 percent of all national advertising. The association works to accomplish the following:

Protect, strengthen, and improve the advertising agency business
Help its members operate more profitably
Further the cause of advertising as a whole
Raise the quality of advertising content
Improve the public's image of advertising.

A second type of association is the advertising agency network. More than 200 agencies belong to one of seven national networks. These agencies are independent; they are not large. They work for a strong network organization and for uniform operation in the hope that individual members will be successful in signing up large national advertisers as clients. They pool their brains and efforts to solve common problems. At meetings they exchange advertising ideas, experiences, methods, policies, and procedures. They discuss agency management, services, and costs. Each offers to serve as a branch office of the other members.

WORKING WITH ADVERTISING AGENCIES

Why manufacturers use agencies

Normally, the larger manufacturers of consumer products will do some consumer advertising and will employ one or more advertising agencies to handle that advertising.

There are *advertising* reasons for this use of agencies. The client gets expert, tailored, well-built advertising because the typical advertising agent is a specialist in creating and scheduling ads which will influence and persuade. The client gets the experience, the talents, and the know-how of individuals such as he does not have within his own organization; the agency can employ and pay high salaries to those individuals because they work for a *number* of clients. Then the client gets the accumulated wisdom of a firm which usually has worked with a large assortment of advertisers, with a diversity of products and services, with all media, in many markets, and with a wide range of promotional problems and goals. Finally, the client gets an outside, objective point of view; he buys outside advertising service in the same way he buys outside accounting, public relations, legal, and research services.

There are *cost* reasons for this use. We have noted that the manufacturer must pay the full media rates regardless. If he does not employ an advertising agency, he must pay full media rates, *plus* the cost of creating and placing his advertising. For manufacturer-agency operation to cost as much as manufacturer-plus-advertising-facilities operation is virtually impossible. In many cases, commissions granted to advertising agencies cover completely the cost of an agency's advertising service for a client.

Selecting the agency

Selection factors. When an advertiser undertakes to select an advertising agency, he first identifies those with adequate facilities to handle his account satisfactorily and to provide the services he wants. Next he looks for agencies which are suitable and appropriate for him. These two features may involve geographical proximity, personnel, absence of competing accounts, size, or policies. The advertiser investigates agency management, wanting its caliber to be high; he is interested in top management *and* in the individuals who will handle his account. The advertiser compares the records of the agencies still in the running, records with previous and with present clients, records of demonstrated creativity and imagination. Finally, certain advertisers insist that the agency eventually chosen have had experience with this type of product or service—automobile, food, banking, transportation.

Use of two or more agencies. Large and diversified manufacturers of consumer products are more likely to use two or more advertising agencies than are small, single-brand manufacturers. Why the use of more than one agency? Some advertisers feel that each agency serves as a yardstick or standard by which the performance of the other(s) can be measured. Then, perhaps each agency tries harder, wanting the business it is not now getting. An advertiser may like to know that two or more sets of brains rather than one are working on his problems. Our very largest advertisers may feel that their advertising funds are just too large to be turned over to a single agency.

Several bases are available on which to set up a multiagency pattern. Product or product line is one. Geography is another. Media is a third. Advertising agency specialization is a fourth. Finally, one type of campaign (product, perhaps) can be placed in one agency while another type of campaign (corporate, perhaps) is placed in a different agency.

For example, at one time the agency picture of Procter & Gamble, our largest national advertiser, was as shown in the table below.

Agency	Account
Benton & Bowles	Crest, Ivory Snow
Leo Burnett Co	Camay, Lilt
Compton	Tide, Gleem
Cunningham & Walsh	Folgers
Dancer-Fitzgerald-Sample	Dreft, Radar
Grey Advertising	Jif, Duz
Honig-Cooper & Harrington	Clorox
Papert, Koenig, Lois	Salvo, Dash
Tatham-Laird & Kudner	Mr. Clean, Bold
Young & Rubicam	Cheer, corporate advertising

Client-agency relations

Few manufacturers of consumer products ever take the position that they will have an advertising department headed by an advertising manager *or* employ the service of an advertising agency. The "either one or the other" concept is unrealistic. The manufacturer usually has his own advertising department *and* uses agency service. His advertising department and the advertising agency work together closely; the relationship is complementary, not mutually exclusive. In an extremely abbreviated way, we can think of a manufacturer as a specialist in making soap and of the advertising agency he uses as a specialist in creating advertising which will help create customers for that soap.

The relationship has been correctly compared to marriage in that the advertiser-agency compact should not be undertaken lightly. There will be a great amount of unavoidable "togetherness" between client and agency. This calls for much cooperation, for much give and take. When he makes his final decision and selects, the advertiser assumes a lengthy association. Indeed, when making his selection, one of the advertiser's most fervent hopes is for mutual confidence and compatibility over the long run. Both parties must be willing to adjust and compromise up to a point. Each must work for a growing understanding of the other, for a relationship characterized by mutuality and reciprocity. Each must expect legitimate differences of opinion about many matters, including the quality and effectiveness of the advertising the agency builds. As with marriage, change and replacement can be quite expensive.

The advertiser owes quite a bit to his agency. He owes the cooperation found only in a real, genuine partnership. He should meddle little or not at all in the agency's operations and do little or no changing of the ads his agency builds. The agency should be able to count on getting adequate information and data from the client, and the client must go as far as he dares in making confidential information available to his agency. The advertiser, of course, is wary about turning over confidential information because of the ever present possibility that the two will part company—that the agency may drop the advertiser and go to work with and for a competitor or that the advertiser may decide to switch agencies. The advertiser must expect his agency to make money on the account. He must let the agency know that it enjoys security so long as it deserves security. Finally, the advertiser must be patient, especially during the first two years of the relationship.

Switching agencies

Causes of turnover. Many times each year headlines in advertising publications scream the news that a certain manufacturer has switched his account from agency A and has placed it with agency B. Less often the headline reports that agency C notified client D that C was resigning account D, forcing D to select a new agency. To fire and replace an advertising agency—to resign an account—both are relatively easy to do. The client-agency turnover rate must be described as high rather than low. Why is it high?

A most weighty consideration is the impossibility of determining just how good or how bad an ad really was. To measure the effectiveness of the typical ad with precision simply is not possible; no yardstick or scale has been perfected which will do this. A magazine ad or a TV commercial may cost $20,000. That cost figure can be determined with satisfactory accuracy. But the other figure needed is entirely too elusive. That other figure is the sales volume produced or caused by that particular ad. For example, just how many tubes of toothpaste did that last Crest ad on the back cover of McCall's sell? Whenever a manufacturer's sales volume, share of market, or profits drop, he is apt to think that weak advertising was a cause, maybe a major cause, maybe *the* cause.

There are, of course, other causes of advertiser-agency changes. Sometimes the agency concludes that the account will never become profitable. Sometimes the agency can sign up a larger, competing account if it resigns a present account. Occasionally a manufacturer wants to begin using a medium with which his present agency is not experienced or wants service the present agency does not offer. Personality clashes and a basic disagreement about policies or strategy can cause a switch; so can personnel changes in either firm. Unreasonableness, client interference, agency neglect, and loss of confidence in the other are additional explanations.

When the client-agency relationship is so unhappy that a parting of the ways is imminent, harsh accusations are often hurled by each party at the other. The client complains about weak advertising, unqualified personnel on his account, agency indifference, general incompetence, waste, excessive charges, and poor service. The agency counters with comments about unprofitability of account, unreasonable demands of the advertiser, incompatibility, serious and continuing disagreement, politics, nepotism, slow pay, too little cooperation but too much interference.

On occasion, an agency has probably been made a sacrificial goat when some client had erred. All this back-and-forth bickering clearly points up the need for a technique which will measure what an ad does to sales volume.

Costs of changing agencies. When an advertiser and his advertising agency part company, costs of various sorts are almost inevitable, costs which can add up to a considerable amount. The advertiser loses the know-how, the marketing information, and the experience on his account of the agency fired. That agency patently had logged enough time to learn something about the advertiser, his product, his competition, and about working with that one advertiser. Usually the client and the agency have gone through a shakedown period and smoothed off some rough corners. The advertiser incurs certain costs when he surveys the field and selects his new agency. While this is going on, there is usually a period of interruption, of uncertainty, of waiting, of diminished effort, of reduced momentum. Then, the new agency must have time to learn what its predecessor had to have time to learn—about the client firm, its personnel, its policies, its problems. Even then, only with the passage of time does the new agency pick up speed and become fully productive.

House agencies. The question sometimes arises as to why a manufacturer does not set up his own advertising agency, staff it with his own personnel, build his own ads, and thus qualify for commissions from media. The attraction of these "house" agencies is essentially financial; there are the media commissions, and there is the hope that the manufacturer's staff can build good ads cheaper than an independent agency could.

Only a very, *very* few manufacturers operate house agencies. Why? Such an agency's experience is narrow rather than broad and varied; that is bad. It has an inside point of view, not outside. Inbreeding is a real danger which could result in ineffective advertising. Normally, the manufacturer cannot budget as much money for staff, including specialists, as can a large independent agency. The personnel of the house agency can hardly feel the keen competition and the heavy pressure to please the client that regular agencies feel. One wonders if the head of a house agency can maintain his independence and retain his integrity—or whether he must be a "yes-man." Finally, the manufacturer has less flexibility, maneuverability, and leverage in that he cannot abolish one of his own departments, and that's what his house agency actually is, as easily as he can fire an independent advertising agency.

QUESTIONS AND PROBLEMS

9–1. What factors does a manufacturer consider when selecting media to carry his ads?

9–2. What factors influence the length of a campaign?

9–3. Advertising agencies sell creativity and imagination. What can they do to increase the number of new ideas they will have?

9–4. Comment on a manufacturer's repeating one or more ads during a campaign.

9–5. List some internal and some external influences or developments that could cause changes in ad plans.

9–6. On what grounds might a manufacturer fire his ad agency?

9–7. What matters do you think should be included in a full-term course entitled Advertising Management?

9–8. A maker of a line of consumer products is thinking about changing advertising agencies. What agency factors or considerations should he check?

9–9. What are some of the more common objectives of advertising campaigns?

9–10. What are some of the advantages and disadvantages of small ads?

PART V

ELEMENTS OF
PERSUASION:
SALES PROMOTION

Stimulating manufacturers' salesmen and retailers

P_{ART} V treats *sales promotion*, an area consisting of all sales stimulants and promotional communication not classified as personal selling or as advertising. Chapter 10 examines how a manufacturer can use sales promotion materials, activities, and methods to generate enthusiasm in, and increase the sales productivity of, his salesmen and the retailers who handle his line of products. Chapter 11 describes how the manufacturer uses sales promotion techniques to stimulate the demand of ultimate consumers and to help them to be better buyers and consumers.

The concept of sales promotion as an area, as an element in the promotional program, is much more recent than the two concepts of personal selling and advertising. Even today the term *sales promotion* has different meanings for different persons. Clearly, sales promotion activities are far less unified, more heterogeneous than is true of personal selling or advertising. Quite a few of these activities are either nonrecurrent or noncontinuous. A salesman usually communicates with a single buyer; an ad typically communicates to a mass of buyers; much sales promotion is aimed at small or middle-sized groups most of which are rather clearly defined and homogeneous. The American Marketing Association defines sales promotion as consisting of those "Marketing activities, other than personal selling, advertising, and publicity, that stimulate consumer purchasing and dealer effectiveness, such as display, shows and exhibitions, demonstrations, and various non-recurrent selling efforts not in the ordinary routine." In the AMA view, sales promotion supplements both personal selling and advertising, coordinates them, and helps make them more effective. Thus the sales promotion manager works for himself *and* for and with the sales manager and the advertising manager.

And that, of course, raises the question of the location of sales promotion responsibility and activities within the manufacturer's organization and elsewhere. One pattern calls for a separate sales promotion department—manager, staff, and budget. In certain firms, the sales promotion budget is approximately one half the size of the advertising budget. A second pattern provides for no separate sales promotion department but assigns some activities (and budget) to the advertising manager and some to the sales manager. A third possibility is a combination department; it might be headed by an advertising and sales promotion manager—or by a sales and sales promotion manager. Other patterns involve outside firms. A manufacturer's advertising agency may have a sales promotion or merchandising department and participate, on a "free" basis or for a fee. Sometimes media join the manufacturer in sales promotion activities. Recently, specialized sales promotion agencies have appeared. Clearly, sales promotion activities and their handling are more important than an organization chart; sales promotion as a program is more important than sales promotion as a department.

Here are examples of purposes or objectives of sales promotion activities as they affect a manufacturer's salesmen and retailers.

Train salesmen to make better sales presentations.
Design and administer sales incentive plans.
Build sales manuals and advertising portfolios.
Generate more interest and "push."
Encourage retailers to do a better job.
Counsel and advise on retail management problems.
Add more retail distribution.
Reinforce the entire promotional effort.

TRAINING AND EQUIPPING MANUFACTURERS' SALESMEN

In some firms, the sales promotion staff trains and equips the sales force. Sales training programs, methods, and manuals may be the creations of that staff. The sales promotion manager may be responsible for building the sales presentations salesmen are expected to master and use. Long-range training as well as introductory training may be his responsibility. Sales training is recognized early in this chapter because the training a salesman gets has great influence on how effective he will be in his basic and important role of stimulating the manufacturer's retailers.

Sales promotion personnel may equip company salesmen with the selling tools needed. Examples are advertising portfolios, demonstration items, visual aids, samples, models, photographs, charts, graphs, slides, and movies.

CONTESTS AND INCENTIVE CAMPAIGNS FOR MANUFACTURERS' SALESMEN

These two types of stimulants may be a sales promotion responsibility. In *contests,* the salesmen compete against each other for a fixed number of prizes. In *incentive campaigns,* each salesman essentially competes against his own past; each salesman's performance and production determine (1) whether he gets a prize and (2) if so, the type of prize. "A" performance gets him one of the top prizes; "B" performance is rewarded with a second-class prize. In incentive campaigns the number of "A" prizes awarded is not set in advance; it is determined by and is equal to the number of salesmen who earn them. A manufacturer may schedule one, two, or three of these stimulants a year. Each may run for one, two, or three months. Less than one month is too short—more than three months is too long. A theme must be selected, forms and records designed, and promotion of the competition planned. Prizes can be tangible (cash, merchandise, travel) or intangible (honor award, recognition, publicity). The method of earning points must be simple, clear, and fair. Dollar sales volume is one base, but, here the star salesmen almost always win. Another base for points is percent of sales increase, but this permits lazy salesmen to bestir themselves enough to win—then revert to sloth. A third base is the sales-to-quota ratio. A final possibility is to credit salesmen with points for stipulated acts or achievements. A salesman's points can be exchanged for prizes, often pictured in a catalog which contains not only personal items but also merchandise for the wife, the children, and the home. Sometimes the catalogs are mailed to the salesman's home. Prizes may be presented at a big ceremony designed for that purpose.

Here are some typical goals of salesmen's stimulants:

Increase sales—in total or in certain lines.
Introduce a new product.
Level out a seasonal sales curve.
Add new retail accounts.

Increase average order size.

Increase product demonstrations made.

Build a mailing list.

Get more point-of-purchase displays installed.

Increase the number of sales presentations made.

FIGURE 10–1. Why travel is popular incentive

THERE are 10 big advantages that travel has as an incentive and which has made it the fastest growing award in the past decade:

1. Everyone loves a vacation even to a destination he has already visited.

2. Travel develops prestige. People love to talk about their trips and take pride in being seasoned travelers.

3. Incentive programs pay for themselves. Until somebody earns a trip, there's no cost other than promotion.

4. Trips are glamorous and exciting—easy to promote.

5. Travel is educational and healthful. It provides valuable background and insight into current events.

6. There is never-ending variety of trips from which to choose. Today, because of transportation speed and reduced costs, anywhere in the world is a possible incentive site.

7. Travel is talked about during and long after the contest. This makes subsequent incentive programs easier to promote.

8. Wives are big boosters with a trip at stake. Wives help— and prod—their husbands to meet their quotas and earn the trip for two.

9. There's carry-over enthusiasm after the trip rather than a letdown.

10. Your best producers have an opportunity to mingle, compare notes and stimulate each other in an informal, relaxed atmosphere.

Source: *SM/Sales Meetings*, January 15, 1969.

Several merits are claimed for these stimulants. Most important is the increase in the manufacturer's sales volume. Then there are the higher earnings and rewards salesmen enjoy. The fun of rivalry and the activity of competition are regarded as favorable. Finally, contests and incentive campaigns can generate greater contact and rapport between management and salesmen.

On the other hand, certain good salesmen loathe these stimulants. To design a competition that will be fair to all, that permits no hanky-panky, is most difficult. Overselling and high-pressure selling may develop, and customer service may be neglected. After the competition, losers may feel ill will, there may be a let-down feeling, sales may drop. For one of these stimulants to be effective and successful, it must have sound design, persuasive promotion, and able administration.

Involve salesmen's wives?

There is disagreement concerning whether promotional material about incentive drives should be mailed to salesmen's wives. Their interest can provide additional motivation—some wives will urge their husbands to work hard to win rewards or prizes. The wife joins her husband's boss as a communicator of reminders about the drive. But, some wives will encourage their husbands anyway, perhaps making mailings unnecessary; this is especially probable if the prize is for the family (TV set) or for husband-and-wife (travel). And some salesmen and some wives will resent the mailings.

Mailings to wives should be light rather than heavy, infrequent rather than too frequent. They are safer if every salesman can win something, more risky if only a few prizes are offered. Salesmen should be informed in advance of any mailings to their wives. Despite the number of complaints they cause, mailings to wives are favored by a majority of sales promotion executives.

Commercial incentive firms

If a manufacturer chooses to, he can pay a commercial incentive firm to design and administer an incentive program for his salesmen. One such is the E. F. MacDonald Incentive Company; the bulk of its business comes from selling incentive programs for manufacturers' salesmen.

In the MacDonald merchandise operation, a full-color catalog shows and describes thousands of products, each with its value expressed in prize points. A salesman earns these points for accomplishing certain of his company's marketing objectives. When the salesman has earned enough points to "buy" the prizes he wants, he orders them from Mac-Donald, who ships them and then bills the salesman's company.

MacDonald sells about 7,500 merchandise prize campaigns a year to companies in such industries as the automotive, appliance, banking, food, soft drink, and industrial equipment; it has distributed merchandise awards worth over one-half billion dollars.

The MacDonald travel division provides tailor-made domestic or foreign travel itineraries for clients who prefer to use travel rather than merchandise. Currently, MacDonald tour conductors escort some 50,000 prizewinners to vacation resorts each year.

SALES MEETINGS FOR SALESMEN AND RETAILERS

Sales meetings are a natural and common feature of the training and stimulating of a manufacturer's sales force. Furthermore, many manufacturers sponsor meetings for and with their middlemen. Because of space limitations, this text must omit treatment of middlemen at the wholesale level and concentrate on the middleman of greater significance in sales promotion, the retailer. Because of similarities between sales meetings for a manufacturer's salesmen and meetings for that manufacturer's retail dealers—and because the manufacturer's salesmen conduct many sales meetings for and with their retailers, this section combines the two types of meeting and is logically located early in this chapter.

Where and how

Some sales meetings are held at the manufacturer's plant or home office. Control can be great, the factory can be toured, executives are on call, and some retailers like to get away from home. But, the cost in time and money is considerable, the size of the group may be unwieldy, and there may be interference with normal operations. A group of retailers may meet with a salesman in a local hotel. Or, when working with a single retail firm, the salesman may hold a sales meeting on the retailer's premises.

As for pattern or format of the meetings, sometimes a group from the home office tours the territory. In contrast, regional retail associations may select a group from their respective memberships to go to the home office, get the word, and then bring it back to the entire membership. Divisional or even district sales managers may conduct meetings in their respective areas. In this last instance and in meetings a salesman may lead for his retailers, those merchants may be particularly encouraged to voice comments and ask questions—to contribute problems, solutions, and experiences.

Suggestions about sales meetings

Every sales meeting needs a plan and a purpose; it needs to be designed to do some specific job for some specific group. It may be designed to

instruct or explain,
foster fellowship,
generate enthusiasm and raise morale,
inspire or excite,
unveil the forthcoming promotion program,
inform, sometimes in advance, or
present new products or models.

Decisions must be made about place, timing, and length of meeting. Persons wanted at the meeting should be notified in good time. The substance and style of the meeting demand careful selection; included here are how the session will be opened, what ideas, information, and concepts are to be presented in what sequence. Irrelevant matters and even matters of minor importance must be excluded. The leader must control the session and keep it focused on the one central theme or goal. How to end the meeting, and what if anything should be distributed for persons to take home, are two other problems. Closed-circuit television is used by some manufacturers for sales meetings. The advantages of large groups, simultaneous communication, and minimum travel cost and time are counterbalanced by the high cost of closed-circuit TV.

Sales meetings must be entertaining, dramatic, and fast moving as well as informative and inspirational. Showmanship contributes excitement. Members of the audience need the time and the facilities to get acquainted. If practicable, their participation should be invited and expected. Sessions that run too long or attempt to cover too much usually fail. Leaders who talk down to or preach at the audience always fail.

Unusual formats

Imagination and creativity are reflected in some of the sales meetings held. Here are three examples.

One company bought three 50-year old railroad cars and outfitted them in the style of the Gay Nineties. The Educator car could accommodate 32 salesmen in training sessions that lasted two days. The Motivator car was equipped to provide an elegant place for cocktails, dinner, and conversation. It contained an upright player piano and an old-fashioned bar. The Innovator car was used for housekeeping needs.

Various companies have put traveling shows on the road, often with Broadway casts, to attract salesmen and retailers to sales meetings. One 14-act musical extravaganza was put on in 32 cities in six weeks.

Tents are being used to house sales meetings. Color, size, and shape offer many choices; so do interior appointments. One advantage of tents is that they can be put up almost anywhere. Tents have happy connotations for many.

DIRECT-MAIL PROMOTION

Manufacturers using direct-mail promotion typically concentrate on two groups—their own sales forces and their retail dealers. There are, of course, some manufacturers who promote their goods and services to some extent through direct mailings to ultimate consumers and to persons who are buying influences; automobile manufacturers are an example. Some firms, furthermore, locate their direct-mail activities in the *advertising* department and budget. But the differences between direct-mail promotion and advertising (newspaper, magazine, television, radio, outdoor, transit) are such as to recommend that direct-mail promotion be assigned to the sales promotion manager.

At this point, three terms need to be described so they can be distinguished from each other. *Direct advertising* goes from seller to buyer directly, making no use of such commercial vehicles as newspapers or television. Some direct advertising, *direct-mail advertising*, makes use of our postal facilities. Direct-mail advertising is a vehicle for sending a seller's story in physical, written form by controlled distribution to a selected group of persons through the mail. The rest of the direct advertising, the nonmail portion, gets from sellers to buyers in various ways. A salesman can deliver it in person; shoppers pick up some off retail counters; some is enclosed in consumers' packages, bundles, and bags; some is placed on or in automobiles and on porches; some is handed to individuals in stores or on sidewalks. The third term is *mail-order selling*. This is actually a complete method of marketing goods and services in that the seller does the entire selling job by mail; he makes no use of wholesalers, retailers, salesmen, or personal selling. The mail-order seller may run newspaper or magazine advertising to induce inquiries—then follow up with letters, catalogs, or other direct mail.

Forms

Direct-mail promotion takes many forms. Cards, letters, reply forms, return envelopes, leaflets, folders, booklets, house organs, calendars, blotters, labels, stickers, and reprints are common. Even the outside envelope which contains these can and often should carry some promotional message.

FIGURE 10–2.   Insurance reply card

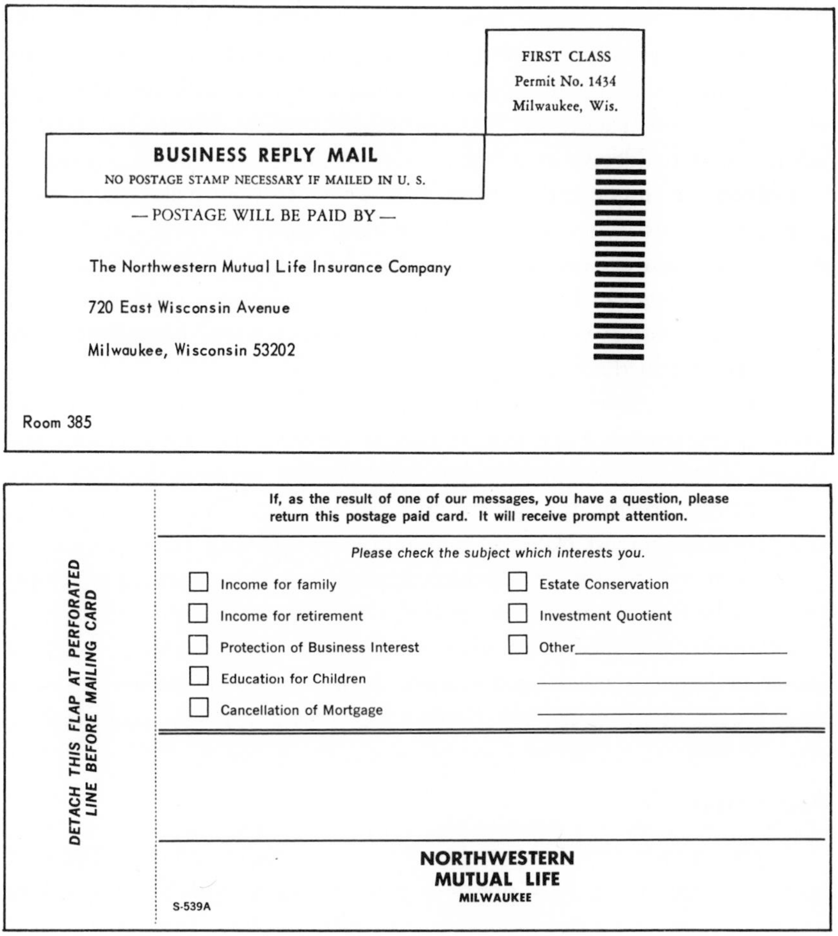

FIRST CLASS
Permit No. 1434
Milwaukee, Wis.

BUSINESS REPLY MAIL
NO POSTAGE STAMP NECESSARY IF MAILED IN U. S.

— POSTAGE WILL BE PAID BY —

The Northwestern Mutual Life Insurance Company

720 East Wisconsin Avenue

Milwaukee, Wisconsin 53202

Room 385

If, as the result of one of our messages, you have a question, please return this postage paid card. It will receive prompt attention.

Please check the subject which interests you.

☐ Income for family	☐ Estate Conservation
☐ Income for retirement	☐ Investment Quotient
☐ Protection of Business Interest	☐ Other_____
☐ Education for Children	_____
☐ Cancellation of Mortgage	_____

DETACH THIS FLAP AT PERFORATED LINE BEFORE MAILING CARD

**NORTHWESTERN
MUTUAL LIFE**
MILWAUKEE

S-539A

Mailing cards can do a good job for certain types of brief message. One can use Uncle Sam's postal cards—or one can design and print his own. Mailing cards are speedy, economical, convenient, versatile. However, the space is limited, the communication is not confidential, the card itself is seldom impressive.

Letters are widely used; they enjoy roughly the advantages of mailing cards and can avoid most of the weaknesses of cards. Letters are exceedingly adaptable. Promotional letters benefit to a significant degree from the high regard we accord personal letters; they move in to share some of the universal interest in personal mail.

Outside envelopes must not be ignored. Basically, these contain and transmit whatever is being mailed, but they can do more. They can use color for attractiveness and distinctiveness. They can make a bid for reader attention with pictures, maps, illustrations, diagrams, and such. They themselves can carry important messages such as slogans, mottoes, or timely statements. They can even give piggyback rides to seals, stickers, and promotional labels. Incidentally, in most instances the *typed* address is more successful than pasted-on mailing labels, handwritten addresses, and addresses stamped onto the mailing envelope by a plate.

Leaflets are simple and inexpensive, even when they make use of color and illustrations. They can be distributed alone, or they can be used as envelope stuffers and get a free ride with such items as letters and invoices. Leaflets can list product specifications, describe product features and satisfactions, even accompany one product while promoting some other product in the line.

Folders are grown-up leaflets; they are the most common of printed promotional forms. They can be had in various folds, sizes, colors, and shapes. They are inexpensive but effective for sending product data.

Brochures are the top-quality form of mailing. They exude prestige and glamour; they are elaborate and impressive *and* they are expensive.

Self-mailers are any items which require no outside mailing envelope; they can be folded, secured in some manner (staple, stamp), and mailed.

Broadsides are the spectaculars of mailings. They measure 17 by 22 inches or larger; some are self-mailers. A broadside is often used to open or to close a series of mailings. Some wind up as displays in retail stores.

Postal class

There are two classes of postal service from which to choose. First-class postage is speedy, enjoys prestige, gets attention, will be returned or forwarded—and is costly and becoming more so as postal rates increase. Third-class postage, the other option, is just about everything first-class is not.

Advantages and disadvantages

Direct-mail promotion has several features of outstanding benefit to sellers. One, of course, is the user's control of circulation; because he controls the mailing list, he decides who will and who will not be sent the mailing. A related plus feature is the personal nature of the communication; the typical mailing is addressed to a specific person at his own individual, unique address. Then, the message sent can be personalized, confidential, and complete. Great variety and great flexibility can be had. Timing can be quite precise. And, if a seller wants to measure the quality of his promotion, he can ask each addressee to get back in touch with him—then divide the cost of the mailing by the number of addresses who do.

Three handicaps deserve mention. Direct-mail promotion is an expensive way to communicate with members of a buyer group when contrasted with advertising. To production costs (creative work, printing) must be added mailing costs (addressing, postage). Too, there is so much junky direct mail that some individuals refer to *all* of it as "junk mail." Finally, unsolicited mail from strangers suffers from low reader interest.

Uses

Direct promotion may be successfully used to

Send out news,
Express appreciation for an order,
Thank a buyer for a payment,
Handle complaints,
Answer buyers' questions,
Whet buyer's curiosity,
Remind,
Influence,
Stimulate,
Make sales,
"Lead" salesmen's calls,

FIGURE 10–3. Two leaflets from a Playboy mailing

DECODE:

HCAE HTNOM EROM
NAHT OWT DERDNUH SEINAPMOC TSOH
SEITRAP TA YOBYALP!

Must the alphabet be from A to Z? Try it the
other way and see. If this message seems to
confuse, give to your children to peruse!

clue

ANSWERS:

"Follow up" salesmen's calls,
Keep in touch with buyers,
Reopen inactive accounts,
Offer catalogs and booklets, and
Welcome new customers.

Mailing lists

Unless the list is "right," each mailing, no matter how excellent, is doomed to failure. If a communication is to be a success, if it is to achieve the results it hopes for, then it must be sent to the "right" persons.

Where do sellers get or find mailing lists? A list of customers can be a most valuable mailing list. Local directories, including, of course, the telephone and the city directories, can provide lists. Some sellers are able to get certain membership lists (clubs, professions, religious groups, political groups, association rosters) and then use them effectively as mailing lists. A list of automobile registrations compiled by county officials offers various possibilities. Salesmen sometimes are asked to build lists and to add names to lists. News stories and want ads in newspapers are potential sources of names. A seller may exchange names with a noncompeting seller; he may rent names through a list broker for about $20–$25 per 1,000; he may buy a list from a commercial list house or from the owner. Visitors to convention booths and visitors who take plant tours may be worthwhile addressees for certain purposes.

Getting a list, however, is not so serious a problem as is keeping a list current—accurate, complete, up to date. Strong efforts must be made to stay accurate. Otherwise there is waste, loss of respect if mailings go to persons for whom those mailings are inappropriate, and less achievement per dollar of cost than there should be.

What can be done to help keep mailing lists up to date? A seller can periodically ask addressees to notify him if they change. He can correct lists from directories when the next directory is issued. The salesmen of many manufacturers can report changes which should be made. News items may tell of changes which should be made in a list. Any first-class mailings returned to the sender identify needed changes. If the list user sends the same mailing to the names on two or more lists, he may be able to check each list against the other for the purpose of seeing that no recipient gets more than one mailing of one batch. If a mailer sends two or three identical mailings in the same mail to the same person, that person's impression can hardly be good. One of

FIGURE 10–4.   Sheet from the catalog of a dealer in mailing lists

FRITZ S. HOFHEIMER, INC.
MAIL ADVERTISING and SALES PROMOTION SPECIALISTS
29 EAST 22nd STREET   NEW YORK, N. Y. 10010

PHONE: OREGON 4-6420
CABLES: EVRIADRESS

	Dermatologists (Leading) (continued)	
	143 Pennsylvania	18.50
	117 Texas	16.50
134	Derrick Mfrs.	27.50
28	Desiccator Mfrs.	12.50
996	Design Engineering Firms	40.00
	106 California	16.50
	125 New York	17.50
7,800	Design Engineers (Individuals)	45.00M
559	DESIGNERS (Fashion)	35.00
64	(Furniture)	16.50
36	(Furs)	12.50
1,274	(Industrial)	40.00M
290	(Industrial, leading)	30.00
119	(Jewelry)	22.50
105	(Optical)	20.00
419	(Packaging)	35.00
120	(Scenic)	25.00
336	DESK Manufacturers (all kinds)	35.00
18	(Children's) Mfrs.	10.00
81	(President's) Mfrs.	16.50
75	(School) Mfrs.	16.50
100	(Typewriter) Mfrs.	22.50
22	DESK Glasstop Mfrs.	11.50
65	Lamp Mfrs.	15.00
69	Pad Mfrs.	15.00
102	Dessert (Gelatin) Packers	20.00
31	Dessert Knife Mfrs.	12.50
11	Detachable Blade Knife Mfrs.	10.00
3,293	Detective Agencies	40.00M
486	DETECTOR (Electronic) Mfrs.	35.00
20	(Flaw) Mfrs.	10.00
8	(Gas) Mfrs.	10.00
2	(Lie) Mfrs.	8.50
43	(Metal) Mfrs.	12.50
43	(Radioactivity) Mfrs.	12.50
574	Detergent Mfrs.	40.00
93	Detergent (Synthetic) Mfrs.	17.50
5	Detinners	10.00
11	Detonator Mfrs.	10.00
50	Developer (Photo) Mfrs.	12.50
3,177	Developers (Real Estate & Land)	45.00M
255	DEVELOPMENT Agencies (Industrial)	27.50
677	Psychologists	40.00
34	Device (Anti-Skid) Mfrs.	11.50
43	Dextrine Mfrs.	13.50
18	Diabetes Remedy Mfrs.	12.50
25	Diabetic Food Mfrs.	12.50
17	Diagnostic Apparatus Mfrs.	12.50
30	DIAL (Clock) Mfrs.	12.50
81	(Watch) Mfrs.	17.50
522	DIAMOND Cutters (Lapidaries)	40.00
1,152	Merchants	45.00M
1	Mine	5.00
43	DIAMOND (Industrial) Mfrs.	15.00
4	(Synthetic) Mfrs.	5.00
46	DIAMOND Bearing Mfrs.	15.00
24	Drill Mfrs.	12.50
55	Powder Mfrs.	15.00
117	Tool Mfrs.	26.50
92	DIAPER Manufacturers	17.50
728	Services	40.00
38	Diaper Bag Mfrs.	10.00
87	Diary Publishers	17.50
27	Dice Manufacturers	10.00
22	Dice Cup Mfrs.	10.00
16	Dictating Machine Mfrs.	10.00
14	Dictionary Publishers	10.00
1,285	DIE Casters	50.00M
220	Casters Rated $500,000 or more	27.50
45	Cutting Machinery Mfrs.	15.00
51	Holder Mfrs.	15.00
4,453	Die Makers	40.00M
	485 California	30.00
	606 Illinois	35.00
	157 Indiana	20.00
	144 Massachusetts	18.50
	811 Michigan	40.00
	150 New Jersey	20.00
	411 New York	30.00
	427 Ohio	30.00

	Die Makers (continued)	
	163 Pennsylvania	20.00
	175 Wisconsin	20.00
142	DIE Makers' Accessory Mfrs.	30.00
252	Maker's Equipment & Supplies	35.00
220	(Perforating) Mfrs.	30.00
497	Sinkers	40.00
34	DIESEL Crane Mfrs.	12.50
108	Engine Mfrs.	22.50
24	Engine Starter Mfrs.	12.50
29	Locomotive Mfrs.	12.50
238	Dietetic Food Mfrs.	32.50
269	Dietitians' Schools	27.50
65	Differential Gear Mfrs.	15.00
76	Diffuser Manufacturers	17.50
38	Diffuser (Air) Mfrs.	10.00
79	Digger Manufacturers	17.50
302	DIGITAL Computer Mfrs.	30.00
51	Plotter Mfrs.	12.50
92	Printer Mfrs.	17.50
66	Recorder Mfrs.	15.00
18	Digitoxin Manufacturers	10.00
1,000,000	Diners Club Credit Card Holders	25.00M
	Min. 10,000—4-up cheshire or gum labels.	
	Sample lit required. Merchandise offers	
	must give option to charge to D.C. account	
219	DINETTE Furniture Mfrs.	27.50
89	(Chrome) Furniture Mfrs.	18.50
35	Dining Car Supervisors	15.00
259	DINING ROOM Furniture Mfrs.	30.00
202	Table Mfrs.	27.50
42	Dioctyl Mfrs. & Distributors	15.00
172	Diode Mfrs.	25.00
66	Diploma Writers	20.00
1,637	DIPLOMATIC CORPS (Foreign in U.S.)	45.00M
4,597	(U.S. ABROAD)	40.00M
61	Dipper Manufacturers	17.50
15	Dipping Table Mfrs.	10.50
14	Direct Mail Advertising Clubs	10.00
582	Direct Selling Firms	40.00
195	Direction Finder (Electronics) Mfrs.	25.00
125,000	DIRECTORS (Larger Corporations)	35.00M
67,422	(Selected Corporations)	32.50M
13,172	(Large New York Corporations)	40.00M
500	Directors (Film)	40.00
714	Directory Publishers	40.00
887	Disability Psychologists	50.00
30	DISAPPEARING Bed Mfrs.	10.50
64	Door Mfrs.	15.50
5,200	DISC Jockeys	40.00M
232	Makers	35.00
12	Gauge Mfrs.	10.50
4,888	Discount Stores	35.00M
	382 California	25.00
	116 Connecticut	16.50
	166 Florida	18.50
	258 Illinois	22.50
	141 Indiana	17.50
	248 Massachusetts	22.50
	253 Michigan	22.50
	184 New Jersey	18.50
	456 New York	27.50
	328 Ohio	25.00
	325 Pennsylvania	25.00
	271 Texas	22.50
408	DISCOUNT Stores (Independent)	35.00
989	Stores (LESSEES IN)	50.00
411	Store Chains	32.50
127	Dish Manufacturers	25.00
52	Dish (Paper) Mfrs.	13.50
38	DISH Cloth Mfrs.	10.50
37	Dish Mfrs.	10.50
116	DISH WASHING Composition Mfrs.	20.00
434	Machinery Distributors	40.00
59	Machinery Mfrs.	13.50
639	Disinfectant Manufacturers	40.00
3,172	Disinfectant & Fumigating Firms	40.00M
612	Dispensaries	40.00
211	DISPENSER Manufacturers	30.00
18	(Coffee) Mfrs.	10.00
70	(Soap) Mfrs.	15.00

43

your authors, incidentally, found five identical airmailed promotional mailings in his mailbox one morning.

Testing

The most experienced, successful users of direct-mail promotion are strong on testing. They are always moving in the direction of a more effective use of this type of promotion. They experiment and then try to determine what is best. Trial and experience should be used in seeking answers to such questions as these:

♦ When should one use first-class postage? Third class? Airmail?
♦ Can "gadgets" (buttons, pennies, rubber bands) increase response?
♦ What specific elements (letter, folder, reply card) should make up a mailing?
♦ How close together should successive mailings be scheduled?
♦ What mailings should be sent to home addresses? Business addresses?
♦ Should reply envelopes be stamped with one stamp—or with several one-cent stamps?

Techniques

Here are five rather common technique patterns:

One shot. This is a single mailing. An example is the announcement a retailer sends his credit customers informing them about the retailer's infrequent sales. Or, a manufacturer notifies persons in a certain city of his annual showing in that city.

Continuous. This promotion continues over an indefinite time period. Publishers of textbooks send mailing after mailing year after year to professors. Media do the same to advertisers and to advertising agencies. Retailers may put enclosures in each month's statements.

Campaign. Here the seller predetermines the number of mailings to constitute the series; four is a common number. Their names are dropped from the mailing list when addressees buy—when, for example, the subscriber to a magazine renews. The list becomes dormant after the terminal mailing.

Wear out. This technique is popular with mail-order sellers. Successive mailings are sent to the names on the list so long as the last mailing was profitable. Mailings stop when the last one lost money.

Cooperative mailings. Small groups of noncompeting sellers sponsor a joint mailing or series. This is less costly than for each to send solo mailings.

HOUSE ORGANS

A manufacturer may ask his sales promotion staff to be responsible for certain company house organs. Just what are house organs? They are publications which appear weekly, monthly, quarterly—or every now and then. Most have adapted the editorial format of the popular consumer magazines, some the format of newspapers. Circulation is controlled, so the issues are free. Only a very few sell advertising space. Size and number of pages vary. One estimate is that 5,000 house organs reach 20 million individuals.

Two types of house organ may be assigned to the sales promotion staff. One is edited for the manufacturer's salesmen, one for his retailers. Both types are sales oriented so as to stimulate buying and selling. They are designed to inform, to inspire, to encourage, to entertain, to build goodwill and prestige.

House organs for salesmen

Salesmen want information about their products and their companies, about production and sales; they want instruction and counsel about how to sell more. They want human interest material—news of other salesmen, of other company personnel, of meetings, conferences, and contests. They want a personal publication, one that builds morale by recognizing outstanding performance and outstanding salesmen.

House organs for retailers

These work for more harmonious relations, greater understanding, and closer contact between manufacturers and their retailers. As to content, they contain product information; details about the manufacturer's promotional policies and plans; tips about how to sell more and even manage better; descriptions, pictures, and offers of point-of-purchase materials; and case histories.

Here is Chrysler's description of its house organ, the *Chrysler-Plymouth Times:*

The *Times* is a sales-oriented tabloid published by the public relations department of the Chrysler-Plymouth Division. It is sent to every Chrysler-Plymouth dealer, his department heads, and his retail salesmen. Others who receive copies are members of the Division's field sales organization and Division and corporation executives.

The *Times* is primarily a means of communication between the Division and its dealers. The emphasis is on selling activities as they relate to automobiles.

An effort is made to describe how a dealer or group of dealers originates a sales activity or campaign, what the advertising and promotion material consists of, how the campaign is executed, and what the results are. Such stories of success are helpful and of benefit to other dealers.

The *Times* also carries:

♦ Information about product features, particularly when new models are introduced.
♦ News about Plymouth successes in stock car and drag racing and high-performance activities in general.
♦ News about individual dealers—awards they receive for community and other activities, plans to build or open new facilities, observance or an anniversary, etc.
♦ News about Chrysler-Plymouth Division personnel that is of interest to dealers and other Division people.
♦ Miscellaneous information and pictures that can be helpful to anybody engaged in some aspect of retail car sales.

The tabloid format is used to achieve good legibility, flexible use of pictures, eye-catching layout, and ease of handling by the reader.

MERCHANDISING THE MANUFACTURER'S PROMOTION PROGRAM

What

Once a manufacturer's promotion program for the coming year has been built, the next job is to see that the program is merchandised to the two most influential groups—to his salesmen and to his retailers. More and more, the sales promotion manager is being asked to play a dominant role in this undertaking. Before attempting to merchandise the company promotion program to the company salesmen, the sales promotion manager must have determined that the men know (1) how advertising operates as a promotional force and what it can and cannot do; (2) how each of the company promotion activities contributes to the overall promotion effort; and (3) how to sell the promotion program to retailers. Such instruction is often a part of the sales training given salesmen.

Briefly, merchandising the promotion program is presenting, telling, and selling the manufacturer's advertising program and his sales promotion program. It is informing salesmen and retailers about those programs, getting them to grasp the essence and objectives of those programs, stimulating them to be enthusiastic about and favorably inclined toward those programs.

Who and how

Several types of personnel present and sell the promotion program. Home office brass are impressive because of their titles—sales promotion manager, advertising manager, sales manager—maybe the vice president in charge of marketing. A manufacturer may expect the account representative and others from the advertising agency to participate. He may expect the media to which he will be paying large sums to take part in person; the star of the manufacturer's television show may be asked to appear, or a magazine might be asked to send out mailings. In the majority of cases, each individual salesman is a key person in that he is expected to sell the program to his respective retailers.

As to *how*, the sales meeting has already been recognized as a useful vehicle; in merchandising the promotion program, these are usually scheduled on a district or regional basis—not on a national basis. Mailings from media have been mentioned; other mailings can be sent by the manufacturer himself. House organs and ads in retail business publications can help sell the program. When salesmen in the field are talking to individual retailers, they use the oral, written, and visual aids salesmen typically use.

Content

Phases of the manufacturer's *advertising* program of interest to salesmen and retailers include:

Media and circulation.   Competitive comparisons.
Campaign theme.   Size of advertising fund.
Any pretest results.   Background for these decisions.
Schedules.

Each salesman and each retailer is primarily interested in the advertising to appear in *his* area or market.

As for the manufacturer's *sales promotion* program, salesmen and retailers are interested in such matters as:

Samples of point-of-purchase materials.
Samples of direct-mail.
Details of any manufacturer-retailer cooperative advertising plan.
Manufacturers' exhibits at trade shows.
Particulars about consumer stimulation (next chapter).

Why

The manufacturer who does not make a serious effort to merchandise his promotion program is remiss. As for his salesmen, they cannot describe unless they know, they cannot explain unless they understand, they cannot sell unless they themselves have bought. Do remember, the salesman is the most frequent manufacturer-retailer contact; often he is the only personal contact.

As for his retailers, the manufacturer wants them to coordinate, to tie in, to synchronize *their* promotional efforts with and to *his*. He hopes they will use the promotional materials he offers and will participate in joint promotional activities. In general, the manufacturer wants retailers to stock, display, and push his brands—to cash in to the maximum extent on his promotion.

PROMOTION MATERIALS OFFERED RETAILERS BY MANUFACTURERS

The section just concluded described how manufacturers merchandise their own advertising programs and sales promotion programs. Part of the sales promotion programs of some manufacturers consists of various types of promotional materials and support those manufacturers make available for use by retailers in their own retail promotion programs. These are logically and commonly merchandised to a manufacturer's salesmen and retailers in the same manner and at the same time he merchandises his own promotion program to them. The present section takes a brief look at the nature and importance of manufacturer-offered promotional materials and aids for use by retailers. This chapter contains separate sections on Direct-Mail Promotion, Manufacturer-Retailer Cooperative Advertising, and Point-of-Purchase Promotion; all three are very close to, and even overlap, some of the matters treated in this section.

Promotional materials and aids

A manufacturer may offer his retailers an advertising mat service. This service makes copy, illustrations, even complete ads of various sizes available; when used, most appear in newspapers. A mat is a papier-mâché form in which newspapers can cast a printing plate which will reproduce or print an ad. Some manufacturers offer actual outdoor posters and car cards; costs may be shared. Broadcast programs and commercial announcements are elements in some of these offerings; once again, manufacturer and retailer may share the cost. Then there is promotional literature of all sorts for retailers to put into the hands of ultimate consumers in all sorts of ways. Examples are envelope stuffers, cards, reprints of ads, counter pickups, handbills, and many of the other items listed in the Direct-Mail Promotion section. Imprinting space on such items is often generous because many retailers like to display their firm names, addresses, and telephone numbers prominently. The manufacturer often supplies this promotional literature, with retailers paying for imprinting, envelopes, addressing, and postage. Sometimes the retailer is billed, but the charge is canceled on his use of the items.

Some items offered are essentially builders of retail floor traffic. Premiums, coupons, contest entry blanks, instruction schools, fashion shows, and demonstrators are examples; some of these are described in the next chapter. Gifts, "free" offers, spectacular point-of-purchase displays, and brief appearances of celebrities are other examples.

A manufacturer of convenience goods may offer a promotional allowance, the amount determined by the volume of the retailer's purchases. The manufacturer pays the entire amount—the retailer is expected to promote the manufacturer's brands by way of handbills, ads, point-of-purchase displays, personal selling, or in special store promotions. Occasionally, a manufacturer will offer aid in such storewide promotions as are scheduled for Christmas and back-to-school time.

Importance of promotion materials for retailers

The importance of an assortment of retail promotional materials and aids to certain manufacturers must not be underestimated. This importance is great enough to demand that each of those manufacturers determine his own competitive strengths and weaknesses, the plus points and the minus points of his brand, and the strong and weak points of his retailers, their goals and their problems. In designing the assortment to

FIGURE 10–5. Ad mat Ford offers its dealers

Pinto—Where little means a lot

$**0000**

Torino 500 Hardtop
with Luxury Extras

$**0000**

Luxury-Equipped
Galaxie 500 Special

$**0000**

Explorer Special with Luxury Extras

$**0000**

POWER STEERING & BRAKES
NO EXTRA COST

White Sale Galaxie 500 Hardtop

We took our best selling Ford Galaxie 500 and Torino . . . added the extras most people want . . . and sweetened the deal with free power steering and brakes.

Save up to $308* on White Sale pickups. Explorer Specials specially equipped with luxury extras!

*Manufacturer's suggested retail prices now reduced up to $308 when you buy a luxury-equipped Explorer Special pickup.

FORD PINTO
It's like a sale price all year long!

The new little carefree car! Saves on gas, on maintenance.

Save with the Ford Team! Look at all you get on White Sale Specials:

Free power steering and free power brakes on special edition Galaxie 500's and Torino 500's! Equip your choice with vinyl roof, wheel covers, whitewalls, special seat trim, special exterior trim, special color . . . the power steering's on us!

Also add air conditioning, tinted glass, automatic seat-back release, deluxe seat belts (Torino) and the visibility group which includes seat belt warning light, remote control outside mirror, luggage compartment light and other niceties . . . also get power front disc brakes—free!

White Sale Torino 500 Hardtop

FORD TEAM
7TH ANNUAL
WHITE SALE

See us for savings

(HOMETOWN MOTORS)

offer, many manufacturers must first determine through which *types* of retail store their brands move and in what quantities; toothpaste, aspirin, soft drinks, shoe polish, and razor blades are examples of products which are sold by several types of store. The manufacturer may have to tailor his offering somewhat in the light of this fact. Then within each type there are A-grade, B-grade, and C-grade stores; the needs of the three grades which a manufacturer should do something about are seldom the same.

The circumstances of large retailers are such that many do not tie in with and support a manufacturer's promotion program. But the small retailer who needs and would use much is the type of account on which the manufacturer must spend little. So, the manufacturer must have a clear picture of his distribution, he must classify and group his retailers, he must design and offer to each group the optimum assortment of promotion materials *for it*. Well to be remembered is the fact that only a very few retailers will use one manufacturer's promotional materials twice during the same season; retailers simply have too many items to sell.

MANUFACTURER-RETAILER COOPERATIVE ADVERTISING

What and why

Manufacturer-retailer cooperative advertising, often referred to as vertical cooperative advertising, is consumer advertising run in the retailer's market, almost always over the retailer's name, featuring the manufacturer's brand, and usually paid for jointly by the manufacturer and the retailer. In the vast majority of cases, the retailer pays the local medium at the local rate and then gets some reimbursement from the manufacturer. Because this promotion is *advertising* in the technical sense, it is found only in the six advertising media—newspapers, magazines, television, radio, outdoor, and transit. Other manufacturer-retailer joint promotional activities are treated elsewhere (Merchandising the Manufacturer's Promotion Program, Point-of-Purchase Promotion, and so on). One estimate is that at least $500 million is spent annually in manufacturer-retailer cooperative advertising, 80 percent of which is placed in newspapers.

This type of advertising promotes a wide variety of products: air planes and ale, shoes and sterling silverware, watches and washing machines.

The common denominator? Exclusive or selective distribution; under intensive distribution the plan is unworkable.

As to *why*, the retailer is the manufacturer's representative in his local market, he stocks and sells so many products that his support and promotion must be selective. Our manufacturer wants *his* brand to get some of that support and promotion. Towle sterling, for example, may be in a store which stocks four other brands of sterling; Towle obviously wants promotion at the retail level.

Because his retail distribution is restricted, the manufacturer is anxious to see that ultimate consumers in each market know from which retailer or retailers the manufacturer's brand can be bought.

A few manufacturers have selectively distributed brands so popular, outstanding, and entrenched—they have "consumer franchises" so strong—that those manufacturers can demand that their retailers participate in vertical cooperative advertising. The manufacturer of the leading brand of watches or cameras might be able to stipulate that retailers cannot handle his respective brand unless they engage in this type of advertising. Most manufacturers desiring this type of promotion, however, can do no more than urge, recommend, and encourage.

This form of advertising can be offensive or defensive; it can be a most effective promotional activity when handled properly.

What the manufacturer does

Because newspapers get the vast majority of this kind of advertising, our treatment which follows is based on the use of that medium.

The manufacturer plans the program and earmarks budget for it. Next he merchandises this program to salesmen and retailers as described in the preceding section, doing so in plenty of time to allow retailers to plan. The manufacturer then adopts whatever controls or rules he deems desirable. For example, he may impose a ceiling on dollar volume; if he markets through wholesalers too, he decides whether the plan should be manufacturer-retailer or manufacturer-wholesaler-retailer. He stipulates which newspaper(s) each retailer must use, what scheduling must be observed, and what copy regulations will apply. He may spell out the merchandise each retailer must buy and in what quantities in order to qualify. Finally, he settles on policies and procedures for the administration and operation of the program. After controls and rules have been determined, the newspaper ads are built, either by the manufacturer's own advertising staff or by his advertising agency. The final step is for the manufacturer to make the ads available to his retailers early enough for them to examine, judge, arrange, and plan. The advertisements are usually in the form of mats.

True, some manufacturers pretest and screen proposed ads when building the assortment from which retailers can select. Test-market testing is the type of research favored by some manufacturers. After he has run the ads in the actual marketplaces and has tried to distinguish between

FIGURE 10–6. Retailers can put their names and addresses in the lower left corner

the stronger ones and the weaker ones, the manufacturer can make a more convincing case for retail acceptance and participation. Reassured retailers run more manufacturer-retailer cooperative ads than do retailers who do not have evidence of advertising effectiveness.

The manufacturer must draw his manufacturer-retailer contracts for vertical cooperative advertising carefully. What the retailer may and may not do, and what the manufacturer will and will not do, need to be spelled out in clear and adequate detail. The agreement must tell the retailer all he needs to know about how to prove his right to reimbursement and at what rate. The manufacturer hopes that his contract will turn out to be both simple and legal—and that's quite a hope.

What the retailer does

Continuing with the newspaper medium, the participating retailer selects the newspaper(s) to use. Often this involves no real choice because (*a*) there is only one newspaper in many markets and (*b*) there may be only one newspaper in the retailer's market approved by the manufacturer. The retailer's second job is to select which ad to run. This choice is made from the group of ads made available by the manufacturer.

In certain cases, the retailer can run a mat as a separate ad *or* include the mat as one element in a larger ad. As a generalization, manufacturers prefer the former. There is no problem of compatibility of products included in an omnibus or group ad; nor is there a problem of unity, layout, or design in an ad controlled and built by a retailer. The retailer usually tells the newspaper what prices if any are to be included. The next step, that of scheduling, involves selection of month, week, day, position, and frequency. Then comes the coordinating phase. Here the retailer harmonizes this promotion with the manufacturer's and with his own other promotion. He checks to see that his stock is adequate. He decides what point-of-purchase promotion should support the ad. He informs his salespersons about the coming effort.

A manufacturer-retailer cooperative ad needs to be soundly built just as does the retailer's other ads. Its core should be a powerful, persuasive promise of satisfaction or benefit. It should tell what the product is and does. Usually it should contain prices and always it should tell ultimate consumers where the brand is available.

The retailer must administer the advertising effort efficiently. He must earmark budget for the effort. He must keep records of sales and costs. He must control all phases of the joint promotion so that he has no trouble qualifying for reimbursement by the manufacturer.

Financial arrangements and operations

Of the four basic plans of paying for this type of advertising, the first three are not common. (1) The manufacturer pays the full cost. One version here is for the manufacturer to run and pay for a typical manufacturer's ad, then insist that his retailer(s) run (and pay for) a tie-in ad, often on the same page of the newspaper. (2) The manufacturer insists that the retailer pay the full cost. This is practicable only if the brand enjoys a strong consumer franchise and gives the retailer a high markup. (3) In case wholesalers are participating, the two common sharing patterns for manufacturer-wholesaler-retailer are 50–25–25 and 25–25–50. This is not too common because many selectively distributed products do not go through wholesalers. (4) In this most common pattern, manufacturer and retailer share the advertising cost, and the most common split is 50–50. The manufacturer often sets a limit or ceiling on how much advertising and how much reimbursement the retailer should plan and expect. A popular limit is 5 percent of the retailer's purchases. For example, suppose the retailer buys $100,000 worth and the limit is 5 percent. Under the 50–50 split pattern, the manufacturer's participation is limited to $2,500; the retailer pays the other $2,500.

Typically, the retailer places the ad and is billed by the newspaper at the local rate, which is usually lower than the general rate. The retailer pays and gets a receipted copy of the newspaper invoice; this he sends to the manufacturer along with a copy of the ad and *his* invoice or bill to the manufacturer. The manufacturer reimburses with a credit memo or with a check.

Advantages and disadvantages

Advantages to manufacturer. There are several possible benefits for the manufacturer. He gets more advertising for less money. Identification with locally respected and prominent retailers is desirable; too, local consumers learn where they can buy the manufacturer's brand. Retail involvement in the manufacturer's promotional program may result in greater retail interest and push. The program may help the manufacturer's salesmen attract and then hold desirable retailers. In theory, at least, the manufacturer exercises some control over retail promotion of the manufacturer's brand, even to adapting and tailoring the advertising market by market.

Disadvantages to manufacturer. One common and major disadvantage to the manufacturer is the large number of retailers who flout the rules and thereby lower the quality of the advertising. For example, the manufacturer may prohibit advertising on Saturday—but discover that retailers run ads on Saturday so as to qualify for the newspaper's largest discount. Or, as another example, a retailer may mutilate the manufacturer's copy or run the brand name in small type. Another disadvantage is the great amount of clerical work needed in inspecting copies of the ads submitted by retailers, checking invoices, reimbursing retailers, and such; this clerical work is involved, time consuming, and costly. Next, the manufacturer cannot know in advance just how much of this advertising will be run—or where; his promotion, thus, can be uneven. Operating and administering the program is expensive. Too many of the manufacturer's promotional dollars may be spent in this type of advertising. Finally, most plans are difficult to abandon.

Advantages to retailer. The retailer, too, gets more promotion for less money. Sometimes this may even free more promotion dollars to put back of *his private brands*. At least he gets paid for promoting a manufacturer's brand. Some retailers benefit from association and identi-fication with the manufacturers of certain consumer brands. Finally, the ads are often of higher quality than those which would have been built locally.

Disadvantages to retailer. Retailers resent the restraints imposed by the manufacturer—his dictating and stipulating about media, scheduling, and copy. Retailers run the risk of neglecting the promotion of brands with no cooperative dollars, brands they *should* promote. Retailers may make the mistake of *buying* merchandise they should not buy just because of its co-op dollars. Some of the ads are too national and manufacturerish in personality and emphasis; they don't look like retail ads. Sometimes reimbursement is slow.

Problems

One of the most vexing problems in cooperative advertising stems from billing frauds. One version is double billing. Here the retailer and the newspaper connive. For example, the newspaper charges the retailer $50 for an ad but gives the retailer a paid invoice for $100. If the manu-facturer reimburses on a 50–50 basis, the manufacturer's reimbursement results in the retailer's paying no part of the cost of the ad. A second version sees the retailer qualifying for a substantial end-of-year quantity discount but not telling the manufacturer about it. In a third version, the retailer does a two-way split run, one ad for manufacturer A's prod-uct, the other for manufacturer B's product—then asks for reimbursement from both as though each ad was in the newspaper's complete issue rather than in just one half. A final fraud is when a metropolitan retailer schedules an ad which contains an intentional error. This appears in the early edition. Then the retailer notifies the newspaper of the defect and the ad is corrected and rerun. The retailer tries to get reimbursement for *two* ads.

A second type of problem is legal in character. One provision of the Robinson-Patman Act is that any advertising allowance must be made available on proportionately equal terms to competing retailers. The manufacturer must not be guilty of discriminating between or among his retailers. The act's wording and provisions are vague and general. Often a manufacturer cannot determine with confidence the legality of some proposed vertical cooperative advertising program.

Retail requests are problems. Some retailers push and push for more favorable terms and for more liberal, less strict, rules and stipulations, for exceptions to certain regulations. A retailer may ask for cooperative dollars even though he uses forbidden media. Closely allied is the problem of the retailer who considers a manufacturer's advertising allowance (not uncommon for convenience goods) to be nothing more than price concessions.

A final problem involves who will build the ads. The manufacturer has a problem of dealing with and through his advertising agency if he wants it to build them. The agency will not get a commission from the newspaper. The agency does not place the ads—the newspaper bills the retailer off the local rate card. So, the agency must build the ads for free or for a fee—or the manufacturer must make other arrangements.

POINT-OF-PURCHASE PROMOTION

Point-of-purchase items are the promotional materials at, on, or in retail stores. The perfect example? Window displays. Most point-of-purchase items are produced for manufacturers and supplied by them to retailers at no cost.

Point-of-purchase is an important type of promotion. New types of products and new brands are offered to retailers every week. The undeniable diminution in effective personal selling in retail stores has been accompanied by an increase in self-service. The shopper now buys more on impulse than ever before; many of her decisions to buy originate and take place completely in the retail store, often stimulated by display. One estimate is that 80 percent of all buying done by ultimate consumers is done on the bases of self-selection and self-service. More and more, point-of-purchase promotion is used to announce, to show, to attract, to remind, to prove, to dispense, to sell. Point-of-purchase promotion is the manufacturer's last opportunity to communicate to and to influence store shoppers. Heavy suppliers of point-of-purchase materials to retailers are the manufacturers of foods, beverages, cosmetics, clothing, drug products, and paper products.

What and where

These are popular types of point-of-purchase promotion:

Reprints of magazine ads	Posters
Jumble baskets	Decals
Easel-back display and price cards	Bins
"Dummy" packages and cartons	Racks
Window displays and streamers	Product masses

Favored materials are cardboard, metal, plastics, and wood.

Supermarkets make much use of posters; floor stands of metal, wire, or cardboard; shelf edgers and "talkers" of cardboard; overwire banners; and metal racks. Incidentally, point-of-purchase displays in the typical supermarket can be seen by more than 5,000 shoppers each week.

As to *where*, we see some stores using *exterior* locations for such point-of-purchase items as banners, flags, and signs. *Interior* locations coveted by manufacturers include windows, counters, shelves, tables, walls; floor space near elevators, the store directory, or the check-out spot; and air space between floor and ceiling.

Uses

Manufacturers use a strong line of point-of-purchase items to get retailers to stock new products and new brands. Manufacturers hope their point-of-purchase assortments will enjoy retail favor to the end that retail goodwill increases; such goodwill can be translated into such desirable developments as better merchandise location in the store, retail support and promotion, better dealer relations, and the like. Through his point-of-purchase promotion the manufacturer hopes to make a last and successful bid for a favorable buying decision—to cash in on all his other promotion, particularly to make his advertising more effective.

Retailers use point-of-purchase promotion on their buildings, in their windows, and on their doors to convert sidewalk traffic into floor traffic. The retailer employs point-of-purchase promotion to support and reinforce *his* advertising, to tie his promotion to a manufacturer's promotion, to move heavy stocks, to help build the retail image he wants. He hopes to stimulate impulse purchases and reminder purchases. All of these mean sales and profits.

Shoppers use point-of-purchase promotion as one source of information about products and their uses. It helps the shopper in her shopping by calling her attention to what is new, by reminding, by suggesting, by identifying bargains. Ideally, it tells her what she wants to know, what she needs to know, what she benefits from knowing.

Distribution of point-of-purchase materials

The normal procedure is for a manufacturer to order the point-of-purchase items he will make available to his retailers. Then comes the job of getting these items to those retailers in the most satisfactory manner. Several distribution techniques are available. Some manufacturers ship point-of-purchase materials direct to retailers and expect installation by the retailers. Some manufacturers' salesmen deliver the materials to their retailers; either the salesman or the retailer installs. Sometimes point-of-purchase items are shipped to wholesalers for distribution by them to retailers. Occasionally certain small items can be packed with the merchandise. Then there are commercial installation firms whose service can be bought if circumstances warrant. Sometimes a manufacturer advertises the availability of point-of-purchase materials and ships only upon request by retailers. The least desirable method is to bundle up a season's quantity and send it, unrequested, to retailers.

Essentials of good display

Good point-of-purchase items are those built on a big sales idea or promise, preferably the same one featured in the manufacturer's current ads. They tell shoppers instantly and with certainty the *type of product* being promoted and the *brand name*. They are simple and powerful, bold and distinctive; they are unified, colorful, and dramatic. Copy is brief, simple, clear, and emphatic. Layout and typography should contribute to communication—not hinder or handicap it. Price should be included unless there is overwhelming reason to omit it.

Interestingly, whether point-of-purchase materials are good or bad depends on the reactions of *retailers* and *shoppers*. Unless the retailer likes the item, he will not install it, and that is bad. Retailers particularly like light and motion—they like point-of-purchase displays which, if appropriate, use sound or scent to appeal to shoppers' senses of hearing or smell. If a point-of-purchase item has no favorable effect on the shopper, that too is bad.

How retailers choose point-of-purchase materials

The retailer is offered and actually gets far more point-of-purchase materials than he uses; he even discards some unopened. How does he decide what to use from this overly abundant quantity?

Some of the influences which bear on him relate to merchandise. If a product is new or new for a certain retailer, its point-of-purchase promotion has a better-than-average chance of being used. If the product gives the retailer a high markup or offers him high potential sales volume, the odds are favorable. Retailers are attracted to window displays featuring products which will build floor traffic. Products often bought on impulse, seasonal products in season, products of which the retailer has too many get their point-of-purchase materials used.

Features of the point-of-purchase materials themselves can help or hurt the chances of use. Here are some positive features. Size is not too large or small. Excellence of item is basically great. Item is sturdy and dependable under wear and tear. Item is easy to get at, assemble, and install. Item encourages the buying of related products. Item is functional ("Please Pay When Served" signs, protective counter mats, clocks). Item strikes the retailer as suitable and appropriate for his store and for the merchandise involved.

Then the relations between a retailer and the competing manufacturers whose brands he stocks constitute an influence. If a manufacturer's retail franchise is valuable, retailers are usually more favorably inclined to find space for some of his point-of-purchase materials. If the retailer's relationship with a particular manufacturer's salesman is unusually cordial, that salesman usually gets some display space. If a retailer regards a manufacturer highly (his national advertising, his aid to retailers), then the retailer tends to favor that manufacturer.

Never forget that each retailer has a very limited amount of space which can be given over to point-of-purchase promotion. The competition among manufacturers for that space is fierce. Each manufacturer would like to "say the last word" to shoppers who have needs, dollars, and a buying frame of mind.

Waste in point-of-purchase promotion

One estimate is that retailers use less than half of the point-of-purchase materials they receive free. A reasonable guess is that 20–25 percent of this free material is not used. This waste can be attacked by two groups, manufacturers and retailers.

Manufacturers can effect some reduction by better buying; the closer they come to the "right" quality (neither too high nor too low) and the "right" quantity (not too much), the less waste there will be. Greater ordering of ensemble displays might reduce some waste; examples are displays built on themes (gardening, picnics) that promote several related products. Manufacturers can place their point-of-purchase materials better, sending it to the right retailers neither too early nor too late. Better promoted point-of-purchase materials, by ads and by salesmen, should be less wasted. Consultation with producers of point-of-purchase promotion and with advertising agencies may reduce manufacturers' waste. Pretesting such elements as size, practicality of use, sales idea, design, ease of installation, and retail reaction—pretesting in a sample of stores should reduce waste. Above all, each manufacturer needs to build a point-of-purchase *program*, well thought out, sound and complete, one tied to his consumer advertising program. Such a program calls for continuous attention and concern, study and research, and above all, for rigorous planning. Here is one manufacturer's schedule:

	Plan	Design	Test	Produce	Deliver
Weeks before use by retailers.......	24	18	15	10	4

Good management will not be achieved so long as point-of-purchase promotion is handled in a hit-or-miss, careless, or neglectful manner.

BUSINESS CATALOGS

There are consumer catalogs—there are business catalogs. Consumer catalogs are treated in the following chapter on consumer stimulation.

We note two types of business catalog. One is for the use of purchasing agents and will be referred to as industrial. Industrial catalogs are much used by those who make and sell, by those who buy and use, industrial and technical products. These catalogs are a major sales tool for industrial salesmen. The other type of business catalog is put together by manufacturers of consumer products and placed in the hands of their retailers, who use these catalogs when buying merchandise for resale.

A catalog is essentially a reference book, booklet, or volume showing and describing merchandise for use or resale. It must be both informative and persuasive. It can be bound or loose-leaf. The business catalog is properly classified as sales promotion, not personal selling or advertising. This is true even though some manufacturers of industrial products spend as much as 25 percent of their *advertising* budgets on their catalogs. This simply reflects an accounting and budgeting decision.

Design

Business catalogs must be designed with three persons in mind. First of all is the person who will buy from the catalog; this person, we have seen, is either a purchasing agent or a retailer. The buyer's point of view is paramount because the role of the catalog is to help buyers buy. The second person is the manufacturer who designs the catalog and makes it available; his catalog must do for him what he wants done. Third is the manufacturer's salesman who uses the catalog in his selling. Because of the interest of these three, because of the catalog's nature and uses, catalogs deserve and demand careful planning and sound design.

Physically, the business catalog should be easy to handle, easy to refer to, and easy to file; 8½ by 11 inches is a popular size because it fits a majority of file drawers. The manufacturer's identification (company name, brand name, trademark) should be bold and instantly recognized on the backbone or spine and on the outside front cover. Each manufacturer must decide how much quality (money) to put into each catalog. Some catalogs should look and be expensive and prestigious—some should be obviously plain and less costly. All should be attractive and durable. Because its life is usually long, the catalog must be easy to keep up to date. One answer is the loose-leaf version with sheets punched to fit in a ring binder. When the manufacturer brings out something new, when he updates the old, or when he needs to correct a mistake, he simply sends the appropriate inserts to buyers.

The catalog's arrangement should be clear and quickly grasped, its organization logical. There should be the optimum number of sections, and each of these should be of the optimum size. Products should be classified and similar items grouped together so the buyer can locate what he is interested in easily and in little time. The index should be cross-indexed, easy to find, easy to use.

Catalog content is mainly a matter of copy and illustrations. The major need of copy is completeness. Descriptions of products should include sizes, colors, styles, packing, uses, price, and transportation costs. The buyer must find the technical information he looks for and needs. Descriptions must be clear, accurate, dependable, and in adequate detail.

The good catalog is illustrated generously. Color, realism, and accuracy contribute. Buyers like pictures which show the product in use *and* persons, provided those persons are not officials of the manufacturing firm.

Uses by buyers and sellers

Buyers file catalogs for future reference about several matters. To them, the catalog is a source of specific, even technical, facts and figures. It gives the buyer a complete picture of the manufacturer's product line, including mechanical details, specifications, performance data and proof, how each product operates, and how each should be used. Buyers use catalogs to check on prices, in selecting a potential source of supply, to buy from. They expect catalogs to contain the answers to their questions about product applications.

For a seller, his catalog functions as a silent salesman in a buyer's office when the real salesman is not there. It is a vehicle which conveys buyer benefits and buyer satisfactions to buyers. As a sales tool, the catalog works toward stronger sales presentations and shorter sales interviews.

Distribution of catalogs

Most business catalogs or buyers' guides are delivered by salesmen, or they are mailed to buyers; a few are offered in publication ads. The manufacturer may lead the actual receipt of the catalog with a telephone call if such is warranted, with an announcement card, a teaser-type communication, or with a letter of advance notification. A card, letter, memo, or band may accompany the physical catalog. Mailing packages or containers should bear identification labels.

Problem of catalog changes

While it will be necessary to make catalog changes from time to time—changes involving products, prices, or correction of mistakes—such changes are costly, and insofar as possible the advertiser should avoid or at least minimize the need for revision. What can be done about changes of prices printed in the catalog? One possibility, obviously, is to omit prices from the catalog and print them on separate price sheets; price can be revised and the price sheets replaced rather easily, particularly if the catalog is of the loose-leaf type. A possible risk here is that the current price sheets may get separated from the catalog. Another method is the changing of the discount structure so as to effect price changes.

Another answer to the problem of change is the infrequent issue of a large catalog, followed periodically by smaller supplements. Still another is to issue a number, perhaps 10, of small catalogs and republish one or two as needed.

TRADE SHOWS, CONVENTIONS, AND EXHIBITS

The toy fairs staged in New York City and the furniture shows staged in High Point, North Carolina, are examples of promotional events to which business buyers are invited. One estimate is that 5,600 trade shows, conventions, and industrial expositions are held annually, that a few manufacturers exhibit in as many as 250. Some trade shows run for a few days only; at the other extreme there are always exhibits and salesmen in the Chicago Merchandise Mart. Professors who attend the annual meetings of their professional associations are familiar with the exhibits and the hospitality of textbook publishers.

Among the objectives that exhibitors may accomplish are the following:

Write up orders.	Check on competitors.
Strengthen company image.	Demonstrate the products.
Build a prospect list.	Distribute samples or literature.
Increase goodwill.	Learn buyers' attitudes.

In an effort to realize these aims, most who show promote their exhibits in a serious manner. How? Their salesmen talk up the exhibits and invite buyers to them. Announcements and invitations are sent to buyers by mail. Ads are run in business or professional publications for the same purpose. Sometimes publicity stories are accepted by editors and appear in those same publications. Once the trade show or convention opens, a manufacturer may resort to door prizes, contests, novelty, live shows, giveaways, dramatic demonstrations, celebrities, or movies in an effort to increase attendance.

Operational features

The manufacturer may start by deciding specifically what he wants to accomplish. For example, he might say, "I want 250 retailers who are good prospects to come to our space, inspect our products, and examine our line. Each is to be asked to fill out a prospect card." Then the manufacturer goes about designing an exhibit which will attract 250 good retail prospects.

His exhibit will benefit from being built on and around a strong idea or theme. Design is so important to success that the sales promotion manager may decide to retain the services of a commercial firm which

FIGURE 10–7. Key questions for exhibit planners

FIFTEEN questions to be asked in planning an exhibit were supplied to attendees at the Exhibit Institute by Dr. Joseph E. Bachelder, director of Marketing Communications Research Center.

They represent a summary of an in-depth study made by the Industrial Advertising Research Institute which Bachelder headed. "If you can answer them you will have a good one (exhibit)," said Dr. Bachelder. "If you can't you'd better not have an exhibit."

He added: "We incorporated here everything that combines underlining factors of memorability and factors involving the play-through of sales ideas."

Here are the questions:
1. What is the story to be told?
   • Product features
   • Product benefits
   • Product applications
   • New developments
   • New design
   • New applications
   • Service features
2. Does the exhibit make an unusual and, at the same time, effective effort to attract visitors?
3. Does this effort to get attention help to tell the product story, or is it merely an attention-getting gimmick?
4. Does the exhibit tell the story by itself, and continuously, or does it depend on intermittent "shows" or word-of-mouth explanations?
5. Does every important element in the exhibit function in telling the product story?
6. Has every distracting or non-functional element been removed from the proposed exhibit?
7. Has it been made as easy as possible for the visitor to absorb and remember the story?
8. Has animation been used as much as possible?
9. Does the animation help to tell the story?
10. Are the product features and benefits clearly spelled out, instead of being left to the imagination?
11. Are the product features and benefits demonstrated, instead of merely being illustrated?
12. Are clear cases of product application pointed out?
13. Is the exhibit well-unitized, instead of being a disorganized display of unrelated, miscellaneous elements?
14. Has the exhibit been simplified, so far as is practical, to tell the story? Has every unnecessary element been removed?
15. Are all statements about product features and benefits believable, immediately acceptable and demonstrable?

Source: *SM/Sales Meetings*, November 15, 1968.

specializes in exhibits. In any event, the exhibit or booth should have attractive eye appeal; it should be different from others yet in harmony with the entire show. By all means the booth should be staffed with personable and able individuals in generous number—individuals who know exactly what to do in order to make the desired impression and to help the exhibitor accomplish what he set out to do.

If his products are too large or heavy for his salesmen to carry, the industrial manufacturer tries, if feasible, to stage as impressive product demonstrations as possible. The trade show may offer such a manufacturer his only opportunity to show and operate his products as he talks with buyers.

Some sort of registration machinery is found in many booths in order to get at least the names and addresses of prospects. One example is the literature request card which the prospect is asked to fill out. This makes certain that the literature reaches the buyer at his office rather than getting misplaced and lost at the show. In addition, the seller gets the buyer's name, title, address, and, perhaps, valuable information about his interests and his problems.

Some manufacturers host a meeting in a retail association trade show city and invite *their* retailers to it; this meeting is usually scheduled for the day before or the day after his type of retailers (drug, hardware, furniture) have their annual trade show or convention.

Comments on trade shows

The value of trade shows is questioned because their effectiveness is questionable. Among the merits claimed for them is the opportunity for face-to-face contact with buyers by home office personnel of seller firms who normally do not see buyers. Seldom are so many prospects concentrated within a single building, including buying influences and top executives of buyer firms who seldom see salesmen. The nature of the trade shows and conventions permits a manufacturer to learn much about the operations of competitors. Buying inquiries and selling leads can be invited and sought. Buyers' attitudes toward competitors and their lines can be sensed. Finally, for some products, the buyer has a rare opportunity to touch a product, to see it in realistic, true-to-life circumstances.

But, there is the other side of the coin. For most exhibitors, the cost is high and the promotional event is brief. Noise, crowds, partying, and the city's attractions can distract. The exhibit of any one manufacturer may turn out to be inferior to competitors' exhibits. Not always are the dates convenient.

In the light of these plus points and minus points, each exhibitor must try to estimate how many of *his* top prospects registered for the show, how many and which of these visited his booth, and what their reactions were. This is not an easy or a precise undertaking.

Here are some comments about trade shows from Mr. T. I. Adams, exhibit manager of Republic Steel:

Republic Steel regards trade shows primarily as an advertising medium rather than as an avenue for direct sales. Many other exhibitors use trade shows as a medium for direct sales, and rightly so; but if we were to attempt to do so, we would probably have very little return on our investment in this medium. The number of specifications that must be agreed upon in the sale and purchase of steel, and the number of persons usually involved in even a single transaction do not favor any sort of "impulse buying" of steel at a trade show.

As a close parallel to the way we use trade publication advertising, we use trade shows as a method of reaching the many buying and specifying influences for steel and steel products that we are unable to reach through our salesmen's calls. The audience that we reach at a trade show is a pre-selected audience of persons with an interest in manufacturing, and in the marketing of the finished products. Steel is usually the material most widely used in these products. In many cases, we can only reach these persons through advertising because we do not know who they are or what their specific influence is in the marketing of steel. Because of this, it is very probable that we would be unable to reach them even through the medium of direct mail. At a trade show we are, in effect, able to "go retail" and set up a store whereby they can call on us if their interest in our products prompts them to do so.

Many advertisers regard trade shows as only a place to introduce new products. Trade shows provide an excellent way to do this; however, we regard trade shows primarily as a way to interest "new people" in our products. Our audience for our advertising is continually changing and new faces are constantly appearing in the ranks of our customers' personnel. Trade shows offer an excellent way to meet these new people and to acquaint them with the advantages which we have to offer them. These advantages may be connected with products which have been marketed for many years.

Our philosophy of exhibiting has a few peculiarities which have worked out very well for us and in which you may be interested. We try to have an adequate space for our exhibit to accommodate the number of visitors to be expected. At most of the shows in which we participate, we are interested in almost 100 percent of the visitors. Of course, we never achieve this primary objective, but we do have some success in attracting from 25 to 35 percent of the visitors. The booth is laid out in such a way that it is obvious to the passersby that we are most anxious to have them come into our booth. The entrance to the booth is well marked, and the path that the visitors will take through the booth is also well marked. We station a girl at the entrance to invite the visitor to come in. In all cases, we have some kind of audience participation in which the visitor must do something to obtain full benefit from the exhibit.

We usually have three or four product demonstrations for the visitor as he proceeds through the booth. We make it very easy for the visitor to ask for literature at the very moment in which his interest in any particular product is aroused. As the visitor leaves the booth, we usually offer him a small premium as a token of our appreciation for his having visited us. This procedure has proved to be very successful over many years of exhibiting.

Of our total advertising budget, approximately 5 percent is set aside for trade shows; but nearly 40 percent of the measurable returns from advertising, that is requests for literature and further information, are attributable to our trade show participation.

As a final thought, it might be interesting to consider the number of methods which can be used to attract and inform visitors at a trade show in comparison to the methods available in other forms of advertising. The whole range of modern audio-visual techniques can be used in trade shows, including motion pictures, slide films, recorded music, as well as the use of professional talent in drama, demonstrations, magic shows, and the like. Of course, printed information, pictures, diagrams, scale models, and other static methods can be used effectively. The appeal to the visitors' senses can include sight, hearing, smell, touch, and taste. Of course, the principal benefit of the trade show advertising medium is that it offers any caller a chance to talk with a representative of the exhibitor company to ask questions, to get acquainted, and in many cases, to buy.

HOW MANUFACTURERS STIMULATE THEIR RETAILERS

Contests for retailers

A manufacturer may turn to dealer contests in his effort to step up retailers' promotion and sale of the manufacturer's brands. Typically the manufacturer plans the contest, promotes it to his retailers, and awards prizes to the winners. Some contests are for the retailers themselves, some for the stores. In addition, a manufacturer may design a contest for a retailer to run within and for his own firm.

Three patterns or bases are popular. Retailers may vie for the best point-of-purchase display. They may compete on the basis of dollar purchases. They may compete on the basis of percentage increase of purchases.

Executive gifts

The trade association representing the advertising speciality industry classifies advertising specialities as advertising novelties, calendars, and executive gifts. We treat the first two in the next chapter as consumer stimulants; executive gifts we treat here.

Executive gifts are distributed in limited quantity to important buyers, buying influences, their families, or their offices and homes. Most cost within the $10–$25 range, but some cost more. The gifts are practical and functional, many are unusual. Some are for short-run consumption—cheese, fruit, beverages, steaks, and tickets; others are for long-term use—desk sets, trays, cameras, glassware, and luggage. Although some carry the recipient's name and a few carry the seller's identification, most carry neither. Executive gifts are given in appreciation of past and in anticipation of future business. The advertising specialty industry describes them as "reminders of a seller's thoughtfulness." Most are distributed by mail or by someone on the manufacturer's staff, perhaps a salesman. Executive gifts are, of course, received by other business buyers than retailers; they are given to such buyers as wholesalers, purchasing agents, buyers of advertising space and time—to business buyers in general.

Trade advertising

Trade advertising is, as the term implies, *advertising*, but because its purpose is to influence, persuade, and stimulate retailers (remember, we do not have space to treat wholesalers), it is placed here.

Trade advertising is run by a manufacturer of consumer products to stimulate the retailers who stock and sell his merchandise. Most manufacturers of products sold by retailers feel pressure to try to influence the attitudes and actions of the retailers they want to stock and sell their wares. Most of those retailers are in a strong position because most do not *have* to carry the brands of any one manufacturer, and most *do* carry the directly competing brands of several manufacturers.

FIGURE 10–8. Cartier's ad promoting executive gifts appeared in *The Wall Street Journal*

Cartier

ALMOST EVERYONE WOULD LIKE YOUR BUSINESS GIFTS TO COME FROM CARTIER

Our world-renowned name enhances the impression made by the gifts that go out in your company's name.

Through our Corporate Sales Division you are offered a comprehensive selection of truly distinctive gifts starting at modest levels. Because they are business gifts, you will enjoy an important price advantage.

A complete Cartier service plan is designed to relieve you of time-consuming details.

Christmas gift brochure on request.

For an appointment, at your office or at Cartier, call PLaza 3-0111.

CORPORATE SALES, DIVISION OF CARTIER INC.
Fifth Ave. at 52nd St., New York, N. Y. 10022

Because the retailer's major goal is to make money, his basic question when making buying decisions is: Will it sell—at a profit? So, a manufacturer in his trade advertising stresses salability, sales volume, gross margin, quality-to-price relationship, terms of sale, relations with suppliers, and, above all, the manufacturer's consumer promotion program.

FIGURE 10–9. Trade ad run by a manufacture and aimed at hardware retailers

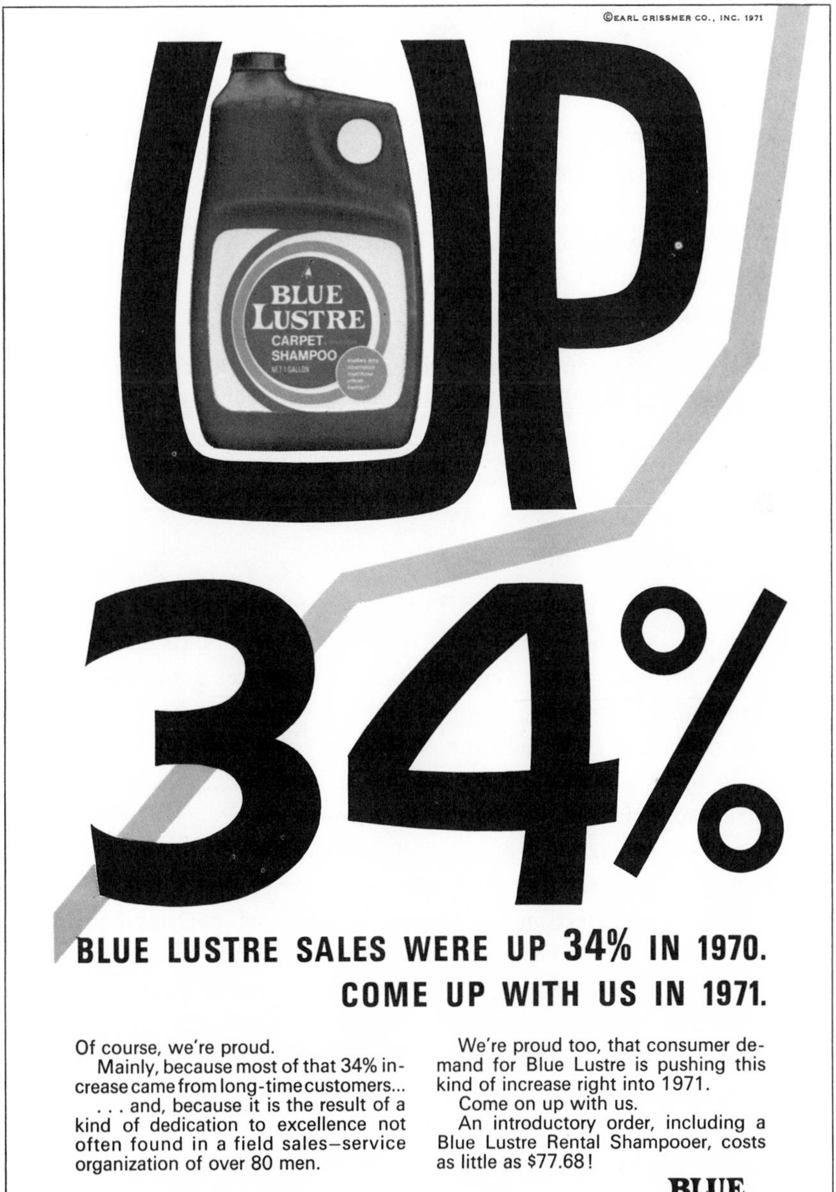
©EARL GRISSMER CO., INC. 1971
UP
BLUE LUSTRE
CARPET
SHAMPOO
34%
BLUE LUSTRE SALES WERE UP 34% IN 1970.
COME UP WITH US IN 1971.
Of course, we're proud.
Mainly, because most of that 34% increase came from long-time customers...
. . . and, because it is the result of a kind of dedication to excellence not often found in a field sales–service organization of over 80 men.
We're proud too, that consumer demand for Blue Lustre is pushing this kind of increase right into 1971.
Come on up with us.
An introductory order, including a Blue Lustre Rental Shampooer, costs as little as $77.68!
EARL GRISSMER COMPANY, INC. • 712 E. 64th ST. • INDIANAPOLIS, INDIANA 46220
BLUE LUSTRE

Source: Reprinted from 1971 *Hardware Retailer* Magazine.

He promises sales and profit, markup and margin, high turnover and low cost of handling, popularity with ultimate consumers because of his advertising and his sales promption activities.

Typical goals of the trade advertiser are to:

Announce new products.
"Sell" his consumer promotion program.
Urge retailers to stock and push the line.
Announce specific deals, specials, or contests.
Get retailers to synchronize their own promotion.
Stress the profitability of the line.

Trade advertising appears in such merchandising or trade publications as *The American Druggist, Chain Store Age*, and *Women's Wear Daily*. The same type of communication can travel from manufacturer to retailers by mail.

Deals manufacturers offer retailers

Deals are special concessions. They may be offered to increase retail distribution, to increase the number of in-store displays, to increase retail inventories, to get greater retail support, to counter some competitive promotion, or, in general, to increase sales and share of market. The offer is usually for a limited time. The most common way for a retailer to qualify for the concessions is to place a large order, the composition of which is sometimes stipulated by the manufacturer.

What does the retailer get that he would not otherwise get? Free goods may be the reward. Reduced prices are sometimes the reward. Closely akin are advertising or display allowances, perhaps equal to 1 percent of the retailer's purchases. The manufacturer may offer some extraordinary point-of-purchase or other promotional material. Or, he may offer the retailer a personal, in-store demonstrator for a certain number of days. The retailer may be allowed certain merchandise on consignment. He may be quoted more liberal dating, billing, or terms.

A final reward will be described in a bit more detail; it is the inclusion of retailers' names and addresses in the manufacturer's magazine ads. Regionalization of magazine circulation has greatly encouraged and facilitated this deal. Manufacturers of furniture and tires are examples of firms using this particular promotion.

Some retail lists are short, some are long. Once in a while, a manufacturer with highly selective distribution will list in one ad retailers in all 50 states. Long lists are usually grouped by states, by listing cities alphabetically under each state, then by listing the retailer(s) in each city. The list of retailers may be the right-hand page of a two-page spread. The listing occasionally is free; sometimes the cost is shared; sometimes the retailer must place a certain order or do a predetermined type of promotion (newspaper advertising, window display) to qualify for inclusion.

TRAINING AND STIMULATING RETAIL SALESPERSONS

Most manufacturers of consumer goods which move through retail stores are to a large extent dependent on how successfully those retailers' salespersons sell. In a real sense those individuals are members of the manufacturers' selling teams; if they are weak, a manufacturer's overall selling effort will be weak. Even if retailers defray part of the cost of the plans and programs developed, the person to take the initiative and the responsibility is the manufacturer.

Training

A few manufacturers operate special sales training schools at the home office and factory, or in regional headquarters, for promising retail salesmen. For example, one runs a 10-day training course at several regional training centers; the retailer pays travel, salary, and living expenses for the period, and the manufacturer pays the rest. Such an operation is seldom feasible except for makers of "big ticket" items—automobiles, large appliances, expensive cameras.

Or, the manufacturer may take the training program to the retail salespersons. Correspondence courses and other direct mail may be used. Sales manuals, films, slides, charts, and literature may be supplied to retailers with which *they* can teach their salesmen. Before-hours or after-hours sales meetings may be conducted by the manufacturer's salesmen. In rare instances, a manufacturer will equip and route a special training bus or trailer that holds 15-20 persons.

Many manufacturers cannot afford to offer any of this training, and many are not willing to try.

Certain facts are discouraging to manufacturers considering or actually doing some sort of training. The typical retail salesperson is not going to study hard, he is not going to drive himself, he is not going to do much homework if any. He probably will be difficult, resentful, and even hostile if he has been forced into the training program. Because

he reads little, communication with him must rely heavily on visual training aids and visual training.

Training content should stress product information, buyer information,
and how-to-sell information. The manufacturer's aspirations must be restrained; he must not try to do too much too quickly. He certainly
must avoid the appearance of running a "school," of scolding, preaching,
or talking down to retail salesmen. Here are topics which have been
handled satisfactorily by various manufacturers:

Courtesy and good manners.
Importance of salesmen.
How to speak effectively.
Determining buyers' wants.
Human relations.
Telephone selling.
How to demonstrate products.
Handling buyers' objections.
Developing a clientele.

Stimulating

The purpose of this stimulation, of course, is to get retail salesmen
to sell more and to do certain jobs which will contribute to more sales.
Sometimes the manufacturer wants greater selling effort in off seasons
or back of his full line.

Many types of stimulants are used. Gifts, allowances, and discounts
are used. PM's (some translate this as Push Money, some as Premium
Merchandise, some just call it "spiffs") may be offered on items the
manufacturer is particularly anxious to move. Then there are contests
and other sales incentive plans. Sales meetings and house organs have
been mentioned. Finally, the better the relations between a manufacturer's
salesmen and the salespersons in his retail firms, the greater the sales
effort put back of the manufacturer's brand.

MANAGEMENT COUNSEL FOR RETAILERS

A manufacturer can encourage his retailers to do a better job by
offering them management counsel. Many retailers need this, and many
expect it. Competitors of the manufacturer may be doing this currently.
We have already admitted the dependence of the manufacturer on a

retailer's salespersons; now we are recognizing his dependence on the retailer himself, on his competence as a manager. The manufacturer in a sense is as strong and as weak as his retailers are, because they see and deal with his ultimate prospects and customers. A particularly relevant and basic fact here is that many manufacturers need the volume of their output which goes through the smaller sized stores. But small retailers are at least handicapped in certain areas and operational phases

FIGURE 10–10. Table of contents from a Johnson & Johnson booklet entitled *Make Customers Stop by Promotions*

STOP

A practical application of the principles

of retail advertising and sales promotion

In compiling and editing this book, Johnson & Johnson made every effort to assure itself of the practical application of its contents. Therefore, to the observations and personal experiences of its own sales representatives in the field and its research staff it added those of . . .

LOUIS E. KAZIN, Ph.G., former Director of the Pharmaceutical Extension of Rutgers University, who has 30 years in drug retailing, 12 years as a drug store owner, and for several years a national drug publication editor.

LAURENCE LOUGHLIN, Vice-President, Advertisers' Exchange, Inc.

when in competition against mass retailers. The situation, then, is that manufacturers need to sell through small retailers who need help from those manufacturers; the more and the better help manufacturers give, the better jobs small retailers can do for their manufacturers.

On a high level, manufacturers offer the same aid that management consultants sell. Counsel on specific matters includes:

Location	Pricing
Organization	Accounting and records
Layout and arrangement	Consumer services
Equipment	Stock control
Buying	Turnover
Display	Storage
Salesmanship	Personnel
Advertising	Planning
Traffic stimulation	Forecasting
Credit management	Budgeting

How is management counsel supplied? Some counsel is offered in printed material—bulletins, house organ for retailers, newsletters, and such. Specialized manuals may be supplied to retailers; for example, an advertising manual might help retailers build stronger ads, select more suitable media, schedule more effectively, budget more soundly. Person-to-person counseling can be done in retail clinics, maybe on a district basis, in the form of conferences, classes, discussions, and seminars. The manufacturer's salesmen may function as counselors.

QUESTIONS AND PROBLEMS

10-1. A manufacturer of a line of consumer products is thinking of beginning a refresher training program for his experienced salesmen. Make some suggestions.

10-2. If a manufacturer does an outstanding job when training his salesmen, how may he recover more than the cost of the program?

10-3. Why might a retailer reconsider a product which he has earlier refused to stock?

10-4. What types of editorial material may be found in a manufacturer's house organ published for his dealers and his salesmen?

10-5. List some sources of mailing lists suitable for use by retailers. For what purposes might retailers mail to those persons on the lists?

10-6. Comment on sales meetings held aboard a cruise ship.

10–7.   Is manufacturer–retailer cooperative advertising a bribe? Blackmail? A valuable promotion tool? Comment.

10–8.   Most point-of-purchase material retailers receive is free. When might a manufacturer ask his retailers to pay all or part of the cost of point-of-purchase items?

10–9.   How do you explain the low quality that characterizes most retail salesmanship?

10–10. Are contests for manufacturer's salesmen good or bad? Are they a bit of both?

CHAPTER 11

Stimulating ultimate consumers

B EFORE A SELLER can hope to increase purchases by ultimate consumers
he must have identified his product or service; his wares must be "known"
to buyers. Otherwise he will be greatly handicapped in trying to stimulate
and serve them. Four of the most common methods of identification
involve brand names and trademarks, trade characters, packages, and
slogans. A brief treatment of each follows. In a sense, brand names, trademarks, and packages are merchandising or product matters; trade characters are clearly more sales promotional in nature than either advertising
or personal selling; slogans are closely related to advertising campaigns.
Publicity, which is another factor in the stimulation of consumer purchases, will be discussed in Chapter 13.

PRODUCT IDENTIFICATION FOR CONSUMERS

Brand names and trademarks

The term *trademark* is the official and legal name for brand names
and pictorial trademarks. Legally, a trademark can be a word, name,
symbol, device—or a combination of these; a brand name, thus, is one
form of trademark. For us, a brand name is a word, a trademark is
a pictorial symbol or device, and a trade name is the name of the firm

or company; the three can belong to a manufacturer, to a wholesaler, or to a retailer.

The selection of a brand name is important for several reasons. The cost to establish a new brand name is high, even for a good one. Promotion costs increase year after year. There are so many brand names, and new ones appear every day. At the moment of selection, the seller intends never to change the brand name, because change is both costly and confusing. So, we can understand why a manufacturer looked at 153,000 brand names before selecting "Corfam."

Some brand names are personal names; the person can be the founder of the firm, a famous deceased person, a person from the realm of mythology. Sometimes the trade name is selected for additional duty as the brand name. The dictionary may supply brand names. Some sellers have appropriated foreign words for use as brand names. Some brand names have been coined. The seller may use letters or numbers. He can add a prefix or a suffix, he can misspell, shorten, or combine words, and he can even build a meaningless brand name. The better brand names are short, appropriate, and distinctive—easy to pronounce, to hear, and to remember. They are suitable in all media and for a family of products. Brand names are weak and unfortunate if commonplace, if they have an undesirable connotation, or if they infringe or misrepresent.

No seller wants his brand name to become generic, to slip into the public domain, to become public property. When does this occur? When the public refers to that *type* of product—to that *class* of product—by the seller's brand name. Such a fate befell such brand names as escalator, cellophane, and lanolin. How can this be prevented? By giving the public a word or phrase for that *type* of product, as Prestone *antifreeze* and Deepfreeze *home freezer*. In addition, the seller can indicate that his brand name is a legal trademark and is so used; he may use the symbol ® or use distinctive lettering for this purpose. In addition, the seller can police the market, protesting and taking action against anyone misusing his brand name.

Trade characters

Since the appearance of television, more and more sellers have sponsored trade characters as an identification and promotion device. Betty Crocker and the Green Giant are two well-known examples. After deciding to have a trade character, the seller has three options: he can choose from the world of animate beings (Chessie, the C&O cat), he can per-

FIGURE 11–1. These three pictures show the modernization of Martha Logan, Swift's trade character

sonalize and animate a mute, immobile object (Planter's Mr. Peanut), or he can rent the use of some well-known character (Peanuts comic strip characters).

Trade characters can be masculine, feminine, or sexless. Each is a unique personality able to move, to talk, to act. Some are named, some are not. Consumers associate some with a brand name, some with the sponsoring firm.

A trade character can give personality to a product or to a company. It can symbolize a product's virtues as Tough Guy does for a brand of piston rings *or* an enemy of the buyer as Dirty Dan Carbon did for a gasoline company. It can endow a seller or his product with warmth, emotion, and friendliness. At least two trade characters were named to tell the public how to pronounce brand names—Sue Shard and Hugh Bline. The Green Giant even gave his name to the company for which he works. Many trade characters deliver advertising messages; many provide a thread of continuity to and through a succession of advertising campaigns.

Packaging

Packaging costs are properly shared by the production budget *and* the promotion budget. For many products the package is one cost of influencing buyers; it is a promotion tool of considerable power. Self-service, open display, and the decline in the use of shopping lists have greatly increased the role of the package; they have made it a real basis for seller-to-seller competition. The sales promotion manager's interest in packaging is natural and understandable. Retail preferences are a dealer matter; retail displays are often built of packages. The package can help or hurt the manufacturer's efforts to stimulate ultimate consumers. Box tops, coupons, cents-off labels, and sample sizes are other package features related to sales promotion.

The package is asked to do three main jobs by the persons most concerned; they are the manufacturer, the retailer, and the consumer. First, it is to protect its contents all the way until they have been consumed. There must be no spoilage, breakage, deterioration, spilling, leakage, or evaporation. Second, the package is to identify. Shoppers in stores and consumers in their homes want to be able to recognize product type and brand correctly and immediately. Visibility and legibility must be good at eye level or floor level, from several feet away, from several directions, to women who should wear glasses but do not. Third, the package is expected to stimulate buying. To do this it must be attractive, provocative, and appealing.

Many packages contain inserts, clearly a sales promotion item. Examples of package inserts are leaflets, samples, folders, decals, booklets, coupons, pictures, premiums, and mailing cards. Circulation is low in waste and rather high in quality. The typical insert is versatile and inexpensive, it travels free.

Much has been heard and read recently about "consumer protection." Packaging is a natural interest of those who speak for consumers and of organized professional consumer groups. The Point-of-Purchase Advertising Institute requested that the following be considered in packaging and labeling:

> List actual ingredients.
> Give ingredients by percent of total.
> State grade of product.
> Give unit price.
> Use readable type.
> Standardize packages.
> Give preparation instructions.
> Convert to metric system.
> List caloric content.
> Use government grade labeling.
> List fat content and kind of fat.
> List nutritional content.
> Note expiration date (perishables).
> Give net weight.
> State number of servings.
> Ban fractions in net weight.
> Discontinue "cents off" packages.
> List safety factors.
> Reduce package sizes.

Slogans

If the advertiser chooses, he can express the theme of each advertising campaign in the form of a slogan. Once in a long while, a slogan catches on so well that the advertiser continues to publicize it campaign after campaign, year after year; "It floats" is such a slogan.

The slogan should be short and simple, clear and catchy, easy to remember and easy to repeat. Puns, plays on words, rhyming, rhythm, balance, and alliteration can be built nicely into slogans. Slogan writers

FIGURE 11–2. Du Pont MSD cellophane safeguards the taste and texture of Levy's rye bread during shipment and the time it spends on a retailer's shelf.

must remember that the deftly turned phrase they compose is intended to be repeated verbatim.

The good slogan says something good about the brand or the seller in not over seven or eight words. It suggests or promises benefit or satisfaction. It avoids being trite, too clever, or subtle—good slogans identify *type of product*, include *brand name*, and promise a *benefit*.

CONSUMER CONTESTS

One estimate is that approximately 400 consumer contests are sponsored annually offering prizes worth $60 million and backed with $500 million of promotion. This powerful sales stimulant is used more in buyers' market than in sellers' markets; it tends to run in cycles. Consumers enter contests in the hope of winning prizes. Cash and travel are two popular types of prizes; merchandise, too, is popular. Merchandise offered may include ordinary items such as swimming pools, automobiles, and appliances or exotic items such as oil wells, islands, and race horses. Evidence of purchase may be requested; if so, one effect is to force sampling at full retail price by contestants who are new users of the product.

TABLE 11–1. Who sponsored contests

	First half 1970	First half 1969	Last half 1969
Soft drinks............................	25	29	27
Meat products.........................	20	20	21
Fats & dairy...........................	17	23	21
Canned & frozen foods.................	8	8	7
Flour, mixes & feeds..................	8	8	7
Spices & condiments...................	6	7	6
Confections & desserts.................	5	7	6
Pet foods.............................	4	5	4
Tea & coffee..........................	2	2	3
Breakfast cereals......................	2	2	2
Other foods...........................	10	14	13
Petroleum & TBA products.............	34	48	39
Health & beauty aids..................	31	35	36
Appliances............................	10	12	11
Publishers & broadcasters..............	8	11	9
Cleaning aids.........................	6	5	5
Clothing..............................	2	3	3
Miscellaneous.........................	83	70	71

Source: *Incentive Marketing*, August 1970.

Types

The sponsor of a consumer contest can choose from several types. One easy to enter and easy to judge is the 25-word statement that begins, "I like (brand name) because . . . ." Another simple type asks the entrant to complete a verse, a jingle, or a limerick; some of these have pulled a delightfully large number of entries. Other contests call for writing a letter, composing a slogan, naming a product or a trade character, word building, solving puzzles, or suggesting new product uses.

In *contests*, the entrant does something that is judged; the less skill required, the larger the number of entries. In contrast, there is the *sweepstakes* format in which the consumer does nothing but see if his number,

FIGURE 11–3a.   Cash offer requirements

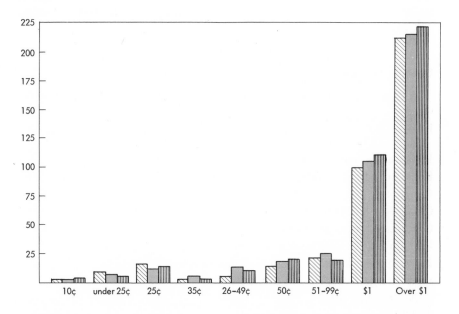

FIGURE 11–3b.   Type of contest

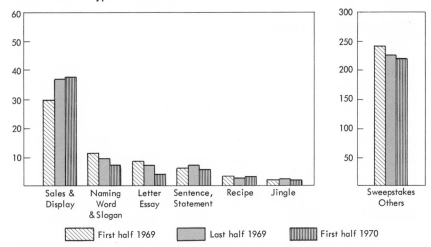

Source: *Incentive Marketing*, August 1970.

his card, or his cutout is a winner. Or, he sends in his name and address on an entry blank to be included in a drawing. Sweepstakes are illegal in some states.

Specific purposes

Although all consumer contests are expected to stimulate consumer buying, the sponsor's objective can often be stated more precisely. Examples:

Increase the unit of purchase.
Build store traffic—retailers stock entry blanks.
Get more thorough readership of ads.
Change an unfortunate sales curve.
Get greater retail distribution.
Perk up interest of consumers, retailers, salesmen.
Increase the number of product demonstrations.
Stimulate new uses for old products.
Build a mailing list.
Get testimonials from consumers.

Merits claimed for contests

Outstanding consumer contests generate mass interest and excitement; entries number in the millions—a soap manufacturer got 11 million in one of his contests. There is publicity, there is showmanship, there is sampling. And the sampling ranks high in favorable attentiveness, interest, and thoughtfulness, because most entrants buy, use, and look for something good about the product. Contests appeal to strong motives—to play, to compete, to win, to get something for nothing. The effects on retailers' *and* manufacturers' sales are positive.

Criticisms of contests

Opponents of contests fear that prizes and contest promotion will overshadow the manufacturer's product and its promotion. They regret that prizes are subject to income taxes. Some critics doubt if contest results justify contest costs, amounts which can be high when the costs of prizes, promotion, judging, clerical, and handling expenses are added. Effects, furthermore, may be a short-lived increase in sales followed by a slump. Winning by professional contest entrants, ill will of losers, legal restraints, and contest scandals of the past are presented as influences against consumer contests. Finally, opponents consider consumer contests to be one of the more risky types of promotion to sponsor because sales volume *and* number of entrants may both fall below the firm's forecasts.

In the late 1960's, "preselected winner" games received some unfavorable publicity. The fact became known that only about 10 percent of the prizes were ever awarded, and most of those given were small. Forms of manipulation were discovered relating to control and direction of winning numbers. The FTC went into corrective action, as did some of the large gasoline companies which were sponsoring such giveaway games of chance.

Suggestions about contests

Single contests should be scheduled to run four to eight weeks; weekly contests should run four, five, or six weeks. Interest tends to lag after six or eight weeks. A hard choice is whether to run one contest for five weeks—or five separate contests for one week each.

As for prizes, the first prize should be relatively huge, secondary prizes relatively modest. If 5,000 or 10,000 secondary prizes are offered, obviously they must be small ones. The manufacturer can get merchandise prizes at less than retail value—sometimes free because of publicity value. Once a $5,000 cash prize outpulled $10,000 worth of merchandise by four to one, but $500 in merchandise outpulled $250 in cash. Merchandise prizes discourage those who make a profession of entering contests.

Every effort should be made to make the contest interesting and easy to enter, to choose a task the consumer can do with relative ease. The task should be tied to the consumer's experience with the product. Proof of purchase should be tolerable—the entrant must not be required to prove that he bought a gross of the product.

Lotteries must be avoided. Any contest resembling a lottery should be attempted only after consultation with lawyers, or by contracting with a specialized commercial firm to handle the entire promotion. It is essential to avoid what the Federal Trade Commission considers to constitute a lottery. The FTC says that a lottery includes (1) *consideration* (such as purchase of the product; this explains the usual option of a "reasonable facsimile"); (2) an element of *chance* rather than skill (temperature readings, depth of snow); and (3) a *prize*. Simply, the FTC claims the promotion is a lottery if the entrant pays to enter for a chance to win a prize.

Rules should be adopted and drafted with great care. They should be clear and simple, fair and complete. Rules involve dates, the entrant's task, who can enter, how to enter, prizes, judging, and announcement of winners.

FIGURE 11–4. Canada Dry offers golf balls as premiums

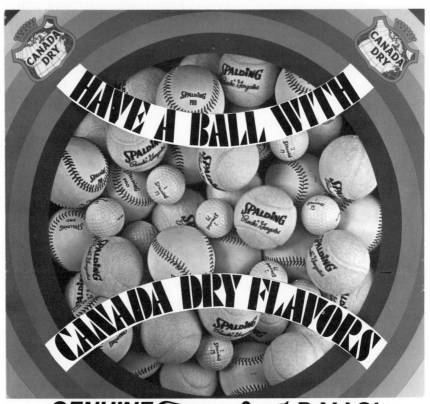

Consumer contests must be promoted just as products are advertised and sold. One type of promotion is directed at salesmen and retailers, one at ultimate consumers. Multiple entries are encouraged by consumers. A single sweepstakes may be backed by a $2 million promotion budget. Television, radio, and magazines are popular advertising media.

Retailers play an important role in many contests. They stock the brand, have entry blanks for consumers to pick up, make product demonstrations. Hopefully, they publicize the contest in their ads and with point-of-purchase promotion. The manufacturer may award prizes to retailers who gave out the entry blanks of the consumer winners.

Judging and the selection of winners must be characterized by competence, objectivity, and integrity. Because of possible complication and difficulty, many large contests are handled by specialized contest firms which include judging as one of their services.

How does the manufacturer evaluate his consumer contest's results? He determines the number of entries, measures the change in sales volume, tries to estimate how many retailers participated, asks for the judgment of his salesmen and retailers.

CONSUMER PREMIUMS

A premium is some item of value offered to a consumer as a bonus or bribe if the consumer makes a certain purchase, watches a product

TABLE 11-2. Who sponsored premium offers

	First half 1970	First half 1969	Last half 1969
Canned & frozen foods	71	70	68
Soft drinks	60	49	50
Confections & desserts	57	54	52
Fats & dairy	43	39	45
Meat products	32	25	30
Spices & condiments	26	22	24
Flour, mixes & feeds	25	25	28
Tea & coffee	20	20	19
Pet foods	19	14	15
Breakfast cereals	17	18	18
Other foods	89	94	87
Health & beauty aids	130	134	127
Petroleum, TBA products	98	92	92
Appliances	41	49	44
Cleaning aids	34	43	39
Publishers & broadcasters	17	26	24
Clothing	14	11	18
Miscellaneous	247	269	272

Source: *Incentive Marketing*, August 1970.

demonstration, or submits to a sales presentation. The premium can be considered something extra which sweetens the offer, an additional reason or special inducement for buying. Essentially the premium is in the nature of a gift—lagniappe. The premium may be "free"; if not, the amount the consumer must pay must be well under market price. When a housewife is charged for 12 rolls but receives the traditional "baker's dozen" of 13, she is getting a premium; when a man buys a suit and gets a "free" tie, the tie is a premium; when a family saves 1,000 coupons and exchanges them for a bridge table, it is a premium. Trading stamps, incidentally, are exchanged for premiums, but they demand and get the next section all to themselves.

Products appropriate for premium promotion

Most convenience products bought by women or children can benefit from premium offers. These products typically are low in price. There is great product similarity, competition among brands is fierce, consumption is regular, and replacement rather speedy. Examples? Soap, food, coffee, tea, and drug products.

Specific purposes

Among the various purposes for which sales stimulants may be used are:

Loading retail shelves and increasing stocks.
Increasing size of purchase.
Meeting price competition, especially off-label price reductions.
Increasing store traffic.
Bidding for the goodwill and support of children.
Promoting a family of products.
Boosting sales in off seasons.
Gaining entreé for house-to-house salesmen.
Selling one unit one time to new consumers.
Increasing brand loyalty through coupon saving.

Selecting the premium

Selecting the premium to offer is a critical decision because some are fantastically popular—some flop. These generally are features of good

FIGURE 11-5.

Standards of Marketing Practice

A premium promotion is a compact between a user (advertiser) and the supplier for the benefit of the consumer. Responsibility for performance must be shared by both user and supplier. The NPSE member, however, bears a primary responsibility in this relationship, and must conduct himself in all transactions in a professional manner which leads to the ultimate satisfaction of the consumer.

We believe the following Standards are essential to this professional performance:

RELATIONSHIP WITH THE USER: The member should maintain the closest possible working relationship with the user throughout the promotion period, including assistance in planning, counseling on the establishment of clear objectives, preparation of advertising, follow-through on details of prompt fulfillment, and evaluation. Complete respect for confidences relating to the user's marketing plans is most necessary.

PROGRAM PLANNING: The member shall insist upon the most complete specifications in all contracts, including:

(a) *Item description* as to contents, features, materials, size, quality, packaging and pricing.

(b) *Retail Values* and comparatives in self-liquidating or free offers should be used only when approved by both the supplier and the user, and when there is no reasonable chance of deception.

(c) *Delivery time and expiration date* should be included in all consumer copy. A procedure for alerting the consumer to delayed delivery of premium merchandise should be specifically provided, with responsibility spelled out as to performance and cost. Consumers' checks should not be deposited until just before the scheduled shipping date. Responsibility and procedures for non-delivery, damaged goods and replacement should also be specified.

PURCHASE COMMITMENT: A fair and reasonable quantity commitment should be specified in the contract, with detail of shipping schedules and lead-time requirements for back-up supplies beyond the original purchase.

DECEPTIVE PROMOTIONS: It shall be the NPSE member's responsibility to avoid participation in supplying any promotional campaign which may be deceptive in nature. In the case of sweepstakes, all prizes should be awarded by drawing; preselected-winner promotions undermine consumer confidence.

SALES REPRESENTATION: The member should insure that staff salesmen, manufacturers' representatives, jobbers and any others who sell his products observe the necessary professional standards in relationships with the user. Manufacturers' representatives' responsibilities by type of promotion, territory assignment, exclusions, commission rates, terms of payment, sample policies and reporting requirements should be detailed by contract.

ADVERTISING APPROVAL: No member shall abrogate or delegate his responsibility and right to approve initial, intermediate and final promotional and advertising materials representing his products, directed at the consumer and the trade.

MEMBER'S RESPONSIBILITY: It should be understood that in all cases it is the professional supplier executive's ultimate responsibility to see that a promotion is properly conducted — and to withdraw immediately from any program if the user refuses to safeguard performance.

•

A member failing to comply with these Standards shall be subject to sanctions and will face disciplinary action as provided by the Board of Directors, including possible termination of his membership.

NATIONAL PREMIUM SALES EXECUTIVES INC.
240 Park Avenue, Rutherford, New Jersey 07070

Source: *Incentive Marketing*, December, 1970.

premiums; few if any premiums can qualify on all counts:

♦ Attractive, appealing, even glamorous. Not available locally.
♦ Useful, usable, and wanted. Known product, needing no demonstration.
♦ Quality brand name. Quickly obtainable. Dependable.
♦ Not instantly consumed. In harmony with the main product.
♦ Not stocked by manufacturer's retailers. Easy and sturdy to distribute.
♦ Worth two to three times what the consumer is charged for it.
♦ Up to date and in good taste. Consumer can accumulate a set.

Self-liquidating premiums appeal to manufacturers making a selection. Here the ultimate consumer is asked for proof of purchase *and* for an amount of money. The price charged covers cost of the premium, handling, packing, and mailing; it does *not* cover costs of promoting the premium, so the manufacturer hopes that additional sales will compensate for that particular expense. Of course, any "free" premium promotion

TABLE 11–3. Types of premiums used most

	First half 1970	First half 1969	Last half 1969
Games, toys & sporting goods*	157	166	161
General kitchenware	101	90	94
Appliances	91	94	96
Wearing apparel	75	75	78
Records, booklets & books	74	74	71
Omnibus catalog offers	67	68	66
Silverware	53	54	51
Soft goods	41	45	40
Cutlery	36	39	36
Jewelry	31	40	38
Glassware & tumblers	31	30	28
Dishes & bowls	28	30	31
Pens, pencils	25	28	27
Paper products stationery	23	21	22
Seeds, plants & bulbs	19	19	16
Plastic-film items	11	11	9
Brushes, combs	3	5	3
Miscellaneous	174	167	175

* Includes Picnic, Barbecue, Outdoor Accessories and Camera Equipment.
Source: *Incentive Marketing*, August 1970.

is self-liquidating if the promotion's total cost is covered by margin on added sales volume produced by the promotion. The price on a self-liquidating premium is often $1 or less; one, however, was a success at a price to the ultimate consumer of $12.95 plus several package wrappers.

These have been successful premiums:

Jewelry	Kitchenware	Cutlery	Textiles
Flowers	Toys	Appliances	Records
Luggage	Books	Pens	Comic Books

Premium distribution

The physical distribution of premiums is accomplished in various ways. Premiums such as dishcloths, dishes, and toys are sometimes enclosed in the regular product package. An adaptation is to secure the premium to the *outside* of the package; this may pose problems (breakage, theft, space) for retailers handling the line. Actually, the package itself can be a premium; cheese spread glasses which have been decorated for later use as fruit juice glasses are an example. When product A is offered to a consumer at a reduced price when he or she buys product B, then the premium A is bought at retail just as regular merchandise is bought. House-to-house salesmen deliver certain premiums. Either the sponsoring manufacturer or a premium service company can mail premiums to consumers. Coupons or tapes can be saved or punch cards can be punched out and exchanged for premiums by mail, in redemption centers, and sometimes in regular retail stores.

Merits claimed for premiums

The overall argument for premiums is that they can achieve the goals identified in the Specific Purposes section. Premiums do convert some prospects into first-time users, some of whom make repeat purchases. They provide a promotional change of pace welcomed by most company salesmen; and, their cost need not be high. Premium announcements in ads may get additional readership for those ads.

Criticisms of premiums

The points made against premiums remind one of those levied against consumer contests. Money spent promoting the premium might better be spent promoting the manufacturer's brand. Premiums are just a shot

FIGURE 11–6.   Bausch & Lomb promotes its sunglasses, telescopes, and binoculars for use as premiums

B A U S C H & L O M B I N C O R P O R A T E D

R O C H E S T E R , N E W Y O R K   1 4 6 0 2

Motivation for sale!

To you, the purchaser, a premium or incentive must be more than just a "thing". You do not buy products; you buy motivation. Beyond what an item can do, how it does it, how it is made, is the <u>one feature</u> with which you are most concerned - desirability.

High quality obviously is an important ingredient of desirability. There is a sure way of being certain that the people to whom you offer a premium or incentive recognize its value: select a name world-famous for excellence. Among these few is Bausch & Lomb.

Desirability, too, must include universal appeal. The products offered here are instruments of fun. They are for the great and growing leisure-time activities - travel, sports, hobbies, outdoor activities. For both men and women, they enhance the pleasures of life, yet they are practical and long-lasting. Everyone who goes outdoors can use sunglasses, a telescope or binocular. Every magnifier has a multitude of uses. In addition, each product has proved itself by being highly successful in retail sales.

A card is enclosed for your convenience in ordering samples or requesting the help of our premium representatives who are among the most experienced in the field.

Sincerely,

L. K. Howard

L.K.Howard:eps   Premium Merchandising Manager
Enc.

☐ Have your local representative call on me.

Please ship and bill me at special premium price a sample of

_____

_____

Name _____

Firm _____

Address _____

_____

CG-18, 096410   PRINTED IN U.S.A.

in the arm—just a costly one-time sampling technique that fails to build brand loyalty. Some premiums are stolen before ever reaching the ultimate consumer; others may hurt a brand's image by cheapening it. Coupon operations are not easily discontinued.

Suggestions about premiums

No premium will compensate for a deficient product. So, the sponsoring product must be sound and fair priced, have merit and repeat purchase value.

The three major groups to whom premiums are offered are children, women as women, and women as homemakers. A manufacturer may better fit a premium to one of these groups and to his circumstances by keeping in touch with persons and firms in the premium industry. These include manufacturers of premiums, commercial firms which offer complete handling of premium promotions, and editors of business publications devoted to the world of premiums. There is a national premium exposition.

When a manufacturer gives the consumer some choice of premium, he is using variety and the power to select in order to widen premium appeal. He is making modest adoption of the operational pattern of the coupon-and-catalog premium users. If he does offer a choice, it should be an easy and not a difficult one.

The premium, itself a stimulant, must be promoted, often heavily. This usually means frequent and forceful ads; radio and newspapers are popular media. Promotional promises about the premium and about its prompt and safe delivery must be honored lest the consumer be disappointed. The same premiums must not be promoted too long.

The pretesting of premiums is recommended strongly.

TRADING STAMPS

Trading stamps are related to premiums because consumers exchange stamps for premiums; even so, the trading stamp as a consumer stimulant deserves its own section and treatment.

About four out of every five families save stamps. Food stores distribute about two thirds of the stamp total; some service stations, drugstores, dry cleaners, and hardware stores give stamps. Shopping goods dominate the premium assortment, with home furnishing items accounting for one half or more. Shopping goods appeal to housewives. In addition, retailers who give stamps *sell* convenience products in the main; they would consider any redemption center or store offering convenience items as premiums to be a competitor. The consumer can usually "buy" a nice premium with the stamps saved over a five-or six-month period.

Stamp operation

The retailer, obviously, must get the stamps to give his customers. A few large retailers have and run their own stamp plans, but most retailers patronize an independent stamp company. The stamp firm sells its stamps to retailers, stocks the premiums for which stamps can be exchanged, supplies premium catalogs, and provides redemption facilities. Redemption centers often look and operate much like retail stores; each premium has its price, and stamps are the medium of exchange.

The stamp company makes money in three ways. It buys the premiums at attractive prices, it has the use of the retailer's purchase money for a period of time, and not all stamps given away by retailers will be redeemed. Most stamp companies follow a policy of franchising a number of noncompetitive retailers in each market.

The retailer pays $1.50 to $3 for 5,000 stamps. He gives one stamp for each 10-cent purchase. The customer saves the stamps and pastes them into a stamp book which may hold 1,200 stamps; she buys premiums with the number of books required. Whenever the retailer is so inclined, he can designate bonus stamp days or bonus stamp products; or, he can give a stamp jackpot to some lucky winner.

Although the typical stamp company promotes its stamps to ultimate consumers locally and nationally, the retailer, too, does some promoting. The retailer pays 2 to 3 percent of gross sales, not net, and may find it difficult to abandon the stamp offering. His hope is that stamps will encourage regular patronage. The addition of trading stamps will not solve retail problems or correct retail weaknesses in such areas as merchandising, assortments, location, pricing, personnel, or finance.

Effects on costs, prices, and profits

Do trading stamps reduce retail costs and increase retail profits? Do they result in higher retail prices? Such hopes or fears cannot be proved nor disproved. Findings are contradictory; conclusions must rest on assumptions and limited data.

If the retailer is to gain any advantage from stamps, the following must occur: (1) His sales must increase enough to reduce his fixed costs per unit sold by an amount greater than the increase in variable costs per unit sold attributable to the stamps. This increase in sales may have to be 10 to 15 percent in range. (2) His other promotional costs, mainly advertising, must drop by an amount greater than the cost of the stamp plan. (3) Otherwise, his selling prices must go up.

Trading stamps may have done well by the *first* retailer in a group (food store, service station) to offer them. As more and more competitors begin to give stamps, the promotional effectiveness of stamps can hardly do anything but decline; the cost burden, however, stays relatively constant. If *all* competing retailers in a market give stamps, then the result almost has to be higher retail prices or lower retail profits. Some retailers, disenchanted with stamps, have abandoned them and have tried to substitute lower prices, more advertising, better display, stepped-up personal selling, and improved all-round operation.

CONSUMER SAMPLING

In a sampling operation, the manufacturer or retailer puts the product into the hands of ultimate consumers for consumption by those individuals. The sample may be free—or there may be a small charge for it. The consumer examines and inspects; he learns by testing and trying the item. Hopefully, he likes the product, he buys it, and he continues to buy it. The sampler's assumption is that a product is its own best salesman, that seeing is believing, and that consuming is convincing.

We have just looked at premiums and the trading stamps which can be cashed in for premiums. How do samples and premiums differ? The sample is always the product itself; the premium may or may not be. Typically, receipt of a sample does not require any purchase by the consumer; premiums usually can be obtained only by making a purchase. Consumers usually receive samples prior to any purchase by them of the product; only rarely is a premium given away before the consumer buys.

Many products and some services are promoted with sampling. Product examples: cereals, cosmetics, beverages, soaps and detergents, toothpastes, candies, gum, razor blades, and newspapers. These items are low in price and bought frequently. But, a retailer may place an automobile in a consumer's hands for a week or a weekend. Many product demonstrations executed by salesmen achieve about the same objectives as those achieved by sampling. Services, too, are sampled. A laundry may offer to do a "free sample bundle," or an advertising agency may make a speculative presentation.

Some general characteristics about sampling are the following. There are two elements of cost, the sample itself and its distribution. In certain distribution methods, the sampler can choose between placing the physical sample in consumers' hands *or* giving consumers coupons which can be exchanged for samples. Retail distribution is a prerequisite; the seller may want his product stocked by at least 50 percent of his type(s) of retail store before launching his sampling operation.

Size and price of samples

A sample can be inadequately small and thereby insult the consumer; it can be extravagantly large and thereby anger the retailers who sell the product. What about size? A sample should be large enough to give the consumer a realistic trial of the product and no larger. For many products this calls for three, four, or five consumption units. This influence often recommends that a manufacturer use his "small" size as the sample rather than his "regular" size. One coffee manufacturer sampled "A" and "B" income families with a half-pound tin. A shampoo manufacturer or a maker of a headache remedy may produce a special sample size which is a miniature of his regular size. A cereal maker can face a real problem in deciding whether he should distribute one extra-large portion for one person to try *or* a larger quantity which will provide a modest serving for each member of the family.

As for price, we recognized that some samples are free, some cost a small amount. There is no single answer here. The free sample gets greater coverage and wider distribution; its volume is big if advertising precedes or accompanies the sampling operation. But, free samples easily get into the hands of nonprospects. A small charge reduces this waste by screening out some of the curious and some of the sample hounds; it may endow the sample with greater psychological value. The larger the sample, the more pressure there is to make some charge. What the consumer pays reduces the net cost of the physical sample, but it increases the handling cost. Any charge, of course, works against the basic idea of sampling and may help defeat the sampling operation.

Distribution of samples

House to house. Samples or coupons can be distributed house to house. Great selectivity is possible, residential area by area, even house by house. Some is done by salesmen, but two types of contract distribution dominate. Each will be described briefly.

FIGURE 11–7. Ad of a company which makes a business of distributing samples

At this moment they're more liable to switch brands than at any time in their lives.

And we have the only plan designed to make sure that the brand the "Switchables" switch to is yours.

They've just moved to a new home. They don't know anyone. They don't know where to shop. They don't know where to turn.

They need food. They need toilet articles. They need laundry supplies. They need toasters, electric broilers, blenders, tools—you name it. They need it. They need everything.

And in a matter of days they'll be establishing buying patterns that will stay with them a long time.

The "Switchables"

They're the "Switchables." And according to Progressive Grocer's authoritative "Consumer Dynamics in the Supermarket" study, 38,000,-000 of them moved last year. (Even more will move this year.)

And they've proven to be the single consumer group most prone to brand switching.

How do you get them to switch to your brand? (Old or new.) By controlled sampling with the New Family Welcome Kit. Selectively, regionally, nationally . . . and inexpensively.

It works this way.

Put your product in our memorable New Family Welcome Kit Doll House. (Your competition won't be in it.) Soon after a new family moves into the area you want covered, we'll have a Doll House personally delivered to them. And we'll get a signed receipt. You pay no premium for our highly selective distribution.

And here's how we distribute. Local companies, such as fuel oil companies, public utilities, banks, CATV companies, etc., distribute the Doll Houses, with their imprint and

any special offer they wish to make to each new family as it moves into the area. They find the Doll House an effective way to get new leads, to build good will among potential customers.

Welcome Kit Franchises

In addition, we are introducing another form of distribution whereby the Welcome Kit is delivered personally to the new homeowner by a franchised hostess. Local stores will also participate in this with coupons redeemable at those stores. Complete merchandising and sales promotion backups included for each franchisee.

Each New Family Welcome Kit Doll House contains more than $10 worth of products, plus a packet for your coupons, literature, swatches . . . and a research questionnaire to check out re-purchase intent and buying preferences.

And by using a full size sample (not mandatory, but we've found it the most effective kind of sample) your prospects quickly establish fa-

miliarity and a use pattern.

Does it work? Ask anyone in any of the companies on the list below.

If you're interested in switching the "Switchables" to your product, send this coupon in now. *Now.* There's still a little room left in the kits going out later this year and in 1970. Better still, call (516) 249-5252 and ask for Mike Keller, President, or Gina Glantz, Director of Marketing. And count yourself in.

Partial list of clients

American Can (Dixie) / Texize Chemicals / Alberto-Culver / Trewax Mfg. / Colgate-Palmolive / Lewis-Howe / 3M Company / Pillsbury / Holland House Brands / Beech-Nut / Fisher Nut (Div. Beatrice Foods) / A. E. Staley / Miles Laboratories / Mead Johnson Labs / General Foods / Berkey Photo / Santa Inc. (Div. of Beatrice Foods) / Bristol-Myers / Schick Safety Razor / Diner's Club / Columbia Record Club / Best Foods / Clairol / Southern Comfort

New Family Welcome Kit, Inc., Farmingdale, L.I, N.Y. 11735 is a publicly held company. Annual Report on request.

New Family Welcome Kit, Inc.
168 Broad Hollow Road—Route 110
Farmingdale, L.I. N.Y. 11735
(516) 249-5252
Please send more information on your
New Family Welcome Kit program.

Name _____

Title _____

Company _____

Address _____

City _____ State _____ Zip _____

☐ I want more information on your other kit programs which include: Survival Kit, Hospitality Kit, Fund-Raising Kit as well as your special marketing services.

☐ I want information on your franchise program.

(1) There are *commercial firms* which sell this service in three versions. (*a*) They will leave a sample at each front door. (*b*) They will ring the doorbell, wait, and leave a sample whether the door is opened or not. (*c*) They will ring and wait but not leave a sample unless the door is opened; to those who open their doors, the distributor gives a personal presentation and makes a product demonstration.

(2) Then there is the *Welcome Wagon*. In its operation, a hired hostess calls on newcomers to a community, she welcomes them, she describes the major features of the locality and answers questions about it, and she leaves samples or coupons good for samples from noncompeting firms. There is more use of the Welcome Wagon service by retailers than by manufacturers.

Advertising the sample.   The first step in this distribution method is the offer of the sample in the seller's advertising. Four of the six media are appropriate: radio, newspapers, magazines, and television; outdoor and transit are not appropriate. One possibility is to use part of a publication ad as a coupon which the consumer can mail in or exchange for a sample. Another possibility is not to use a coupon but to stress, to feature, to emphasize the sample offer. A third possibility in publication ads is to use the so-called "hidden" offer. Here the offer is buried in the body of the copy, perhaps in the next-to-last paragraph. Because hiding the offer works against the basic idea of most sampling, this third pattern may be more of a testing or research technique than sampling.

Cost per sample distributed through the use of advertising is often high because response is often small. Most requested samples are mailed to consumers asking for them, but some are distributed through retailers; these techniques are the next we examine.

Mail distribution.   Many samples are mailed; some were requested by consumers, some were not. Mailing offers several advantages. Selectivity can be high, minimizing the number of samples going to the "wrong" individuals. There is certainty of delivery. There are no personal distributors to be supervised. There is no problem of housewives who do not open their doors to strangers. Of course, the sampler must have a mailing list; if his product is liquid, his mailing package can be expensive; then there is postage to pay.

Rather than mail a physical sample, some sellers prefer to mail a coupon which can be redeemed for a sample. This involves no package, it is speedy, and many nonprospects receiving coupons will not redeem them. Redemption builds store traffic if retailers have the samples.

Distribution through retailers.   Sometimes a manufacturer puts his own representative in a retail store to distribute samples to shoppers. Sometimes he arranges for the retailer to do the job of physical distribution. A toothpaste maker may even produce a very small size of his brand for stocking and selling by variety stores, considering this a form of sampling and hoping only to break even on this distribution.

This technique can send shoppers to stores and thus build goodwill. But, some retailers have been guilty of *selling* certain samples, some have been known to *give* quantities of the samples to store employees. Retailers expect to be paid well for handling coupons.

Miscellaneous distribution methods. One firm makes a business of packing a group of samples together and placing the assortment into

FIGURE 11–8. By renting the bus, Diet-Rite is able to distribute samples in many locations

the hands of homogeneous consumer groups. Gift assortments have been designed for brides, students, new mothers, hotel guests, and new homeowners.

Manufacturers of gum, candy, or cigarettes may choose some version of "pass out" sampling. A pretty girl may be stationed on a busy corner and give samples to sidewalk pedestrians. Samples may be passed out at ball games, from fair booths, in business offices, or on the campus. A sample package of cigarettes may be on the airline's luncheon tray;

a small cylinder of tooth powder may be in the package with the tooth-brush.

Trial offers are a form of sampling. Retailers have been known to sample television sets, vacuum cleaners, and even mattresses in this manner.

Detail men are missionary salesmen representing ethical drug manufacturers. They "detail" doctors and other medical personnel, explaining the products in their lines. Commonly, the detail man leaves samples for doctors to give their patients.

Merits claimed for sampling

Sampling reflects the seller's superb confidence in his product; it is a powerful proof of his promotional promises, particularly of his advertising claims. Manufacturers' salesmen like sampling because it helps them launch new products, enter new markets, and increase share of market. Retailers know the power of sampling, often relying on a sampling operation to justify their stocking new brands. Consumers like samples, especially of products which promise taste satisfaction or smell satisfaction. They like to try new products and new brands at no risk. Finally, we have recognized that keyed sample offers in ads are useful in testing and comparing.

Hostility toward sampling

Some claim that the cost of sampling is excessive when related to what sampling accomplishes. In addition, there are cases histories of sampling operations in which retailers became irritated at the sampling manufacturers; sometimes retailers thought the sample entirely too large, sometimes the retailers felt underpaid for the role they had to play in the project. Then there is the ubiquitous problem of waste which occurs when samples get into the hands of those for whom the samples were not intended.

DEMONSTRATORS

Product demonstration is a basic promotional technique used in various situations. In the chapter on personal selling, we recognized its worth to and use by salesmen. Many television commercials are built on demonstrations of products. Manufacturers demonstrate, retailers demonstrate.

But here we are not thinking of the vacuum cleaner salesmen cleaning a living room rug, or a salesman demonstrating an adding machine in an office, or a tractor salesman showing what his machine can do on a farm. Instead, we have in mind a special type of demonstrator hired by certain manufacturers to work in certain types of retail stores.

The cosmetics industry serves well as an example. A manufacturer of cosmetics may elect to list the most important, the most impressive department and specialty stores through which he wants substantial sales volume. One possibility is for him to hire and train a group of demonstrators. He offers to assign these demonstrators to the select group of stores, with salary paid by the manufacturer. The individuals would look, dress, and act as regular retail salespersons; shoppers could not distinguish them from retail employees. Each demonstrator's big assignment is to push *her* manufacturer's brand; she will, of course, make other sales just as do the retailer's own salespersons.

Because the cost of demonstrators is high, they can be placed only in retail stores of high traffic and high sales potential. Demonstrators who work in food stores may do some sampling in addition to demonstrating. In providing the services of demonstrators, manufacturers must beware lest they violate the Robinson Patman Act.

CONSUMER DEALS

In the preceding chapter we saw that manufacturers offer deals to retailers. Now we look at the deals manufacturers offer consumers, most often on grocery and drug products.

The consumer deal is essentially a sales stimulant; it bears some resemblance to the premium. The manufacturer hopes the promotion will induce retailers to buy in large volume because of anticipated heavy buying by consumers. While the consumer deal can be helpful in converting ultimate prospects into first-time customers, in adding new retail distribution, and in entering new markets, it can also benefit the established product which has reached a sales plateau or leveling-off point. A good question: Do consumer deals increase brand loyalty—or do they merely result in consumers' buying the big deal of the moment?

Cents-off coupons

These certificates are placed in consumers' hands through door-to-door distribution or through direct mail; they can be part of a newspaper or magazine ad; they are in some packages, on some packages. When the consumer buys the promoted item and presents her coupon, she gets the item for less, perhaps 5 cents less, perhaps 15 cents less. Punched card size and dollar bill size are popular. Some coupons are coded so that machines can be used in the final sorting and processing.

FIGURE 11–9. Cents-off coupon that appeared in an ad run in newspaper supplements

Choose.
He who hesitates is out 10¢.

Nothing good comes easy.
In the case of these two mild natural cheeses, you must choose one to use the coupon: either the mild colby or the mellow cheddar.
Both are wrapped in Saran™ and dipped in wax to preserve their mild flavor. Both come bagged for easy opening and re-wrapping. Both have the fine taste of longhorn-style cheese.
Eeny, meeny . . .

10¢ 6/70

SAVE 10¢
WHEN YOU BUY
a 12-ounce
half-moon of
Kraft Cheddar
or Colby Cheese

(KRAFT)

Division of **Kraftco Corporation**

10¢

STORE COUPON

To the grocer: You are authorized to act as our agent in redeeming this coupon. We will reimburse you for the face value of this coupon or, if coupon calls for free goods, we will reimburse you for the regular retail price of the free goods plus 3¢ for handling each coupon, provided you and the customer have complied with the terms of this offer. Proof of purchase of sufficient stocks of Kraft product specified to cover coupons presented must be furnished upon request. We will not honor redemption through outside agencies, brokers, etc., except where specifically authorized by Kraft. The customer must pay any sales or similar tax on the product received. Coupon void if use is prohibited, restricted or taxed. Cash redemption value of coupon is 1/20¢. Redemption on other than product specified constitutes fraud.
Kraft Foods, P. O. Box 1600, Clinton, Iowa 52732

REDEEM THIS COUPON PROMPTLY   6/70

10¢

10¢

The A. C. Nielsen Company is the source of these figures:

Number of companies using coupon promotions   800
Number of coupons distributed annually . . . .   10 billion
Number of coupons redeemed annually . . . .   1 billion

Distribution methods:

42% by newspapers   9% in and on packages
31% by direct mail   3% by Sunday supplements
12% by magazines   3% by other methods

Retailers are not totally enthusiastic about redeeming these coupons. The checking-out process in supermarkets is slowed down. Time is required in sorting, handling, and counting. Then the retailer must do his redemption job. His money is tied up for some time. He claims that the two- or three-cent handling allowance typically allowed by the manufacturer does not cover his costs.

Misredemption is a problem for the manufacturer, a serious problem in certain markets. Misredemption takes place when the shopper checks out, hands the cashier a handful of coupons, and gets cash or credit regardless of whether she bought the products covered by the coupons.

Pandemonium may result at newsstands if one issue of a magazine costing the consumer $0.50 contains coupons worth $2.50 on the purchase of foodstore products.

Cents-off package

This is a variant of the cents-off coupon. Rather than do a couponing deal, the manufacturer may prefer to feature the discount deal on the regular package. On occasion, competing manufacturers have fought each other fiercely in this arena. A small jar of instant tea, for example, had a "5 Cents Off" on its label *and* a "25 Cents Off on Next Purchase" coupon secured to the jar with a rubber band. At times, the Federal Trade Commission has moved to get the leading firms in an industry to drop their on-package cents-off labels.

Cash refund

In this deal, the consumer buys the product and pays the full retail price. She then sends proof of purchase to the manufacturer—a label, a box top, a wrapper. The manufacturer then makes a cash refund to the consumer; the amount may be the amount the consumer paid, or it may be some other amount, even including postage. Retailers love this type of deal for obvious reasons.

One-cent sales

Here the consumer buys two units for the price of one plus 1 cent, or three units for the price of two plus 1 cent. Close kin but technically a premium is the "buy one and get one free" offer.

ADVERTISING SPECIALTIES

The advertising specialty industry divides its items into *executive gifts, calendars,* and *novelties.* Because executive gifts are given to business buyers, they were placed in the preceding chapter. Although there is some business use of calendars and novelties, their nature and use seem to justify their being classified and treated as ultimate consumer stimulants. Both differ from premiums in that premiums seldom carry the seller's name, and premium offers usually demand a purchase by the consumer.

Calendars

Of the dollars spent annually for advertising specialties, calendars account for about one third, making calendars the most common form of advertising specialty. Of the three calendar types (pocket, desk, and wall) one type, the wall calendar, deserves a few comments.

A popular and rather costly version has a separate entire sheet for each month, each with a different illustration, each including last month and next month on a smaller scale in addition to the current month. A bit more modest is the calendar which consists of four illustration sheets each with three *month* sheets attached. A third, economy model has a single illustration plus the current month on each date sheet. Consumers like color; they favor suitable illustrations of objects currently popular. There is a preference for large date sheets which can be folded back or over and thus kept; there is also a preference for memo space for each day.

As for distribution, some calendars can be picked up in retail stores, some are mailed, some are delivered by salesmen.

Consumers need, they want, they expect, they use calendars; over 75 percent of those distributed are kept and used. All types repeat the seller's message over a 12-month period; none requires upkeep. Wall calendars in a sense are small indoor posters for which there is no space charge.

Novelties

Advertising novelties are *not* advertising according to our classifications, but the term crept in and seems likely to remain. Actually, these novelties are *gifts;* they are products of value useful to and enjoyed by consumers. Usually the novelty is imprinted with the seller's name, address, and a brief promotional message. Many are kept and used over a substantial period of time. Cost may be a few pennies or a few dollars, making them resemble the modest prizes given to the least fortunate contest winners. Some occupy the consumer's wall (thermometer), some stay on desk or table (ashtray), some stay in sewing closets (yardsticks),

FIGURE 11–10. Assortment of advertising specialties used by one company

some are carried on the consumer's person (pens). Here are other examples.

Address book	Comb	Ruler
Key case	Litter bag	Balloon
Fan	Pencil	Knife
Paperweight	Bottle opener	Yo-Yo

As for selection, the great degrees of variety and flexibility can be inferred from the number of items available—10,000. Many of the characteristics of good premiums are equally valid here. Quality and utility must not be too low. The novelty should not be a strange, unknown item. Frequency of use is desirable over a relatively long life. Despite these, price per unit must be modest if not even low. Other selection considerations include: identity of the recipients, competitive promotional activities, our seller's promotional program, and the objective of the novelty distribution.

The big, overall objective is to build goodwill, but this breaks down into more specific jobs or goals. Here are some:

To open doors to salesmen.	To introduce salesmen.
To say please and thank you.	To remind.
To invite.	To make mailings more effective.
To identify prospects.	To build retail traffic.
To increase distribution.	To recognize birthdays.

Novelties must be distributed. Mail, salesmen, retailers, or advertising offers may be used. Whichever the method, the seller tries to control the distribution by preselecting his recipient group. Selective circulation means less waste; this is a significant consideration because novelties are too costly for indiscriminate circulation.

MATCHBOOK PROMOTION

Approximately 15 billion matchbooks reach ultimate consumers each year, 90 percent of which are received free. Matchbooks are in the home, in the office, in the automobile, and in the consumer's pocket. Over 70 percent of all adult consumers habitually carry these books, and the adults using them use 143 books per year on the average. Three hundred thousand firms use these matches to promote a wide variety of products and services.

The typical matchbook is a packet of paper matches with a cover and a strip on which a match can be struck. Many contain 20 matches per book and are packed 2,500 books per case. Both the inside and the outside covers can carry promotional copy; these covers are used by manufacturers and retailers on both a national and a local basis.

Resale matches

One technique involves what are called *resale* matches; these books usually have four-color outside covers, one-color inside covers. Resale matchbooks are given away by retailers, most of whom sell tobacco products; or, they are sold by the carton in retail stores. The matchbook manufacturer sells the covers to other sellers for their promotional messages, but he controls the distribution of the matches with two limitations; the seller who buys the use of the covers can specify (1) the geographic area to which the matches go and (2) the time of year for the distribution. Resale matches can provide wide coverage at low cost because the dispensing and selling retailers stand 75 percent of the cost. These matches are frequently used by manufacturers of convenience goods.

Reproduction matches

Reproduction matchbooks are designed and bought outright by the sellers who will use them for promotional purposes; the sellers do not buy just the space on the covers. After adding his promotional story,

FIGURE 11–11.   Reproduction matchbooks used by Phifer Wire Products

the seller distributes the matches to a prechosen group or groups. Manufacturers of industrial products, makers of consumer goods, sellers of services, retailers—all are included in the group of sellers using reproduction matches. Dry cleaners, motels, and banks are prominent users. The user may dispense the matches in his own place of business, through his salesmen, or by mail. Reproduction matches are available on airlines, at banquets and meetings, in trade show booths, and at conventions.

Reproduction matches can be distinctive and unusual in various ways. They can be personalized with each individual buyer's name or initials if the seller wants to spend that kind of money. They can be imprinted with the names and addresses of individual retailers. Circulation is under better control than is true of resale matches. The cost, of course, is higher. Inside covers are often used as coupons or as maps of the area the seller covers; they can carry lists of sales offices or show product details.

TWO TELEPHONE PROMOTIONAL FACILITIES

Yellow Pages

As has been hinted on several occasions, sales promotion as an area poses difficult decisions about what should be classified where; two telephone promotional services, Yellow Pages and Western Union Operator 25, are examples of this difficulty. Both are used by business firms to some extent, but, in the opinion of your authors, both should be treated as ultimate consumer stimulants.

A telephone directory is furnished to each resident customer and to each business customer. Four thousand different directories are issued annually with a total circulation of over 75 million. The Yellow Pages contain approximately 14 million listings and ads telling "where to buy it." Products and services are arranged alphabetically as classified headings. Wholesale and retail firms *and* brand names are listed alphabetically under each heading. So, the consumer can check on (1) a product or a service *or* (2) the firm(s) offering it. Manufacturer and retailer may share the cost; for example, the manufacturer may pay for *his* trademark—the retailer may pay for *his* listing. The fact that he, his brand, and his retailers are listed in the Yellow Pages may be included in the manufacturer's advertising.

Yellow Page promotion has certain attractions. It enjoys 24-hour availability. Its life expectancy is the same as that of the directory containing it. When he or she refers to the Yellow Pages, the consumer is often ready to buy—usually ready to shop. This is localized promotion for a distant manufacturer, directing buyers to the wholesalers and retailers handling his brands by giving their names, addresses, and, of course, telephone numbers. A manufacturer can buy space in any or all of the 4,000 directories; he can buy any space unit available to local retailers.

Western Union Operator 25

This service is available in 20,000 markets. It allows a consumer to telephone his Western Union office and ask for Operator 25. The consumer can then ask that operator where a certain brand is available; he can ask for the names and addresses of nearby retailers handling that brand. If retailers are few, Operator 25 identifies all of them. In larger markets, retailers are grouped into units of four or fewer, and the operator rotates the groups as she reports. Thus, in larger markets, each retailer gets the same number of mentions. Operator 25 sometimes limits her identification to retailers in the postal zone in which the inquirier lives. Once again, the manufacturer may refer to this service in his ads; he and his retailers may share the cost.

CATALOGS FOR CONSUMERS

Because business catalogs were examined in the previous chapter and because all catalogs have many similarities, this section on consumer catalogs can be extremely brief.

Consumer catalogs range in size from 4 pages to over 1,600 pages. They are a promotional tool which presents and promotes an assortment of consumer items. There are illustrations, descriptions, and prices. By contrast to business catalogs, the consumer catalog contains more illustrations, more color, and shorter, harder hitting copy. This copy must be persuasive and complete; it must tell consumers what they want to know about sizes, colors, other product details, and prices; it must be clear and easy to read about terms of sale, shipping costs, and guarantees. The catalog must be well indexed and easy to order from.

A big mail-order house such as Sears issues two large and several smaller catalogs a year; Sears recently mailed about 12 million catalogs of 1,684 pages in 11 regional editions. A specialized mail-order firm such as L. L. Bean issues seasonal catalogs during the year. Department and specialty stores such as Neiman Marcus may distribute several specialized catalogs each year, of which the most elaborate is the Christmas one.

FAIRS FOR CONSUMERS

General comments

There are county fairs, state fairs, and world's fairs.

A seller may participate in a fair to secure direct sales or income; sellers of food, producers of shows, and promoters of races immediately come to mind. But, this is selling rather than sales promotion. Another seller may sponsor a booth or an exhibit primarily to get leads for his salesmen. Still another may see in a fair the opportunity to do some market research. Some sellers sign up because their competitors have signed. But, the great explanation of why most sellers participate is the assumption that the publicity and public relations values of exhibits will have good effects on sellers' images.

Consumers attend fairs to be entertained, to relax, to learn, to be excited and thrilled, to savor uncommon experiences, to be stirred emotionally.

There are three common patterns of participation. (1) A seller can exhibit individually. (2) His can be one element or part of his industry's exhibit. (3) He can join one or more related sellers in sponsoring a complementary, noncompetitive exhibit.

In September, 1970, when Expo '70 ended a run of six months in Osaka, Japan, attendance stood at a record 64,218,770. This was the first universal exposition to be staged in Asia. The visitors were thought to have left 19,700 tons of trash. At this writing, there is talk of a bicentennial fair in Philadelphia in 1976.

CONSUMER EDUCATION AND SERVICE

Consumers need a certain type of information and counsel which the seller's sales promotion staff should supply; two items are recognized here, *tags and labels—consultation and advice.*

The typical consumer has doubts and fears. There are so many types of products, so many brands, so many sellers, so many promotional claims. No wonder the consumer needs help and information about what to buy and about how to use and care for it. The seller has a real concern here. If the ultimate consumer buys the wrong product, if she or he uses it in the wrong manner, then the consumer blames the seller and his brand. That is bad. Product types that come to mind at once, in which consumer education and service are especially important, include: appliances, foods, cosmetics, furnishings, and decorating material. By informing the consumer properly, the seller bids for goodwill which leads to happy purchases which increases goodwill which leads to more happy purchases.

Tags and labels

Tags are tied, wired, or sewed to the product; labels are sewed, pasted, stamped, or printed on the product or its package. The purposes of both are to identify, minimize confusion and uncertainty, promote with selling copy, reduce buying mistakes and returns, and make buying safe and speedy.

Information on tags and labels includes:

- ◆ Brand name; manufacturer; amount; quality
- ◆ What the product is made of, is, and does; how the product is made
- ◆ Characteristics and construction; specifications and composition
- ◆ Product performance; how to use the product; care the product needs
- ◆ Promotional copy; cautions; guarantee; price

Consultation and advice

When you buy an automobile, you ge a booklet telling you about the vehicle and how you should treat it. When a housewife has a floor-covering problem, she can fill out a questionnaire, mail it to a manufacturer of floor coverings, get her problem studied, and be given recommendations.

So, consumers need counsel, and sellers give counsel. Some is sent by mail. Some is available in consultation clinics. Some sellers operate service centers where help, literature, even product repairs and maintenance are available. Makers of certain appliances send home economists into the home to demonstrate and instruct. Some sellers sponsor a speaker's bureau, offering to send a representative to speak to certain types of groups on certain subjects; if not speakers, the sellers may offer films. Finally, there are courses and schools, one session or a series. Typical are decorating schools, sewing classes, and cooking schools.

Inward WATS

Various companies have recently made *inward* WATS (wide area telephone service) available. For example, suppose you see a product advertised in the *Reader's Digest* and want to know which dealers stock it in your market. If the ad contains an inward WATS telephone number, you can dial it at no charge to you and learn the identities of three dealers within your zip code area. The *Reader's Digest* service operates round-the-clock, seven-days-a-week. Media covered are TV, radio, and magazines.

Several versions of this service are operational. One manufacturer solicits consumer attitudes on an item being test marketed; the label tells consumers the number to call; their comments are tape recorded. At least two makers of appliances offer the service to owners needing emergency service information. Ship lines and motels offer the service for making reservations. Stock brokers, insurance companies, trucking firms, and rental car companies are among the business firms interested in and using inward WATS.

QUESTIONS AND PROBLEMS

11–1.   What might cause a manufacturer to change his brand name?

11–2.   List some examples of sampling done by retailers.

11–3.   A manufacturer of consumer products is to add to his family of products. In selecting a brand name what features or characteristics should he hope to incorporate?

11–4.   Contrast the jobs premiums are asked to do when offered to ultimate consumers with their assignments when offered to middlemen.

11–5.   Suggest some guidelines for banks thinking of sponsoring premium promotions.

11–6.   What are some package inserts found in today's packaged products?

11–7.   Why do so many ultimate consumers continue to buy from catalogs?

11–8.   List some pressures a firm may feel to change or even drop its trade character.

11–9.   A service station operator is thinking about beginning to offer trading stamps to customers. What questions should he ask?

11–10. What are some desirable characteristics and some common uses for advertising novelties?

ELEMENTS OF
PERSUASION:
INDIRECT PROMOTION

Public relations

W<small>E HAVE LOOKED</small> at three elements of persuasion—at personal selling, at advertising, at sales promotion. To us, these are three forms of *direct* promotion because the great bulk of each promotes *brands* of products and services. Now, in Part VI, we take up our fourth and final element of persuasion, *indirect* promotion; this promotion does for the *sellers* of brands what direct promotion does for the brands themselves.

Indirect promotion will be treated in two chapters. Chapter 12 takes a brief look at public relations, a phrase sometimes abbreviated to its initials, PR; Chapter 13 examines the two major mass-communication tools of PR, *publicity* and *institutional*, or as it is often called, *corporate* advertising.

We are going to see that the overall job of PR, like that of direct promotion, is to influence the opinions, attitudes, and beliefs of individuals. Communication is the essence of both PR and of direct promotion. Salesmanship and brand ads, publicity and institutional ads are nothing if not communication.

There must be close coordination and unity among the four elements of persuasion. They should complement each other, not clash or be in conflict.

A product is more than just a physical item; it is also something offered for sale by a certain seller. Because PR insists that the selling firm be sound and be known as sound, PR makes easier and more successful the jobs of the sales manager, the advertising manager, and the sales promotion manager. Each of you can recall purchases you have made in which the identity and the character of the seller were as important as the image you had of the brand bought.

His direct promotion affects the PR of a seller. Does a manufacturer's salesman give good advice and counsel to his wholesale and retail customers? Is the manufacturer's advertising helpful and in good taste? Do the tags and labels of his products give adequate and clear information to ultimate consumers? If any answer to such questions is negative, then direct promotion is damaging the firm's PR.

We must recognize that brand (direct) promotion can help or hurt company (indirect) promotion, and vice versa.

NATURE OF PR

Social responsibility of business managers

There are two views of how management should function. One sees management's responsibility as that of increasing the firm's profits and maximizing the market price of each share of the firm's stock. Decisions are made on the basis of how the owners of the business would be affected. If a certain course of action promises greater profits, then that course of action is the one to adopt. The only group to which management has obligations and responsibilities is the owner group. It is recognized, of course, that all operations must be within the law.

The other view, which can be thought of as the PR view, assumes that management cannot do a good job for the owners unless it does a good job of helping to improve the quality of life for our entire population. Some stockholders, indeed, are demanding this. Under this second view, business management is expected to play a prominent role in working toward solutions for today's numerous and mammoth social problems; management must do something about them. There must be concern, involvement, and contribution on the part of business concerning such problems as unemployment, urban renewal, education, housing, pollution, and conservation.

So this second attitude is that what business firms do must be consistent with the public welfare—must be good for society. And, the larger the corporation, the more watchful, even suspicious, is the public.

Here are the views of the president of the Gulf Oil Corporation:

The times demand that businessmen present their views—not only about how we see our responsibility to society, but most importantly—how we are fulfilling that responsibility.

The traditional responsibilities business has to society have been long established by the nature of our free enterprise system: the responsibility to provide profits to our shareholder investors; to produce quality products desirable to customers, fairly priced and honestly advertised; to provide employment and to reward employees for their contribution to the success of the enterprise; to contribute a percentage of our income directly to the communities in which we operate; and to otherwise retain the goodwill of the local and national publics that permit us to conduct our business. These have been, and continue to be, quite basic responsibilities that business must always meet.

Essentially, these have been the full scope of our responsibility—until now. Today, maximum financial gain, the historical number one objective, is forced into second place whenever it conflicts with the well-being of society. We now must examine the proposition that the *first* responsibility of business is to operate for the *well-being* of society.

Corporate image

Perhaps in our examination of what PR is, we should refer again to *corporate image*, first recognized in Chapter 7. Just as *brand* image is what individuals perceive the brand to be, *corporate* image is what individuals perceive the seller of the brand to be. Whereas personal selling, advertising, and sales promotion as we viewed them are mainly concerned with *brand* image, PR and its major tools of mass communication, *publicity* and *institutional advertising*, are mainly concerned with *corporate* image. The better its two images, the better off is the company.

Every seller has his own personality. Persons like or dislike the image they see in exactly the same way they like or dislike people. There are people with whom you would not spend your time—there are sellers with whom you would not spend your dollars. Your impression of and your attitude toward a seller are important to him. Each seller hopes his image is attractive.

The seller himself is responsible for the image individuals have of him just as he is responsible for his brand's image. He must qualify for and achieve a good corporate image—then maintain it—then publicize it.

One of our largest manufacturers recognizes these as some of the determinants of his corporate image: product quality; advertising; research; treatment of employees; profits; dividends; performance of his retailers; concern about noise and pollution; dealings with government; what the public learns about him through newspapers, TV, and radio.

Meaning of PR

Public relations is a philosophy, a pattern of behavior, a way of living. It is the belief that the firm's interests and well-being run parallel to society's interests and well-being. It is the assumption that the welfare of individuals is important enough to weigh heavily in management's decisions. It is the fundamental conviction that business must be socially responsible.

Good PR rests on the foundation and criteria adopted for company policies. This demands the adoption and implementation of policies which will benefit both the firm *and* society. Management should develop and then live by policies which are appropriate to and in accord with the public interest. The starting and most basic of all policies for all sellers is to offer buyers a sound product or service, a fair amount of utility and satisfaction at a fair price.

Top management recognizes and respects the significance of *all* of its activities which affect the public's attitudes toward the company. Management realizes that the company is a part of and depends on the society and the economy in which it operates. The company, therefore, should contribute to society as well as to the economy. Recognizing that business and society share a common fate, PR merges company interests with public interests.

Once a company has adopted the PR way of operating, the next step is to communicate this fact. Communication describes company policies, explains the company's courses of action, interprets the company's behavior. The company *informs* the public so that the public will know, it *explains* so that the public will understand. Incidentally, policies and behavior are a top-management responsibility. Communication is mainly a PR responsibility.

What is PR *not?* PR is not a panic button to hit in an emergency. It is not a pose or façade which will mask or whitewash company indifference, insincerity, hostility, or guilt. It is not a smoke screen to hide unfairness, unsoundness, or defects. It is not a way of deceiving the public into seeing "bad" as "good." Above all, it is not a slick way to con or manipulate the public. The director of public relations at B. F. Goodrich disagrees with those who hold that PR's first purpose is to *mold* public opinion. He says,

Its primary function is to execute a program of action that will *earn* the public's understanding. PR people are not engineers of public consent, but are communicators and stimulators of public acceptance.

We are now ready for definitions. Among the short ones are these:

Doing right and getting credit.
Good conduct effectively reported.
Good works well communicated.
P = performance; R = recognition.

A fuller definition is:

> *Public relations is the management function which evaluates public attitudes, identifies the policies and procedures of an individual or an organization with the public interest, and executes a program of action to earn public understanding and acceptance.*

Note that *doing* and *communicating* are implied in each definition.

Recently the Public Relations Society of America sponsored a research project in which top business executives were asked to comment on various phases of PR. Here are three of the questions and the answers:

1. What mental image does the term *public relations* stimulate in your mind?

Publicity	50.0%	Advertising	4.5%
Communication	27.0	Press agentry	4.5
Counseling	27.0	Overselling	4.5
Product promotion	18.0	Phoniness	4.5
Liason	13.5	Education	4.5

2. How important is the public relations function in your company?

Very important	91.0%
Important but not vital	4.5
Not too important	4.5

3. Is the value of public relations more significant to your company today than it was five years ago?

More important	86.0%
About the same	14.0
Less important	.0

PR objectives

1. The *being* and *doing* goal is: To be and operate—so as to deserve and encourage—goodwill and respect, support and patronage—for the products, policies, and personnel of the firm.

2. The *communicating* goal is: To inform the public so it can think and act intelligently—to increase understanding and appreciation of the role of the firm in our society and economy.

Armour-Dial's PR:

(1) seeks to evaluate attitudes of those individuals and groups with whom we deal, our publics, (2) identifies and relates company objectives, policies, and procedures with the interests and these publics, and (3) plans and acts to earn understanding and acceptance of those whose favorable attitudes and actions we value in the conduct of our business.

Here are the objectives of Westinghouse's PR activities:

To build the reputation of Westinghouse as an efficient producer of quality goods and services, as a good company to do business with, and as a good place to work.

To establish the reputation of Westinghouse (1) as a valuable asset to the industrial, social, and economic life of the nation and to the communities in which it operates; and (2) as a well-managed enterprise which serves the best interests of customers, owners, employees, and public.

To elevate the prestige of Westinghouse in research, product development, and scientific advancement.

To achieve and maintain understanding of the Company, its policies, problems, and activities by all publics.

To publicize among all publics the leadership of Westinghouse in the fields of engineering, manufacturing, and distribution.

WHO NEEDS GOOD PR

Every commercial firm, many associations, and certain individuals must pay attention to PR. Our major concerns are the commercial firms (manufacturers, wholesalers, retailers, sellers of services) and the commercial trade associations (serving such groups as public utilities, transportation firms, mass media, financial institutions, tourism interests, labor unions). Names that come to mind for trade associations include: Chamber of Commerce of the United States, National Association of Manufacturers, National Retail Merchants Association. Politicians and performers are individuals with PR problems.

Nonprofit organizations seeking good PR include: Red Cross; Boy Scouts and Girl Scouts; churches and religious groups; educational institutions; and government agencies, including branches of the military service.

A COMPANY'S "PUBLICS"

The *public* of public relations demands segmentation because a company deals with a number of groups and needs to enjoy good relations with each. So, we must first ask, "What is a 'public'?"

FIGURE 12–1. This statement contains profit goals *and* PR goals

---

OBJECTIVES OF ARMOUR AND COMPANY

To conduct all of our affairs according to the higest standards of ethics and business integrity.

To provide high quality products at reasonable prices for the consumer.

To strive constantly, through research and through better methods, to improve our products and create new ones.

To maintain relations with dealers and with livestock growers and other suppliers that will help them, as well as ourselves, to grow and prosper.

To provide steady employment at fair wages and under safe and healthful working conditions.

To be good industrial neighbors in our local communities, and to be good citizens through helping to serve the nation's best interests in every way possible.

To conduct our business so that we earn a reasonable profit and are enabled to provide shareholders with a fair return on the money they have invested in our company.

FIGURE 12–2. The Television Information Office is the public relations arm of the TV industry

TELEVISION INFORMATION OFFICE

What is the Television Information Office?

TIO was established in October, 1959, to provide "a two-way bridge of understanding between the television industry and its many publics."

Who supports TIO?

The three major television networks (ABC, CBS, NBC), individual commercial stations and groups, educational stations and the National Association of Broadcasters.

Whom does TIO serve?

TIO provides a continuing information service to meet the needs of educators, students, government agencies, the press, the clergy, librarians, allied communications professionals and the general public, as well as broadcasters.

Why?

Television is an increasingly powerful social force in today's world. TIO's purpose is to increase knowledge and understanding of the medium among those individuals and groups who have a direct interest in its impact upon our society.

How does TIO do this?

Nationwide, TIO maintains an extensive, affirmative and long-range educational program. Through frequent and varied national mailings, speeches and direct participation in conferences and other activities, TIO keeps in continual contact with individuals and groups representing a wide range of special interests. It provides its sponsors with materials for pursuing the same activities at the community level.

For us, a "public" is a group of persons with some common denominator, with some unity, with some homogeneity. A public is a commonality; its members have roughly the same interests, goals, problems, and circumstances; each member is similar to the other members. There is a sense of awareness of group identity—even of a common future. Most members have the same attitude toward any controversial subject. As will be seen, some publics are small, some are large. There is overlap across a company's publics. *Employees* and *stockholders* are two publics we recognize, yet one third of Westinghouse employees are also stockholders. The *gen-*

FIGURE 12–3.   Union Carbide recognizes its stockholders as an important public

UNION CARBIDE Stockholder News

THE DISCOVERY COMPANY

No. 70-1   June, 1970

Over 900 people at annual meeting; keen interest shown in pollution-control efforts

Stockholders exhibited a keen interest in many of Union Carbide's varied activities, including its pollution-control efforts, at the Annual Meeting on April 22, attended by about 950 people. Questions posed to Chairman of the Board Birny Mason, Jr., who presided, covered such subjects of public concern as the recent Apollo mission and the Corporation's unique new process for treating municipal wastes (see story on page 4).

The meeting was held in New York at Hunter College. Although the college was not in session that day, because of the Jewish holidays, the proceedings were briefly interrupted during the latter part of the discussion period by a small group of students who forced their way into the auditorium to protest Union Carbide's presence there. They were removed by security guards.

A total of 46,919,292 shares was voted at the meeting, representing 77.58 per cent of the outstanding shares.

There were two items of business on the agenda: election of Directors and the selection of auditors. Stockholders reelected the 12 nominees for Directors (see page 4) named in the Proxy Statement. The selection of Hurd-
(Continued on page 2)

President F. Perry Wilson at the lectern in the Hunter College Auditorium reports to stockholders on operations for the first quarter. (Right above) At the close of the meeting, Birny Mason, Jr., Chairman of the Board, stops to talk with one of the stockholders.

Stockholders told sales at record high

Sales of Union Carbide reached a new first-quarter high of $725.9 million in 1970, President F. Perry Wilson reported at the annual meeting. Stockholders were told that this result, representing an increase of 7 per cent over 1969 first-quarter sales of $680.9 million, was achieved in spite of the slowdown in the domestic economy, which has affected most of the Corporation's business. Overseas sales were up 13 per cent, while in the United States they were up 4 per cent.

Earnings for the quarter were $42.6 million or 70 cents a share, down 16 per cent from the 84 cents reported in last year's first quarter. The figure for 1969, however, included a 9 cent-a-share nonrecurring gain from the sale of Neisler Laboratories, Inc.

In commenting on operations, Mr. Wilson said that earnings are expected to improve as the year progresses. One reason they fell below the previous year in the first quarter was that the 1.2 billion-pound-per-year ethylene plant at Texas City, damaged in an explosion last October, did not get back into operation until the first week in April, later than expected. Also, as anticipated, costs in some areas continued to rise faster than the Corporation could offset them through improvements in operating ef-
(Continued on page 2)

A shine with a bonus The 1970 version of Union Carbide's PRESTONE car wax and cleaner, which has a colorful "mini" racing car packed in plastic on top of it, features a heavy-duty silicone formula. This results in a better shine and easier application. Also, the cleaner's proportionately higher wax content gives long-lasting surface protection. For those who want to know how brightly their car shines, the new PRESTONE product provides a "shine meter" to measure the intensity of surface reflection.

eral public is another public; all adults are members *and also* are usually members of other publics.

Each of a corporation's publics hopes for—may even expect—certain behavior of the corporation. The rest of this section lists a firm's publics and indicates what each wants from the firm. Because of our limited space, this seems the best way to picture the PR pressures on the firm.

The desirability of good relations with these publics is obvious because relations with them can affect sales volume, or costs, or both. So, profits reflect these relations.

Communities

These are the cities and towns in which a company has factories, plants, branches, stores, offices, and such. They are sometimes referred to as "plant cities." Within each are local civic leaders, prominent persons, opinion leaders, and civic groups.

Communities look to their companies for regular employment and payrolls. They expect a company to buy locally when such purchases are appropriate. They want civic concern and support for charitable, cultural, and community undertakings. They expect companies to pay fair taxes. They hope plants and grounds will be kept clean and attractive.

That firms are aware of this public is clear in this statement by the president of one of our largest corporations:

We must get out of our office and board rooms and get into our communities. This is the only way we truly can meet society's needs and earn its understanding and support—by recognizing and reacting to changing social needs and by communicating our business goals, problems, and actions.

Competitors

Its competitors want ethical behavior by the firm, behavior which promotes the industry. They want contact, cooperation, exchange, and two-way communication. In trade associations, competitors expect membership, attendance, support, and participation in association activities.

Customers and Prospective Customers

This public is of major interest and importance to us. Much about it has already been covered in earlier chapters. Buyers expect satisfaction from the products or services the company sells. They want vendors to have sound policies concerning products, distribution, prices, and promotion. They hope their dealings and relations with the seller will be pleasant.

Educators

Contact, cooperation, speakers, personnel exchanges, and advisory boards are examples of what educators want from business. They want teaching aids and materials. They want job offers for their graduates. Educational institutions hope for financial support—scholarships, endowed chairs, buildings, grants, and endowments.

FIGURE 12–4. Booklet of materials available to colleges and universities from U.S. Steel

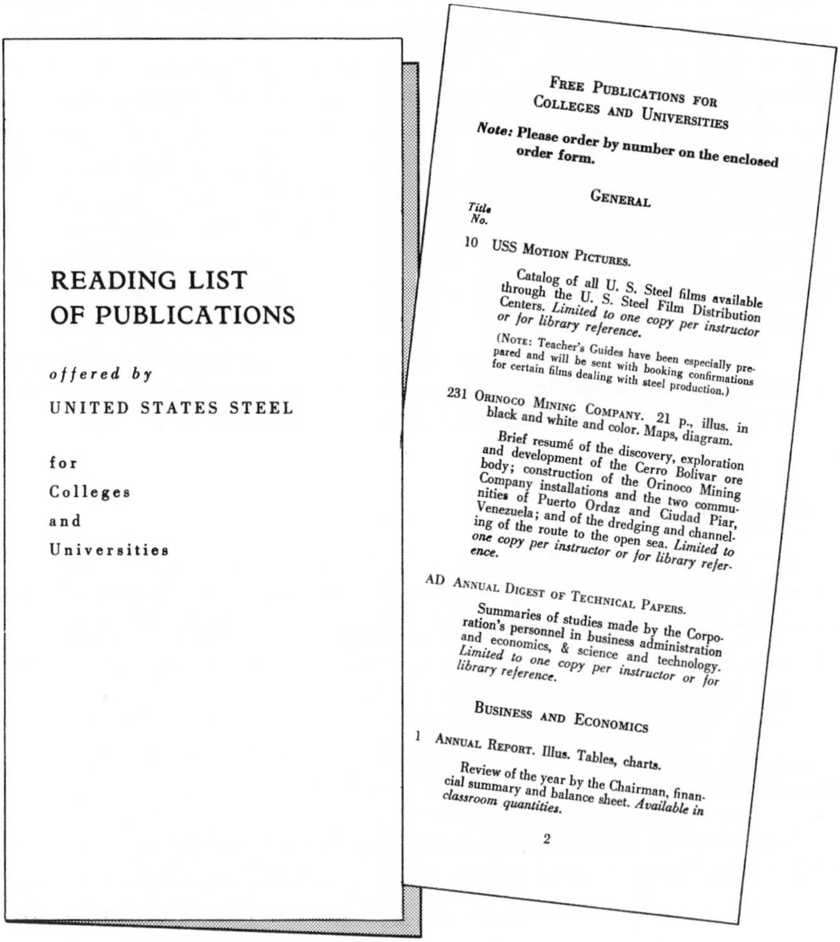

READING LIST
OF PUBLICATIONS

offered by
UNITED STATES STEEL

for
Colleges
and
Universities

FREE PUBLICATIONS FOR COLLEGES AND UNIVERSITIES

Note: Please order by number on the enclosed order form.

GENERAL

Title
No.

10 USS MOTION PICTURES.

Catalog of all U. S. Steel films available through the U. S. Steel Film Distribution Centers. *Limited to one copy per instructor or for library reference.*

(NOTE: Teacher's Guides have been especially prepared and will be sent with booking confirmations for certain films dealing with steel production.)

231 ORINOCO MINING COMPANY. 21 P., illus. in black and white and color. Maps, diagram.

Brief resumé of the discovery, exploration and development of the Cerro Bolivar ore body; construction of the Orinoco Mining Company installations and the two communities of Puerto Ordaz and Ciudad Piar, Venezuela; and of the dredging and channeling of the route to the open sea. *Limited to one copy per instructor or for library reference.*

AD ANNUAL DIGEST OF TECHNICAL PAPERS.

Summaries of studies made by the Corporation's personnel in business administration and economics, & science and technology. *Limited to one copy per instructor or for library reference.*

BUSINESS AND ECONOMICS

1 ANNUAL REPORT. Illus. Tables, charts.

Review of the year by the Chairman, financial summary and balance sheet. *Available in classroom quantities.*

2

Employees—present and prospective

Present employees are interested in wages, working conditions, communication, and treatment. Security, benefits, grievance handling, and personal promotion are other concerns. Employees want a sense of identification, to feel that they belong. Salesmen, expecially, want to be adequately informed so that they can harmonize with the company image and operate in line with company policies. A salesman hopes his company's promotion program will be outstanding.

As for *prospective* employees, here is the opening paragraph from a recruitment booklet of Carnation:

We're searching for young men who aren't afraid to work for a company that's different. We didn't plan to be different, but now that it's happened, we couldn't be happier. Like most companies dating from the 1890's, Carnation was founded by people who believed in rugged individualism. But while other companies have grown up into impersonal, unwieldy bureaucracies—the kind that smother a man with red tape and paper work—Carnation has kept its character. We're different. The last of the little ol' billion-dollar food companies, you might say. We're big and prosperous, but we still believe in the sacred right of the individual to do his thing. To have room to breathe. To make decisions, to learn by doing, even to make mistakes. We don't believe there's any substitute in the world for actual responsibility. We'll throw you the ball and let you run with it. From day one. At Carnation, YOU make the difference. You're a living, breathing human being with strong feelings about things and ideas of your own about getting things done. We like it that way. If you share our faith in the individual, join us.

General public

This public consists of everybody. It is particularly important because all voters are members *and* all ultimate consumers are members. The general public wants much that communities want. Perhaps we can sum up by saying that the general public expects good corporate citizenship of each firm.

Government officials

Top executive officials, legislators, and personnel in regulatory agencies (Food and Drug Administration, Federal Trade Commission, Federal Communication Commission) are the main government officials who "expect" from the business firm. They are involved in such problems as poverty, health, ecology, taxation, transportation, and consumerism.

Government officials want two-way communication with business. They want understanding, cooperation, and support. They hope business participation in joint efforts will be informed and enlightened. As a president of the Parker Pen Company, when also chairman of the National Association of Manufacturers, told a Washington audience: "Both business and government are intended to serve the people. They are *not* ends in themselves."

Mass media

Our interest is in the six advertising media—newspapers, magazines, TV, radio, outdoor, and transit—we looked at in Chapter 8; they are sometimes referred to as the "press."

The publication and broadcast media look to PR directors for news material. They expect responsible reporting and fair treatment.

Middlemen

One of many manufacturers' most important publics consists of the wholesalers and retailers who handle their products. In an overall way, they want whatever contributes to profit. They are interested in such matters as promotion by a manufacturer, margins, service, management counsel, fair treatment.

Stockholders

Stockholders think much about earnings, dividends, and the market price of a share; they hope these three will increase. They want to be kept posted on corporate affairs, including current operations. They want annual reports they can read.

Suppliers

Suppliers want from a manufacturer much the same things as do his middlemen. Sources of supply want profitable sales, prompt payment, only reasonable requests, considerate treatment of their salesmen. Armour says, "The reputation of Armour as a customer assumes almost the same importance as the image of Armour as a supplier."

Newspapers and radio stations, like any other businesses, have their own policies and should not be asked to violate them. Following is a list of Don'ts which should be remembered when working with news media:

1.

Don't ask newspapers, TV or radio stations to submit pictures or stories for approval before they are printed or go on the air unless you feel it is a matter of vital importance to the Company. Even then such a request should be handled with extra tact.

2.

Don't ask for a "break." You will receive consideration from press, TV and radio if you have maintained friendly relationships with them and if the statement or story has news value.

3.

Don't submit releases accompanied by advertising. Advertising contacts should be made with the advertising department and news stories should be placed with the editorial or news department.

TO **SELL** MORE - **TELL** MORE

MAKE NEWS!

11

FIGURE 12–6. This table of contents indicates the types of material contained in annual reports

The B.F.Goodrich Company Annual Report

Table of Contents

PUBLIC OPINION

The opinion of any public about an issue, a problem, a decision, or a course of action is the consolidation of the opinions of the members of that public. Some experts hold that as *opinions* become stronger, they develop into *attitudes*—that as attitudes become stronger, they develop into *beliefs*.

Public opinion stems from and reflects the consensus of reference groups, social classes, and even the culture. Public opinion is the composite of the ideas, views, assumptions, and convictions of the individuals comprising groups, classes, or culture about some subject. Often the subject is a controversial one; beverage alcohol, sex, religion, careers, prices, and advertising are examples.

A company obviously prefers to operate in a friendly environment rather than in one that is hostile. A seller can be hurt badly—even put out of business—if public opinion is strongly against him. If the company is to live and prosper, the opinion the public holds of it must be good. Sales, otherwise, will come hard, or costs will be high, or both. Suppose the dairies in a market raise the price of milk. Normally, the public's reaction will be unfavorable, but the dairy hit hardest by this reaction will be the one rated lowest by public opinion.

Public opinion, then, either favorable or unfavorable, is a powerful influence on a firm's success. Here's how the president of the American Oil Company put it:

How well we fare in the continuing battle to improve our rate of return; in the face of uncertainties posed by the decade of the '70's, may well be determined by how effectively we deal with public opinion.

THE PR PROCESS

In a telescoped version, the PR process consists of two steps: (1) behaving right, and (2) communicating that fact. Our treatment calls for a bit more detail, for eight steps.

Step No. 1. The beginning of the PR process is the firm's solid, complete, and permanent commitment to the PR way of life. Management assumes its social responsibility in all sincerity. Then it identifies its publics and rates them according to (*a*) their importance and (*b*) their expectations.

Step No. 2. This consists of a complete, fact-finding examination of the firm. Is it guilty of sins of omission? Of commission? In executing this PR "audit," the management must fight against bias, preconceived ideas, rationalizing. It must be braced to discover unpleasant facts or unsatisfactory conditions never suspected.

Step No. 3. This consists of corrective action. Unsoundness is replaced with soundness. All company conditions, practices, and policies are made the best practicable. The company stops what should be stopped, it starts what should be started.

Step No. 4. Whereas Step No. 2 was essentially internal, Step No. 4 is mainly external in that it calls on the firm to determine, then evaluate, the attitudes of its "publics" toward the firm. Here the firm first discovers, listens, and learns where the firm now stands in the opinions of its "publics." This includes uncovering the *why* of those opinions. In evaluating, the firm then studies, analyzes, and weighs what those public views and impressions call for from the firm. As in Step No. 2, management must be objective, thorough, and accurate. Research methodology is, of course, beyond the scope of our treatment.

Step No. 5. Once again, as in Step No. 3, management decides what *can* be done—then what shall be done. This involves revisions, adjustments, modifications. If some bad feature or condition can't be corrected at the moment (interruption of service, shortage of consumer products in wartime), then short-run action may be indicated. Advertising that explains is one such action.

Step No. 6. Phase one of PR ends at the conclusion of Step No. 5, and phase two, the communicative phase, starts. In Step No. 6, the company explains and interprets its policies and its behavior to its publics. It reports, it informs; it describes, it educates. Informed publics are preferred over ignorant ones. Public understanding and acceptance demand this communication. After all, unless a company communicates knowledge of its actions, a public cannot give it credit for living right, for being human, for being concerned; just *being* right is not enough.

Step No. 7. After communicating, once again the company checks on the attitudes of its publics, just as it did in Step No. 4. It evaluates by asking, "How did our Steps No. 5 and No. 6 work out"?

Step No. 8. In this last step, the firm sets up facilities and techniques for continuous monitoring of public opinion against any future need for Step No. 5. In addition, it plans for continuous communication to its publics. PR communication must not be casual or erratic, impulsive or hit-or-miss. This Step No. 8 is essentially a research-respond–research-respond continuing process.

The PR process is summed up nicely by the American Oil Company:

> We gain and hold a good company reputation *first* by our actions, conducting our business in a way that merits approval and respect; *second* by good communication, telling people what we are doing and why, so as to gain their understanding.

COMMON PR TOOLS

This section recognizes only the more common tools used by companies in performing their PR activities and in achieving their PR goals. It does not attempt to be complete and exhaustive.

Forms of *publicity* (mention in the *editorial* section of advertising media in contrast to the *advertising* section) are not included here. The news release, for example, is widely used in PR, but it is treated in the next chapter in the section on publicity.

Publicity and institutional advertising are, of course, tools used by the PR director to communicate to publics; in most cases, they are his *major* tools. Because they are so important, the next chapter is devoted to them.

Many of the activities listed here as tools lead to publicity. Two examples: (1) a contribution to a school—reported on a TV news show; (2) a speech by the company's president—summarized in a newspaper.

Now for the more common tools, other than publicity and institutional advertising, used by companies.

Community activities can contribute to good PR by improving corporate image. For example, some companies hold an annual Christmas party for the children of the community. Participation in United Fund drives is another example. Company executives may be prominent in such service clubs as Rotary or Lions.

Contributions are a PR tool. Some are made to employees, some to communities, some are donations to various worthy causes. Some take the form of disposal of surplus or substandard products.

Films are produced and made available by some companies. Films may be of a public service nature, or they may be designed mainly to entertain. Many theaters run such films, and most TV stations show several PR films each week. There are commercial firms which distribute films to such publics as educational institutions, civic clubs, and women's organizations.

Two types of *house organs* do PR duty. The internal type is edited for the firm's employees, the external type for ultimate consumers.

FIGURE 12–7.   Film available from The B. F. Goodrich Company

---

*   *   *

"TOMMY LOOKS AT TIRES"

16mm, color, sound, 20- 1/2 minutes.
Recommended for intermediate, junior and senior high viewers.

Produced with an eye to both entertainment and educational values, the film shows
step-by-step processes in the manufacture of passenger car tires and covers high-
lights of research, development and testing. Viewers experience the equivalent of
a guided tour through a modern tire factory and witness behind-the-scenes activity
in research and tire-testing laboratories.

The film is the only known pictorial record that shows the scientific skills, planning
and equipment required to produce tires of today's advanced designs and capabilities.
By continuing its "Tommy" character in the present film BFG enlivens what might have
been simply a conventional documentary. The teenage-driver-related domestic
situation depicted is encountered in most American families today. The film places
the spotlight on one of the 20th century's most taken-for-granted industrial marvels -
the tire.

Produced by The B.F. Goodrich Company, Akron, Ohio.

Distributed by Sterling Movies, U.S.A., Inc., Central Booking Exchange,
43 West 61st Street, New York, New York   10023

A-298   LITHO. IN U.S.A.

Here is Chrysler-Plymouth's description of its *Plymouth Traveler:*

The Plymouth Traveler magazine builds Plymouth car owner loyalty by
creating good will between the dealership and the Plymouth car buyer and
by appealing to a major interest of the American family—vacation travel
and tourism by car.

Each issue is a tour guide of a major city, a state or a region. Pictures
and introduction provide a general background. Other sections of the issue
describe recreation facilities and activities, places to visit, accommodations
and restaurants. The inside back cover usually contains a list of local Plymouth
dealerships.

The reader is invited to obtain additional information, maps, brochures
and other travel aids without charge by sending in a travel service coupon.
(After request is filled, the coupon is sent to the dealership nearest the reader.)

The *Traveler* usually carries only three full-page Plymouth ads and a
service ad on the back cover. The dealership's imprint—names, address and
phone number—appears on the back cover near the name of the person
receiving the magazine.

Of the ten issues each year, the one in October is a new-car issue consisting
of text and pictures of the Plymouth models. The new models are presented
in an editorial manner consistent with the style and format of the *Traveler*.

FIGURE 12–8.   Front page of a typical house organ.

JOBS 70 – 3 SUCCESS STORIES

Bewildered newcomers eased into useful roles

One of the men is Black and so is the girl. The other man is Cuban. When they came to Cyanamid, the only thing they had in common was an uneasiness about their strange surroundings.

Today Rudolph Fowler, Sylvia Mason and Jose Hernandez are efficient members of the Cyanamid community — the men at Bound Brook, the girl at the Princeton Agricultural Center.

What brought them to this stage is a training program sponsored jointly by the federal government and Cyanamid to turn the disadvantaged unemployed into productive citizens. Since 1968, the government-financed program has enriched Cyanamid with hundreds of useful new employees.

In some ways, Fowler, Miss Mason and Hernandez are typical of all the employees who make the grade after undergoing the training program, referred to as JOBS 70, which is being given at a number of locations. In other ways they are not. Miss Mason, for instance, is one of the few females hired under the program. Hernandez, like many of the Bound Brook trainees, spoke only Spanish when he started. But while he is a Cuban, most of the others are Puerto Rican.

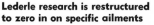

It didn't take Sylvia Mason long to master some difficult requirements.

All suddenly found themselves for the first time plunked down in the middle of a bustling, noisy plant complex, surrounded by people they could not understand. Even for Blacks born in the U. S., this experience is unsettling. Some are barely out of the rural South and have never seen a large factory complex such as the one at Bound Brook, and many have not previously heard the quick Northern speech.

Their situation brings to mind the ordeals of the immigrants from Central Europe in the early 1900's. But few of those earlier immigrants were lucky enough to have a Ralph Vargas to help them.

Vargas is a pleasant young man who is the Bound Brook trainees' teacher. Attached to a New Brunswick, N. J., company that was hired by Cyanamid under the JOBS 70 program, Vargas started in 1969 to teach basic English to Puerto Ricans. Last year, the course was expanded to include basic education, orientation and counselling for all those hired under the program.

Anxious to get ahead, Rudolph Fowler is planning to go to night school.

But Vargas, who is "professor" to students like Fowler and Hernandez, is far more than their teacher. He is a guidance

(Continued on page 7)

Lederle research is restructured to zero in on specific ailments

PEARL RIVER, N. Y. — The organization of pharmaceutical research and development at Lederle has been restructured for a concentrated effort against four major disease areas, it was announced today by Borden R. Putnam, Lederle general manager.

He said the move is responsive to the pressing need for new drugs to treat the major diseases which still prematurely kill or incapacitate. These are mainly the chronic and degenerative illnesses requiring long-term therapy which contribute substantially to today's high costs of medical care. Another target area is the critical need for new anti-infective drugs which are more effective against the continuing threat of emerging bacterial resistance.

Dr. Ira Ringler, Lederle's

director of research, has established interdisciplinary forces whose efforts will be directly aimed at heart, stroke, infective, mental and arthritic diseases. Lederle research had previously been organized along lines dictated by the boundaries of science areas such as organic chemistry, chemotherapy, and experimental therapeutics.

The new groupings and their respective directors are: Infectious Disease Therapy, Dr. Martin Forbes; Cardiovascular-Renal Disease Therapy, Dr. John J. Denton; Central Nervous System Disease Therapy, Dr. William D. Gray; and Metabolic Disease Therapy, Dr. Edward C. DeRenzo. These mission-oriented units will be supported by the Toxicology Section directed by Dr. John F. Noble and the Process and

(Continued on page 3)

Shulton agreement signed

C. D. Siverd, left, and George L. Schultz, chairman of the board of Shulton, Inc., sign merger agreement. Shulton stockholders are expected to meet toward the end of March to approve the merger of the leading maker of toiletry, fragrance and cosmetic products with Cyanamid. Operations will continue with present management.

The people behind the bottle: a visit to the Breck plant
See center spread

Cyanamid news

AMERICAN CYANAMID COMPANY
WAYNE, N. J. 07470
VOL. 15 · NO. 1   JANUARY, 1971

Plastics Division consolidated with Industrial Chemicals unit

WAYNE, N. J. — The Plastics Division was merged Jan. 1 with the Industrial Chemicals Division to form a major new unit called the Industrial Chemicals and Plastics Division, with headquarters at Wayne.

Howard E. Nehms, formerly general manager of the Industrial Chemicals Division, has been named general manager of the Industrial Chemicals and Plastics Division. G. A. Forlenza, formerly general manager of the Plastics Division, has been appointed assistant general manager of the new division.

T. P. Turchan, vice president

responsible for these segments of the company's business, said the consolidation will permit more efficient alignment of manufacturing, technical and marketing functions and will reduce operating costs.

Plant to Continue

The Wallingford, Conn., plant will continue as one of the major manufacturing units of the new division.

Products of the division will include chemicals for industrial processes, paper-making and water purification, chemicals and explosives for mining and construction uses, and such plastics products as molding compounds, resins, adhesives, and Acrylite® acrylic sheet.

Department managers in the new division are R. B. Latimer, chemical products; C. E. Austin, industrial products; F. W. Miner, plastics.

Reporting to Latimer are:

Forlenza   Nehms

R. M. Goddard, marketing manager, process chemicals; C. L. Pulsfort, marketing manager, explosives; W. B. Kauffman, technical director, process chemicals; and V. J. Wilhousky, production manager.

Reporting to Austin are: R. E. Logan, marketing manager, paper chemicals; R. T. Schoepflin, marketing manager, water treating chemicals; D. E. Withers, marketing manager, mining chemicals; J. L. Hillman, technical director, paper

(Continued on page 6)

The blond in the construction office

CHARLOTTE, N. C. — The potbellied, cigar-chomping boss who barks orders at his construction workers is undergoing a change.

In his place could very likely emerge a small blond such as Anne Sanford, who became the University of Florida's first female BBC in December. Two days after she earned her Bachelor of Building Construction, she was in Charlotte, N. C. on

the payroll of The Ervin Company as a management trainee. (Cyanamid's acquisition of Ervin Sept. 1 spearheaded a major company foray into the construction industry.)

But Anne Sanford insists she didn't set out to blaze any trails. Instead, she is just fulfilling an ambition for a career in the construction field. She has been assigned to work with the

(Continued on page 3)

Anne Sanford doesn't think a girl in construction field is unusual.

The fact that the *Traveler* visits a different city, state or region in each issue encourages the reader to save his copies for future reference. Some public libraries maintain files of the magazine and teachers use it in geography classes. It is regular reading fare in such public places as doctors' waiting rooms, beauty parlors and barber shops.

Local chambers of commerce and service organizations request copies of an issue devoted to their city or area for distribution with their own promotional materials.

Professional and businessmen's societies and associations planning to meet in a city covered in the *Traveler* write for a quantity of that particular issue.

All of this gives subscribing dealership prolonged exposure.

Plymouth dealerships can purchase any quantity of subscriptions or order copies in bulk quantities for showroom use, or both. The dealership furnishes the *Traveler* circulation department with an initial list of its customers and prospects.

If it does not have one, the magazine prepares without charge an initial list. Names of the dealership's subsequent Plymouth buyers can be added automatically.

At least once a year, the *Traveler* circulation department sends each dealership a proof of its subscription list and suggestions for up-dating it.

Editorial and printing standards are set by the public relations department of the Chrysler-Plymouth Division, which is responsible for the operation of the magazine.

For a modest price, subscribing dealerships have their names associated with a magazine that has been cited for its widespread appeal and which promotes good will and communication between dealers and motorists."

Literature of various types can do various PR jobs. The annual report to stockholders comes to mind at once. Certain printed items are used to answer requests for company information from students and instructors. Titles of booklets available from the American Oil Company include: "The Price of Gasoline"; "What's Your Public Relations Quotient?"; "Clean Air Research"; "Urban Unrest"; "Tips From Pro Drivers."

Mailings are used for PR purposes. Direct mail has already been covered, in Chapter 10.

In some PR activities, there is no substitute for *personal contacts.* Company executives may visit with mass media personnel or with other opinion leaders. Lobbying demands much face-to-face exchange. All contacts of all the company's employees with all publics can work for better relations. PR possibilities exist when salesmen call on buyers.

FIGURE 12–9. Twenty-page guide to Indiana history available from American Oil Company

AMERICAN TRAVELER'S GUIDE TO INDIANA HISTORY

AMERICAN OIL COMPANY

FIGURE 12–10.   Mailing sent by Sears to credit customers who pay promptly

FIRST to Sears *... then to school*

January 7, 1972

Dear Mr

We take sincere pleasure in thanking you
for the excellent manner in which you have
handled your account. It is rated A-1 outstanding and additional credit is available
whenever the need should arise.

We wish to invite you to shop at Sears for
many new and exciting fashions. Our buying
organization has gone all out to ensure your
entire family of the very latest in styles
and colors.

You can count on us to accept your judgment
as to your satisfaction with the values you
select. May we count on you for an early
visit?

                    Yours very truly,

                    Manager

Sears, Roebuck and Co.

FIGURE 12–11.   Keynote address delivered to the Marketing Conference of the National Conference Board

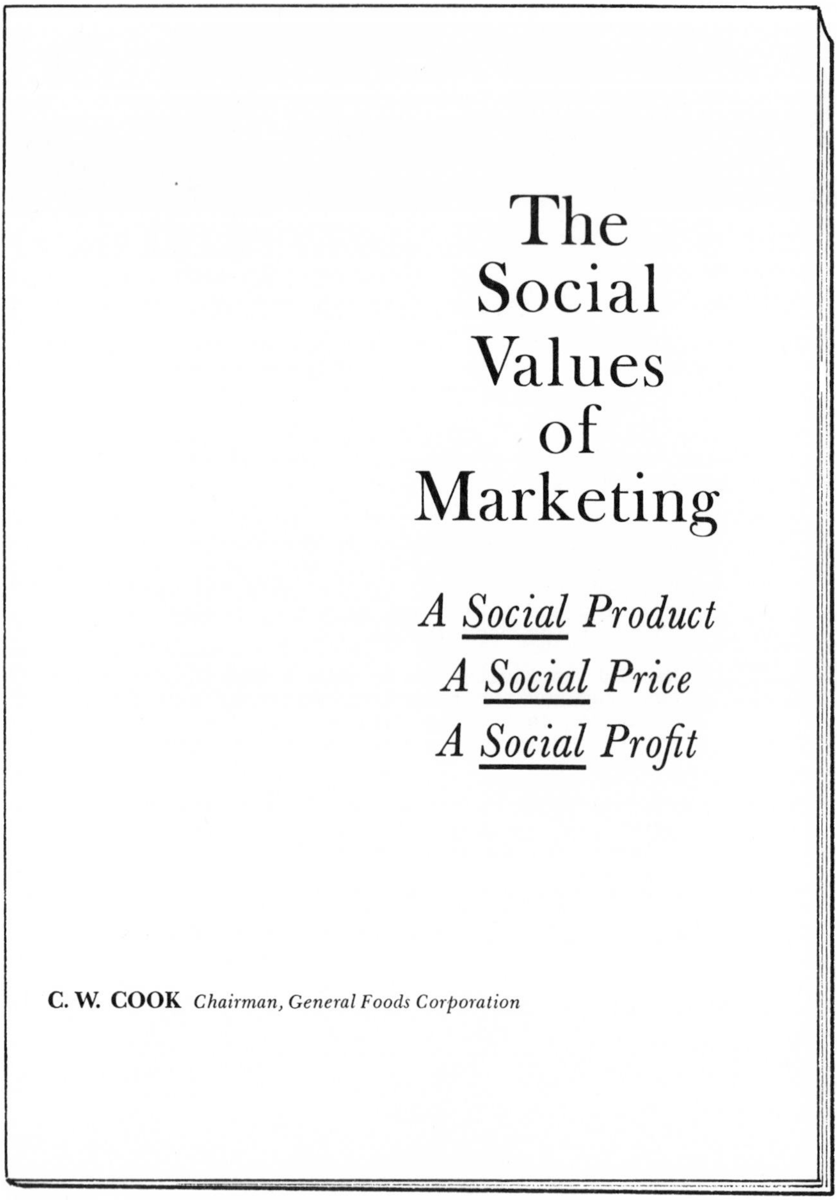

The Social Values of Marketing

A Social Product

A Social Price

A Social Profit

C. W. COOK *Chairman, General Foods Corporation*

Some *open houses* are held annually, some are nonrecurring. At the former, employees and their families—indeed, even the entire community—may be invited to meet company executives and to see the physical aspects of the business. An example of the latter is the initial, official opening of a new plant, store, or other facility.

Plant tours are often made available on a daily basis; open to public, they are planned, standardized, and conducted. Visitors are usually shown how some product is made and may be given a sample of it.

FIGURE 12–12. This 15-minute show was offered to radio stations

FAMED ACTRESS LILLIAN GISH TALKS ABOUT FILMS AS AN ART FORM...

AND ABOUT ONE OF THE ALL TIME GREAT DIRECTORS, D.W. GRIFFITH.

New York reporter Stan Burns interviews the famed actress, Lillian Gish, in connection with her new book "Lillian Gish, the Movies, Mr. Griffith and Me." The publisher is Prentice Hall.

The cue in: "This is Stan Burns in New York...."

Time: 14:30

Out cue: "...this is Stan Burns in New York."

The enclosed tape recording is provided without cost to you. Please return it in the enclosed envelope along with the postage-paid card which indicates whether you plan to broadcast this material.

We would appreciate your comments.

All of the costs involved with this production were paid for by Prentice Hall Publishing Company. Thank you.

* * * * * * * * * *

Speeches have PR potential. Some are made to college classes, some to service clubs, some to banquet or convention groups. If it chooses, the firm may operate a speaker's bureau complete with speakers, promotion of engagements, and booking facilities.

Some companies sponsor *staged events* for PR reasons. Examples: visits by prominent persons; fashion shows; parades; company picnics; anniversary celebrations.

Companies are not unaware of the PR ramifications of their *trade association activities*. These can be reflected in membership, support, cooperation, and participation.

PR ORGANIZATION

PR is company-wide

By now we have sensed that PR is a philosophy which must be all-pervasive, that it must permeate the entire company, that it truly needs the participation and support of every employee. This ubiquity has given rise to the observation, "A company can get along without a public relations department, but *not* without a public relations philosophy." Examples of the wide range of items that can have a PR effect: the way the property looks; all company ads; telephone manners; salesmen's contacts with buyers; what production employees tell their friends; the letters the company mails; how company products are serviced; even the way company truck drivers drive.

Being a companywide service department, the PR department is available to work with all other departments. It helps mold all company policies and operations. The top PR executive of B. F. Goodrich is described as being:

". . . extremely conscious of the need of the rapport which should exist between his department and other segments of the company, particularly those in the communications business—Employee Relations, Employee Communications, Union Relations, Customer Relations, College Relations, Government Relations, Advertising, and Sales Promotion."

The comment continues:

We cannot communicate effectively with publics outside the company unless we do some internal communicating among ourselves. Our objectives are the same: To gain favorable attention and recognition for BFG; to improve our industry and position; and to increase BFG sales and profits.

PR demands a location at the top-management level because PR is a policy-level function. The PR head should work closely with the company head who is responsible for setting company tone and shaping company image. As Gulf says:

The chief executive who must manage a multi-national corporation depends upon his public relations executive for a regular reading of the public pulse, identification of problem areas within company operations that may quicken that pulse, recommended preventive medicine or at least adequate emergency treatment, then the part that shows: public announcement of the progress, prevention, or cure that results.

PR is a staff function which helps top management evaluate public opinion, then offers suggestions about modifications of policies, and about how to communicate most effectively with company publics. It is not an operating function such as sales, or production.

Organizational structure

Much variety is found in the location of PR in organization charts and as regards titles. Some companies have separate PR departments, some combine PR with some other function, usually with advertising, occasionally with sales promotion. Here are a few actual examples:

- ♦ PR director reports to VP-PR and advertising.
- ♦ VP–advertising and PR reports to chairman.
- ♦ PR director reports to manager–advertising and sales promotion.
- ♦ Manager–advertising and PR reports to general marketing manager.
- ♦ Director–advertising and PR reports to VP–marketing.
- ♦ Manager–PR reports to director–advertising and PR.

The PR function is usually located in the home office of large firms, seldom in the firm's divisions. The function is most often headed by a director of public relations, an increasing number of whom are trained behavioral scientists.

Here is a statement from Armour-Dial:

Public relations management at Armour-Dial has been identified as a separate function since 1968.

In its most recent positioning, after several shifts, PR management is a part of Marketing Services, and is identified as Advertising/Public Relations. The other two parts of Marketing Services are Merchandising, and Marketing Research.

Marketing Services is structured as one of three departments comprising marketing functions of the Grocery Products Group of Armour-Dial. The other two marketing departments are Product Management, and Sales.

The coordinating of PR activities with marketing activities, and the direction of certain PR efforts toward the attainment of certain marketing goals are common in large companies.

Public affairs

Recently the top management of certain companies, mostly large ones, felt a growing need for more information about—for more counsel on—

FIGURE 12–13. Swift's Director of Public Relations reports to the president

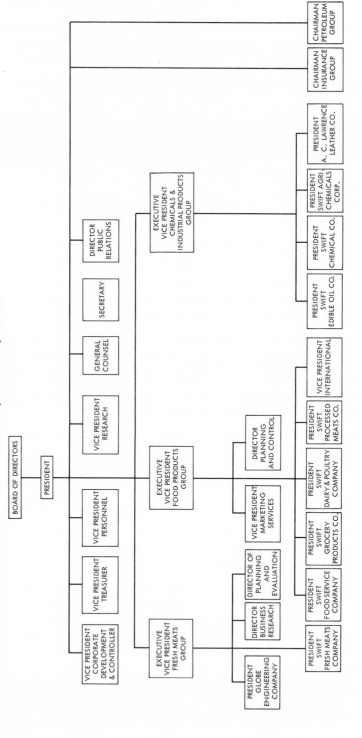

relations between business and government. The number of such companies is increasing. The response of some companies has been to expand their facilities for dealing with government officials, including legislators. Other companies, however, have created a new unit, a public affairs department, headed by a public affairs director or a public affairs manager. This new department and function reflect the upgrading of the stature and significance of two publics we have already recognized, the *government officials* "public," and the *general public* "public."

Here are the major objectives for which a public affairs department works:

1. A better environment in which our free enterprise system can continue to operate.
2. Employees better informed on matters political and economic, civic and social.
3. Greater employee involvement and participation in politics.
4. Closer contact, increased cooperation, and more effective communication between business and government. Some companies have established Washington offices for these purposes.
5. Greater business concern with problems, and greater business support for programs relating to public health, education, and welfare.
6. A stronger voice in influencing government legislation and regulation affecting business.

Public affairs is a high-level function. Here are examples of line relationships:

♦ Director–PA reports to VP–public relations and public affairs.
♦ Manager–PA reports to VP–personnel and public affairs.
♦ Director–PA reports to VP–public relations and advertising.
♦ Director–PA reports to VP–public affairs.

OUTSIDE PR COUNSEL

If a company chooses, it can employ the services of an outside firm specializing in PR work. One such is Daniel J. Edelman, Inc., one of the few leading international public relations firms. Edelman is credited with being an innovator and leader in PR. In a *Gallagher Report* poll, Edelman was named as one of the four outstanding national PR firms. As PR counsel to business and industry, associations, and civic and welfare organizations, Edelman, Inc.

. . . develops and executes programs for its clients encompassing a broad range of PR activities including corporate, financial, marketing, and governmental relations; social involvement; and community and employee relations.

Here is what Goodrich says about its PR counsel:

As an extended arm for BFG Public Relations, Carl Byoir & Associates has loyally served as PR counsel for 34 years. The firm keeps two staff writers quartered in Akron. But Byoir personnel in New York City Headquarters and in six branch offices over the U. S. also give nationwide support in areas important to the company. The Byoir agency supplies in-depth services by specialists who can call public attention to the BFG name and interests. Whether the PR projects concern financial expertise, news reports, feature articles, news photography at the scene of an event, or personal placement of material with editors, qualified Byoir personnel can be called into prompt action.

A group of top executives was recently asked in a research project sponsored by Daniel J. Edelman, Inc., what services they look for from a PR firm. Their answers are given below.

	percent		percent
Publicity	50.0%	Creativity	13.5%
Communication skills	45.0	Flexibility	9.0
Counseling	41.0	Research	4.5
Knowledge of media	36.0	Press agentry	4.5
Product promotion	23.0	Advertising	4.5
Marketing	18.0	Detail handling	4.5
Government relations	18.0	Problem solving	4.5

A company can use a PR firm on a continuing basis, as Goodrich does, or it can use a PR firm for large, nonrecurring projects. A common financial arrangement is for the client to pay the PR firm: (1) a fixed retainer, plus (2) a personnel time charge for hours worked for the client, plus (3) the cost of any outside services bought in serving the client.

PROMOTION MISTAKES HARMFUL TO PR

So much for PR per se. This, however, is a book on promotion, so we need to be fully aware of the close relationship between the two. This relationship could be approached in various ways.

Our approach is to point out how certain promotion mistakes or errors, not unknown in actual operation, can work against good PR. We limit ourselves to 10 in personal selling, 10 in advertising, and 10 in sales promotion; that number could, of course, be larger. Many of the 30 mistakes listed affect more than one public.

Personal selling mistakes

1. Overaggressive, high-pressure selling.
2. Manufacturers' salesmen inadequately informed about wholesalers' and retailers' needs.
3. Salesmen's playing favorites among buyers.
4. Salesmen's criticizing the company to other employees.
5. Salesmen's refusal to participate in community affairs.
6. Poor service to customers.
7. Salesmen's circulating of false, damaging rumors about competitors.
8. Blaming suppliers unjustly for company mistakes.
9. Abuse of the reciprocity selling point.
10. Textbook salesmen who do more visiting than selling.

Advertising mistakes

1. False, deceptive, and misleading promises.
2. Ads created to please someone other than buyers.
3. Manufacturer's failure to localize manufacturer-retailer cooperative ads.
4. Refusal to supply illustrations to textbook authors.
5. Arrogance in dealing with ad media and agencies.
6. Ads that are offensive or in bad taste, that brag or boast.
7. Advertising illustrations that have been "doctored."
8. Copy too critical of competitors by name.
9. Ads that "talk down," insulting buyers' intelligence.
10. Ads that overdo the "keep your money at home" theme.

Sales promotion mistakes

1. Charging too high an admission price to a World's Fair exhibit.
2. Shipping cases that do not store conveniently in warehouses.
3. Samples that are too large or to small.
4. Mailing lists that are incomplete or outdated.
5. Inadequate sales training.

6. Manipulated, deceptive "giveaway" promotions.
7. Trade characters whose behavior is silly or irritating.
8. Tardiness in answering inquiries about the product.
9. Premiums that are defective.
10. POP displays too complicated for easy installation by retailers.

QUESTIONS AND PROBLEMS

12-1. List some "staged" PR events.

12-2. What are some PR goals of a college?

12-3. List some firms or groups with PR problems.

12-4. Suggest some causes of bad public relations between a manufacturer and his suppliers.

12-5. Why should the PR director be a top-level executive?

12-6. How can the PR budget be defended to a stockholder?

12-7. List some common PR mistakes of small, independent retailers.

12-8. Should a firm's ads be cleared by the PR department? Explain.

12-9. Should the goodwill generated by good public relations be carried as an asset on the balance sheet? Why?

12-10. Why is public relations more important today than just a short time ago?

CHAPTER 13

Publicity and institutional advertising

THE PRECEDING CHAPTER gave us a very brief glance at PR. *This* chapter treats the two major tools PR uses in the communicative step or phase: *publicity* and *institutional advertising*.

On pages 380–81, you recall, there was a breakdown of the PR process. We assume at this point that Steps No. 1 through 5 have been taken—that the firm is now ready to undertake mass communication.

PART I: PUBLICITY

What

An advertising medium consists of two parts, the *advertising* portion, and the *editorial* portion; every element of the medium is either advertising, or it is editorial content. The advertising media which carry almost all publicity are newspapers, magazines, TV, and radio. In newspapers, editorial material includes: news stories, feature stories, photographs and drawings, comics, cartoons, editorials, letters to the editor, and "name" columns. In magazine editorial space we find: articles, stories, illustrations, recipes, question-and-answer departments, and reviews of books, movies, and plays. In the two broadcast media, the main editorial time contains: programs, shows, and newscasts. Other than word-of-mouth publicity, we think of publicity as being, in the main, communication that appears in the editorial space and time of advertising media, particularly in the

FIGURE 13–1. Publicity issued by General Electric's Press Relations department

The new projector called Color Print Viewer blows up 3½-in. square snapshots onto its own 10 × 10 in. screen. The compact device just announced by the General Electric Company shows up to 50 prints without reloading and has storage space in back of device for 150 more. The viewer is designed especially for showing prints made with Instamatic cameras and other square format cameras. It looks like a TV but weighs only 11 lbs. The device is 14 in. wide, 9 in. deep, and about 18 in. high.

Source: The General Electric Company, Cleveland, Ohio.

four mentioned. Media *sell* advertising space and time; they do *not sell* editorial space and time.

IBM, for example, buys a full-page ad in *The Wall Street Journal;*

that is advertising. *The Wall Street Journal* runs a news story about IBM's current earnings, or about the new product featured in the full-page ad; that is publicity. Or, a publisher runs an ad for one of his books in *The New York Times* Book Review section which contains a review of the book. The ad is advertising, the review is publicity. A Sears TV ad—TV news coverage of the opening of a new Sears store; ad—publicity.

Common subjects of publicity? Generic type of product or service; person; place or geographic area; drives or causes; organizations; government; ideas or points of view; events or attitudes. The two big subjects for us are (1) the seller who makes or retails a product or offers a service, and (2) the brand name; thus publicity relates to both *corporate* image and *brand* image.

Publicity is mild, subtle, low-key promotion. Except for word-of-mouth publicity, it is nonpersonal. The message is more informative than promotional. Sellers' identity may not even be disclosed. For example, an article on funeral customs may encourage the sending of flowers but not name any florists.

Now for a definition:

Publicity is the nonpersonal stimulation of demand for a product, service, or business unit by planting commercially significant news about it in a published medium, or obtaining favorable presentation of it upon radio, TV, or stage that is not paid for by the sponsor.[1]

Publicity versus Advertising

In relating publicity to advertising, maybe our best approach is to highlight the differences.

1. Unlike advertising, publicity designed as news stories demands a *news* slant.
2. Ads can be scheduled close together. The bases for much publicity (the opening of a new business firm, the selection of a new president for the company, the merger of two firms) do not permit *any* repeat communication, or only infrequent reuse.
3. Advertising media refuse to run proffered publicity far more often and far more casually than they refuse to accept ads. Sellers, thus, cannot schedule publicity in any regular, consistent way. Many more publicity items are refused by media than are used.

---

[1] Ralph S. Alexander *et al., Marketing Definitions: A Glossary of Marketing Terms* (Chicago: American Marketing Association, 1960), p. 9.

FIGURE 13–2. Here is a news release as issued—here is what an editor did with it

FROM: Daniel J. Edelman, Inc.   FOR: SPECIALTY ADVERTISING ASSOCIATION
       221 North LaSalle Street   740 North Rush Street
       Chicago, Illinois   60601   Chicago, Illinois   60611
       Phone: (312) 782-9250

For further information contact John DeFrancesco or Clif Drozda

FOR IMMEDIATE RELEASE

SPECIALTY ADVERTISING FIRMS REPORT SALES UP

10 PER CENT IN FIRST THREE MONTHS OF 1970

CHICAGO, ILLINOIS, JUNE 30, 1970 -- In a business period generally considered soft in most markets, a survey answered by better than 40 per cent of member firms of the Specialty Advertising Association (SAA) revealed an average gain in sales of nearly 10 per cent during the first three months of 1970. The survey requested percentages of sales increase or decrease only, and not dollar volumes.

Of the firms which responded, increases in sales out-numbered decreases by more than 2.5 to one.

As the trade association for the specialty advertising industry, SAA represents some 1,200 companies. Specialty advertising includes imprinted specialties, calendars and business gifts used as a medium for advertising and sales promotion.

SALES UP according to a survey answered by more than 40% of member firms of the Specialty Advertising Association (740 N. Rush St., Chicago, Ill. 60611) revealing an average gain in sales of nearly 10% during first three months of 1970. Survey requested percentages, not dollar volumes. Increases in sales outnumbered decreases by more than 2.5 to one. Specialty advertising included imprinted specialties, calendars, and gifts used as a medium for ads and promotions.

4. Media do not edit or redo ads unilaterally; they do not hesitate to rewrite the publicity items they receive and decide to run.

5. Media have complete control over *when* they run a publicity item, over *where* they place it, and over *how much* space or time they give it. Advertisers control those three variables for ads.

6. The source of an ad is perceived to be a seller whose aim is obvious and clear. For that reason, the ad may encounter skepticism, raise questions, or be met with buying defenses. The source of publicity, however, appears to be an editor; this endows publicity with more prestige and greater acceptability, often greater credibility.

7. Buyers assign publicity the value, the image, and the rating of the medium in which it appears to a much greater extent than is true of advertising.

8. Sellers expect quicker response to their brand advertising than to their publicity.

9. Media have rate cards and sell advertising space and time; they do not charge for the space or time occupied by publicity. Publicity is "free" only in this sense. If advertising and publicity are thought of as girls of different types, *publicity* is the girl sellers flirt with and make passes at—advertising is the one they marry and support.

10. The foregoing nine points make clear that publicity is *not* free advertising, nor is it a substitute for advertising.

We must recognize, of course, that both publicity *and* advertising are intended to inform and to influence a firm's publics. Each needs to be in harmony with the other; what is implied in both must be compatible and consistent, not in conflict. They need to be coordinated as regards both substance and timing. Both need PR approval and clearance.

Publicity media

Earlier we pointed out that there are six main advertising media—newspapers, magazines, TV, radio, outdoor, and transit and that of these, newspapers, magazines, TV, and radio carry the great bulk of publicity, outdoor and transit being less well adapted for the purpose. We noted, too, that in regard to publicity, the print media, newspapers and magazines, differ from the broadcast media, TV and radio, in that *space* is more adjustable than is *time*. So, we find much of the total volume of publicity in newspapers and magazines. TV and radio, of course, must make a certain percentage of their time available for "public service." The publicity director is interested in a medium's circulation in the same way and for the same reasons that the advertising manager is interested.

FIGURE 13–3. Example of radio publicity

(Format to be used for radio spot announcements if your company
should sponsor a public service event in the community.)

PUBLIC SERVICE SPOT ANNOUNCEMENT:
 FOR USE NOW THROUGH (date of event)

                                        TIME: 30 seconds

        ANNCR: Enjoy an evening of music under the stars . . .
                  when the Gateway Festival Orchestra, under the
                  direction of William Schatzkamer, presents
                  a FREE Bicentennial concert on Sunday, August
                  16, starting at 8 p.m. Sponsored by Anheuser-
                  Busch, the concert will be given on the city's
                  historic riverfront . . . in front of the
                  Gateway Arch. You will hear everything from
                  the delightful calliope in an original medley
                  to the familiar classics. There will be some
                  community singing, too. Park FREE on the levee.
                  Bring camp chairs or cushions. Remember --
                  next Sunday, August 16, at 8 p.m.

The newspaper is the leading carrier of publicity. Included here are regular newspapers, such as *The New York Times,* and business newspapers, such as *The Wall Street Journal.* On regular newspapers, the city editor is responsible for all local news.

News magazines (such as *Time*) and business magazines (for example, *Forbes*) are vehicles for publicity. Corporation activities and changes in consumer products are frequently sufficiently news worthy to gain coverage in the news magazines and other magazines read by consumers. By their very nature, business magazines do contain many editorial items about persons, companies, and brands.

Bases for publicity

Every publicity item must have its own subject. Examples:

Accomplishments	Interviews
Activities	Meetings
Anniversaries	Mergers
Awards	New Products
Companies	Open houses
Developments	Parades
Elections	Persons
Events	Places
Executive appointments	Records
Expansion plans	Retirements
"Firsts"	Sales and earnings
Guests	Speeches

Instead of waiting for publicity to "happen," the seller should study his publicity potential, plan for and create continuing publicity, and then carry out his plan. Quite helpful in this endeavor will be a calendar datebook. As the term implies, this is a schedule or program for next year; it is a plan, a program.

Use of a calendar datebook starts with the seller's spotting known publicity events and marking them on the calendar. Examples of such events are annual reports, anniversaries, retirement ceremonies, and new annual product models. Once these annual, dependable bases have been put on the calendar, the seller then identifies and schedules any nonrecurring bases available next year. Then he plans to create "fill-in" publicity, particularly for the longer in-between periods which at that time contain no planned publicity bases. Publicity is thus planned, created, and programmed; it is not left to chance.

Publicity forms

All publicity forms are versions of news or of information. News has not changed since Kipling described it as telling Who, What, Where, How, and Why. The three most important requirements of news are (1) that it be timely or current, (2) that it be of interest to many persons, and (3) that it be accurate and true. If, in addition to these three, it is dramatic and arouses emotion, that's all the better. The pub-

FIGURE 13–4.   Anheuser-Busch's publicity check list

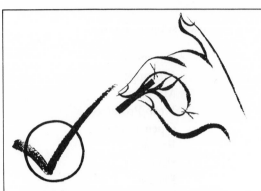

A PUBLICITY CHECK LIST
FOR YOU ABOUT YOUR COMPANY

PERSONNEL

1. New people join your organization.
2. Promotions.
3. Retirements.
4. Awards for safe driving, courtesy, etc.

FACILITIES

1. Addition of new or unusual equipment . . . (new trucks, new office or warehouse equipment, etc.)
2. Addition of new office or warehouse space . . . Groundbreaking ceremonies.
3. Remodeling.
4. Change of location.

SERVICES

1. Increase in service.
2. New kind of service.
3. Any special or unusual service.

COMMUNITY RELATIONS

1. Any special service to the community or organizations.
2. Civil Defense activities.
3. Contribution to Community Chest, United Fund drive, etc.
4. Picnic or Christmas party for orphans or needy.

FIGURE 13–4. (*Continued*)

ABOUT YOUR PEOPLE

HOBBIES AND SPORTS

1. Fishing enthusiast makes record catch.
2. Week-end golfer makes hole-in-one.
3. Bowler rolls perfect game.
4. Any sports achievement in any field that is more than routine.
5. Unusual hobbies or projects that are interesting or help
   others. Any with a company tie-in?

SOCIAL

1. Engagement and marriage of one of your employees, or son or
   daughter of one of your employees.
2. Any special social function in which one of your employees is a
   principal . . . dance, reception, tea, or coffee hour.

COMMUNITY RELATIONS

1. One of your employees is chairman of Community Chest
   or other community fund-raising drive.
2. One of your people is elected president, or to other office, of
   service club — Kiwanis, Optimist, Lions, Boy Scouts, etc., or other
   worthy organization.
3. You or one of your employees is making a speech at a
   civic or community group.

OTHER ACTIVITIES

1. One of your people is drafted, wins honor or performs outstanding
   service in the armed forces.
2. Son or daughter of one of your people . . .
   a. Wins university scholarship.
   b. Named exchange student to foreign country.
   c. Becomes Eagle Scout, etc.
   d. Is elected to campus office, or wins other
      honor at college.

FIGURE 13–5. Discovering a story

A continuous flow of publicity from an organization is necessary for maximum results. The person in charge of the preparation of publicity well begins by developing a checklist of source material that can be evolved within the company and by planning a production flow around this list. The following suggests the scope of material available in most companies.

Marketing developments
New products.
New uses for old products.
Research developments.
Appointments and changes of marketing personnel.
Large orders received.
Successful bids.
Awards of contracts.
Special events

Company policies
New guarantees.
Changes in credit terms.
Changes in distribution policies.
Changes in service policies.
Changes in prices and pricing policies.

News of general interest
The annual election of officers.
Meetings of the board of directors.
Anniversaries of the organization.
Anniversaries of an invention of the company.
Anniversaries of the senior officers of the organization.
State or national holidays that can be tied into the organization's activities.
Annual banquets, luncheons, parties, and picnics.
Local pageants in which the organization participates.
Special weeks, such as Candy Week, Clean-Up–Paint-Up Week, and
Local sports events in which teams from the organization compete.
    so on.
Festive occasions, such as Valentine's Day, Mother's Day, Father's Day, feast days, etc.
Founders' Day.
Foundation meetings.
Conferences and special meetings.
Welfare activities.
Open house to members of the community.

FIGURE 13–5. *(Continued)*

    Athletic events.

    Successful bids.

    Awards of contracts.

    Training course graduation ceremonies.

    Father and son golf tournaments.

    Awards of merits to employees.

    Cornerstone laying.

    Opening of an exhibition.

Reports on current developments

    Reports of work on new experiments.

    Reports on conditions of the industry.

    Progress reports on the company.

    Employment, production, sales, and other statistics showing trends.

    Reports on new discoveries, inventions, and safety devices.

    Tax reports.

    Speeches by principals.

    Predictions and analyses of economic conditions.

    Employment gains.

    Financial statements.

    Organization appointments.

    Opening of new markets, both foreign and domestic.

Personalities—names are news

    Visits by famous personages, including well-known customers, noted educators, local, state, and Federal government officials.

    Personal accomplishments of individuals.

    Winners of company contests.

    Employees's and officers' advancements.

    Interviews by company officials.

    Company employees serving as judges for various contests.

    Interviews with employees.

Slogans, symbols, endorsements

    The company's slogan—its history, development, aim, and fulfillment.

    A tie-in of company activities with local slogans.

    Creation of a slogan for a particular purpose or occasion.

    The company's trademark.

    The company's name plate.

    The company's trade character.

    Endorsements of company policy, products, or methods by prominent people.

Source: Frey, Albert W. (ed.). *Marketing Handbook* (2d ed.; New York: The Ronald Press, 1965).

FIGURE 13–6. Typical news release and what happened to it

NEWS RELEASE

THE DISCOVERY COMPANY   **UNION CARBIDE CORPORATION,** PUBLIC RELATIONS DEPARTMENT
270 PARK AVENUE, NEW YORK, N. Y. 10017 · TEL. (212) 551-3875

FOR RELEASE: IMMEDIATELY

CONTACT:
Gertrude Scharding
Tel. (212) 551-3771

R. MANNING BROWN, JR., ELECTED A DIRECTOR OF UNION CARBIDE

NEW YORK, May 27 -- R. Manning Brown, Jr., president and chief administrative officer of New York Life Insurance Company, has been elected a director of Union Carbide Corporation, it was announced today by Birny Mason, Jr., chairman of the board of Union Carbide.

Mr. Brown joined the New York Life Insurance Company in 1951 as assistant vice-president in the real estate and mortgage loan department. He was named vice-president in charge of real estate and mortgage loans in 1955 and in 1962 was elected an executive vice-president. He was elected a director in 1967 and president and chief administrative officer in 1969.

He is also a director of The Great Atlantic & Pacific Tea Company, Morgan Guaranty Trust Company of New York, Louisiana Land and Exploration Company, Avon Products, Inc., Union Camp Corporation, Union Theological Seminary, and the Economic Development Council of the City of New York. He is a trustee of the Metropolitan Museum of Art, the Lincoln Center Fund, the John Simon Guggenheim Memorial Foundation, and Princeton University.

Born in Elizabeth, New Jersey, Mr. Brown was graduated from Princeton University in 1936. He and his family live in Princeton.

- END -

Union Carbide Corp. (New York)—R. Manning Brown Jr., president and chief administrative officer of New York Life Insurance Co., was elected a director of this chemicals concern.

The Wall Street Journal, May 28, 1970.

licity director must always be clear about whom he hopes to inform and influence, which medium or media he hopes will carry the publicity, the publicity form to use, and the response or reaction he wants.

Here are some main forms publicity can take:

1. The news or press release. This is the most useful, most common type of communication from the business firm to mass media. Ideally, the release or story will be newsworthy, perhaps even helpful, to a high proportion of the medium's circulation. Many news releases are pre-planned and scheduled well in advance; some are unplanned—about such an emergency as an explosion, or a strike, or a lawsuit. Goodrich sends out over 800 news releases each year featuring products, persons, or the Goodrich firm; many are accompanied by photographs.

2. The news or press conference. This event is scheduled only when the company has a major announcement or a really important story to tell. Each conference should be planned carefully. The list of media persons to be invited demands thoughtful building. If practicable, the top executive should preside, and, if appropriate, his associates should be present. Answers to probable questions should be given advance attention. Publicity material is often distributed to each media representative.

3. The feature article or story. This item does not have to be *current* news. Running from 500 to 2,500 words, feature articles can present more color, more depth, and more detail than does the news story. Business magazines are good vehicles for feature articles. An issue of *Chemical Week*, for example, pictured J. Peter Grace on its cover and contained an eight-page article on W.. R. Grace & Co. Some feature articles are written by reporters, some by free-lancers. Sometimes an idea or an outline is suggested to an editor; if his reaction is encouraging, then the writing is started.

4. Photographs. Many of the publicity items found in newspapers and magazines have their own photographs. Editors prefer photographs that combine the familiar with the unusual, the everyday with the exceptional. Qualities of good photographs include action, color, beauty, realism, and human interest. The popular physical form is the 8-by-10-inch glossy with caption attached.

5. Letters to editors. These are useful to express opinions; they are good to publicize company position.

6. Editorials. These are rare and difficult to get. On its 100th birthday, an outstanding firm might be recognized by an editor's devoting an editorial to it. Some editors welcome background material for editorials.

FIGURE 13–7. Typical press release

NEW FAMILY
WELCOME KIT, INC.

168 BROAD HOLLOW ROAD – ROUTE 110
FARMINGDALE, NEW YORK 11735 - (516) 249-5252

PRESS RELEASE

NEW FAMILY WELCOME KIT, INC., ENTERS FRANCHISE FIELD
WITH UNIQUE DISTRIBUTORSHIP OFFERING...

NEW FAMILY WELCOME KIT, INC. of FARMINGDALE, NEW YORK, (a public company since November, 1968) specializing in sampling, marketing research, couponing, sales promotion, and premiums announces its expansion into FRANCHISING.

The company distributes product samples, special offers, and coupons coast-to-coast for consumer goods manufacturers interested in reaching new families. Through their broad distribution pattern, reaching directly into the new home, NEW FAMILY WELCOME KIT eliminates the high cost of product sampling for the manufacturers.

The WELCOME KIT is a unique DOLL HOUSE filled with top-brand name household, cosmetic, drug and grocery items. Up to now, the distribution of the kit has been effected by companies selling services direct to the consumer's home, such as Fuel Oil Companies, Public Utilities, CATV Companies, etc. They find the DOLL HOUSE most effective for getting leads, building goodwill and winning new customers. Many banks and home builders also distribute the WELCOME KIT ... all over the U.S.

The new Franchise Hostess Plan will phase in a new method of distribution, commencing February, 1970. WELCOME KIT will be delivered directly to the new homeowner by a franchised hostess. * Local stores will also participate, with coupons redeemable at the stores. Complete merchandising and sales promotion back-up is to be included for each franchised distributorship. Franchise prices are scheduled to start at $10,000.
* Note: More than a dozen "pilot" towns already in operation in New York and New Jersey.

The Franchise Hostess Plan will also develop valuable marketing research data for manufacturers who provide product samples for the NEW FAMILY WELCOME KIT, as well as other localized consumer sampling-advertising-trade relations services. The present methods of WELCOME KIT distribution will continue until the new Franchised Hostess Plan meets complete acceptability.

A partial list of manufacturers currently participating in WELCOME KIT programs includes:

AMERICAN CAN COMPANY..............with Dixie Dispensers, Aurora & Northern Tissue
TEXIZE CHEMICALS, INC.............with Fantastik
ALBERTO-CULVER...................with VO-5 Creme Rinse
COLGATE-PALMOLIVE COMPANY.........with Axion
HUNT-WESSON FOODS.................with Snack Pack (Peaches & Chocolate Pudding)
3M COMPANY.......................with Kitchen Scrub 'n Sponge
HOLLAND HOUSE BRANDS, INC.........with Whiskey Sour Cocktail Mixes
BROOKE BOND FOODS.................with Red Rose Tea
SANNA INC...(DIVISIONS OF)........with Swiss Miss Cocoa Mix
FISHER NUT..(BEATRICE FOODS).......with Sunflower Nuts
DOW CORNING......................with Sight Savers
A.E. STALEY CO...................with Sta-puf Fabric Softener
MILES LABORATORIES...............with Bactine Skin Cream, S.O.S. Soap Pads
MEAD JOHNSON LABS................with Vi-Sol plus Safety Plug for Children
GENERAL FOODS....................with Tang
THE NESTLE CO....................with Taster's Choice, Nescafé, Decaf

For more information about NEW FAMILY WELCOME KIT Programs contact:

Mr. Myron Kaller, President

PR-10-0   SAMPLING, COUPONING, MAILING AND RESEARCH PROGRAMS REACHING NEW FAMILY MOVE-INS.
January, 1970

Features of good publicity

Good publicity must qualify on many counts. It must be timely and fresh, factual and accurate, brief and specific. It must be informative and interesting to many persons. It must rank high in news value or in human interest. Sex, food, money, travel, society, and adventure are popular subjects.

Each item must be written and organized so that an editor can easily read, summarize, excerpt, or rewrite. Editors condense publicity rather than expand it. Publicity must conform to the medium's image and style. Otherwise, the medium's readers, viewers, or listeners will not see or hear it. The editor accepts only those items which meet his standards and qualify on his criteria. He has preferences even about physical form.

Media relations

Importance.   The publicity director needs good relationships with the media he hopes will carry his publicity. But, first, we must remember certain facts that are relevant.

Editors are gatekeepers. Editors control the space and time publicity directors want. In magazines, there will be an editor in chief who ultimately controls the editorial content, and there may be subject editors as well. In the newspaper medium, the key man may be the city editor, or, he may be a more specialized editor—the business editor, the food editor, the society editor. In broadcasting, the news editor and the program director control time.

No newspaper has enough reporters to cover and process all local news. So, newspaper editors depend on publicity men for material and for information—about what *is* happening, about what *will be* happening. Editors, of course, have their defenses up; they are wary; editors are responsible for, and are judged by, the editorial fare they feed to their circulations. And do remember, editors reject, they throw away more publicity stories than they accept and run.

The smart publicity director knows and respects the restraints under which editors operate. The amount of space or time an editor "owns" is limited. Suppose a newspaper decides that its space shall be allotted 60 percent to advertising and 40 percent to editorial material; for every 60 pages of advertising sold, the editor gets 40 pages. The competitors for these 40 pages are many, and their competition is fierce. And, issue after issue, month after month, the contents of the 40 pages must reflect balance and fairness to all.

So, publicity directors need the goodwill of editors, reporters, commentators, and cameramen.

Guidelines.   No publicity director should try to disguise advertising as "news." So-called news releases which are too commercial or too promotional do harm, not good. References to the seller or to his brand must be subdued.

Neither the publicity director nor the advertising manager should approach a medium with an ad in one hand and a publicity item in the other. Any suggestion of bribe, threat, or pressure infuriates editors; they are incensed by the implication that their space or time "belongs" to their advertisers. Of course, we must be realistic and admit that newspapers *may* give retailers publicity in proportion to the amount of space retailers buy. Magazines, too, have been accused of favoring their heavy advertisers in editorial columns.

Publicity directors should never beg or complain, scold or blame.

Editors expect fair and equitable treatment from each publicity director. They do not want him to play favorites. Instead, they want him to be fair and available to all.

The publicity director must learn each medium's audience. Only by so doing can he tailor his publicity to the interests of each audience, telling each what it wants to read, see, or hear.

In the same way, the publicity director must know each editor, his policies, and his needs. This calls for personal contact; it also calls for a study of the types of publicity material he accepts and uses. Editors resent their time being wasted. They frown on duplicate items to competing media, and on any carbon copy of an item—wondering just *who* got the original.

Good relations demand that publicity directors "make" media's deadlines. Schedules must be met. Magazine editors, in particular, must get material well in advance of publication.

A final guideline for the publicity director is to plan for the long run. He must be both patient and persistent. He must be an honest and accurate service arm to the press. Confidence, trust, and respect must be worked for and earned, and that cannot be achieved overnight.

What about "bad" publicity?   All or most of the bases recognized thus far are bases for *favorable* publicity. Events or developments, however, *can* give rise to unfortunate, damaging publicity; most such events are entirely outside the firm's control. Examples: investigation by the government; fires, explosions, deaths; a manufacturer's recalling defective products; lawsuits or unfavorable court decisions.

Three steps should be taken before any of these happen. The starting step, obviously, is to try to prevent such experiences.

Another step is to draft a plan, in advance, for contingencies—then hope it will not be needed. Such a plan avoids surprise and insures preparation. The W. R. Grace & Co. tells its personnel:

In event of emergencies, each operational unit of the company (plant, sales office, laboratory) should have a current, detailed emergency plan for handling explosions, fires, floods, and other disasters. A vital part of such a plan is provision for keeping press and public fully informed on the state of affairs following the emergency. Information handling in an emergency should be governed by prompt disclosure of the consequences, within the limitations of legal and insurance requirements.

The third step is to set up techniques and procedures for fact-finding, techniques that are thorough yet speedy, whenever emergencies occur.

Once the event strikes, management should contact the press at once. Seldom is it smart to ignore the situation, or to try to conceal it; never is it smart to try to hide from the press. Some situations demand the calling of a press conference; some recommend that a top executive get in touch with one or more editors. If editors are asked to suppress bad news, ugly rumors can result.

If the press initiates the contact and asks questions, a "No comment" response is a grave mistake. This from Goodrich:

On occasions when circumstances may produce undesirable or controversial news, an attempt to give a satisfying response must be made. Unless the information is confidential or might jeopardize the Company's business position, a "No Comment" is held to be the worst and most damaging answer to be given. Stone silence will be judged as a cover-up, or, at the very least, an indication of unwillingness or inability to cooperate.

Instead of evasion, there should be a report to the press of facts that have been determined. This report should be full and frank, simple and courteous. Guesses, assumptions, and predications should not be made. Reports covering the event should be helped in whatever ways are practicable; their suspicion and resentment are aroused if their coverage is made difficult. As more information is learned, follow-up facts should be fed to the press.

If vicious or untrue rumors are circulating, the company may consider using ads that explain, that stress the positive, that may even offer rewards if anyone can prove the allegations. Examples of such rumors: a certain product is contaminated; a certain firm will not hire workers of some ethnic group.

Word-of-mouth publicity

In textbook writing, positions must be modified sometimes, and exceptions must be made. Such is the case now.

We have said thus far that publicity appears in the editorial portions of newspapers, magazines, TV, and radio. But, there is a different kind of communication—a different kind of publicity—we must recognize at this point. Its common title is *word-of-mouth* publicity; for sellers, it can have the effect of favorable promotion, or unfavorable. So, a quick glance at word-of-mouth publicity.

What.   The best concept of word-of-mouth publicity for our purposes is that of conversation, of two-way communication. It is two housewives evaluating supermarkets across the fence that separates their yards. It is three students discussing the quality of some TV show. It is two instructors arguing about which textbook is best.

Word-of-mouth publicity takes various forms. It can be an expression of opinion, a report of some personal experience, the recommendation of some course of action. An important feature is that the communicator is *not* seen by the receiver as representing or working for a seller. That explains part of its power to affect attitudes and to influence behavior.

As a promotional force, word-of-mouth publicity is more subtle and more informal than is advertising or even publicity in mass media. It is always person-to-person, often face-to-face. It can travel or spread quickly; the more emotional its content, the speedier it is.

Receivers and senders.   Many receivers are opinion followers who depend on opinion leaders in such areas or specialties as fashion, food, or travel. Whereas the opinion follower can get mainly facts from ads, he can get judgment and evaluation from opinion leaders. The more reluctant a person is to adopt a new course of action, the more he depends on, and is influenced by, word-of-mouth publicity.

The seller wants his salesman or his ad to influence an opinion leader favorably—for the opinion leader to buy, consume, and like—*then to circulate favorable word-of-mouth publicity* about the seller and his brand. Senders frequently volunteer and start the process. Or, a sender may send after being asked for information, often about a matter of common interest. Opinion leaders, of course, engage in word-of-mouth exchanges between and among themselves.

W-O-M and manufacturers.   Manufacturers want favorable word-of-mouth publicity, particularly makers of consumer products; they want to avoid the unfavorable. This is because W-O-M publicity can help or hurt both brand image and corporate image. This power is great because, as noted, the sender is *not* viewed as being commercially involved, as *not* having an ax to grind. Instead, he appears to be reporting on his experiences, to be sharing his knowledge, to be giving friendly and trustworthy advice.

The manufacturer is not able to generate and sponsor this force in any controlled way. He knows that it can be distorted, can degenerate into the transmittal of false and damaging rumors. So, much is still to be determined about W-O-M publicity.

PART II: INSTITUTIONAL ADVERTISING

What

We have just looked at *publicity*. Now we look at the other major tool used in PR to communicate to large numbers of persons, to one or more "publics," *institutional advertising*. Some refer to this as *corporate* advertising.

FIGURE 13–8. Photo and caption distributed by American Oil Company

Lead-free gasoline greatly extends spark plug life, as photo illustrates. The clean plugs (right) were operated in an engine using lead-free fuel for over 80,000 miles without a change. Thick lead deposits coat the contacts, nearly closing the gap, of plugs used for about 12,000 miles in a car fueled by leaded gasoline.

Brand advertising, as we have seen, promotes a product or a service; institutional advertising promotes the seller of that product or service. Brand advertising strives for a favorable attitude toward a brand; institutional advertising works for goodwill and friendly feelings toward the advertiser. The creative techniques and ingredients of both types are essentially the same. The media are the same.

The users of institutional advertising are the same as those included in the discussion of the sponsors of PR in the "Who" section of Chapter 12. Our main concern here, as there, is the commercial seller of goods or services. Most sellers using institutional advertising also use brand advertising; corporate image *and* brand image are influenced by both. A seller's brand advertising and institutional advertising must be compatible; content, substance, and promises must be consistent and complementary.

Institutional advertising promotes the idea that the seller himself—not just his brand—is worthy of consideration, is attractive, is a real influence when consumers make buying decisions. It deals with something more abstract and less tangible than food, for example, or beverages, or automobiles. It is indirect action advertising. Both brand and institutional advertising are bought and run for the same reason, to make the adver-

FIGURE 13–9. Gulf photo and caption

Opportunities Industrialization Center trainees and Gulf Oil service station employees in Philadelphia share a course in auto mechanics. The 40-hour course covers carburetion, alternator-generator and tuneup work.

FIGURE 13–10.   This ad which ran in 1908 is thought to be the first institutional ad of a patronage nature

Twenty Million Voices

A PERFECT understanding by the public of the management and full scope of the Bell Telephone System can have but one effect, and that a most desirable one —a marked betterment of the service.

Do you know what makes the telephone worth while to you—just about the most indispensable thing in modern life?

It isn't the circuit of wire that connects your instrument with the exchange.

It's the Twenty Million Voices at the other end of the wire on every Bell Telephone!

We have to keep them there, on hair trigger, ready for you to call them up, day or night—downtown, up in Maine, or out in Denver.

And to make the telephone system useful to those Twenty Million other people, we have to keep *you* alert and ready at this end of the wire.

Then we have to keep the line in order—8,000,000 miles of wire—and the central girls properly drilled and accommodating to the last degree, and the apparatus up to the highest pitch of efficiency.

Quite a job, all told.

Every telephone user is an important link in the system—just as important as the operator. With a little well meant suggestion on our part, we believe we can improve the service—perhaps save a second on each call.

There are about *six billion connections* a year over these lines.

Saving a second each would mean a tremendous time saving to you and a tremendous saving of operating expenses, which can be applied to the betterment of the service.

The object of this and several succeeding magazine advertisements is *not to get more subscribers.* It is to make each one of you a better link in the chain.

First, give "Central" the number clearly and be sure she hears it. Give her full and clear information in cases of doubt. She is there to do her utmost to accommodate you.

Next, don't grow fretful because you think she represents a monopoly. The postmaster does, too, for the same reason.

The usefulness of the telephone is its *universality, as one system.* Where there are two systems you must have two telephones—and confusion.

Remember, the value of the service lies in the number of people you can reach *without* confusion—the promptness with which you get your response.

So respond quickly when others call you, bearing in mind the extensive scope of the service.

The constant endeavor of the associated Bell companies, harmonized by one policy and acting as one system, is to give you the best and most economical management human ingenuity can devise. The end is efficient service and your attitude and that of every other subscriber may hasten or hinder its accomplishment.

Agitation against legitimate telephone business —the kind that has become almost as national in its scope as the mail service—must disappear with a realization of the necessity of universal service.

American Telephone & Telegraph Company

And Its Associated Bell Companies

One Policy—One System Universal Service

UNITING OVER 4,000,000 TELEPHONES

tiser's operation more successful; the two types just take different approaches to the same goal.

In small companies, one advertising department may handle both brand and institutional advertising. In large firms, an institutional advertising unit may be housed in the PR department and be responsible for all institutional advertising. A company may assign its institutional advertising to an advertising agency *not* doing any of the firm's brand advertising.

Because the top PR executive is much concerned with the total corporate personality, his interest in institutional *and* brand advertising is obvious and understandable. The need to coordinate the two types is clearly present when PR department personnel administer institutional advertising but *advertising* personnel administer brand advertising.

Here is an excerpt from a booklet prepared by the Magazine Advertising Bureau:

PIONEERING CORPORATE ADVERTISING

Pioneering effort highly successful

The summer of 1908 saw the launching of what was probably one of the first large-scale efforts to "educate the public" in behalf of an American corporation—in other words, Corporate Advertising. In this period, shortly after the turn of the century, this type of advertising was far more likely to be called public-service or institutional advertising. This pioneering corporate advertising effort was launched in 1908 by the American Telephone and Telegraph Company.

The sustained AT&T advertising campaign was neither planned nor written to increase business directly. Its objective was to make known and understood the purposes, problems, and policies of the telephone system. It educated people in the use of the telephone and how to get the best service from the system. However, such public service and corporate image advertising not only accomplished its overt public service objectives admirably, but at the same time packed considerable sales wallop. During the first five years of the campaign, the company gained over two million new subscribers—a substantial increase in rate of growth.

Number and skill of advertisers grew

Soon this strange new phenomenon of public service companies assuming a friendly, public-spirited attitude and using advertising to increase public understanding and goodwill became quite common. Streetcar companies advertised to teach the rules of the road and to allay prejudices. Power companies interpreted electricity as a public servant. Railroads promoted "safety first."

Gradually at first, then with increasing momentum, more and more corporations launched corporate advertising efforts. Objectives of this kind of advertising grew along with the numbers of corporations involved, as did their skill in strategy and execution of the advertising.

Patronage advertising

Patron advertising is the most widely used type of institutional advertising. In it, the seller communicates about himself rather than about the products or services he sells. He tries to convince buyers that his operation entitles him to buyers' patronage, that he is a good source

FIGURE 13–11. Early patronage ad introducing Martha Logan, Swift's trade character

FIGURE 13–12. Sears patronage ad

FIGURE 13–12. *(Continued)*

Your first house–how Sears can help you make it a home

Old house or new house, Sears has everything you need to make it a home. Decorating tips, guide books, expert advice, remodeling ideas. All *free*. Read the many ways Sears, Roebuck and Co. can help you get settled faster.

ANYONE who's ever tried fixing up a house from the bare walls out will tell you that it's a tough job for amateurs.

Sears can help by lending a *professional* hand.

First, Sears will give you free guide books written by decorating experts: "Decorating Made Easy","The Kitchen Idea Book", "The Fashion Bathroom Show-case", and "Home Improvement Ideas".

Then Sears will give you follow-up advice on topics like these:

• How to choose an exterior paint color that suits your house and its surroundings (Sears Color-Scape Plan).

• How to find a wall paint that's an exact match for your favorite Aztec gold rug (Sears Color Bank of 820 shades will help you).

• How to blend colors all through the house (simply follow Sears Harmony House Color Plan).

Expert advice

Would you like expert advice on plans for updating your kitchen or bath, a new central air-conditioning system, re-shingling the roof? A phone call to Sears will bring the appropriate specialist to your door.

Other Sears specialists can show you how to disguise problem windows with draperies, how to pick the most practical wall-to-wall broadloom for your living room. And they'll have fabric samples along so you can study them right where you'll use them. All this advice is absolutely *free*.

Expert installation and service

After the advice, Sears is ready, able and willing to follow through with *installation*—anything from a whole room to a single appliance.

When Sears modernizes a kitchen or bathroom for you, *everything* can be handled from the plumbing out. Quickly, carefully, with a minimum of fuss.

When Sears installs an appliance, the man just won't leave until you're satisfied that everything looks right, works right, *is* right. And you can rely on Sears appliance servicing to make sure it *stays* right.

Choice of credit plans

Sears has a tremendous selection of furniture, appliances, furnishings. Even original oil paintings.

Sears has a variety of credit plans, too. One of them is the Modernizing Credit Plan, which allows you up to *five years* to pay for major home improvements—with no money down.

In fact, Sears has *everything* you need when you're turning a house into a home. Including this famous pledge: *satisfaction guaranteed or your money back.*

◄ *First meal in their first house—and a whole lot of work ahead before it will be a home. Sears can help them fix it up—and help them stretch their budget. It is Sears constant aim to give equal quality for less money, or better quality for the same money.*

FIGURE 13–13.   Kodak public relations ad

We want to be useful
...and even interesting

Staying out of trouble

Even if Kodak were holier than thou or than business in general, to admit it would merely inspire the cynics. What makes the system work is fear of the dissatisfied consumer's most terrible form of revenge—indifference to our brand name.

The consumer never sees the little piece of tape which our Judy Austin holds here. While stretching a buck the consumer can also strain that little piece of tape when he tries for a 21st picture from a 20-exposure 135 cartridge. Trace amounts of copper, iron, or nickel compounds in the adhesive can cause the tape after a while to weaken its grip and yield part way. *If it doesn't yield all the way and leave him with loose film,* he wins. After he sees the results, he may write us a caustic letter about streaks along most of his 21 pictures. You would hardly expect him to know that the yielding tape left a little of its adhesive on the velvet lips of his cartridge to streak over the whole film as it was wound back.

So Judy Austin has to figure out how to keep track of traces of copper, iron, and nickel in the raw materials that go into that adhesive. Actually Mrs. Austin (who came as a chemist) figures out how computers should keep track of some 200 different physical tests on some 150 products in addition to the unseen bit of tape. (Since we make far more than 150 products, she isn't the only Kodaker with such duties.)

Tests are started when someone foresees the possibility of dissatisfaction. Unforeseen trouble discovered by the consumer breeds intramural panic. Having been in business, a long time, we have learned many lessons.

Nevertheless, Judy with her computer programs works on ways to accomplish more with half a million items of data per year than just ward off complaints. It all goes even further than early warnings to manufacturing departments and suppliers of raw materials.

Consider this: One of our major advantages in the marketplace is uniformity of product. When variations occur in components, it takes big (figurative) holding tanks to even them out. The less in the tank, the less money stands idle in inventory.

That's what one woman's job is about.

FIGURE 13–14. Public service ads sponsored by the Advertising Council

PUBLICATION DATE
TUES., JULY 28, 1970

Should this date be inconvenient, please run this
public service message on the earliest date available.

Your kid shouldn't know more about drugs than you do.

You can do some quick catching
up with the straightforward, easy
to read Federal source book:
"Answers to the most frequently
asked questions about drug
abuse."

Write for your free copy. Send
in the coupon below.

```
• • • • • • • • • •
• Drug Abuse Questions and Answers •
• National Clearinghouse for Drug •
• Abuse Information •
• Box 1080, Washington, D.C. 20013 •
•                                   •
• Name:_____          •
•                                   •
• Address:_____          •
•                                   •
• City:_____          •
•                                   •
• State:_____          •
•                                   •
• Zip:_____          •
• • • • • • • • • •
```

 advertising contributed for the public good

Lysergic Acid Diethylamide does not go in your car battery.

And it shouldn't go in your child
either. Learn more about LSD in
the Federal source book: "Answers to the most frequently asked
questions about drug abuse."

Write for your free copy. Send
in the coupon below.

```
• • • • • • • • • • • •
• Drug Abuse Questions and Answers •
• National Clearinghouse for Drug •
• Abuse Information •
• Box 1080, Washington, D.C. 20013 •
•                                   •
• Name:_____          •
•                                   •
• Address:_____          •
•                                   •
• City:_____          •
•                                   •
• State:_____          •
•                                   •
• Zip:_____          •
• • • • • • • • • • • •
```

advertising contributed for the public good

 Thank you for your past and current support.
AND PLEASE SEND US TEARSHEETS
We want to publicize your support!

from which to buy. Thus, patronage advertising complements and re-inforces brand advertising.

Advertising themes that have been used by manufacturers include:

Research	Problem-solving ability
Quality control	Growth
Competence of personnel	Production facilities

Themes appropriate for retailers include:

Customer services	Size
Personnel	Merchanidse variety
Innovations	Performance

Public relations advertising

A second type of institutional advertising was unfortunately labeled *public relations* advertising. This can be a bit confusing because *all* adver-tising has PR goals and PR effects. Specifically, the public relations ver-sion of institutional advertising is asked to communicate to one or more of the advertiser's "publics" the advertiser's position on some current problem or issue.

Sample objectives:

1. To present the company's position during a strike.
2. To correct inaccurate assumptions.
3. To prevent or reduce ill will.
4. To oppose proposed legislation.
5. To explain temporary product shortages.

Public service advertising

The final type of institutional advertising to be discussed is *public service* advertising. Here the advertiser contributes to the welfare of the general public by stating publicly his position on, and by advocating, some socially desirable action. The advertiser usually has strong convic-tions on the matter and wants to make his belief known. His support for some public cause strengthens his reputation for social responsibility.

The issue is usually not controversial. Examples:

Pollution	Highway safety
Better schools	Conservation
Health	Accident prevention

QUESTIONS AND PROBLEMS

13-1. How can a firm get maximum promotional utility from a favorable bit of publicity?

13-2. What topics or subjects are common in *financial* publicity?

13-3. View a 30-minute newscast and list 5 recipients of publicity on it.

13-4. List 5 situations recommending the calling of a press conference.

13-5. What are the basic differences between brand advertising and institutional advertising?

13-6. Why might a company place its institutional advertising in a different ad agency from the agency handling its brand advertising?

13-7. Find 5 *patronage* ads and summarize the theme or "big idea" of each.

13-8. Find 5 *public relations* ads and summarize the objectives of each.

13-9. Find 5 *public service* ads and summarize the objectives of each.

13-10. Should religious groups sponsor public service advertising? Comment.

MANAGEMENT OF THE PROMOTION PROGRAM

CHAPTER 14

Promotion goals
and strategies

WE TURN, now, in Part VII, from a study of single elements of persuasion to the broader dimensions of promotion management. In considering the promotional mix or blending of those persuasive elements, we
must be of necessity concerned with total marketing strategies as well.
As we noted in Chapter 1, the promotion mix is but a part of a more
complex marketing mix which combines promotion with decisions about
products, locations and channels, and price. We will be studying the
management of the promotion mix in the chapters to come, but realistic
management of promotion can be achieved only through careful coordination with the other elements of the marketing mix.

Because management is a goal-directed activity, we must begin with
an examination of goals, then proceed to explore alternative strategies
by which goals may be achieved. That is the mission of this chapter.
In Chapter 15 we look more closely at the promotional planning process
to carry out the strategic designs of the firm. Next, in Chapter 16, the
plans are made specific through budgeting and scheduling. Finally, in
Chapter 17, our study of the management task comes full cycle with
a look at evaluation and control of promotion.

COMMUNICATION STRATEGY

Before beginning, let's take an overview of communication strategy
so that we can appreciate the role of each step in the planning process.

Put simply, the firm's communications strategy prescribes the role to be played by every persuasive element used to communicate with customers about the firm, its products, and its services. To do this, consideration must be given the following:

1. Assessing communication needs.
2. Formulating promotion goals.
3. Evaluating promotional alternatives.
4. Allocating persuasive tasks.

ASSESSING COMMUNICATION NEEDS

Like every other marketing management task, the starting point is the consumer. No realistic promotion strategy can be devised without a hard look at the consumer and customer groups to which the effort is directed. Moreover, as we have already noted in the buyer behavior discussion in Chapter 3, the way in which consumers reach decisions about purchases cannot be ignored. Questions such as these need the manager's best thoughts:

Are there several segments to the market or just one?
Do segments differ in socioeconomic characteristics?
Does prior ownership of our brand or similar products affect buying decisions? How?
How much information seeking does the customer normally employ?
Is the purchase decision made by the buyer alone or is it a joint decision between husband and wife, or purchasing agent and design engineer?

Answers to questions like these require much the same type consumer analysis as the marketing manager uses to formulate overall marketing strategy, but often in greater detail. The main point to remember is that design of effective promotion strategy requires a detailed knowledge of target customers and their buying habits.

Assessing the communication needs can be helped if special attention is paid to the products' life cycle, the nature of the demand-creating task to be performed, and the information appetite of target customers.

Product life cycles

A most useful idea which helps one understand the need for different marketing and promotion strategies is the concept of a products' life cycle. The product-life-cycle concept applies to the product as a *class* or *industry* whole, not for a specific *brand* within the industry. Perhaps the most widely used version of product life cycle divides the life of a product into four stages: introduction, growth, maturity, and decline.[1] Figure 14–1 shows these four stages graphically and includes some scale numbers which may help clarify the concept. The segments are not equal in size, and actually each life cycle has its unique dimensions. But generally a successful product will enjoy a longer market maturity stage, as we shall see.

FIGURE 14–1. Product life cycle and demand creation tasks

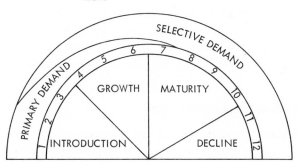

In the *introductory* stage, a new product class has been created and brought to the marketplace. Acceptance of the product may not occur, and the cycle terminates at this point. If acceptance does occur, it is likely to be slow at first, and at points 1 and 2 on the scale, the company may still be sustaining losses as heavy promotion budgets and product launching costs exceed returns. As sales volume increases, however, profits should begin to accrue.

The profits, or promise of profits, attracts competitors, and the *growth stage* begins. At points 4 and 5 the competitive pace quickens as new brands appear. Total industry demand is rising as more and more prospects move into the user category. Later in the growth stage, at point 6, the rate of growth slackens, and quite often some marginal firms either drop out or are absorbed through merger into healthier competitors.

The maturity stage is characterized by market saturation, usually by

---

[1] Jay Forrester, "Advertising, A Problem in Industrial Dynamics," *Harvard Business Review*, March-April, 1959, p. 108.

a large number of competing firms in an industry—or in any event, intense competition—and by declining profits. Brands have tended to become more alike; and to achieve product differentiation and attract more customers, the firms must intensify promotional efforts and resort to product innovations, all of which increases costs. That the television industry has reached the market maturity stage is evidenced by the estimated 96 percent of all households that have sets—a high degree of market saturation. Automobiles, standard home appliances, and groceries are among products that have reached market maturity as shown by similarity of makes and brands, intensity of competition, changes in models or product characteristics, and emphasis on promotion and other forms of nonprice competition.

The maturity stage is the longest stage, because a product may stay here until some new development comes along to make it obsolete. And for products like grocery staples, toothpaste, and similar consumer goods, the expected duration of market maturity may be long indeed.

Nature of the demand creation task

The demand-creating task facing the firm is closely related to the product life cycle. In Chapter 1, as we discussed general marketing goals, the twin concepts of *primary demand* and *selective demand* were introduced. Primary demand, you recall, is the demand for the product type or class, whereas selective demand is the demand for a particular brand of that product class. Figure 14–1 suggests how these factors are related. In the early stages of a product's life cycle, the emphasis on primary demand suggested by Figure 14–1 is necessary as potential customers are being introduced to the new concept and informed about the features and benefits of the new-product class. This primary demand task continues through later stages even into late maturity because new prospective customers are entering the market and need to be "sold" on the product class or type. Selective demand creation begins early, in anticipation of competition, and dominates the maturity and decline stages of the life cycle.

If a manufacturer decided to bring out a new brand of toothpaste, he must recognize that while his *brand* is new, the product class is in the maturity stage of the life cycle. The demand creation task for him, then, is clearly to stimulate selective demand. Moreover, he knows that in the maturity stage heavy emphasis on promotion and other nonprice competition is necessary, so he must be prepared to enter with a large promotion budget.

Information appetites

A third area of consideration in assessing communication needs has to do with the information needs or appetites of target customers. As a product reaches maturity, the level of information already acquired by customers is at a quite high level compared to that at the earlier stages. The communication strategy must take into account the difference between information already possessed and that needed to prompt a sale. Failure to do so can result in more than simple wasted communications; it may lead to expenditures for promotion that bores or even antagonizes prospects. Where communication gaps are found, opportunity to close the gap and satisfy information appetites exists.

Research on the message receivers is one way to uncover the information gaps. A study of objections encountered by salesmen is another, since objections are often strong clues to lack of understanding or comprehension of product benefits. Study of competitor's messages is yet another way for the manager to keep abreast of the information needs of target customers.

In the market maturity stages, the customer's information needs are likely to be met by past promotion programs. The lack of a clear information gap does not mean that no appetite for more information exists. Rather it means that the manager must find the creative spark to say the same things more effectively than his competitors. This, of course, is why we began this discussion with emphasis on consumer analysis and research.

Finally, the concept of information appetite relates to our discussion in Chapter 2 and 3 about buyers. The perceived need for information will most likely vary with the newness of the buying decision and with the products' perceived importance to the buyer's self-concept. Thus, for high self-risk products (or expensive purchase decisions frought with the bivalent feedback of losing scarce dollars), the buyer needs and wants information to assist him in evaluating the product and in reassuring him of the wisdom of his selection.

FORMULATING PROMOTION GOALS

General types of promotion goals

A goal is a target or objective. It is a statement of *where* management wants to be at some future point in time, of *what* management expects to achieve. Because promotion goals are a part of the total marketing goals of a firm, we need to note some general marketing goals a firm might set for itself. These may be expressed in such *absolute terms*, as "sales of $125 million this year," or in *relative terms*, such as "a 10 percent increase in sales and a 4 percent increase in after-tax profits." Promotion goals, in turn, are statements of what management expects its promotion efforts to achieve. We will look at three broad categories: action, message, and communication goals. These are alternative ways of looking at the goal-setting task, but we must emphasize that they are not exclusive categories. A firm does not decide on an "action" goal to the exclusion of "message" or "communication" goals. Rather, all three may be simultaneously pursued. This will be easier to see after a brief look at the three categories.

Action goals. Promotion, never forget, is marketing's persuasive communication with buyers and buying influencers. One useful classification of goals, then, is what action or response the promotion seeks to evoke. *Direct action* promotion is that which seeks an immediate response. The direct action goal is to get the prospect to *do something:* to buy now, to clip a coupon and mail it in, to visit a dealer, to call and ask for more information, to try a new use for the product. Promotion may have *indirect action* goals. These do not seek an immediate response, but rather hope to keep a brand name differentiated and loaded with positive valences so that when a prospect reaches the listing stage, our brand is easily recalled. Indirect action promotion may seek to build, over time, a need for our product in the mind of potential customers. No one message or effort is expected to result in specific, measurable response, but the cumulative effort of continuous messages is aimed at developing a feeling that the buyer's self-concept will be enhanced or protected by purchase of the product and brand.

An industrial salesman, for example, may be expected to achieve direct action goals by reaching quotas for the various products he sells and by having a high sales-to-calls ratio. Salesmen who sell heavy industrial equipment, computer systems, and the like may be pursuing indirect action goals on most of their sales calls to a firm. They are developing a long-run rapport and nurturing a potential demand that may not be realized this week or even this year. In sales promotion, a contest may have direct action goals related to consumer purchase of the product as a requirement for entering the contest. An exhibit at a world's fair, however, may be designed to achieve indirect action goals of improving company image or brand image. The retail ad may seek sales tomorrow, or simply seek an indirect action goal of getting shoppers to think favorably about the store.

FIGURE 14–2. Direct-action advertisers put in coupons for immediate response

Message goals. Another way to classify promotion goals is according to the nature of the message being communicated. The promotion effort may seek to *inform*, to *persuade*, or simply to *remind*. The goal may be to *inform* prospects of the benefits of a product class or the features of a brand. As Figure 14–3 suggests, this goal is a common one in the early stages of a product's life cycle where primary demand stimulation is necessary. Later, when the firm feels that prospects are already informed about its product, the goal may be to *persuade* them that its brand is superior to competing brands. There is an element of persuasion in primary demand stimulation, of course, because there is always some competition for the consumers' dollars. The emphasis on persuasion increases, however, in the growth and maturity stages of the product's life cycle. If the consumer is likely to list several well-known brands for possible purchase, the persuasion goal is important if the firm's brand is to survive the screening process. Finally, the goal of some promotion is merely to *remind* prospects of the brand and its benefits. Well-established products in the market maturity stage may use some reminder promotion (simple outdoor advertising with nothing more than the brand name displayed) and firms with products in the sales decline stage may eventually do nothing but remind customers of those products while

FIGURE 14–3.   Relation of message goals to product life cycle and demand types

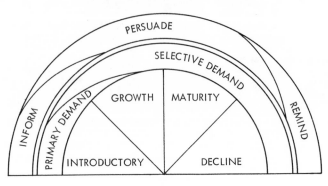

placing greater promotional emphasis on the new products in the introductory or growth stage.

Communication goals.   A third way of looking at promotion goals is according to the communication goals of the effort. Promotion may seek to create *awareness*, to impart *knowledge*, to influence *attitudes*, or to stimulate *response*. In the early stages of the product's life cycle, awareness that such a product exists, or that a firm's brand exists, may be the goal of introductory promotion. This awareness goal may also coincide with reminder-type messages. If knowledge about the brand, its features and benefits, is to be communicated, this may be the goal of a promotion effort or campaign. To influence attitudes is more difficult. This goal requires a promotion effort which seeks to shift customer and prospect attitudes to a more positive valence for the firm's brand. We want them not only to be aware of the brand and to know what the name stands for but also to have a positive valence for the product or brand. Finally, the communication goal may be to get the customer to say "I want" or "I'll buy now," and this can happen only after attitudes are positively influenced.

Sales goals.   Although sales are a special and important form of direct action goal, they are commonly used as a statement of promotion goals. "This promotion effort is expected to generate X dollars in sales." The sales goal for promotion efforts is appropriate only if all other elements in the marketing mix remain unchanged. Otherwise, use of sales as a measure or goal is more appropriate for the total marketing mix of the firm than for one of the components of that mix. There are many situations, however, in which product, place, and price do remain unchanged, where the only variable actively changed is promotion. In such instances, sales (in dollars, market share, or units) may appear to be a reasonable goal.

Need for specific goal statements

Mention of sales as a goal brings us to a recognition of the need for making goals concrete and specific. Too often management sets sales as a goal without realizing that sales goals are often too general and vague (even when stated in dollar amounts) to guide the planning of promotion efforts. Suppose, for example, that a firm stated as a goal "Increase sales $400,000 in the next 12 months." If the firm has been selling all that it can produce with present plant capacity, this might be a production goal. If excess capacity exists, then it may be a sensible general *marketing* goal but not necessarily a good promotion goal. The sales increase could come through a reduction in price, introduction of a new model, expansion of geographic territory served, more intensive distribution within present territories, or shifts in promotion.

Perhaps the firm is more specific and states: "We do not plan to change products, locations, or prices, nor do we wish to spend any more dollars in promotion efforts, but we want to increase sales $400,000 and increase our share of the market thereby from 11 percent to 13 percent." This certainly is a more precise goal statement, but it still leaves much to be desired if the goals are to become: (*a*) guides to strategy and planning, and (*b*) standards for control and evaluation. What the firm needs to do is to make explicit the subgoals that underlie the main sales goal they are enunciating. For instance, any or all of the following might be appropriate promotion goals which would help achieve the marketing goal of a $400,000 sales increase:

1. Get buyers of other brands to try our product.
2. Keep buyers of our brand loyal and cut down on the losses to other brands.
3. Get present customers to use more of our product by:
    a) Serving it more often (new recipes).
    b) Extending the seasonal use (iced coffee).
    c) Discovering new uses (use detergent to wash the car and windows as well as clothes).
4. Get dealers to display the product and push it more vigorously.
5. Attract new customers from the prospect pool.

In summary, promotion managers must define clearly the goals of the promotion activity and efforts of the firm. These goals must recognize the product life cycle and demand alternatives, and they must be precisely spelled out if they are to serve as guides to planning and as standards for control.

EVALUATING PROMOTIONAL ALTERNATIVES

Once the goals of promotion have been spelled out, the promotion manager must consider the alternative *strategies* by which the goals might be reached. The strategy chosen is the broad plan of attack the firm will use in the coming period; it is a promotion mix selected from the alternative combinations of persuasive elements open to the manager.

Although the number of alternative strategies is virtually infinite because of the vast array of media, personal selling tactics, and sales promotion stimulants available, we can divide them into three broad categories. These are: push strategies, pull strategies, and combination strategies. Our discussion of these alternatives will be from the viewpoint of total promotional efforts and not from the viewpoints of the substrategies of advertising, personal selling, and sales promotion. There is a very good reason for this. Our study of communication systems suggested that there are multiple channels of message transmission and that all should be in harmony for maximum effectiveness. Thus our look at promotion strategies must necessarily be from a broad enough perspective to assure that all our persuasive communications are coordinated and supportive.

Alternative strategies

Push strategies. The first broad alternative consists of relying on pushing the product down through the channel of distribution to final customers. Figure 14–4 will be helpful in considering all these alternatives: It suggests the scope of the promotion problem for a manufacturer several levels removed from final customers, as well as some marketing situations where the customers are more directly accessible. A push strategy places heavy emphasis on personal selling at each level in the channel until goods reach customers. Here are some marketing situations in which a push strategy might be appropriate:

A manufacturer sells large quantities of machinery or parts to another manufacturer. There are few customers, orders are large in dollar value,

FIGURE 14–4. Promotion strategy alternatives

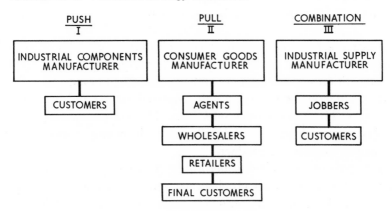

some technical or engineering help may be needed to sell prospective buyers, and shipments go directly to the customer.

A manufacturer sells a common supply item with little brand differentiation, on a price and delivery basis, through wholesalers, to business and institutional buyers. Examples might be nails, mops, buckets, or memo pads.

A manufacturer sells to middlemen and places their brands on the products.

A manufacturer sells a standard household product like ladders or dustpans through agents and wholesalers and retailers to final customers.

Push strategies would seem appropriate, then, in situations where the channel of distribution is fairly direct and the unit of sale large or where the product is highly standardized with little or no brand recognition or differentiation.

Pull strategies. The basic idea of a pull strategy is to create enough demand at one level of the distribution channel to force the next higher level to carry the product. Thus we would expect the consumer goods manufacturer in Figure 14–2 to aim his promotion efforts at final customers to create a demand for his product. Consumers would be urged to "ask your dealer for it if you don't see it" or "ask your dealer to write to us." The strategy owes its name to the effort of manufacturers to "pull" their product through the channel of distribution by forcing retailers and wholesalers to carry the product in response to customer demand.

A pull strategy places heavy emphasis on mass communication with prospects. Advertising dominates the promotion mix of firms attempting this promotion strategy. Here are some appropriate marketing situations in which a pull strategy might be appropriate:

A manufacturer is entering a new channel of distribution to sell a product in the late growth or market maturity stage of its life cycle in competition with well-known, heavily advertised brands.

A manufacturer sells to a widely dispersed market and does not wish to develop his own extensive sales force. He will use brokers and other middlemen and depend on the pull of his advertising to convince these middlemen to carry the product.

A manufacturer is introducing a new product concept that threatens established products with obsolescence and is meeting trade resistance. He focuses his effort on consumers to create the *primary* demand for the product idea and *selective* demand that will force dealers to carry the new product.

Pull strategies, then, would seem appropriate for new products sold in complex channels of distribution to widely scattered target customers.

Combination strategies. In competitive markets, manufacturers often wish to use all means available to achieve persuasive communication. They seek a promotion mix that employs both pull and push strategies in some combination deemed effective for the goals of the firm. The firm may employ regular salesmen to push the product to wholesalers, missionary salesmen to work with dealers and train retail salesmen in better sales (pushing) methods, and advertising to help pull the product down and through by creating demand for its brand. Moreover, sales promotion may be used in combination with the pull and push tactics to coordinate and supplement the primary efforts. Combination approaches to promotion strategies are most common in actual practice. The variations range from very *heavy* emphasis on push with a *little* pull support (as in industrial selling supported with modest advertising effort to develop leads for salesmen and to establish confidence in the name of the seller) to very *heavy* emphasis on pull with *some* push support (as in consumer goods such as toothpaste where missionary and sales efforts aim mostly at keeping good shelf position for the demand created by massive advertising efforts).

Factors influencing strategy choice

We have already noted that the promotion strategist must have detailed knowledge of his goals and of his target customers. There are, in addition, other influences that deserve mention. Some of these, one may argue, are merely dimensions of the target customer identification problem. No matter. They are important in the shaping of promotion strategies and should be noted even at the risk of redundancy.

Nature of the market. The customers for a firm may be small in number and geographically concentrated, or they may be large in number and widely dispersed. The nature of the number and location of prospective customers is an important consideration to the promotion manager. Small, concentrated markets may be served direct with a push strategy; large, dispersed markets require complex distribution channels and a reliance on pull techniques. Quite obviously, as we have noted throughout this book, the social, economic, educational, occupational, and other characteristics of target customers are important determinants of communication content and of selling techniques.

Product complexity. Some products are simple enough for customers to understand without extensive demonstration and explanation. Others are technically complex and subject to a host of buyer questions that cannot be effectively answered through mass communication. A 1-quart carton of milk, for instance, is not a very complicated product idea to sell. The machine that takes coated cardboard and forms the cartons, on the other hand, may require extensive explanation and demonstration to a prospective dairy manager.

Competition. As with all other elements of the marketing mix, promotion strategies must be designed with a keen awareness of the practices of the competition. Sometimes the strategist may choose to ignore conventional practices, as does the seller of Electrolux vacuum cleaners when he stresses the push strategy of door-to-door selling over the heavy pull strategies of General Electric and Hoover. We still argue that creative deviation from competitive practices requires a thorough understanding of what one is deviating from.

ALLOCATING PERSUASIVE TASKS

This chapter began by stating that the communication strategy prescribes the role to be played by every persuasive element used to communicate with customers. The final step in laying out a promotion strategy involves making explicit assignment of roles. To do this, the manager must consider both internal and external resources and talent available or procurable for strategy execution. For each avenue, certain costs and benefits are inherent and must be considered. We need to briefly look at some of the options in each major promotion sphere.

FIGURE 14–5. This ad allocates to the company representative the task of full explanation of the program

Do we need the Retailer Educational Program?

Chain Drug Management answers: "We certainly do!"

Read's Inc.
Serving the Baltimore area since 1883.

Jacobs Pharmacy Co., Inc.
Read's expanding chain serving cities in Georgia, Alabama, South Carolina and Mississippi.

Read's Inc. and Jacobs Pharmacy Co., Inc. welcome the Retailer Educational Program to our present systems of employee training and development. Job related International Correspondence Schools Home Study Courses will enrich highly motivated career employees, assist in teaching trainees and also help us recruit desirable new personnel. "Continuing Education" for front-end personnel will naturally enable employees and the stores they operate to attain the goals of our management."

Increase Your Investment... In People! Decrease Turnover... Of Valued Employees!

Since 1890 more than 8 million individuals have taken advantage of the curriculum offered by International Correspondence Schools, Scranton, Pennsylvania. Liggett & Myers has selected 13 Home Study Courses from the ICS libraries and makes them cooperatively available to our retail drug customers. You select the "student"—we provide the scholarship.

Available ICS Courses—Retail Merchandising, Retail Business Management, Practical Business Administration, Personnel-Labor Relations, Basic Inventory Control, Office Management, Accounting, for Management Decisions, Advertising, Retail and Local, Market Research, Modern Executive Management, Practical Accounting, Clerk-Typist, Modern Woman as a Supervisor (combined with Personality Development).

How ICS Home Study Works:

1) Student selects the course; 2) Periodic exams sent to ICS faculty for grading; 3) Certificate of completion awarded to student.

Continuing Education

Many pharmacists are utilizing our Retailer Educational Program to reinforce their own business-administration backgrounds. Others are applying these home-study benefits to valued Front-End Managers. How you add this on-the-job training to your company is your own decision. The retail drug industry acknowledges *continuing education* in business administration vital to insuring *continuing success* in today's competitive retail community.

Ask your Liggett & Myers representative to tell you more about his Retailer Educational Program.

Notice to all Retailers:

Liggett & Myers Incorporated periodically offers promotional, advertising, merchandising and display programs on proportionately equal terms to all retailers regardless of size. For further details contact your Liggett & Myers representative or write to Liggett & Myers Incorporated, P. O. Box 1969, Durham, North Carolina 27702.

Liggett&Myers
Incorporated

Advertising

Most of the advertising role is assigned internally to the firm's ad department or to its quasi-internal partner, and ad agency. Thus, a pull strategy to launch a new product with a goal of establishing 50 percent brand awareness by the end of the first year will assign a heavy role to mass communication for most consumer products.

The external possibilities are in the area of dealer cooperative spending. For many lines of consumer goods, the practice is so thoroughly intrenched that the manufacturer has little choice but to assign some communication role to the co-op campaigns. For as has been noted, once established, the ad allowance becomes a part of the price structure from the retailers' point of view and he may insist on competitive allowances.

Personal selling

The general role personal selling is to play will have been decided as the strategy is laid out. The specific assignment of duties and responsibilities is the logical conclusion of that assignment. Once decided, however, it is critical that the responsibility be communicated and accepted. This calls for close coordination between departments of the firm, and failure to do so can thwart the best-laid plans.

External sales roles may be assigned, but this is more a question of total marketing strategy. Quite often, for instance, the internal sales force is augmented by sales representatives or agents paid a commission and assigned specific territories. Promotion strategists must take care to see that both the internal and external sales staffs are assigned appropriate roles in the campaign. If retailer salesmen cannot be relied on, the strategy must contemplate stimulating them or supplementing them with demonstrators or other trained talent.

QUESTIONS AND PROBLEMS

14–1. Use the product life cycle concept to explain the variation in message goals.

14–2. A manufacturer of electric toothbrushes wishes to know what communication gaps he needs to fill. How can he go about finding out consumers' information needs?

14–3. Bring three consumer magazine ads to class which seek to stimulate indirect action, and three which are direct action in appeal.

14–4. How would the allocation of communication tasks differ in a large firm as opposed to a small firm? To a consumer goods firm as opposed to an industrial machinery manufacturer?

14–5. Why do some firms operate without clearly defined goals?

14–6. How would the promotional task allocation shift as a product moves from the growth stage to the market maturity stage of its life cycle?

14–7. "Some products will never leave market maturity." Comment.

14–8. How does the knowledge of postact dissonance as a possible trait of his buyer's behavior affect the communication goals and strategy of an appliance maker?

14–9. Why might a firm adopt a heavy push strategy in an industry characterized by pull strategies?

14–10. What strategy would be appropriate for the manufacturer of (a) roof shingles, (b) a new toy, (c) carbonless paper.

CHAPTER 15

Planning promotional
programs

WHEREAS strategy is the broad plan of attack for achieving promotion goals, *plans* are the detailed tactics or procedures necessary to carry out the strategy and reach the goals. The making of plans, planning, is an essential element of the promotion manager's job. Indeed, *planning* is usually identified as one of the four major tasks of all management. The management process may be thought of as a system of related activities such as that diagrammed in Figure 15–1. Management, according to this view, is a process of planning a course of action designed to achieve a goal, organizing the individuals appropriately, directing these individuals as they carry out the plans, and evaluating and controlling the process to assure that the efforts are "on target" and proceeding as planned.

In this chapter we need to look at some general requirements of good plans, then turn briefly to some sales forecasting issues that are an integral part of promotion planning. Then we return to the broad promotion planning issues and look at the campaign concept as a key building block to promotion planning.

REQUIREMENTS OF GOOD PLANS

There are some generally accepted requirements of good plans that need to be understood in order to appreciate fully the process of planning

FIGURE 15–1. The manage-
                      ment
                      process

for promotional programs. Good plans are: (1) appropriate, (2) feasible, (3) comprehensive, (4) management-specific, (5) time-specific, (6) dollar-specific, and (7) regularly reviewed. Each of these requirements will be discussed.

Appropriate

A good plan is appropriate both for the goals and strategies of the firm and for the particular organization. A plan is appropriate if it will lead to achievement of the goals established by management. Falling too far short of the goal reflects an obvious failure in planning; exceeding the goal by too wide a margin is less obvious, but just as real a problem. For example, if the promotion plan results in demand for the product far in excess of dealer inventories or production capacity, we would feel that the plan fails the requirement of appropriateness. Customers have been stimulated to seek but cannot find, and they may (as we know from our buying model) substitute competing products to relieve the frustration of being unable to obtain a firm's product. The other dimension of appropriateness is related to the nature of the firm. Plans should be in harmony with the firm or organization mounting the promotion effort. A promotion plan suitable for a soap manufacturer or toy producer may be highly inappropriate for an exclusive dress salon or for a manufacturer of guided missile components.

Feasible

Closely related to appropriateness, feasibility is the second test of good plans. The successful planner designs programs that are feasible in light of the monetary and the human resources of his firm: the plans can be carried out with the financial resources of the firm and with the human talents and abilities available to the organization. While many firms state a sales goal, they also have a profit goal in mind. Feasible plans help accomplish the sales goal without trespassing on the profit goal. Promotion plans are often carried out through wholesaler and retailer members of the marketing team. A plan which commits these dealers to a kind or degree of cooperation they are either unwilling or unable to provide would not pass the feasibility test.

This latter point cannot be overemphasized. Too often students of marketing study channels from the viewpoint of the manufacturer and assume that he can order up at will any cooperation he desires from members of his channel team. Experienced managers know better. With the growth of large-scale buying units, such as chains of huge discount outlets or department store groups, real power or channel control is often more in the hands of the dealers than of the manufacturers. Thus the feasibility test must be carefully applied to plans involving dealer use of point-of-purchase techniques, cooperative funds, and similar promotion tools.

Comprehensive

A good promotion plan is a complete, detailed prescription for action. Just as we defined the strategy in Chapter 14 as prescribing the role of all persuasive elements, so the plan builds in that detail for all aspects of the campaign. Nothing is left to be ironed out later; all problems in implementation are anticipated; coordination with other parts of the marketing organization or firm is planned for and spelled out.

A simple matter of a package change affords a good example of what comprehensiveness requires. A change in package will require coordination among these groups or areas:

1. Promotion—to allow changeover and schedule new package.
2. Purchasing—to procure packaging materials.
3. Inventory control—to phase out old package with least dumping or repackaging cost.
4. Advertising—to promote new face to trade and consumer.
5. Sales—to introduce new package to dealers and insure their inventory changeover to new design.
6. Sales promotion—to coordinate for P.O.P. displays and shelf maintenance as campaign breaks.

The promotion plans for such a decision must cover all these aspects if it is to be comprehensive.

Management-specific

A good plan leaves no doubt as to *who* is to do *what*. Not only are the promotion tactics planned, but the means for their implementation are clearly set forth. This leads, as Figure 15–1 reminds us, to better evaluation and control as the plans are executed. Responsibilities clearly pinned down in the plan can be followed up if something goes wrong. Promotion managers have to be especially sensitive to this requirement. The total promotional mix utilizes the talents of individuals in advertising, personal selling, and sales promotion. The promotion plans must specify what each of these is expected to do. The statement, "Oh, I thought *you* were supposed to do that, now me," is a classic symptom of a plan failing the management-specific requirement.

Management-specific plans obviously need concurrence of other department heads within the firm if they are to be truly feasible. A plan that requires a week of special sales force execution just at the same time that force is scheduled for another duty will fall apart in execution. Simply writing the specifications is no good unless the sales manager has been apprised of the plan and approves of the assignment.

Finally, management-specific plans protect the firm against manpower losses. The good manager so plans as to insure that should something happen to him, the work can and will go on. Making plans management-specific provides a blueprint for action that others can follow in his absence.

Time-specific

Promotion planning involves synchronizing and coordinating many activities within one element of persuasion as well as within the total persuasion campaign. It is not surprising, then that we insist on plans passing the time-specific test; there must be no doubt about *when* who is to do what. If a television commerical is to be run at 29½ minutes after 8 P.M. on a specific date, the film must reach the station by 2 P.M. on that date, not the next morning.

Making plans time-specific is a scheduling function, and it is so important to successful planning that a large portion of Chapter 16 is devoted to the issues involved. The kind of detailed scheduling required is hinted at in the foregoing example of the TV commercial. We give it greater consideration in Chapter 16.

Dollar-specific

No less important is the requirement that plans include specific cost expectations. The chief finance officer of the firm must manage the flow of funds, which means he has to plan for financing the activities of all departments. This, in turn, means that he must have precise guides to the spending plans of the promotion manager. The connection between this requirement and the requirement of feasibility needs to be noted. If plans are thoroughly dollar-specific but those dollars cannot be made available for promotional spending, the plan fails.

Making plans dollar-specific also helps make possible one of the major functions of management: control. The dollar-specific plan, or budget as it actually becomes, affords both financial and marketing managers some benchmarks for controlling the promotion program. Variance above budgeted amounts can be spotted quickly and corrective actions taken so that the firm doesn't get three fourths through a campaign and run short of funds because of overages in the early production expenditures.

Regularly reviewed

A good planner is constantly looking over his plans to evaluate them against requirements such as we have been discussing. Plans ought to be reviewed when being evolved, when they are completed, and while they are being executed. When they are being made, plans need to be reviewed to insure that this segment or that segment is not out of tune with other elements of the plan. When they are completed, the plans should be reviewed to insure that they are feasible, comprehensive, and specific as to responsibility, time, and dollars. Finally, plans ought to be reviewed while being executed to assure their continuing appropriateness. Competitive conditions can change rapidly, and these changes can force modifications of plans. A firm cannot stick stubbornly to plans that are no longer appropriate or feasible.

SALES FORECASTING

There is a kind of "chicken-and-egg" aspect to the role of sales forecasting in promotion planning. The dilemma runs somewhat as follows.

How can management set realistic goals and design programs without a sales forecast which takes into account economic, industry, and competitive trends?

On the other hand, how can you forecast sales until you know what sales-stimulating programs management plans to use during the coming year?

There is no disagreement, however, on the importance of sales forecasts as an aid to management planning. The finance officer forecasts cash flows, the production officer plans his production schedules, the purchasing agent plans his procurement schedules, the personnel officer bases his hiring needs—all on the basis of the sales forecast. Sales forecasts are probably the most essential planning documents the firm produces.

While there may be no firm or final answer to the "Which comes first, promotion program or forecast?" question, you may find it helpful to stop thinking of a forecast as a *thing* and start thinking of forecasting as a *process*. Forecasts range from five year, to annual, to quarterly or even more often. Thus, in January the second-quarter forecast may be revised on the basis of new information and the annual forecast adjusted accordingly. In April the third-quarter forecast is made, with necessary revisions for the remainder of the year. The result is a continuing process of forecasts that are ever more immmediate and (hopefully) accurate. The promotion planner may have made one forecast of next year's sales under the assumption that nothing drastic would change in the marketing mixes of any competing firms. In setting goals the firm may accept the forecast, or it may set goals in excess of the forecast. The promotion plans are made to achieve the new goals, and a forecast of sales must be made which takes into account the changes in promotional forces planned. As new information is received about competitor's mixes and the impact competition is making on the market, further revisions in the sales forecast will be necessary.

Types of forecasts

The modern business firm not only makes a number of revised forecasts during a year but it also constructs several types of forecasts. Let's take a brief look at some of the major types of forecasts and try to understand why these various types are needed for planning and control management.

Total sales. The most basic sales forecast is that of total sales for the firm. These are usually made on an annual basis, with semiannual or quarterly review and revision. Total sales forecasts are especially helpful to top management in making plans for plant expansion, financing, and other corporate planning.

Seasonal forecasts. Many firms sell products that have seasonal fluctuations in the volume consumed. Wrist-watches and other gift items, for instance, have a sales peak in May and June as customers purchase them as gifts for graduations and weddings, and again in November and December during the Christmas sales season. Seasonal forecasts for each product the firm sells will aid in the timing of promotion campaigns, scheduling of production, contracting of warehouse space, hiring of part-time or extra workers, and planning for bank loans or other short-term financing help.

Product forecasts. If the firm sells more than one product, then specific forecasts for each product (by season) are called for. Hidden in a total sales forecast figure may be trends in product consumption that alter production and promotion plans. Product A may be declining in sales while new product B is growing rapidly. The result is a total sales increase, but the breakdown of the sales composition is hidden in the total figure. Forecasts by product or at least for groups of allied products provide management with clearer guides to planning and control.

Geographic forecasts. Many companies sell their products in all 50 states; others sell over a regional territory of several states. For these firms, forecasts by territory are helpful. A multiproduct firm may sell more of one product in a northern region and more of another in a southern territory. The quantity and timing of these sales by territory are essential guides to promotion strategy and management. A tire manufacturer, for instance, may need to forecast sales of snow tires, farm tractor tires, bus and truck tires, plus a variety of passenger vehicle tires. The markets for these vary from region to region, of course, and his geographic forecasts aid in planning both for inventory and production *and* for promotion of the various lines.

Customer forecasts. For some firms a useful breakdown of the sales forecast is according to customer, or at least classes of customers. Sales to large-quantity buyers such as chain stores require a different promotion strategy than sales in small quantities through wholesalers. Some firms may sell to a number of markets, with different classes of customers in each. Take a light bulb producer, for instance:

The maker of a standard 100-watt light bulb is selling both an industrial good and a consumer good. The industrial product is identical to the consumer bulb, but the marketing requirements differ. The industrial bulb may be a routine supply item purchased by business and institutional customers to light their premises. Such sales are generally made through jobbers or wholesalers. Some buyers, however, such as the government, purchase enormous quantities of light bulbs and deal directly with the manufacturer. Other direct sales may come from manufacturers who incorporate the bulb into products they make and sell.

Forecasts of sales by customer help the producer plan to serve the major types of customers better and guide his promotional planning accordingly.

Uses of forecasts in promotion planning

We have suggested several ways in which sales forecasts may be made to serve management better. Let's now look at some specific uses of these sales forecasts by promotion managers. While our list of examples will by no means be complete, it should serve to illustrate some of the potential uses of forecasts in promotion planning.

Total sales. The total company sales forecast serves all promotion managers as a general guide to the level of marketing activity that must be expected in the coming period. The sales manager may need to plan to add new salesmen to his organization to stimulate and service a forecast increase in demand; the advertising manager will be similarly guided in his plans by the total sales forecast. We shall note—but not recommend—in the next chapter the practice of many firms of using the sales forecast as a means of setting the total sum of money to be spent in advertising by means of a fixed percentage of sales allocated to advertising.

Seasonal forecasts. The seasonal fluctuation in sales is of genuine concern to promotion managers who must decide on the timing of the several campaigns that make up the total promotion program. The sales manager, for instance, may design his compensation plan to cover expected slow seasons with a salary component or a "draw." The retailer needs to know when to add extra help to take care of seasonal rushes. Seasonal forecasts may serve as an aid to the timing of special sales contests or incentive plans. The advertising manager needs to know when to start and stop campaigns. He needs to know when to plan for heavy advertising efforts and when to attempt counterseasonal campaigns to help even out the sales flow. The sales promotion manager needs to know when to plan his direct-mail campaigns, cooperative advertising, consumer contests, and all the other stimulants for which he is responsible.

Product forecasts. If the forecast by products indicates a growth in technical products and a decline in the sale of routine or standard products, the industrial sales manager may have to revise his job description and specifications and begin to hire a larger number of technically oriented salesmen. If he pays his men a varying commission by product line, the product sales forecasts may suggest that he needs to increase the commission on one product and decrease it on another. The advertising manager will use the product sales forecast as a guide to media selection (especially if the firm sells both to the industrial and consumer markets), and as to what should be featured in the company's product advertising.

Geographic forecasts. These are of particular concern to the sales manager, who must balance territories and establish quotas for his salesmen. Extreme shifts in demand may require redrawing of territorial lines and assignment of extra help to cover expanding territories. The advertising manager is equally concerned, for he wants to select the media most likely to reach prospects. His newspaper ad schedules, for example, will be heavily influenced by geographic forecasts. The sales promotion manager is no less concerned. The continued growth of electronic manufacturing in the southwestern United States, and in Florida, for example, places increased pressure on manufacturers selling to these markets to exhibit at regional conventions and trade shows. Direct-mail plans and catalog distribution are similarly affected.

Customer forecasts. A forecast of marked change in sales to a class of customers affects all promotion activities. Just think for a moment of the changes in promotion planning that would accompany a forecast increase in the sales in supermarkets of an item that had traditionally been sold in some other type of outlet. The sales manager must be prepared to cover both the chain buying offices and the major wholesalers serving independent supermarkets; the advertising manager must consider the impact of a shift into self-service outlets on his need to presell customers on the brand and its features; the sales promotion manager must gear his cooperative advertising, dealer mailings, and contests—whether dealer or consumer—to the new outlets.

We have noted the extreme importance of sales forecasts in all management planning, and the particular use of various types of forecasts by promotion managers. Let's now turn our attention to the basic problem of making a sales forecast.

Steps in forecasting sales

We must be brief. Yet we cannot even briefly summarize the magnitude of the problem. Ultimately, we know that our sales will result from all of our marketing mix, our competitors' mixes, the competition of other industries, the general economic environment, social and cultural mores and whims, the impact of weather and climate, and even the policies of the government on the international scene—to name a few of the factors that influence sales. In the face of all this uncertainty, we are called upon to be certain. All that is possible is to attempt to reduce the uncertainty in a systematic way.

Rather than discuss in detail all the approaches to sales forecasting used in modern businesses, we are going to concentrate on one approach that seems to have considerable merit and support, following it through a series of steps. It is not *the* way to forecast sales; but it is *a* way that seems fruitful. Then we will mention briefly some of the other major approaches employed. For a firm that sells more than one major product, the step-by-step process must be used for each product.

Analyze. The first step in sales forecasting is to study all available past data on company sales, industry sales, market share performance (the percent of industry sales made by our firm), and the general economy. Are industry sales rising, stable, or falling? Is our sales position moving in the same or a different direction? The sales forecaster must study the past data in an attempt to understand what has been happening in our market; he will use this understanding to help reduce our uncertainty about the future.

Isolate. From this analysis the forecaster seeks to isolate factors that will help him predict the future. Industry sales may move up or down as some other indicator varies. The "other indicator" might be national income, population, sales of a related product, or any of a host of influences. Generally, sales forecasters seek to find a relationship between industry sales and some well-established national indicator or figure such as gross national product, national income, population, or the like. The reason for this is that forecasts of these are constructed and published by professional statisticians and economists, and the sales forecaster can use these professionally prepared forecasts to begin to estimate total industry sales for his particular product.

Estimate. After the sales forecaster decides which factors will best serve to predict total industry sales, he collects forecasts of these factors or constructs his own. Then, using the forecasts of the factors, he estimates the total industry sales. In many cases he can rely on the assistance of his industry trade association staff, for many trade associations hire professional economists to prepare forecasts of industry sales.

Apply. The next step is to apply a share of market percentage to the total industry sales forecast. In the first step the forecaster studied past data on company market share. If he found, for instance, that his firm had held 32, 33, 33, 32, and 33 percent of the total industry market in the last five years, then he would multiply the total industry sales forecast by either 32, 32.5, or 33 percent to arrive at a total company sales forecast. He is justified in doing this if no other firms have entered the market and if he can reasonably assume that past conditions will continue to prevail. Knowledge of a new-product feature, or of a competitor's pending innovation, might cause him to modify the share-of-market figure he applies.

Forecast. Although he has developed a *total* company sales forecast in the preceeding step, the forecaster now needs to construct other types of sales forecasts. He applies *seasonal* percentages learned from step one to the total sales forecast, and similarly breaks the total figure into *geographic* and *customer* sales forecasts. Each time he applies a percentage to the total forecast, he is making a forecast of the relevance of that percentage. If sales to chain stores have been growing so that chain stores sales have accounted for 18, 20, 21, 22, and 23 percent over the past five years, he may decide that 24 percent or 25 percent is an appropriate percentage to use. If sales in the Midwest have been growing and sales in the South declining, he will reflect this in his territorial forecasts.

Applying the steps

Let's take an example and apply the steps listed above to make sure they are understood. While the data are hypothetical, they will serve to illustrate this step-by-step approach to sales forecasting.

The sales manager of the Wilson Company, which makes garden tractors, had assembled the data shown in Tables 15–1 and 15–2 and was to prepare a sales forecast for year $n + 1$. In addition, not shown on the table, he had secured (from U.S. Government publications and economic forecasts) the following estimates for the year $n + 1$: Population, 184.1 million; disposable personal income, $357.8 billion; and personal consumption expenditures for durable goods, $44,200 million.

Analyze. The sales manager had studied past company sales by quarter and determined that the year's data in Table 15–2 was typical and repre-

TABLE 15–1. Selected data for Wilson Company

Year	Population (millions)	Disposable personal income ($billions)	Consumer expenditures for durable goods ($millions)	Total garden equipment industry sales ($millions)	Total Wilson sales ($millions)
$n - 10$.....	151.7	$207.7	$30,351	$26,750	$2,675
$n - 9$......	154.5	227.7	29,421	25,974	3,117
$n - 8$......	157.0	238.7	29,099	25,653	3,848
$n - 7$......	159.6	252.5	32,875	29,600	5,032
$n - 6$......	162.4	256.9	32,398	28,500	5,415
$n - 5$......	165.3	274.4	39,632	34,935	6,987
$n - 4$......	168.2	292.9	38,545	33,972	7,134
$n - 3$......	171.2	308.8	40,355	35,578	7,827
$n - 2$......	174.1	317.9	37,297	33,106	7,284
$n - 1$......	177.3	337.3	43,358	38,226	8,792
n.........	180.7	354.2	43,600	38,386	8,444

TABLE 15–2. Wilson Company sales by quarter

I................	$2,462
II...............	3,693
III..............	1,143
IV...............	1,194
Total.......	$8,792

sentative of quarterly sales. He then set about analyzing the information he had collected. So that he could study variations in patterns of growth and change, he converted all the numbers into index numbers, using year $n - 10$ as the base year. Tables 15–3 and 15–4 show the results of those calculations. In addition he calculated his firm's market share, which is also shown in Table 15–4. Using these data, he could then see that in a year, say $n - 5$, population had risen 9 percent, while disposable personal income was up 32.1 percent, from the base year.

Isolate. Looking over the index number data, the manager noted the extremely close relation between the two sets "Personal consumption expenditures for durables" and "Total garden equipment industry sales." The relation is so close, in fact, that he is willing to use it as a basis for further sales forecasting.

TABLE 15–3. Wilson Company data in index number form

Year	Population	Disposable personal income	Personal consumption of durables
$n-10$........	100.0	100.0	100.0
$n-9$.........	101.8	109.6	97.1
$n-8$.........	103.5	114.9	95.9
$n-7$.........	105.2	121.6	108.3
$n-6$.........	107.1	123.7	106.7
$n-5$.........	109.0	132.1	130.6
$n-4$.........	110.9	141.0	127.0
$n-3$.........	112.9	148.7	133.0
$n-2$.........	114.8	153.1	122.9
$n-1$.........	116.9	162.4	142.9
n............	119.1	170.5	143.7

TABLE 15–4. Industry sales in index number form and company market share

Year	Industry sales	Market share
$n-10$........	100.0	10
$n-9$.........	97.1	12
$n-8$.........	95.9	15
$n-7$.........	110.7	17
$n-6$.........	107.5	19
$n-5$.........	130.6	20
$n-4$.........	127.0	21
$n-3$.........	133.0	22
$n-2$.........	123.8	22
$n-1$.........	142.9	23
n............	143.7	22

Estimate. Since he has a forecast of durable expenditures for next year, he can use that to forecast total industry sales. He does this by finding the index number of the durable expenditures figure as follows. He divides the $n+1$ forecast of \$44,200 by the $n-10$ base year amount from Table 15–1 (\$30,351) to get the $n+1$ index number 145.6.

Next, he multiplies the base year "Garden equipment industry sales" of $26,750 (Table 15-1) by the new index number (145.6) to get the expected industry sales of $38,948.

Apply. Now that he has arrived at the forecast of industry sales, he must review the company's position in the industry. He knows that in the last 10 years his company has grown to a fairly steady 22 percent of the market. Last year $n - 1$ it had 23 percent (as Table 15-4 shows), but he knows that part of that was because of a strike which held back a competitor's sales. He believes that 22 percent is the best estimate of market share. By multiplying the industry sales forecast of $38,948,000 by 22 percent, he gets the company sales forecast of $8,568,560.

Forecast. Because, in this example, we limited ourselves to a single-product firm, we will not make separate product forecasts. But data on quarterly sales are provided, and the sales manager will want to use these data to break down his forecast into quarterly components. He can do so by applying the quarterly sales percentages (I = 28 percent, II = 42 percent, III = 13 percent, and IV = 17 percent) to the total company forecast.

The final set of company sales forecasts is, from the above description, really a complex set of forecasts about broad economic factors, industry sales, company share of market, and seasonal and geographic trends. One variation on this approach, where regional data are available, is to estimate total industry sales in each region and apply the appropriate regional market share to estimate company sales. This has much appeal because most firms do not enjoy a consistent market share from region to region, and the average national figure may be far from the mark in a critical region.

Can a retailer use this method? Yes, but on a reduced scale. The department store is interested in the factors (population, income, bank deposits, employment, and so on) in the trading area it serves. From these it attempts to forecast total retail sales and to estimate the market share the store will have in the coming year. The steps are essentially the same, however.

Other forecasting methods

Three other sales forecasting methods deserve our attention because they are used in many business firms. One of these, as we shall see, is a special application of the approach set forth earlier.

Ground up. One approach is to build the forecast from the ground up. That is, to ask each salesman to forecast sales of all products in his territory, then build a total forecast from these reports. Proponents argue that in this type of forecast, the forecast is made by the persons in closest contact with the market and in the best position to reflect special local conditions which influence sales. Critics complain that salesmen are either too optimistic by nature and overforecast, or they are always trying to slip a low forecast by in order to make their subsequent performance look good, or they are just not competent to analyze the local market and come up with a meaningful forecast.

Trend extension. Another approach is to project future sales from past trends. Data are gathered for several years, plotted on graphs, and projected into the future for forecasts of sales. Proponents argue that these can be done by highly trained personnel at the home office and that future sales are never drastically different from past trends. Critics argue that this method misses the crucial turning point in many business cycles. They assert that to project increased sales on the basis of past performance when the economy is making a downturn can lead to disastrous overproduction and planning.

Mathematical models. By far the most promising technique is the construction of mathematical models using the facilities of a computer to perform the extensive computations involved. Such models generally build in the major factors used in the general approach described in this chapter but are capable of handling vast amounts of data to sharpen the forecast that results. Larger individual firms are turning to this approach, and many trade associations are beginning to explore the use of these techniques, both for industry forecasts and on a service basis for members. However complex and sophisticated the approach, the process is still one of attempting to reduce uncertainty. This cannot be done entirely; but mathematical approaches may yield the greatest reduction in uncertainty.

PLANNING CAMPAIGNS AND PROGRAMS

Promotion programs, as we have discovered, are fairly complex creations that utilize a variety of communication media and elements of persuasion. A firm's promotion program for a given year may include a number of campaigns, or subprograms, which must be planned, coordinated, and evaluated. The sum of all of these campaigns for a year is

FIGURE 15–2.   Part of the Crest campaign is aimed at dentists in professional journals

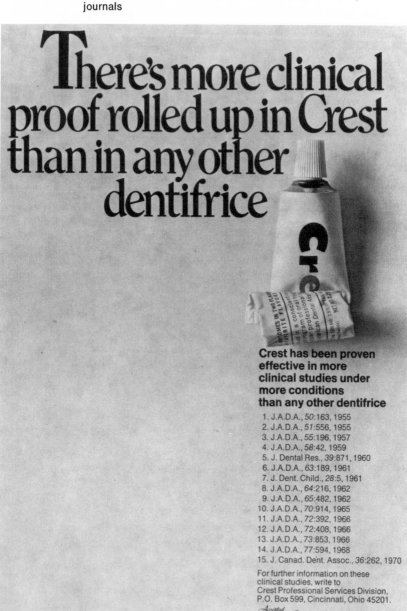

There's more clinical proof rolled up in Crest than in any other dentifrice

Crest has been proven effective in more clinical studies under more conditions than any other dentifrice

1. J.A.D.A., 50:163, 1955
2. J.A.D.A., 51:556, 1955
3. J.A.D.A., 55:196, 1957
4. J.A.D.A., 58:42, 1959
5. J. Dental Res., 39:871, 1960
6. J.A.D.A., 63:189, 1961
7. J. Dent. Child., 28:5, 1961
8. J.A.D.A., 64:216, 1962
9. J.A.D.A., 65:482, 1962
10. J.A.D.A., 70:914, 1965
11. J.A.D.A., 72:392, 1966
12. J.A.D.A., 72:408, 1966
13. J.A.D.A., 73:853, 1966
14. J.A.D.A., 77:594, 1968
15. J. Canad. Dent. Assoc., 36:262, 1970

For further information on these clinical studies, write to Crest Professional Services Division, P.O. Box 599, Cincinnati, Ohio 45201.

Confidence is Crest®

©1971 PROCTER & GAMBLE 280071

FIGURE 15–3. Part of the Crest campaign is aimed at consumers, like this *Ladies Home Journal* insertion

How many cavities can you expect if you brush with Crest?

One? Three? More?

Frankly, we can't name a figure that would apply to each individual.

Because people are different.

They eat different things. They take care of their teeth differently.

So there's a difference in what Crest will do for them. Some people may get no cavities between checkups; some only one; some lots more.

But we do know this.

In nineteen years of testing among thousands and thousands of people, Crest has proved that it can reduce cavities importantly. In these tests, half of the group used Crest, the other half used the same toothpaste but without Crest's fluoride formula.

And these tests were conducted among all kinds of people in many different parts of the country.

Time and time again, the facts tell us: Crest reduces cavities.

And right now 700 people are involved in still more testing. We don't know how each individual is going to do, but we are confident the Crest groups will have fewer cavities.

We know Crest works. And it works best when you do your part. We recommend that you watch between-meal treats, see the dentist regularly, and brush often with Crest. If you do, you're going to have good checkups.

And that's the whole idea behind Crest.

Fighting cavities is the whole idea behind Crest.

©1971, The Procter & Gamble Company.

the promotion program. A retail store, for example, may plan and carry out the following campaigns as a part of its promotion program:

♦ A campaign of day-to-day or weekly advertising of the general merchandise carried by the store.

♦ A specific campaign for each of several special sales or occasions such as Back-to-School, Christmas, January White Sale, Easter, or store anniversary.

♦ A campaign to herald the opening of a new branch store.

♦ An institutional campaign to promote the image of the store rather than to sell specific goods.

♦ A campaign to attract new full-time sales personnel and to train them for more effective selling.

Campaigns. What is a campaign? It is a definite, planned effort, with specific duration, to achieve a defined goal. Alderson and Green put it this way:

> A campaign which is extended over time would bear the closest resemblance to a musical composition. It will have a beginning and a conclusion, and the development of a major theme and subordinate themes in between. It will have tonal texture resulting from coordination of all the instruments or voices at each point in the composition.[1]

Manufacturers may mount several campaigns during a year to help achieve their overall promotion goals. Sales managers, for example, may have their regular sales campaign, a summer contest campaign to boost sagging sales, a campaign to introduce a new product with extra commissions for first sales to an account, a campaign to increase loyalty and cut salesman turnover, and a campaign to select a dealer salesman of the year. Any of these is an effort that deserves planning which meets all of our requirements of good planning. Take the summer sales contest as an example:

It must be appropriate and feasible, suitable for a firm's salesmen and the kind of company involved. It must be planned comprehensively so that each home office and field sales manager knows what he is to do, when, and how much he is authorized to spend doing it. Like a musical composition, the summer sales contest will have an opening to set the theme and make salesmen aware of the program. Letters, sales meetings, brochures mailed to salesman's wives, and articles in the company newspaper or magazine will all join in introducing the campaign. The contest will continue for a specified period, with publicity and communications rising to a climax in the final weeks as the dealine nears. Thus the pace and intensity of the campaign is indeed similar to that of a musical composition. If elements of the plan enter at the wrong time, or in the wrong key or theme, the composition is spoiled; the campaign suffers.

---

[1] Wroe Alderson and Paul E. Green, *Planning and Problem Solving in Marketing* (Homewood, Ill.: Richard D. Irwin, Inc., 1964), p. 372.

Programs. The promotional program, or mix, is the whole of a firm's efforts at persuasive communication. Planning programs requires careful coordination of the component campaigns. The firm would probably not want two special campaigns being run simultaneously, nor would it want conflicting campaigns. For example, a campaign to promote the quality, prestige image of a store might suffer from a campaign to clear stocks through drastic reductions promoted as a Hot Diggity Sale Day.

QUESTIONS AND PROBLEMS

15–1. The ABC Company suddenly discovers that its sales forecast is 25 percent too low. What are some of the probable consequences of this error?

15–2. How would a geographic sales forecast help the promotion manager?

15–3. When might the running of simultaneous campaigns by the same advertiser be justified?

15–4. If you were the manager of a campus store selling books, supplies, and similar merchandise, what type of campaigns would you want to plan for the coming academic year?

15–5. Total enrollment at Mythical U. has been 8,000, 8,800, 9,680, 10,748, and 11,823 over the past five years. Enrollment in the course in Russian history has been 240, 440, 581, 645, and 709 for the same period. How would you go about forecasting enrollment in this course for next year? What is your forecast?

15–6. What dangers are there in using salesmen's estimates to forecast sales when the forecast will be the basis for the quotas established for the compensation system by which these salesmen are paid?

15–7. Why might a manufacturer continue a campaign for more than one year?

15–8. What implications are there in the looping nature of the management process which shows an arrow from planning to directing to controlling and back to planning? How does this control connection affect planning?

15–9. Suppose the Wilson Company, described in this chapter, expected a labor dispute to keep them shut down three months during the coming year. What factors might cause the Wilson Company to think about expecting a 25 percent share of the market in the coming year? How would these factors affect their promotion planning?

15–10. What clues does management have that its planning is not comprehensive?

CHAPTER **16**

Budgeting and scheduling promotion programs

T HE MANAGER is asked to be time-specific and dollar-specific when planning the activities under his charge. Through sales forecasts he attempts to make *income* both amount- and time-specific. Through budgeting and scheduling, the manager seeks to make his planned *expenditures* equally specific. Top management tends to ask two questions of the promotion manager: (1) "How much?" and (2) "When?" These are, indeed, quite reasonable questions if the firm is to have available the right amount of funds for promotion at the right times. *Budgeting* is that part of the planning process that makes plans dollar-specific and answers the question "How much?" *Scheduling* lays out the timing of the campaigns and promotion efforts and answers the question "When?" Answering these two questions has the further beneficial result of setting some bench marks for the control phase of the management process. Actual expenditures can be checked against the budgeted amounts to insure that plans are being followed by the members of the organization.

"Are you right?"—is the third question top management asks the promotion manager; it is at the same time both reasonable and impossible to answer. The question is reasonable because management ought to search constantly for optimal decisions throughout the firm—in inventory control, in production schedules, in financial management, and in promotion management. But the question is also impossible to answer because the manager of a promotion activity can never prove, as we shall discover in Chapter 17, how right or wrong his final expenditure figure is. His dilemma is summed up in a quotation from the folklore of advertising, in which a corporate president is supposed to have said, "I'm pretty sure half my advertising dollars are wasted, but I am not sure which half."

There are two extreme deviations from being "right": (1) gross inadequacy, which means that potentially profitable sales are lost, and (2) wanton extravagance, which results in loss of profits to the firm. The manager of a promotion activity can never know for sure the answer to the question "Are you right?" He *can* avoid the extreme errors through careful budgeting and scheduling and seek to be "nearly right." Because his budgeting forces him to consider how much he will spend on each product, in each market, for each element of persuasion, in each campaign, the budget process helps to protect him from extreme error. Moreover, because he must schedule these expenditures by day, week, and month, he seeks to be as "nearly right" in the timing of his efforts as reason, experience, and know-how will permit.

BUDGETING PROMOTION EFFORTS

As it was with planning and forecasting, so it is with budgeting and scheduling: the question as to which comes first is moot. Our discussion will treat *budgeting* first as we attempt to make planning dollar-specific. Then we will turn to the *scheduling* which makes the plans time-specific. In actual practice, firms may do both simultaneously, building from the schedule the budget required. Many firms, however, establish the budget first, then proceed to break it down into a detailed schedule. After we discuss both budgeting and scheduling, we will look at an example of each sequence. But before we do anything, a little basic review will be helpful.

Promotion and profit relationships

As a review of some basic accounting relations, consider Table 16–1 for a moment. Note the location of the promotion expense on that statement. Note also the general relation which is basic to any income statement: Profit = Gross margin *less* expenses.

TABLE 16–1.   Relation of promotion budget to the income
statement of a firm

Gross sales....................	\$xxxxxxxx
Less: Returns................	xxx
Net sales.....................	\$xxxxxxxx
Less: Cost of goods...........	xxxxxxx
Gross margin..................	\$ xxxxxxx
Less: Expenses	
Administrative............. xxx	
Promotion................. xx	
etc...................... x	
etc...................... x	
Total expenses...........	xxxxxxxx
Net Profit (or Loss).............	\$ xxxx

Thus, an increase in expenses reduces the amount of net profit the firm will earn *unless the expense results in increased gross margin greater than the increase in expense.* Now, how can money spent as an investment in promotion increase gross margin? Here are a few ways:

1. More units of the product can be sold at the same price (either to new customers or by persuading present users to use more of it); this increases gross sales.
2. As a result of increased volume, the cost of goods sold may be reduced by volume purchases and discounts, economies of scale in producing, or automation.
3. Dollars spent for an improved quality of salesman may result in both an increase in gross sales and a decrease in merchandise returned from dissatisfied customers. The effect, then, is a two-edged increase in net sales.
4. Sales volume in units can be maintained at a higher price for some products where prestige image is important and promotion contributes to the prestige aura of the brand.

Promotion expenditures can also affect net profit by making possible reduced expenditures in other areas of the firm's operations. For the retailer, as an example, it may be more profitable to advertise to attract customers to a side-street location than to pay the rent for a main-street location. Within the promotion mix itself, some ad expenditures may have the effect of lowering personal sales expenditures by increasing the effectiveness of the present sales force.

One final word on the promotion/profit relationship. Dollars are invested in promotion in the expectation and on the assumption that the promotion activities will contribute to net profit *in the long run.* Too often this is forgotten. Management may be quite justified in spending more for promotion in the early stages of a product's introduction than can be expected in the form of increases in gross margin during the first year. This first year's operation, indeed, may show a loss—even a large loss. Once the product is successfully launched and establishes its place in the market, the expectation is for a return in profits for those promotion dollars expended in preceeding periods. Because promotion dollars are spent to create future streams of income, we have used the phrase "investment in promotion expenditures." Rather than asking, "How much will our promotion cost?" management is better advised to ask, "How much should we invest in promotion to create the flows of sales income we want to achieve?"

Two major budget elements

Assigning a total dollar value to plans and programs has two major dimensions. The first is the total amount of money to be spent on the activity; the second is the distribution of those funds to the component activities of the program.

Determination of the budget is the first consideration. The budget represents the total allocation of funds for the total promotional mix planned to achieve the goals of the firm. Setting the total promotion appropriation is an answer to the question "How much?"

Distribution of the budget, once determined, is the next item on a budgeting agenda. The total promotion fund must be distributed or allocated to the component elements of persuasion.

Each of these dimensions needs to be explored in greater detail. As we do so, keep in mind that this discussion will highlight some major budgeting considerations and approaches and *will not* seek to give you a "how-to-do-it" formula for budgeting. The scope of the budget problem varies too much from firm A, of size B, in industry C to firm X, of size Y, in industry Z, for any attempt at a standard approach to budgeting.

Budget determination

Let us turn now to some of the influences on, and approaches to, the decision of how much to spend for promotion. We must recognize that no one approach is best for every firm and that many firms use various approaches for personal selling, advertising, and sales promotion.

Influences on. Several factors influence budget determination. If the promotion manager is to be realistic in his planning of how much to spend, he must take these factors into account. Some of the more obvious influences will receive brief comment; the reader can doubtless add to the list.

Product class. In Chapter 1 we noted the common system of classifying products as convenience goods, shopping goods, or specialty goods. The class of the product influences how much should be spent for promotion, because the entire market mix is affected. A convenience good such as laundry detergent, for example, would have a wide market, intensive distribution, and a need for heavy promotion expenditures to presell shoppers before they enter self-service stores.

Stage in life cycle. The amount of funds budgeted for a product in the growth or maturity stages of its life cycle would differ from the amount budgeted for a product in the decline stage. A product in the introductory stage can build its market somewhat gradually. A firm launching a new brand onto the market for a product class in the maturity stage may not have the option of gradual increase in promotion. Indeed, some observers feel that it would take $10 million in promotion efforts to launch a new laundry detergent or toothpaste in the United States.

Competition. The reason large expenditures are necessary in the maturity stage is the nature of competition in that stage. At any stage, competition must be considered in planning promotional budgets. Note that word *considered.* We don't believe in blind imitation of competition, or sheeplike acceptance of industrywide average expenditures. On the other hand, the manager cannot ignore his competitors' promotion stance; he can use industry statistics as a guide to competitive thinking.

What can be afforded. The size and resources of the firm are a definite short-run influence on budget determination. There are two aspects of this influence that should be noted. First, the dollars available are a constraint to be reckoned with. Second, the productive capacity of the firm cannot be ignored. Even if dollars are available for promotion, the resulting demand might exceed production capacities and the promotion therefore be wasteful.

The funds available may require the seller to plan a "roll-out" introduction for a product. Rather than launch national distribution, he plans to roll out gradually from one region or area to the next. Judicious purchase of spots and regional additions of magazines help make this possible.

FIGURE 16–1.   The total budget includes funds for merchandising the ad campaign to dealers

Your customers will see Blue Lustre on CBS⦿ this spring.

CAN THEY GET IT FROM YOU?

Let's talk about it...

■ Thousands of Blue Lustre dealers **NET** more than **$500 a year** with the Blue Lustre Program, the **advertised** carpet cleaning program. Let's talk about it at the National Housewares Exposition, or any of the following shows: Budrow Buyathon, Los Angeles, January 24; Ace Hardware Convention, Chicago, January 17; Wallace Hardware Market, Morristown, January 19; Decatur Hopkins Bigelow Dowse Dealer Show, Boston, January 30; and, the Oklahoma Hardware Company Spring Market, Oklahoma City, January 30.

Or write or phone
Charles Durkee, Executive Vice President, The Earl Grissmer Company, Inc.,
712 E. 64th Street, Indianapolis, Indiana 46220, AC 317 251-9528.

AS ADVERTISED IN HARDWARE AGE, HARDWARE RETAILER

⦿Earl Grissmer Co., Inc. 1971

Once the product is established in a region and profit promise is near, the next area can be tackled.

Economic environment. A final influence is the state of the economy as a whole. Manufacturers tend to increase budgets when business is good and cut back when business falls off. There are several reasons for this. Management may view promotion as expense, and all expenses are cut in downswings. Some expenses are fixed and cannot be cut, but promotion expenses are more variable (except for salaries) and therefore more vulnerable to top management's knife. The practice is fairly general; it may stem from a feeling that in times of recession, consumers cannot be readily persuaded to part with dollars, so firms should wait until the buying mood improves.

Percent-of-sales approach. Essentially an answer to the question, "What part of my sales dollar should go for promotion?", this approach can be applied in two ways. The first is for management to decide on a multiplier, such as 5 percent, and apply the multiplier to sales to determine its promotion budget. If sales are $500,000 and the multiplier is 5 percent, then the promotion budget is $25,000. The sales figure can be past or present sales, but more realistic would be future or expected sales so as to keep expenditures in line with needs. Basing next year's advertising on this year's or last year's sales can be ill advised if business fluctuations occur. A sudden recession could find the firm spending large sums (based on last year's record sales) at exactly the time sales are plummeting.

The second application of this approach is to decide upon some fixed sum per unit of product sold. This might be 10 cents for a bushel of produce or $12 for each deluxe electric refrigerator. Using unit sales instead of dollar sales, the manufacturer simply multiplies the units by the fixed promotion sum and determines his total promotional outlay. As with a percent of dollar sales, the fixed sum per unit can be applied to past unit sales, but it would probably best be applied to forecasts of coming sales.

In either case, this percent-of-sales approach is widely used because it is relatively simple and easy to understand and to apply. There are problems, however. Selecting the multiplier to use is one; keeping it flexible and current is another. The firm may imitate competitors in selecting the multiplier or may use an average of the amount spent in the firm's most profitable years. But market conditions, the economy, the product's life cycle, and competition are always changing. There is danger that top management will come to believe that the multiplier is a sacred decision figure which should not be changed. Finally, there is a hint of cart-before-horse thinking. The notion, especially if applied to past or current sales data and not to future expectations, seems to treat promotion as a *result* of sales and not their cause. The thinking seems to be, "Because sales are high, we can afford more promotion; if sales go down, we cannot afford as much promotion."

To find the "normal" percent of sales, most sellers rely on trade association data. These groups conduct research on member's activities, pool findings to protect identity, and publish "average" operating statements by broad size category. Other associations of advertisers do the same thing for several industry groups.

Promotion task approach.   This approach to budget determination asks not "How much promotion can we afford?" but rather, "Given our goals, what promotion budget will be necessary?" Thus the approach is not bound to or by the past but is geared to the job to be done as that job has been defined in the planning process. The task approach takes the goals, strategies, and plans that promotion managers have made and determines the cost of the needed promotion programs. That sounds easier than, in fact, it is in practice. Usually the planning has spelled out the general nature of the strategy and program, but work remains to make those plans concrete in detail so that costs can be estimated.

The task approach is basically a "buildup" approach to constructing the promotion program and schedule and then determining the budget. For example, a manufacturer may have as one of his goals: increase collect telephone sales orders by 15 percent. The task approach to this program would be to plan a program for achieving this goal, sum the costs of the elements of the program, and arrive at a budget figure for the operation. The program might look like this:

♦ One-half page ads in each of four trade publications every month for three months, then alternate months for three months, so that two are scheduled every month in the last three months.
♦ Direct-mail broadside mailed to 500 active accounts at the beginning of the second month.
♦ Reminder sticker for customers telephone book or file to be delivered by salesmen on regular calls to the accounts in the second and third months.

After the program has been spelled out, the costs associated with each element would be computed. For the trade paper ads, for instance, the space costs (less discounts), production charges, and other expenses not covered by the agency commission would be totaled. The direct-mail component of the campaign would be similarly costed as to printing, addressing, and mailing charges. Finally, the cost of preparing, distributing, and motivating the salesmen to deliver the reminder sticker would be estimated, and the sum of the costs of all these "tasks" would be the budget for this part of the promotion program. Similar processes would be followed for the entire promotion plan.

FIGURE 16–2.

THIRD QUARTER ADVERTISING SCHEDULE

Introduction of the new KODAK INSTAMATIC X Cameras is the highlight of the third quarter advertising schedule. (Details of the ad support for the new line of cameras are provided in the July issue of Kodak Dealer News.)

POPULAR STILL AND MOVIE EQUIPMENT

KODAK INSTAMATIC 124 Camera and Kodak Film

Life	7/10
TV Guide	7/18
Look	7/28

KODAK INSTAMATIC 44 Camera

Life	7/3

KODAK INSTAMATIC M9 Movie Camera/
M109 Movie Projector

New Yorker	7/4, 8/22, 9/12
U. S. News	7/6, 8/10, 9/7
Saturday Review	7/25, 9/26
Time	8/3
Newsweek	7/6, 9/14
Natural History	June-July
Harper's	July
Atlantic	July
Golf Digest	July
(See Photo Fan listing also)	

KODAK INSTAMATIC X-90 Camera

Newsweek	9/14
Time	9/21
U. S. News	9/28
Sports Illustrated	9/28
Boating	September
Car & Driver	September
Flying	September
Esquire	September
Holiday	September/October
Playboy	September
Stereo Review	September
Sunset	September

KODAK INSTAMATIC Reflex Camera

Natural History	June/July and August/September
Realites	September
Venture	September
(See Photo Fan listing also)	

KODAK CAROUSEL Projector

Time	7/27, 9/28
Newsweek	7/13, 8/24
Venture	July-August
New York	7/13, 8/24
U. S. News	8/17
New Yorker	7/25
Sunset	August, September
Harper's	August
Atlantic	August

(The following insertions feature ads for the new KODAK CAROUSEL 760 Projectors and

140-slide tray)

Life	7/31, 8/21
Time	8/31
Newsweek	9/21
U. S. News	9/14
New Yorker	9/19
New York	9/21

NEGRO NEWSPAPERS

1000-line black-and-white ads running in 25 papers for the KODAK INSTAMATIC 44 Camera (8/24) and KODAK INSTAMATIC X Cameras and Film (9/14)

YOUTH PUBLICATIONS

Seventeen	August, September
Ingenue	August, September
Teen	August, September
American Girl	August, September
Boy's Life	July, August, September
Jr./Sr. Scholastic	9/21
Co-ed	September

COLOR PRINT & PROCESSING (MAILERS)

National Geographic	July

PHOTO FAN ADVERTISING

KODAK INSTAMATIC Reflex Camera

August issues of Camera 35, Modern Photography, Popular Photography, and PSA Journal.

KODAK INSTAMATIC M9 Movie Camera

July issues of Modern Photography, Popular Photography, and PSA Journal.

KODAK Film

July, August, and September issues of Modern Photography, Popular Photography, and PSA Journal. Plus Camera 35, August; and Travel & Camera, September.

TELEVISION

KODAK INSTAMATIC 44 Camera

Merv Griffin (CBS)	7/1, 7/2, 7/8
Tonight (NBC)	7/16, 9/6
Happy Days (CBS)	7/23
Today (NBC)	7/31
My Three Sons (CBS)	8/1
Bewitched (ABC)	9/3

KODAK INSTAMATIC 124 Camera & Kodak Film

Medical Center (CBS)	7/1
Bewitched (ABC)	7/9, 8/6, 8/20
Friday Movie (CBS)	7/10
Comedy Tonight (CBS)	7/26
Tonight (NBC)	7/29
Today (NBC)	8/19

KODAK INSTAMATIC 124, 314 & 44 Cameras

Mannix (CBS)	7/4
Today (NBC)	7/9
Tuesday Movie (CBS)	7/14
Mission Impossible (CBS)	7/19
Bewitched (ABC)	7/23
Tonight (NBC)	8/14

KODAK Film

Mannix (CBS)	7/4
Ed Sullivan (CBS)	7/5
Today (NBC)	7/9, 7/31, 8/19
Bewitched (ABC)	7/9, 7/23, 8/6, 8/20, 9/3
Comedy Tonight (CBS)	7/12, 7/26
Tonight (NBC)	7/16, 7/29, 8/14
Thursday Movie (CBS)	7/16
Happy Days (ABC)	7/23
My Three Sons (ABC)	8/1

Color Print & Processing (Mailers)

Merv Griffin (CBS)	7/1, 7/2, 7/8
Friday Movie (CBS)	7/10

KODAK INSTAMATIC X Cameras and Film

TV

9/14	Today	NBC-30"
9/19	Mission Impossible	CBS-60"
9/22	Julia	NBC-60"
9/23	Man from Shiloh	NBC-30"
9/24	Ironsides	NBC-30"
9/26	Mission Impossible	CBS-60"
9/29	Marcus Welby	CBS-60"

All this, of course, is hard work. The firm deciding upon the program described above had to have research data on the effectiveness of various approaches to select that combination of printed ads, direct mail, and reminder sticker. A decision on one-half page every month in four publications had to be made instead of full pages in alternate months. And when all is said and done, the task technique is under the control of a maximum percentage of sales. If the budget, as determined by the task approach for raising telephone sales by 15 percent turns out to be far more than the expected gross margin or increase in net profit from those sales, revisions must be made. The manufacturer may settle for a lower increase in telephone orders or decide to achieve the increase gradually over time instead of through a special campaign.

For all its difficulties, however, the task approach is winning approval from more and more firms as *the* correct way to determine the budget for promotion activities. It is the most rational approach in principle; it is the most difficult in practice.

Other approaches. There are numerous other approaches to the problem of budget determination, although the two just discussed are the major ones in terms of numbers of firms using them. A *minimum-job approach* seeks to provide enough funds for the smallest task worth doing. This approach may be utilized in times of rationing, or in severe economic downturns. *Follow the leader* is an approach that gears all determination to matching competitors, especially the industry leader, if one can be identified. *Net profit* is occasionally taken as the base from which to estimate promotional expenditures. While it does consider the company's financial condition, little else can be said in favor of this approach.

We need to repeat an earlier assertion that companies may use more than one approach to budget determination for the same promotion program. At least many do. What often happens is that personal sales budgets are built up by the task approach because many salaries are fixed and commissions can be accurately forecast on the basis of product and customer sales forecasts. At the same time, the firm may use a percentage multiplier to arrive at the advertising and sales promotion appropriations. The approach may even vary according to product lines, with some large-price items using a fixed sum per unit, others receiving some percentage of forecast sales, and sales promotion figures being arrived at through a minimum-job approach.

Budget periods. There is no general agreement as to the proper period for which promotional efforts should be budgeted. Many sellers, indeed, do not think of promotion in terms of specific time periods. These are usually smaller firms without specific planning in the sense that we have been describing the planning process. Larger or more progressive firms do budget for specific periods of time as an aid to planning and control. The only recognizable pattern of budget periods is the tendency for larger manufacturers to have annual promotion budgets drawn up a few months before the start of the promotion period. The necessity for establishing the promotion budget some months before the programs are to be initiated will be clearer later on in this chapter, after we discuss scheduling. For now let us merely note that some publications carrying consumer ads insist that printing plates be on hand six to eight weeks before the publication date, and we know from our study of advertising that weeks of work in copy, illustration, and layout precede the making of printing plates.

Budget distribution

The second major dimension of the budgeting task is the allocation of promotion funds to the various components of the total program being planned. In discussing budget distribution, three topics are of concern: (1) expense classification, (2) appropriate breakdowns, and (3) reserves for flexibility. Let us examine each of these in turn.

Expense classification. One difficulty in budget distribution is in deciding just what promotion expense belongs in what part of the promotion budget. If the manager of advertising, or sales, is to be responsible for his portion of the total promotion budget, he is understandably concerned with what expenses are to be charged against his budget. In actual practice, one can find little consensus. For example, if a firm decides to prepare some catalogs for salesmen's use, where should such an expense be charged? A survey by *Printers' Ink* magazine revealed the following state of disagreement:

36% of the firms would charge the catalogs to *advertising.*
30% would charge them to *sales.*
32% would charge them to *sales promotion.*[1]

Thus, there are no clear-cut, generally accepted rules telling what goes where in budget distribution.

Printers' Ink has constructed some extremely helpful guides to expense classification; they are found in Figures 16–3 and 16–4. The *white* list in each figure is for items or expenses which clearly belong in the particu-

---

[1] "Is Your Ad Budget Up to Date?" *Printers' Ink*, December 16, 1960.

lar account or budget. The expense items in the *black* list do not belong in the budget named at the top of the list, even though often lodged there by firms. Managers ought to resist such invasions or raiding of their budget dollars to cover expenses in the black list. Such items either belong some other portion of the promotion budget or in some other area of the firm's operation entirely. Finally, there is a *gray* list of border-line items that may or may not be appropriately charged to the department.

In Table 16–2 may be found some excerpts from the *Printers' Ink* survey mentioned before. These examples help illustrate that budget distribution, like other aspects of planning, is an easier-said-than-done affair.

TABLE 16–2.   Selected survey results on what charges belong in which promotion budget

Expense items	Percent who would charge item to:			
	Advertising	Sales	Sales promotion	Public relations
Financial advertising............	53%	0%	0%	31%
Samples; door-to-door distribution costs......................	33	34	33	0
Cost of deal merchandise (10 cents off, and similar deals)........	11	51	32	0
Gift of company products to organizations...............	11	17	11	25
Test marketing programs.........	44	29	5	0
Local cooperative advertising......	69	11	13	1

Source: "Is Your Ad Budget Up to Date?" *Printers' Ink*, December 16, 1960.

Appropriate breakdowns.   We are concerned here with the distribution of the total promotion allocation to more detailed categories of marketing effort than merely selling, advertising, and sales promotion. If a budget is arrived at by the task method, if it is the result of careful study of each product, each promotion task, each market, each persuasive element, each day, week, and month, then the distribution of the budget has been accomplished in the buildup of the total amount. If, on the other hand, the promotion manager has a total sum to be distributed, he must see to it that the planned distribution is in sufficient detail to serve management planning and control.

WHITE LIST: These charges belong in the sales department account.

Sales executives' salaries	Automobile ownership operation and insurance for salesmen	Stationery and office supplies in branch offices	Consumer booklets
Sales executives' commissions	Salesmen's other travel expenses	Branch office sales promotion	Sales-promotion department overhead
Sales executives' bonuses	Salesmen's entertainment	Rent of meeting place for sales conventions	Dealer displays
Sales executives' dues in national sales clubs	Salaries of Clerical staff	Travel of salesmen and headquarters' staff to conventions	Price lists
Social Security taxes on sales executives' salaries	Bonuses of Clerical staff	Convention props and special material	Showrooms
Sales executives' travel and entertainment	Social Security taxes on salaries of clerical staff	Ad reprints, brochures, slide films, records of radio commercials for salesmen, distributors or dealers	Demonstrators
Salesmen's salaries	Prizes for clerical staff	Expenses of advertising department personnel at sales conventions	Samples
Salesmen's commissions	Cost of training new salesmen	Sales-promotion department salaries	Sales service
Salesmen's bonuses	Share of rent, heat, lighting, etc.		Space at trade shows
Salesmen's prizes	Telephone and telegraph expense		Exhibits at trade shows
Salesmen's dues in national and local sales clubs	Gratuity allowance		Salaries of personnel attending trade shows
Social Security taxes on salesmen's salaries	Fleet auto rentals		Securing of market data reports
			Investigation of new markets
			Shipping of sales-promotional material
			Shipping of samples

BLACK LIST: These charges do *not* belong in the sales department account although too frequently they are put there.

Retirement fund for salesmen and clericals	Development expense on new products
Expenses of expediters in factory	Testing laboratory
Bad credits	Freight, express, cartage on regular merchandise
Damage to goods in transit	Trucking
Insurance on goods in transit	Chauffeurs' salaries
Political contributions	Packing
Legal costs (such as FTC and Fair Trade)	Spoiled stock
	Refrigeration
	Cost of damage in transit
	Pilferage

GRAY LIST: These are borderline charges, sometimes belonging in the sales department account and sometimes in other accounts depending on circumstances.

Stock participation or bonus stock for executives and salesmen	Administrative entertainment
Group or other benefit insurance for executives, salesmen and clericals	Sales billing
Outside education for sales executives	Re-packing cost
Expense of tracer staff	Extra cost of special orders (labeling, shipping, warehousing, etc.)
Sales accounting	House organ
Return goods	Differential in price for a special sale
Manufacturer's sales tax	Policy adjustments on price
Warehousing	Research into advertising effectiveness
Shipping cost	Labor expense for handling product at sales branch

Source: *Printers' Ink.*

FIGURE 16-4.

WHITE LIST: These charges belong in the advertising account.

Space and Time:

Paid advertising in all recognized media, including:
- Magazines
- Business papers
- Farm papers
- Car cards
- Theater programs
- Outdoor
- Radio
- Television

Point of Purchase material
Novelties
Booklets
Directories
Direct advertising
Cartons and labels (for advertising purposes, such as in window displays)

Catalogs:

Export advertising
Package inserts (when used as advertising and not just as direction sheets)
House magazines to dealers or consumers
Motion picture and slides (including talking pictures) used for advertising
Dealer helps
Reprints of advertisments used in mail or for display
All other printed and lithographed material used directly for advertising purposes

Administration:

(Note: In some companies these charges go into an Administration account)

Salaries of ad dept. executives and employees
Office supplies and fixtures used solely by ad dept.
Commissions and fees to advertising agencies, special writers or advisers
Expenses incurred by salesmen when working for ad dept.
Traveling expenses of department employees engaged in departmental business

Mechanical:

Art work
Typography
Engraving
Mats & Electros
Photographs
Radio & TV production
Package design (advertising aspects only)

Miscellaneous:

Transportation of advertising material (including postage and other carrying charges)
Fees to window display installation services
Other miscellaneous expenses connected with items on the White List

---

GRAY LIST: These are borderline charges, sometimes belonging in the advertising accounts and sometimes in other accounts, depending on circumstances.

Samples
Demonstrations
Fairs
Canvassing
Depreciation of equipment used by advertising department
Telephone, rent, light, heat and other overhead expenses, apportioned to advertising department
House magazines going to salesmen
Advertising automobiles
Premiums
Membership in associations or other organizations devoted to advertising
Testing bureaus
Advertising portfolios for salesmen
Contributions to special advertising funds of trade associations
Display signs on the factory or office building
Salesmen's catalogs
Research and market investigations
Advertising allowances to trade for co-operative effort

BLACK LIST: These charges do not belong in the advertising account although too frequently they are put there.

Free goods
Picnic and bazaar programs
Charitable religious and fraternal donations
Other expenses for good-will purposes
Cartons
Labels
Instruction sheets
Package manufacture
Press agentry
Stationery used outside advertising department
Price lists
Salesmen's calling cards
Motion pictures for sales use only
House magazines going to factory employees
Bonuses to trade
Special rebates
Membership in trade associations
Entertaining customers or prospects
Annual reports
Showrooms
Demonstration stores
Sales convention expenses
Salesmen's samples (including photographs used in lieu of samples)
Welfare activities among employees
Such recreational activities as baseball teams, etc.
Sales expenses at conventions
Cost of salesmen's automobiles
Special editions which approach advertisers on good-will basis

Source: *Printers' Ink.*

Rather than think of the total mass of target customers, managers try to break the whole down into market areas. Distribution by *market area* is an appropriate breakdown because sales quotas, media schedules, and a host of other marketing activities are planned on a market-by-market basis. If market A accounts for 80 percent of sales and market B, 20 percent, most planners would want to give market A continued support by spending a majority of promotion dollars in that area.

Distribution of the budget by *product* is equally helpful. Some products sell well in certain market areas and not at all in others; some may need heavy advertising and little personal selling while for others a reverse strategy would be appropriate. Out of many products sold, a few may account for the bulk of a firm's sales and thus should receive a majority of promotion efforts. The retailer will need to pay particular attention to a budget breakdown by departments or lines of products he sells.

Budgeting by *time period* is most important. We noted the need for careful timing in promotion planning to insure that financial management can so manage the firm's funds as to have the dollars available when needed. Then, too, the seasonal aspect of sales strongly urges budgeting by time. In the sales forecasting example of Chapter 15, the Wilson Company sales ranged from a high of 42 percent occurring in Quarter II to a low of 13 percent in Quarter III. Promotion that runs counter to well-established seasonal variation must be very carefully evaluated. Most marketers feel that their promotion should take advantage of the seasonal rises, and our study of perception suggests that buyers will be more aware, and will be more likely to be seeking buying information, during the peak sales seasons.

Other appropriate breakdowns include budget distribution by *type of customer* to insure that all targets (for example, consumers, dealers, professional groups, stockholders) are covered by the promotion program. Still another breakdown, one for mass promotion, would be by *media* to insure that the balance between print, broadcast, and supporting media planned in the early stages of strategy and planning design are followed in the actual accomplishment of the promotion program.

Reserves for flexibility. Our treatment of the planning process in Chapter 13 stressed the need for the promotion planner to review continually his plans, both while they are being made and while they are being executed. If this review reveals a need for a change in plans, some flexibility in budgeting should have been anticipated. Budgets are not carved on tablets of stone and blindly adhered to in the face of changing conditions. Competitors' marketing mixes may change, media availability may shift, and market potentials by area or product may vary during the course of a year. Management dare not let the budget become a master instead of the useful servant it is intended to be.

One approach to flexibility is regular review of the budget. Firms have to establish annual plans to guide and assist in the coordination of the many facets of the total promotional effort. But having done this, many firms set a regular—say quarterly—review of the remainder of the budget and can thereby effect changes in plans as needed. The danger in such a process lies in *overreacting* to short-run changes in the market. The well-designed plan may need to be modified, but not without careful thought. Regular review should not become a means of scrapping sound plans for hasty substitution of new approaches in response to every little changing condition in the marketplace.

Another useful approach is to build into the budget a reserve fund unallocated at the outset but designed to allow management to meet changing conditions with funds available for additional promotional efforts. How large this reserve should be depends on experience, present circumstances, and future conditions. Generally, if a balance remains in the reserve account at the end of the budget period, it reverts to the company's general account.

SCHEDULING PROMOTION EFFORTS

Whereas budgeting attempts to make promotion plans dollar-specific, scheduling makes them time-specific. We expect good plans to make clear who is to do what, and when. The degree of coordination needed for truly effective communication with prospects can be achieved only through careful scheduling. Before discussing some of the basic concepts and problems of scheduling, perhaps we should take a look at a simple scheduling problem that might occur for an oil company that plans to run a short two-month campaign to promote winter changeover in its service stations. The firm has regular campaigns to promote the brand name, the quality of service at the stations, and several products sold in the stations. This particular campaign, however, is designed as a special seasonal promotion to persuade customers to have their cars serviced for the coming cold-weather months (i.e., heavy-duty lubrication, winter-weight oil, antifreeze and cooling system checks, etc.).

The firm sells in states along the eastern seaboard of the United States from Georgia to Maine. The winter checkup campaign is to be run in the northern half of the territory during September and October, and in the southern half during October and November. The strategy calls for consumer advertising in television, newspapers, and outdoor, with support from point-of-sale displays in the stations, a mailing to regular credit card users, and trade advertising to dealers. Company salesmen will take orders for point-of-sale material, stocks of antifreeze, and other supplies needed for the winterizing operation.

FIGURE 16–5.   Initial schedule for a special promotion campaign

PROMOTION TARGET	MEDIA	JUNE	JULY	AUGUST	SEPTEMBER	OCTOBER
CONSUMERS	NEWSPAPER				▶ Begin September 9	
	TELEVISION				▶ Begin Evening of 9th	
	OUTDOOR				▶ Change August 30	
	DIRECT MAIL	▶ Show to Regional Sales Managers			Mail in August Bill	▶ Mail in September Bill
DEALERS	TRADE PAPERS MONTHLY		▶ In July and August Issues			
	WEEKLY		▶ Begin July 15 Issues			
	POINT OF PURCHASE		▶ Samples for Salesmen on July 15	▶ Mail to Dealers August 20	▶ Install Tuesday after Labor Day	

In Figure 16–5 the major elements of the campaign are blocked out as the scheduling process begins. Because the northern area campaign begins first, it will control the timing of many elements; we can focus our attention on the northern schedule. Note in Table 16–3 that the introduction of the consumer advertising is really the last major phase of the schedule, because many elements precede this activity. Thus, trade paper advertising to service station dealers appears in the summer, point-of-sale materials are delivered one to two weeks before the consumer ads start, and direct-mail materials are scheduled for insertion in August and September billings, which go out at the end of each month.

The information in Figure 16–5 is of the broadest kind in terms of scheduling. True, general times are spelled out, and some specific dates are detailed in that rough schedule. Now, however, each element of the campaign must be made time-specific. The newspaper advertising will serve as an example. In Table 16–3 a portion of the newspaper schedule that might be established is shown. In each area, specific papers must be selected and ads scheduled for specific days during the campaign. This must be done for each market area, for every newspaper ad planned for this campaign. Similar scheduling must be done for TV spots, by station and market, by day and hour.

The manufacturer has scheduled sales meetings on a regional basis on July 15, at which time the winter checkup campaign will be outlined and the salesmen shown the point-of-purchase materials, consumer ads, and dealer promotion scheduled. These materials will have been shown

TABLE 16–3. Portion of newspaper schedule for the special-purpose campaign

Market and media	Date	Size	Ad to be run
Massachusetts			
Boston metropolitan area			
Herald	9/6	1 p bw	Intro
	9/7	1 p bw	Intro
	9/9	½ p bw	Intro
	9/11	½ p bw	Last Minute Charlie
	9/13	1 p bw	Turnpike
	9/16	¼ p bw	Turnpike

to the regional sales managers at their June 15 meeting, with samples sent to each regional officei n time for its July 15 meeting. Thus, for scheduling purposes, the June 15 date is a deadline for finished production of all advertising materials. In order to have the finished direct-mail piece by June 15, a schedule must be made similar to the one in Table 16–4. In like manner, every item in the promotion program must be scheduled so that all converge on the June 15 deadline for showing to regional sales managers. The schedule for one small direct-mail promotion item to be inserted in the customer's September gasoline bill may begin with a March 20 conference in order to be ready for showing at a June sales meeting. The printed forms would be delivered to regional billing offices in early August, in time for insertion in the statements mailed at the end of the month.

For this one campaign, lasting only two months, similar schedules must be prepared for all elements of the promotion program, with dual delivery and insertion dates for the two market areas (northern states and southern states) defined by the company for this campaign.

Three basic concepts

With this brief look at a simple scheduling problem, we are now ready to turn to three basic concepts which underlie the scheduling of promotion efforts. They are: (1) coverage, (2) frequency, and (3) continuity. After a brief look at each of these concepts, we can turn to more specific discussion of how the concepts affect the scheduling

TABLE 16–4.   Production schedule for direct-mail material in special campaign

June	15	Show to regional sales managers
June	12	Deliver finished work to home office (200 pieces, store rest)
June	1	Approve final proof and order printing
May	20	Review first proofs from printer
May	15	Printing plates to printer; copy to printer
May	8	Finished art work to engraver for plates
April	15	Order finished art work; review copy
April	10	Approve final layouts and illustration ideas
April	3	Rough layouts started
March	20	Copy conference to agree on theme

of personal selling, advertising, and sales promotion. While each concept will be discussed separately, do keep in mind the fact that these are interrelated ideas. Coverage, frequency, and continuity compete among themselves for scarce promotion dollars; each of the three is dependent upon the other two.

Coverage. The basic questions of coverage, or reach, are: (1) To whom should promotion be directed? and (2) How large should the audience group be? You will recall that in Chapter 1 three broad categories of individuals were suggested: nonusers, prospects, and users of the product type. If management must decide to whom promotion efforts will be aimed, then these categories are a helpful starting point. Certainly *users* are logical targets of the promotion effort; users of the firm's brand must be kept happy and loyal, and users of competing brands must be persuaded to shift. *Prospects,* those individuals who qualify on the basis of age, income, and potential benefit from the product, are a second

FIGURE 16–6.   The selection of specific market areas is key to the scheduling task

DMA-THE PROBLEM SOLVER

Allocating advertising dollars to specific marketing areas. Matching time and space buys with client sales areas. Evaluating overall marketing plans. These are only a few of the difficult and time-consuming tasks that can be simplified through the use of Nielsen's DMA concept.

DMA (Designated Market Area) is a carefully studied way of dividing the country into some 200 non-overlapping county groupings. The groupings are, in general, created by assigning each county exclusively to the one market whose TV stations dominate viewing within the area. Sales quotas, product distribution, marketing plans, advertising weight and expenditures and consumer sales, all can be evaluated within one common area.

Three years ago NSI started reporting TV audience and TV ownership estimates by DMAs to meet this need. Today others see the need too. For example, newspapers and magazines now relate their circulation to DMAs.

What about you? Is DMA part of your program? If you're selling TV time, it should be. National advertisers and agencies have proven DMA's value as an efficient means to plan, buy and evaluate spot TV advertising.

For more information, phone, write or wire

 **Nielsen Station Index**
a service of A. C. Nielsen Company

CHICAGO 60601	NEW YORK 10019	HOLLYWOOD 90028	SAN FRANCISCO 94104
360 N. Michigan Ave.	1290 Avenue of the Americas	6922 Hollywood Blvd.	68 Post St.
(312) 372-3810	(212) 956-2500	(213) 466-4391	(415) 986-6437

major group to be covered. The concept of coverage is that of reaching the maximum number of users and prospects.

In the management of promotion, the question of coverage is closely allied to the firm's productive capacity and distribution policies. A company that sells in six New England states would not be concerned with coverage in the Southwest. In a sense, this is a special application of criteria to distinguish between nonusers and prospects. Prospects for this firm are limited to the markets in which it has, or is seeking, distribution.

Frequency. The second scheduling concept has to do with *how often* persuasive communication is attempted with prospects. As the goal of scheduling is to make plans time-specific, frequency is a most basic concept. Promotion efforts are costly; thus, one factor which influences frequency decisions is the amount of money available for the campaign. Another important influence is the nature of the product and its customer buying pattern. Low-cost, frequently purchased *convenience goods,* for example, may require relatively high frequency of promotion to insure that the brand name is constantly differentiated by prospects who will not spend much time in the listing stage of the buying model. In personal selling, as we shall discover, frequency questions involve decisions about how many times per *year* or per *month* customers will be contacted, whereas in broadcast media the frequency questions may involve times per *day*. Our oil company example indicated very frequent use of newspaper ads, with six insertions in the first 10 days alone. Direct mail, in contrast, was limited to two exposures at monthly intervals.

Continuity. The regularity of persuasive communication is at issue in the concept of *continuity*. How much time should elapse between messages? Between campaigns? A most important influence on continuity is the nature of the demand for the product. A firm which sells a highly seasonal good like antifreeze need not plan a program of promotion to prospects aimed at making sales during the spring and summer months. Our oil company had other promotion campaigns running during the entire year *plus* special seasonal campaigns such as the winter checkup promotion we discussed. Products needed, purchased, and used *continually* require more continuity of total effort than those with irregular patterns of sales.

Within the sales period, however, there is another dimension to continuity. In the oil campaign, the newspaper exposure could be obtained through multipage ads in a two-day period, or by varying intervals. In Table 16–4, for instance, we note daily insertions in the opening of the campaign, then a tapering off to less frequent insertions after the opening. Direct mail could be sent in weekly mailings, but the decision in the illustration was to use a monthly interval to allow greater continuity of effort.

By now it must be quite apparent that these three concepts are all highly interrelated. If the dollars available for newspaper advertising in our oil company example were limited, for instance, the company's promotion manager might consider a number of alternatives. Here are a few:

♦ He could maintain his frequency and continuity in major metropolitan markets and cut out some cities of lesser population. This would reduce coverage, of course.
♦ He could maintain coverage and continuity but reduce the frequency of insertions to two or three per week.
♦ He could try to maintain coverage and frequency, but concentrate his newspaper ads in the first two weeks of each month, at a sacrifice of continuity.
♦ He could maintain frequency of insertion throughout the time period in all markets but reduce the size of each insertion.

The variations of alternatives is nearly limitless. Recognizing that these three basic concepts *are* interdependent, we need to turn now to the scheduling of our three major elements of persuasion. And since we have also recognized that this interdependence leads to unlimited variety of approach, our treatment of scheduling will not attempt to prescribe *the best way* to schedule these persuasive elements. As we shall find in Chapter 17, evaluation of promotion is so complex a problem that we must honestly admit that there is no way to know *what* the best scheduling for a given company is or should be.

Scheduling personal selling

First, the question must be asked: should personal selling be scheduled at all? Given our discussion in Chapter 5 of the variety of salesmen's jobs, and the comments in Chapter 6 on directing salesmen, we must recognize that no single answer will serve all situations. In broadest terms, of course, personal selling must be made time-specific to the extent that general guides to coverage, frequency, and continuity are established. Salesmen must know what management expects of them if they are to plan their time efficiently. In practice, however, the range of scheduling runs from sales managers setting detailed sales routes that specify what the salesman is to do each day with which customers, to their giving fairly freewheeling independent salesmen a general assignment of only the broadest coverage expected, such as "You have North and South Dakota."

Coverage questions. The issue of coverage, as we have noted, is partially answered by the distribution decisions the firm makes in designing the marketing mix. Decisions about *intensive, selective,* or *exclusive distribution,* as we discussed in Chapter 1, are in a sense decisions as to coverage. The scheduling of supporting salesmen (such as missionary salesmen or technical specialists), on the other hand, is a duty of the sales manager or sales promotion manager. Will these men be deployed to all customers or only to accounts of a certain size? Will they be used throughout the markets served or only as aids in developing new or weak territories?

Frequency and continuity questions. How often should salesmen call on an account? Analysis of sales data by customer, as we shall note in Chapter 17, quite often reveals that a relationship like the following exists: 20 percent of the number of customers account for 80 percent of dollar sales volume. Quite obviously, then, the high-volume customers deserve more frequent calls than the accounts that may not even earn their own way. If there are seasonal fluctuations in sales, both frequency and continuity must be considered. Some nominal customer contact may be desired in months when no sales are expected. This is especially true in industrial selling where, in a recession or slowdown, few sales are expected all year from some accounts but rapport must be maintained for the expected upturn in business activity.

One approach, widely used, is to classify accounts according to both volume and profitability (because a moderate sales volume earned through a large number of small orders may actually be unprofitable) and set call schedules accordingly. Class A customers are called on every two weeks, class B customers are called on monthly, class C firms are contacted quarterly, and so on.

Scheduling benefits. Application of the three basic concepts to personal selling scheduling does contribute to better planning and more efficient management. For one thing, the sales force is planned according to customer needs and the realities of market demand. The number of salesmen needed can be more accurately determined and justified if these concepts have been used. For the new firm, as an example, the knowledge that there are 1,000 potential customers to be reached every month by salesmen who can probably make 24 calls a week on a regular route can lead to accurate estimation of salesmen required. Finally, the firm may decide that in some areas where coverage is desired, the use of agents instead of company salesmen may be more suitable until the territory develops enough potential to support a new man.

Scheduling advertising

While there may be some division of opinion as to how thoroughly personal selling can or should be scheduled, there is no doubt that advertising *must be scheduled.* The only exception to this would be the small business that does not have a clearly defined program of promotion but rather advertises occasionally if space or time salesmen can persuade the owner to do so. Some of the major questions of advertising scheduling were discussed in Chapter 9. The importance of scheduling advertising efforts is so great, however, that we feel entitled to risk redundancy in the present chapter.

Coverage. The goal is maximum exposure of clearly identified prospects and users of the firm's product. The first basic question, then, is: What types of media should be used? The answer must consider the availability, suitability, and cost of media. In our oil company example, three broad types of advertising were selected: newspaper, spot television, and trade paper media. Certainly others were available, suitable, and within range of the company's financial resources. These three were chosen to adequately *cover* the target market.

Having selected the type of media, the next coverage question is: Which individual media shall we use? Here the promotion manager must consider the quantity and quality of circulation offered by potential media. A related coverage question is the matter of *duplication.* In setting the newspaper schedule for the winter checkup campaign, should the oil company use the *Boston Herald,* the *Boston Globe,* the *Christian Science Monitor;* or some combination of these to reach the Bostom market? The promotion manager is concerned with the cost of media, of course, but his milline rate computations must be tempered with judgments about the quality, prestige, or influence of media with similar circulations in the same market. The goal is always: Cover target customers—users and prospects.

Frequency. As was true for coverage, and as will be true for continuity, there is no magic formula which will determine the ideal frequency for scheduling advertising messages. The number of media to be used, the length of the ad campaign, the size of the ad to be run,

FIGURE 16–7.   Seasonal appropriateness affects scheduling and layout

and the size of the advertising budget are all factors which influence decisions about frequency. We know that buyers can focus on but a part of the perceptual field at any given moment and that only a fraction of a medium's total circulation will bring the message into figure. This leads to a powerful argument that high frequency will increase effective coverage, help prevent the brand from slipping into ground, and be available to a passing parade of buyers reaching the listing stage or screening stage at any given moment of time.

On the opposite side is this fact: frequency costs more money. If the dollars available are limited, the size of the ad (or length of broadcast time per message) must be reduced if frequency is to be maintained. The alternative is to maintain the size and cut the frequency. Both large-size and small-size ads have points in their favor. The *large ad* is an attention getter, is likely to have a better position in the publication, and may help earn some discounts. The message can be longer and more complete. The *small ad*, however, may allow the advertiser to achieve greater coverage (through more media), more frequency (in all media), and greater continuity (through longer continued exposure).

Continuity. The concept of continuity has connotations of consistency and regularity. At the most extreme, the problem might be this: If an advertiser can afford only 12 pages in *Fortune* magazine, should he have 1 page every issue during the year or a 12-page spread in a single issue? Most students of promotion would favor the 1-page, 12-issue alternative because the continuity achieved is important. Continuity adds momentum to a promotion campaign as each ad builds on past efforts. Communication can be gradual, as each message adds to the buyer's store of knowledge about the product or brand, hopefully increasing the positive valence he associates with the product.

Related to the general question of overall continuity is the scheduling matter of starting and stopping campaigns. Should the manufacturer schedule his television advertising for 39 weeks and "take the summer off"? Should the new campaign start in September and end in January, or May, or *when?* If sales are seasonal, the timing of advertising efforts may be extremely critical. Thus, like all other matters in promotion planning, scheduling for continuity depends on other factors: the funds available, the nature of the market for the product, the advertising practices of competitors—all influence decisions about continuity. In the end, a workable compromise must be reached between what is desired and what can be afforded, and between the conflicting claims for coverage and frequency in the advertising schedule.

Scheduling sales promotion

In making his sales promotion plans time-specific, the promotion manager seeks to maxmimize the coordination of the other two elements of persuasion. All that has been said about coverage, frequency, and continuity for personal selling and advertising applies to this third promotion force as well. The sales promotion manager must decide *to whom* promotion efforts will be aimed (coverage) and when they will take place (frequency and continuity).

The example earlier in this chapter of the oil company can again be used to advantage. In that small campaign, you recall, two major sales promotion efforts were planned: point-of-purchase materials and direct-mail stimulation of final customers. The *timing* of the use of each was critical. Direct mail was to be used *after* trade paper ads to dealers and salesmen's calls had stimulated the middlemen to stock up on what they needed to sell during the campaign. The direct mail was to be concurrent with the newspaper and television spots as an added reinforcement to these communications. The point-of-purchase promotion was timed for delivery to dealers about one week in advance of the start of consumer advertising. Too early delivery might result in loss of materials or soiling of them around not-too-clean stations. Too late delivery would impair coordination of all channels of communication and cause a loss of effectiveness.

Like all promotion scheduling, the scheduling of sales promotion activities seeks to have the *right message*, delivered in the *right medium*, to the *right people*, at the *right time*, for the *right duration* for maximum effectiveness. There are questions of *coverage* (Which trade shows are important enough for exhibits? Which houses should receive free samples?); there are questions of *frequency* (How often should premiums be offered? How many mailings to the list selected?); and there are questions of *continuity* to be answered (How often should a consumer contest be run? When should Christmas point-of-sale material be installed?). The application of the three basic concepts to this third element of persuasion are so similar to the application in other persuasive elements that the similarity need not be belabored further.

Scheduling indirect promotion

Because public relations and institutional promotion are viewed as ongoing, there is a danger of being lulled into careless management habits so far as these persuasive elements are concerned. But coverage, continuity, and frequency are the guiding lights here, too. Indeed, the real key to success in these areas is *timing*. A careful scheduling plan means that a spacing of newsworthy events can be planned and that other indirect promotion elements take the fullest advantage of timeliness.

BUDGETING AND SCHEDULING INTERRELATIONS

From time-to-time in this chapter the term "buildup" approach has been used. We need to conclude our treatment of budgeting and scheduling with a recognition of the two broad approaches to the joint problem of making plans time- and dollar-specific. The two approaches are: (1) buildup, and (2) breakdown.

The buildup approach

We discussed a number of ways to arrive at the promotion budget. The task method was essentially the buildup approach. In this approach the job to be done and the plans for achieving it are studied, then the plans are made concrete by building step by step the elements needed to achieve the goals. After the elements are selected, a summing of their costs provides the budget—by product, market, media, time period, promotion element, and in total. In the process, decisions about coverage, frequency, and continuity are made for each element of the promotion mix. The end result is a custom-tailored promotion program designed to achieve the goals established for the promotion portion of the marketing mix.

In the buildup approach, then, the schedule is painstakingly designed piece by piece until the final result is a promotion program with a price tag (or budget figure) attached. The process is rational; the results should be effective. The process is also very, very difficult, as we noted in discussing the task method.

The breakdown approach

The alternative is to start with a budget figure for promotion and proceed to break it up into little pieces. The percent-of-sales approach, or some other budgeting method, may yield a manufacturer a total promotion budget of $1 million. If salesmen are salaried and sales management expense is fixed, the firm may deduct $400,000 to cover these. The remainder of $600,000 is the budget for other promotion items (assuming, of course, the firm set the original figure with this 60/40 ratio in mind).

The $600,000 sum may be split by product (according to the percent of total sales each product is expected to contribute, for example), then by media and sales promotion effort, then by time. For example, the firm may decide to spend 20 percent in magazines, or $120,000. Next, the firm may decide on a group of publications, and allocate $70,000 to magazine A. Since this might purchase only two pages in magazine A, the schedule may be set at 12 one-eighth-page ads for maximum continuity. As a result of this series of breakdowns, a schedule is finally arrived at which allocates the funds provided in the initial budget decision.

We have been discussing the management of promotion and the need to make reasoned plans to achieve specific goals. In the process, we found it useful to insist that the plans specify who is to do what, when, and at what cost. Our look at the management process suggested that the details of the planning process will serve as bench marks against which promotion efforts can be evaluated. In seeking to make plans time- and dollar-specific, three basic concepts of coverage, frequency, and continuity were considered. They interrelate, as do the processes of budgeting and scheduling of promotion. What is apparent, then, is that we are describing in frozen paragraphs and finite words a lively, continuing process that defies fragmentation. It is management.

QUESTIONS AND PROBLEMS

16–1. How can an increase in promotion expense contribute to an increase in net profits for the firm?

16–2. Under what conditions would a firm wish to spend more as a percent of sales for promotion than its competition is spending?

16–3. For the campus store manager you assisted in Problem 15–4 at the end of the last chapter, suggest the major scheduling matters he must consider for the campaigns you outlined.

16–4. When is coverage more important than continuity?

16–5. How does the method of compensation affect the scheduling authority exercised by the sales manager?

16–6. Design a dealer campaign to last 13 weeks with a prize of a trip to Bermuda for the winning dealer and his wife, and for the company salesman serving that dealer and his wife. Sketch out the schedule for such an event, and assume that $100,000 is appropriated for the contest expenses and promotion budget.

16-7. How can a firm determine which customers deserve more attention from the sales force and which deserve less or even no attention?

16-8. What factors outside the firm restrict scheduling freedom?

16-9. How should promotion budgets and schedules be *used* by management?

16-10. When is a breakdown approach to promotion budgeting justified?

CHAPTER **17**

Evaluation and control of promotion

THE WORD *management* is derived from the word *manage*. One of Webster's definitions for "manage" is "to control and direct." The planning (which gives a firm goals and direction), and the organization (which marshals and coordinates the human efforts to reach these goals), are essential elements of management; so is control. And how does Webster define control? Somewhat like this: to check or regulate; to keep within limits; to exercise restraining or directing influence over. Clearly, then, the evaluation and control of promotion is a basic responsibility of the promotion manager if he is to fulfill his *management* duties.

A promotion manager, whether he is advertising manager, sales manager, or sales promotion manager, cannot exercise directing, guiding, or restraining power over promotion activities unless he is well supplied with information upon which to evaluate these activities. This chapter will begin with a look at the basic steps in the control process, survey the kinds of information managers need to assess the effectiveness of their efforts, and then comment on the evaluation and control in the three specific areas of the promotion mix—personal selling, advertising, and sales promotion. We will close the chapter with a note on the complexity of evaluation and control.

THE CONTROL PROCESS

The process by which a manager controls the activities for which he is responsible is essentially the same whether we are discussing the

494

management of promotion, of production, of finance, or whatever. Before we consider specific applications of control techniques to promotion, an understanding of the basic control process is indicated because it will be helpful.

Steps in the control process

This directing, guiding process we call "control" can be broken down into five steps: (1) goal definition, (2) plan of action, (3) information feedback, (4) corrective action, and (5) reevaluation. The first two items on the list are our old friends "goal definition" and "planning." Thus control is inextricably linked with planning in a kind of endless cycle. The information feedback allows evaluation of progress toward goals *only* if some criteria or bench marks are established through clear, precise goal definition in the planning stage.

A simple example from retailing will illustrate the process:

The manager of Smith's Family Store notes that he still has a large inventory of sweaters on hand in February, near the end of the winter season. He wants to clear out this stock of sweaters at a profit in order: (1) to make room for the swimming suits and casual wear he plans to sell for spring and summer, and (2) to convert this inventory into cash so that the summer wear lines can be paid for in time to earn a cash discount. As the first shipments will be arriving on March 1 (with payment less 2 percent accepted until March 30), he realizes that the sweaters must be sold soon.

The manager decides to run a special sweater promotion using daily newspaper advertising in the local papers and spot radio ads on two stations. He plans to start the newspaper campaign on Sunday, with radio spots beginning Monday morning. His estimate is that two weeks will be required to clear the stocks; he plans his advertising schedules accordingly.

The sweater promotion gets underway on Sunday, February 20, with a quarter-page ad in addition to the regular store advertising planned for that day. Near the cash register in the sweater department the manager places a clipboard and instructs the clerks to make a check mark in one of three columns (men's, women's, children's) every time they sell a sweater.

At the end of each day the manager adds the check marks, compares the sales with the inventory of sweaters in each category at the end of the previous day, and computes a new inventory. The ads were originally planned to feature all three categories of sweaters equally. At the close of business on Wednesday, February 23, the manager discovers that nearly all the women's and children's sweaters have been sold but that men's sweaters are still overstocked. Because it is too late to change Thursday's ads, he lets them run as planned but orders changes in the newspaper and radio ads remaining on his schedule. The ads will feature only men's sweaters. By Monday, February 28, the manager of Smith's finds that only a dozen men's sweaters in odd sizes remain. While he had originally planned to run the campaign until Saturday, he decides to cancel all sweater ads after the Tuesday morning paper and the noon radio spot.

This illustration of a special promotion activity by a retailer will allow us to examine the steps in the control process in more detail.

Goal definition. One cannot regulate or control unless he knows what he is trying to achieve. For the manager of promotion, as we noted in Chapter 14, a broad, vague goal such as "increased sales" is of little use, either for planning or control. The goal definition stage is thus doubly important: it aids planning, and it establishes the criteria for control. The manager of Smith's, for example, had goals of moving a specific number of a specific item by a target date at a profit. For this small promotion effort, he established crisp, clear goals.

Plan of action. The plan of action specifies how the goals are to be achieved. The retailer decided what kinds of promotion he would employ (newspaper and spot radio), when he would use each (morning newspapers starting on Sunday, with radio spots beginning on Monday), and how long the effort would be sustained (two weeks). The plan provided for equal effort for all three categories of this specific inventory item. In short, his plan of action was *comprehensive* and detailed; and it was *tailored* to the goals spelled out for the effort.

Information feedback. If control is to take place, information must be provided on which to evaluate progress. The information flows necessary to plan and control promotion activities will not come to the promotion manager automatically. He must *create* information flows which feed back to him the data he needs for decision making. The manager of Smith's counted the inventory at the beginning of the campaign. Then he created a special information system to provide him with daily information on the progress of the campaign. Moreover, he designed the checklist to allow him to control not only all sweaters, but men's, women's and children's sweaters within the sweater group.

Corrective action. In a control system, information must be *used.* The promotion manager must study his information feedback and be able to make two kinds of decisions: he must know *when* corrective action is needed, and *what kind* of action is appropriate. On Monday and Tuesday afternoons of the first week of the campaign, the manager of Smith's studied the sweater sales and took no action. On Wednesday he decided to shift the emphasis of the campaign to men's sweaters beginning Friday morning.

Reevaluation. Finally, the manager of promotion needs to know if he is "on the right track" after taking corrective action. Continuing information flows are a necessity because they allow for timely corrective action and for evaluation of the outcome of the actions taken. The shift in campaign emphasis to men's sweaters dictated by Wednesday's information was evaluated by sales data on succeeding days; as a result, the entire campaign was terminated four days early by the manager of Smith's because he felt his goals had been achieved.

Observations about the control process

Three observations are in order as we conclude our overview of the control process. The first is that control is *basic* to *any* management activity. A student who has as his goal passing a course in promotion with a "C" or better may plan to spend six hours a week studying for the course, earn an "F" on the first test (feedback), spend more hours studying (corrective action), and make a "B" on the next test (reevaluation). An industrial salesman must use the control process to meet or exceed his quota (goal). Wherever there is goal-directed activity, there must be control.

The second observation is that control is a *continuous* process. Control is most definitely *not* a year-end activity or a one-shot operation. Promotion managers dare not wait until the end of a year, or campaign, to evaluate their progress toward goals. Continuous evaluation, correction, and reevaluation are necessary. The retail manager did not wait until the end of the two-week campaign; good students do not ignore feedback and rely only upon final grades for control.

Finally, as we have seen, control is an *active* process. The process we have described is anything but the passive perusal of progress reports or profit statements. Promotion managers must be prepared to make decisions as to *when* and *what* corrective action is necessary. The exercise of restraining or directing influence is an active function for the manager to perform.

TYPES OF INFORMATION FOR CONTROL

By now it is apparent that a willingness to take appropriate action on the basis of information available is a prime requirement for effective promotion management. We need to pay special attention, then, to the kinds of information available to help the promotion manager control his function effectively. In our analysis, we will classify the types of information in three ways: (1) by the type of information or measure, (2) by the timing of the information, and (3) by the nature of the research design that generates the information. While more elaborate breakdowns might be suitable for an intensive study of promotion evaluation, these broad categories will help us explore the variety of information without getting bogged down in the subject.

By type of measure

A most obvious classification of information is that of grouping measures of similar type or kind. A cost ratio, for example, is essentially the same whether we are measuring advertising costs, personal selling costs, or direct labor costs in the production department. Breaking information down into types suggests the following subdivisions of interest to promotion managers: sales, market share, cost ratios, performance ratios, awareness measures, and attitude measures.

Sales. Measures of sales, in either dollars or units, are commonly used in business. Even the smallest firm, with the least sophisticated accounting system, will have some record of sales. *Total sales* are the simplest form of this measure. If the firm sells more than one product, then total sales by products is the next most commonly used sales measure.

Another analysis of total sales is to compare *this* year's figure with the sales for the same period of *preceding* years. A decline in July sales of product Q may not be significant if comparison with past sales data suggests a normal seasonal slump for this product in the summer. The past year's data provides some basis for interpreting the current information.

Another variation on the use of total sales data is to compare *actual* sales data with *forecast* sales or quotas. Salesman Jones may sell $200,000 worth while salesman Smith sells $500,000 worth; how do we evaluate these men? If our planning included forecast sales by territory or sales-man, we might compare these sales figures with the expected or planned sales. Thus, Jones may have sold 120 percent of his expected sales while Smith's $500,000 was only 85 percent of what was expected of him.

Manufacturers and wholesalers find analysis of sales by customer es-pecially helpful. The experience of a great many firms is that a minority of the *number* of customers accounts for a majority of sales revenue. The data in Table 17–1, while hypothetical, will help illustrate this kind

TABLE 17–1. Sales analysis by customer

| Customer | Sales | Cumulative percent: | |
		Of customers	Of sales
A..............	$ 300,000	10%	30%
B..............	300,000	20	60
C..............	200,000	30	80
D..............	100,000	40	90
E..............	30,000	50	93
F..............	20,000	60	95
G..............	15,000	70	96.5
H..............	15,000	80	98
I..............	10,000	90	99
J..............	10,000	100	100
Total.....	$1,000,000		

of analysis of sales. In Table 17–1 a firm which has only 10 customers has listed them from largest to smallest. Next, cumulative percentages have been computed for both number of customers and dollar sales volume. Thus customers A, B, and C represent 30 percent (3/10) of the number of customers, but they represent 80 percent ($800,000/$1,000,000) of the sales volume for this firm.

Any information that predicts a decline in sales to customers A or B would form the basis for far more "corrective action" than a potential decline in sales to customers H or I. Like our past year's sales data, analysis by customer provides a basis for interpreting current information.

Market share. Although analyses of sales are important measures for control purposes, they are essentially inward looking. Even if the firm has increased its dollar sales in every major category, there may still be cause for concern. Why? Because it may not be keeping pace with the total market growth. The firm may be growing in sales dollars but declining in market share. Market share is usually expressed as a percentage that compares the total sales of the firm with total sales for the entire industry or product category. If a company's sales are $100,000 this year and total industry sales are $500,000, then we would say this firm has a 20 percent share of the market (100/500). If the company's sales increased to $110,000 next year, but industry sales rose to $611,000, the firm would have lost some of its share of the market, for the new market share percentage would be only 18 percent.

If data are available on total industry sales by region or territory, similar market share figures may be prepared for these submarkets. Indeed, it is often quite necessary to do so. The total share-of-market figure may conceal some important details in local market performance. One soap manufacturer, for example, was satisfied with his market share nationally but became concerned when regional breakdowns indicated a steady erosion of market share in the West Coast markets. The corrective action in this instance turned out to be a product change to adapt to water hardness in these markets.

A firm may prepare total market share data using its own sales records in combination with total industry sales as collected by the trade association, government, or some other external source. Finding information to allow market share computation on a regional or local basis is more difficult. Two major commercial market research firms do prepare such information, however, and deserve mention. The A. C. Nielsen Company prepares market share reports on the basis of a regular audit of store inventories and purchase invoices in a sample of food, drug, and variety stores. The purchaser of this service is told the market share for his brand or brands by type of store, region of the country, and other broad categories. The Market Research Corporation of America (MRCA) collects market share data from a panel of housewives who record their weekly purchases in a diary.

Proponents of the Nielsen reports stress the accuracy of the actual store audits on which they are based and the fact that the data collected are not subject to memory error or faulty reporting by untrained housewives. Proponents of the MRCA method note that MRCA includes one major food chain omitted in Nielsen samples and stress the fine breakdowns available from MRCA data. MRCA may compute market share by type of household, occupation of husband, or any of a number of methods using the diary method. One additional benefit from its household diary data is the possibility of analyzing repeat purchases and brand loyalty. Whichever approach is used, however, the important measure—share of market—is computed. And as we have seen, share-of-market percentages are a most useful type of information for evaluation and control.

Both sales and market share data are commonly used to evaluate total marketing programs. There are a number of reasons, as we shall discover, why these are not generally successful approaches to the evaluation of specific components of the market or promotion mixes.

Cost ratios. A cost ratio or expense ratio is a figure that expresses the relation between the activity being measured and sales. The convention is to use net sales dollars as the base for computing such percentages in marketing analysis. Sales expense as a percent of sales is a common example. If personal selling expense generally runs 12 percent of sales for firms our size in our industry, the information that our sales expenses are 18 percent may require some corrective action. Further investigation, of course, into the causes or need for such a high ratio would be in order before taking any action. Advertising expenditures as a percent of sales is another common measure employed. As noted in the preceding chapter, this figure may even become the basis for advertising appropriations in many firms.

How do you decide that this percentage, or that percentage, is "out of line" and a cause for concern? We have hinted at one approach: compare with industrywide percentages. These operating ratios by size of firm are typically gathered and published by trade associations or university research bureaus and are a helpful guide to interpreting the firm's information. Another very useful guide is to compare current percentages or ratios with past ratios from the firm. The procedure may take this form:

1. Compute the percentage for a number of periods (months or quarters, typically).
2. Array the ratios from the past 5 to 10 years from highest to lowest.
3. Establish the midpoint of this array and locate the dividing lines between the upper and lower quarters of the ratios collected.
4. Construct a chart with the midpoint and quarters marked on it.
5. Plot current percentages on this chart, using as tolerance limits the upper and lower quarters (quartiles).

For example, suppose you had computed the sales expense percent for your product for the past 10 years, with these results: 16.5, 15.0, 12.0, 14.0, 15.0, 11.5, 11.0, 10.2, 11.3, and 11.4 percent. If you now array these from highest to lowest, you can establish the upper and lower tolerance limits, as Figure 17–1 indicates. Current percentages can be computed and plotted on this chart, as figures for years *w*, *x*, *y*, and *z* were done on Figure 17–1.

The figures for years *w*, *x*, and *y* were all within the range on the chart and occasioned no concern for the manager. When he plots year *Z* on the chart, however, its location may cause him to look into the

FIGURE 17–1.   Construction of tolerance limits and chart of sales expense performance

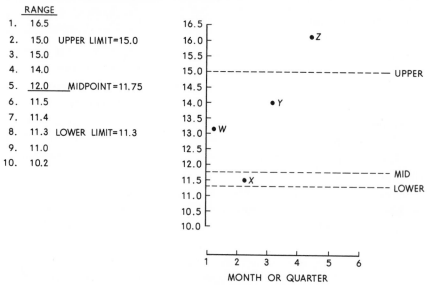

Source: Adapted from M. S. Heidingsfield and Frank Eby, *Marketing and Business Research* (New York: Holt, Rhinehart, and Winston, 1962), chap. 4.

sales expense situation more thoroughly. While our example has been set in terms of years for simplicity's sake, in actual practice a more continuous series (probably by month or quarter) would be prepared.

Ratios are a helpful control device because they convert dollars into relative expressions that can be studied over time. Cost ratios rank as a most important type of information for the evaluation and control of promotion activities.

Performance ratios.   Another useful measure of promotion activity is the performance ratio, which compares output to input. In sales management, for example, a commonly used ratio is the sales/call ratio. The number of calls a salesman makes is divided into the number of sales (note that it is the *number* of completed sales and not their dollar sum) he records in the same time period. Salesman Abernathy, for instance, may have a sales/call ratio of .20, while salesman Bernard's sales/call ratio is .80. The ratio tells us that in five calls Abernathy will make one sale and Bernard, four sales.

In advertising, the purpose of a campaign might be to introduce a new brand name to the market. A measure of the campaign's performance might be the percent of housewives who know the brand name after four weeks. Television rating services provide performance measures of the audience attraction of network programs and of stations within a local market area.

Awareness measures. The promotion manager is also interested in information concerning customer awareness of his product. The goal of a promotion campaign for a new brand or product may be stated in terms of awareness, or more specifically, as the proportion of an audience that has acquired a concept. Surveys of target markets are taken to determine what percentage of the group recognizes the brand name, slogan, product benefit, or whatever element is being tested.

Attitude measures. A final class of information reflects the communication dimension of the promotion task. We are concerned not only with how many people know our brand or product but also with *what they think of it*. If one of the goals of promotion is to increase the positive valence potential customers attach to our brand or product, then attitude measures are an important guide to evaluation of the effort. To measure customer attitudes, however, you must interview a representative group of customers. Such studies take both time and dollars to execute. Their results, on the other hand, are indispensible for assessing the firm's progress toward its communication goals.

An example from the banking industry may help. The marketing officer of a bank once studied the image of his bank held by people in the trading area and discovered that the bank suffered from an old-fashioned, conservative, unfriendly image. A campaign was mounted with the goal of changing the image of the bank in order to make it more attractive to depositors and loan customers. At the conclusion of the campaign, some senior banking officers pointed out that no appreciable increase in savings deposits had resulted from the campaign. The marketing manager, in an effort to provide continuous information for control, had arranged a follow-up study of the bank's image. He was able to cite data to show a positive attitude shift in a significant percent of the population. He also pointed out that in another area of the marketing mix, interest rates paid on savings deposits, their bank was not competitive with other banks. Thus the campaign achieved its attitude goal, but the marketing effort suffered from a price handicap that prevented the bank from achieving its deposit goal.

By timing of information collection

The information available for evaluating the promotion efforts may also be classified according to the timing of the measurement. Certain techniques and measures are available to the promotion manager at different times in the life of a campaign. He may wish to use measures gathered at several times to sharpen the effectiveness of his efforts. Indeed, if continuous flows of information are to be developed, he *must* do so.

Pretesting.   An important time to measure effectiveness is *before* major expenses are incurred and the campaign is launched. Elements of persuasion may be tested on small segments of the market before they are introduced on a mass scale. In advertising, copy and layout tests may be conducted with panels or small groups of typical consumers. We will discuss other pretesting techniques as we consider specific evaluation and control problems for the components of the promotion mix. A final point to note at this time is that pretests or "before" measures are necessary to establish a basis of comparison with later information. The manager of Smith's retail store, for instance, had the beginning inventory against which to measure the sweater campaign's effectiveness. The bank officer had the image data gathered before the campaign was run as a base for evaluating the results of the image campaign.

Concurret testing.   The alert promotion manager seeks information while the promotion efforts are underway. Weekly, or even daily, sales data may be sought in the early stages of a campaign; dealer reorders may be carefully noted. It was through concurrent measures of performance that our retail manager was able to sense when a change in emphasis from all sweaters to men's sweaters was needed. And it was the continuing flow of information that enabled him to save four days' advertising expense by terminating the effort as soon as the goal had been reached.

Posttesting.   Measurements taken after the campaign ends are the third category of information classified by time. The sales that resulted, the ending market share, and the cost and performance ratios discussed earlier in this chapter are most likely computed on a posttest basis. The division of information types into three time dimensions should not imply that there are exclusive techniques for each of these dimensions. To the contrary, many measurement techniques are common to all three time periods.

By nature of research design

Still another way to classify the information used in the evaluation and control process is according to the type of research design or information collection plan being utilized. We look at two broad types: (1) after-only measures, and (2) before-after measures.

After-only measures. As the name implies, the information is collected after something has occurred. That "something" may be the introduction of a new sales compensation plan, a new advertising campaign, or simply shifting scarves from aisle three to aisle five in a retail store. Having taken some action, management decides to "see how it came out." The after-only measure is particularly useful in a new product or new campaign situation. The reason is that in a new situation there is an implied "before" measure of zero. For instance, if a new slogan is being introduced, management may assume that no customer knows the logan until the campaign begins. A survey of housewives taken after some time interval will yield the percent who recognize the new slogan and identify it with the firm's product.

Many of the cost and performance ratios are, by their very nature, after-only measures. At the end of a week, month, quarter, or year the measure is computed. The first application of any information technique is in a sense an after-only measure because all that went before in the life of the company and its promotion may have influenced the measure obtained.

Before-after measures. Much more desirable are information flows that permit measurement before and after a promotion activity. Because of the continuous need for information, most firms make before-after measures available to management. If you stop and think about it, the regular use of after-only measures results in a before-after series because last year's "after-only" measure becomes the "before" measure for this year's effort.

Serious application of before-after measurement of promotion activities helps overcome some of the problems of measuring marketing effort caused by external factors. For example, suppose a manufacturer wants to evaluate some point-of-purchase promotion material for his cooked cereal. He can introduce the material in retail stores and measure the resulting sales as an after-only measure. Or he can measure sales for two weeks before any point-of-purchase materials are installed, then take an after measure of cereal sales covering two weeks after installation. But so many other factors may be at work. To name a few: Competitors may have raised prices, shifting sales to his cooked cereal as a result of price and not point-of-purchase effectiveness. Competitors may have started a heavy ad campaign coupled with a price decrease, to the end that his loss of sales should not be blamed on point-of-purchase materials. The weather may have simply turned cold so that consumers ate more cooked cereal. In carefully designed before-after measures these "other factors" can be largely accounted for by using two stores, or two groups of stores, in which to test the materials.

The manufacturer will select two stores of equal sales in the same city so as to control for weather, competitors' market mixes, economic conditions, and so on. In both stores he will take "before" measures of cereal sales. In only one of the stores will he install the point-of-purchase material to be tested. At the end of some weeks, he will measure sales in both stores. The results may look something like those given in Table 17–2.

TABLE 17–2. Before-after measurement of a store promotion problem

	Control store	Experimental store
Sales before test...............	100	100
Point-of-purchase materials......	(no)	(yes)
Sales after test................	110	130
Change.......................	+10	+30
Net change...................	—	+20

From the table we note that sales rose from 100 boxes per week to 130 boxes per week in the store which featured the new point-of-purchase materials. But note also that sales rose to 110 boxes per week in the control store. We may conclude that the point-of-purchase materials caused an increase in sales of 20 boxes a week (the 30 in the experimental store *less* the 10 which the control store suggests would have happened anyway).

Before-after measurement is a natural outgrowth of continuous information collection. Its benefits are a sharpening of the evaluation of specific promotion practices and a clearer interpretation of the current information.

EVALUATION AND CONTROL OF PERSONAL SELLING

We are now ready to explore some specific evaluation and control techniques. Beginning with *personal selling* and continuing with *advertising* and *sales promotion*, our discussion will be divided according to the three-way time dimension suggested earlier in this chapter.

We have not included a separate discussion of evaluation and control of *indirect* promotion because many of the techniques discussed for the other three promotional elements are potentially useful for this one, and the reader deserves to be spared the obvious duplication that would be involved in a separate treatment.

Pretest information

Some evaluation and control of the personal selling efforts of a firm can take place before salesmen are allowed to come into contact with buyers. Selecting salesmen is, in a sense, a step in exercising control over the input to the firm's selling effort, because it seeks to screen out undesirable individuals and potentially ineffective sales techniques. In addition, limited field testing of new approaches or policies can be considered a pretest information source.

Selection control. Training salesmen is expensive; companies may invest from $5,000 to $20,000 in each salesman before he actually begins to sell in the field. Evaluation and control of personal selling, therefore, must begin with the recruitment and selection procedures used to insure that the investment in sales training is worthwhile. There are various approaches to this aspect of control. Some firms study the characteristics (age, education, experience, height, marital status, and so on) of their best and worst salesmen to attempt to provide some selection guidelines in the hiring of sales trainees. Another approach is the use of psychological tests of aptitude and interest. Information from the applicant's test performance, in addition to other normal selection procedures of application and interview, may help screen out bad risks. The goal of all these approaches is to insure that men recruited for sales training are likely to complete the training program successfully and become productive salesmen.

Sales technique evaluation. During the course of a salesman's training, evaluation of his progress and sales competence takes place. Role playing, in which the trainee attempts to sell either another trainee or an experienced salesman, is one approach to evaluating his progress. Supervised sales calls may also be used; here the trainee actually calls on a customer accompanied by an experienced salesman or manager. Field-testing of prepared sales presentations are often used to select one so-called "canned" sales talk for novice salesmen to use.

Management policy evaluation. The sales manager may select one or two districts or territories in which to test new compensation plans, new expense report forms, or other administrative procedures before introducing them to the total sales force. Through the use of a before-after approach, the performance of men in these test territories after the new idea is introduced is compared to their performance under the prior system.

Concurrent information

Evaluation and control of personal selling should, like any other control process, be continuous. Year-end reports are useful, but effective evaluation and control depends upon continuous feedback of information on which progress may be judged. The management of personal selling can be most effective when regular flows of information are established back from the field to the manager's office.

Report analysis. In our earier discussion of sales management in Chapter 6, the use of daily and weekly call reports by salesmen was mentioned. These reports provide a vital information flow for concurrent analysis and evaluation of sales efforts. These reports may be used at two levels of management. They may become the basis for evaluating the salesman through computation of sales/call ratios and sales/expense ratios; they may also become the basis for broader assessment of the total selling effort. What a single salesman sees as an isolated event may appear to promotion managers as another link in an emerging pattern of sales activity. For instance, the information that salesman Roberts' sales are running above quota in all product lines except line X may suggest that Roberts needs to pay more attention to line X; but if *all* salesmen seem to be having trouble with X this year, or if all salesmen in a particular region are falling below quota on this product, further investigation would be called for.

Field trips and follow-ups. Sales managers need to go out into the field and travel with salesmen from time to time to evaluate the performance of each man and to keep in personal touch with the marketplace. Sales manager–salesman calls are not confined just to new or novice salesmen; they are often necessary on a continuing basis. Customers appreciate the personal attention of the sales manager. A variation is for the sales manager to call by telephone shortly after a salesman's call to see if the customer has any complaints or needs any further service. In this manner he can learn customer complaints while they are fresh and at the same time check on his salesman's performance. When such

FIGURE 17–2. Salesmen's reports provide a means of control

DISTRICT
Salesman's Name

WEEKLY CALL RECORD

FOR WEEK ENDING________

	THIS WEEK	YEAR TO DATE
TOTAL CALLS		
SPECIAL REPORTS		

CUSTOMER	AMH	FMG	CITY	DATE	Special Report	COMMENT

99.080 REV. 9-64
SALESMAN'S COPY ☐
REGIONAL V.P. COPY ☐
GEN. SALES COPY ☐

Initialed By ________ DSM

follow-up calls are planned, salesmen should be informed in advance as a matter of good faith.

Retailing offers a somewhat unique opportunity for concurrent testing of personal selling efforts. Many retail managers have their stores "shopped" as a check on selling effectiveness. This involves hiring professional shoppers to visit the store, act as ordinary consumers, buy or look at merchandise, and then file a report on the quality of the selling, treatment, and service they encountered. One manufacturer of carpets hired a nationwide team of shoppers to evaluate the selling efforts of retail carpet salesmen and their knowledge of the manufacturer's new fiber currently being advertised. The information was so alarming that the manufacturer introduced a training program for retail sales personnel at once in order to improve the effectiveness of the remainder of the introductory promotion campaign.

Posttest information

A number of types of information may be gathered and analyzed quarterly, at year-end, or at the conclusion of a campaign. One obvious comparison is actual sales versus forecast sales by lines and territories. Comparison of actual and budgeted expenses is another analysis that is commonly done on a posttest basis.

Ratio analysis. Computation of a number of ratios on a posttest basis is feasible. Sales/call and sales/expense ratios (often on a concurrent basis as we noted) are examples. These are often computed for purposes of annual review of both salesmen and sales programs.

Quota attainment. The quotas by product, customer, and territory that evolved in the last planning stages may now be used in posttest evaluation. Sophisticated systems of sales control information provide each salesman and his sales manager with a statement of performance which lists the various quotas and the actual performance. An index of attainment can be computed for easy analysis and interpretation.

Returns and complaints. A most useful posttest evaluation is the analysis of returned merchandise and customer complaints. In retailing, returned goods may result from such causes as improper sales advice, from poor buying of goods to sell, or from sheer customer whim. An unusually large amount of returned goods in any one department, however, may signal a need to investigate the operation of that department. Complaints from customers are another check on the quality of the sales effort. Salesmen out in the field may be promising too much either in performance of products or in delivery and service. Study of complaints may well be classed as a concurrent information approach, but a tally of total complaints by salesman for a year is a useful check on the salesman's performance. We should note, however, that the *absence* of complaints may not automatically indicate that high-quality selling is being done. The other measures of quota attainment and ratio analysis are better indicators on the positive side of the evaluation of personal selling.

Turnover. When the number of salesmen leaving the company is excessive, corrective action may be necessary. Recalling the cost of training a salesman to a productive level, excessive turnover means that this

FIGURE 17–3. By changing the postal box number in the last sentence, response to this specific ad can be measured

Love and Marriage and a job!

Today's couples with a marriage and two jobs are on a tight schedule. Happily, the old-fashioned labels "man's work" and "woman's work" are relaxing—to make life easier for husband *and* wife. By working together, planning ahead and taking advantage of shortcuts, the working couple makes a loving partnership of marriage. Here are a few ideas that'll keep your kitchen a smooth-running part of your busy lives.

Start breakfast the night before. A good breakfast *is* important— no matter how rushed you are. But how to add interest to the quick "juice/toast/milk" routine? Bake apples while supper's cooking, basting them with maple syrup! Next morning surround them with TOTAL and milk. Why TOTAL? It's the whole-wheat cereal with more vitamins than any other!

A little bit of home in a bag—that's what a lunch should be. Make your sandwiches and desserts on the weekend and freeze them. Brownies are always a favorite. Give yours a personal touch by folding ½ cup cookie coconut into our Fudge Brownies before baking. You'll find them extra moist and chewy. Then, each day, think up a special "little extra." Tuck in a few SLIM JIMS, for example. They're cellophane-wrapped sticks of spicy dried beef. Or, fill a plastic bag with ONYUMS. They're our zesty new snack that looks and tastes just like crisp onion rings!

A girl can have a hard day at the office, too. So why not teach your husband a few "masculine specialties" he can fix on those— hopefully—rare occasions! We've just introduced 5 wonderful new Betty Crocker Serving Sauces that would make an easy beginning: Hollandaise, Bordelaise, Cheese, Newburg and Mushroom. Keep them on hand for everything from Fish Sticks Newburg to Burgers Bordelaise. They're quick and delicious. (And he'll probably pretend he's slaved for hours!)

This little pig went to market. She's the symbol for our budget-minded Betty Crocker *Piggy Bank Recipes*. Watch for her economical meal ideas on General Mills packages. You'll find her on packages of our Potato Buds, Au Gratin and Scalloped Potatoes right now!

That *man* in your kitchen. For a treasury of fun recipes for Him—*and* Her, send for our FREE booklet, *Cooking for Two by Two*. It features great meals you do together. Write Betty Crocker of General Mills, Box 248D, 400 2nd Avenue South, Minneapolis, Minnesota 55460.*

*Offer expires June 30, 1970

Betty Crocker

OF GENERAL MILLS

training investment is being lost. High turnover may be a result of faulty selection, improper training, inadequate compensation plans, indifferent sales management, or some combination of any or all of these. Annual turnover rates may be computed (1) for each sales district as a means of evaluating the district manager, and (2) for the company as a whole as a means of evaluating total corporate personal selling management.

The discussion of the evaluation and control of personal selling has divided the measures or types of information according to the timing of the measure. It should be stressed that this listing is neither complete nor perfectly exclusive. Information we have listed under one time class may be used in another from company to company, or in special situations. The methods employed by promotion managers may include other types of information not discussed in this brief statement. We hope, however, that the variety and nature of information to aid in the control process of this activity have been indicated.

EVALUATION AND CONTROL OF ADVERTISING

Our discussion of specific evaluation and control procedures continues with a look at some measures of advertising effectiveness. Again, we will be looking at measures grouped according to the time at which they are most commonly used. If an advertiser is to avoid defective or weak ads, if year after year he is to raise the effectiveness of his advertising, if he is to accumulate a satisfactory fund of advertising knowledge, then he has no option but to attempt to engage in testing and evaluating. There is often a wide range of quality between two ads which cost the same amount of money. If the advertiser can select the more effective of the two before they are run, his ad dollars will be more effectively invested.

Advertising research is indicated for just about every facet of advertising. Here are five appropriate subjects for research:

Ads (benefits, illustrations, copy, etc.)
Media (types, features, audiences, etc.)
Scheduling (frequency, position, space or time units, etc.)
Budgeting (flexibility, reserve policy, allocation, etc.)
Campaigns (themes, length, types, etc.)

Because this is an *introduction* to promotion management, we must limit our discussion to the more common methods of evaluation and control of advertising.

Pretest information

Because advertising campaigns often involve expenditures ranging into millions of dollars, and because they often support sales of hundreds of millions, there is great incentive for promotion managers to use a variety of measures in the pre-exposure stages of advertising.

Checklists.   This approach to evaluation measures a proposed ad against a checklist of characteristics. First, the researcher must make a master list or inventory of features or elements believed to be present in productive ads. The list may include such traits as attention value, conviction value, or memory value. Or, it may consist of questions like these: Is the ad clear? Believable? Persuasive? Or, again, it may involve such readability standards as length of words, phrases, and sentences, or the number of personal words (you, they, our, etc.) used. The composer of the list decides what items to include, *and* what weight (15 points, 10 points, etc.) ought to be given each item.

In operation, a proposed ad is put in the hands of the composer of the checklist, he scores the ad and its elements against the list, and he indicates where the ad should be strengthened. Obviously, then, checklist testing is only as sound as the person who originates the list and makes the evaluation.

Consumer juries.   In this technique a group of prospects is asked to react to two or more ads. They rank the ads in order of quality or performance. In earlier years simple "like-dislike" questions were put to the jury to measure its reaction. More sophisticated attitude measures are now available to help the researcher probe the response of each jury member to the ads. Critics of the technique wonder if the jury members change character when they grade ads, ceasing to be ordinary consumers and playing the role of "advertising expert and critic." Proponents of the technique argue that with careful selection of jury members and with the use of more sophisticated attitude measures applied to a series of ads to be tested, the results do provide the advertiser with meaningful reactions and fill some of the feedback gap in the communication process.

Eye-camera studies.   A technique for evaluating layout and impact of printed ads uses an eye camera to study the movements and changes of a consumer's eyes as he examines an ad. Some of these studies use motion pictures to follow the eyes' path through the ad as a check on the structure of the layout. More recent developments include a camera which records the pupil dilation of the subject as he views the ad, an outgrowth of psychological studies which indicate that pupil dilation is strongly associated with degree of emotional involvement in the subject matter being viewed. Again, the sampling problem is acute, as critics of this method point out. Viewing an ad through a complex optical measuring device is, they charge, a most unusual circumstance that is so far removed from the normal exposure conditions as to invalidate the findings. Proponents of the technique reply that they are seeking to improve structural components and to select among approaches, and that these techniques give information which is both useful and otherwise unattainable.

Computer analysis of media.   Selection of a mix of ad media is a difficult task. Some advertising agencies and researchers have begun to develop computer programs to select optimum combinations of media according to some specified list of goals. The computer is fed data on circulation, audience characteristics, cost per page (or minute, or whatever the appropriate cost measure), and the goals of the advertising campaign (minimize cost, maximize exposure, minimize duplication). The computer then attempts to select the best combination of media for the dollars available.

Test runs.   Just as some sales presentations and some point-of-purchase items are pretested before being used nationally, so advertising may be pretested in small runs. Alternative versions of a newspaper ad, for example, may be run in an attempt to discover which ad gets the best results (measured by telephone calls, orders, coupons mailed in, or some similar response measure). Examples of the variables which could be tested are the benefit to promise buyers, the media to use, the intensity of the advertising scheduled. Take intensity. Two test markets and two control markets might be chosen. Assume the advertiser has a 10 percent share of the market in all four markets. In one test market he may run a television commercial 5 times per week, and in the other he runs it 10 times per week. If he finds no significant change in the 5-per-week test market but a jump to 20 percent of the market in the 10-per-week market, he may feel justified to go national on a 10-per-week frequency in all television markets he serves.

Concurrent information

In our discussion of communication process in Chapter 4, we noted that the advertiser might be weeks, months, or even forever removed from feedback in response to his communications. Concurrent information techniques are designed to shorten the feedback process and allow corrective action to be initiated quickly—even during the course of an advertising campaign if necessary.

Coincidental surveys. Broadcast advertising efforts are subject to a special type of concurrent measure which uses a telephone survey technique. A sample of households is selected, calls are made during the time period the advertiser's program is being aired, questions as to listening or viewing are asked, and the results are tallied to show the share of audience the advertiser is reaching. In addition to asking whether or not the program (either radio or television) is being received at the household, the survey may also ask the number watching or listening and may seek to find out if the respondent can identify the advertiser or brand sponsoring the broadcast. The major limitation of the technique is that it excludes households which do not have a telephone listed, a bias against lower-income families which may be both listening to the program *and* appropriate target customers of the advertiser.

Diaries and recall surveys. Two other survey-type measures of broadcast media deserve our attention. The diary method consists of a log or diary of daily listening or viewing kept by a sample of households. In the diary the respondent records the time, station, program viewed, and number and ages of people attending the broadcast. The diaries are mailed in weekly, with participants being paid either cash or trading stamps for their prompt and regular participation. The technique, according to its critics, is subject to memory and literacy bias. But according to its proponents, it affords a more precise evaluation of the type of audience being attracted than does instrument measure.

Recall surveys are made the day following a broadcast. Respondents are asked to identify the programs listened to or viewed from a list of programs scheduled on all stations in the area. The interviewer determines that the respondent has a set in working order and that it was used sometime during the past 24 hours, then shows the respondent the program listing from the daily paper and asks that programs be checked or circled on the schedule if they were attended.

Instruments. Measuring devices attached to radio and television sets collect concurrent information about broadcast media which is subsequently analyzed and reported to advertisers. The best known of these is the Audimeter, a patented device of the A. C. Nielsen Company. The Audimeter records on a paper disk or tape what times the set is turned on, to what station or frequency, when changes in channel or

FIGURE 17–4. Sometimes audience ratings can be the subject of promotion

The CBS Television Network ranks far ahead of both of its competitors by every significant measure of daytime audience leadership. In 1961 it has achieved ★

■ Television's biggest average daytime audiences–15% greater than NBC... 91% greater than ABC ■ More of the most popular daytime shows than the other two networks combined ■ As many daytime shows reaching three million or more families as the other two networks combined. CBS–10...NBC–9...ABC–1 ■ The biggest average audience in more quarter-hour periods than the other two networks combined. CBS wins in 18...NBC in 13...and ABC in 4 quarter hours.

Women, the members of the family who do most of the buying, concentrate their daytime viewing between 10 am and 5 pm. This is known as "Housewife Television." This year, during these hours, the CBS Television Network has delivered:†
■ The biggest audience of the nation's women. 23% greater than NBC...166% greater than ABC ■ The biggest average audience of the nation's housewives. 22% more than NBC...166% more than ABC ■ The biggest average audience of young women (age 18-39). 23% more than NBC...and 135% more than ABC.

When it comes to cost, the CBS Television Network also ranks best, delivering★
■ The lowest cost-per-thousand homes of any network. CBS–$1.73...NBC–$1.91 ...ABC–$1.79 ■ The lowest cost-per-thousand women of any network. CBS–$1.78 ...NBC–$2.12...ABC–$2.39 ■ The lowest cost-per-thousand housewives of any network. CBS–$2.06...NBC–$2.39...ABC–$2.75 ■ The lowest cost-per-thousand young women (age 18-39) of any network. CBS–$4.68...NBC–$5.31...ABC–$5.59.

These are compelling facts for any advertiser whose products are bought by the nation's housewives. Self-service dealers of the nation rate daytime television first over five other advertising media. And, for the fifth consecutive year, housewives of the nation rate the CBS Television Network first in daytime television.

In sum, the most efficient and effective way to move your products through the nation's checkout counters is to advertise to your women customers on the daytime schedule of the CBS Television Network.

★ Audience data: National NTI; 7 am—6 pm, Monday-Friday, January 1-June 1, 1961.

† Audience data: available ARB audience composition figures applied to National Nielsen AA homes reached; 10 am— 5 pm, Monday-Friday, January 1-June 1, 1961.

★ Audience data: available ARB audience composition figures applied to National Nielsen AA homes and costs; 10 am— 5 pm, Monday-Friday, January 1- April 11, 1961.

frequency occur, and when the set is turned off. At frequent intervals the paper record is returned to Nielsen and a new one inserted by the set owner. Proponents of this source of information note that actual set usage is recorded and that that information is not subject to memory error or deliberate distortion by respondents. Critics of the technique argue that the sample is too small, that the set may be turned on although no one is in the room watching or listening, and that no measure of the number of viewers is gathered.

A more exotic instrument measure is available in certain major metropolitan areas where a sample of sets is connected to a central compuer that provides minute-by-minute measure of audience shares throughout the course of the broadcast day. Another approach is to use a roving truck equipped with electronic equipment capable of sensing television sets turned on and the channel to which they are tuned. These latter two techniques are not as common as the other measures we have discussed, but they do provide measures of broadcast advertising that are even more concurrent than the others.

Sales or inquiry logs. We have already encountered this technique in our example of Smith's Family Store earlier in this chapter. A tally of sales resulting from a campaign, or of inquiries stemming from ads, may be kept as a concurrent measure of advertising effectiveness. An industrial ad may contain a coupon keyed to the ad which can be used by buyers to request more information about the product or service. A tally of these inquiries according to the ad and medium provides concurrent measures of both ad design (if different ads are being run) and media (if the same ad is being run in several business publications). Direct-action retail ads and mail-order advertising are also likely to be checked by this technique. Where broadcast media were used, a count of telephone sales or calls to a number mentioned in the ad is a similar use of the technique.

Traffic counts. A final concurrent measure which deserves mention is the count of traffic passing by a display or outdoor advertising location. Observers stationed near the location count traffic passing the site in an oncoming direction as a measure of the exposure potential of the outdoor display. A variation is to substitute a movie camera and analyze the pictures for not only the number of cars passing the site but also the number of passengers who seem to be looking in the direction of the sign.

Concurrent measures of advertising are limited, for the most part, either to broadcast media or to direct-action advertising which bids for

FIGURE 17–5. Award-winning outdoor posters selected by posttest evaluation of expert jury

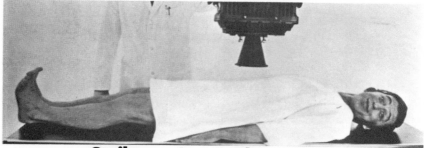

an observable response. This, of course, excludes much of the advertising effort in printed media.

Posttest information

Continuing along the time dimension, we come to information gathered after the advertising effort. Before discussing specific approaches, we repeat the observation that classification of a technique into "concurrent" or "posttest" categories is for the most part arbitrary. Under some circumstances the same technique may be used for both time periods. These measures are classified according to their common usage, but the reader is urged to remember that variations in use of information are frequent and appropriate. For example, the broadcast surveys we discussed as a concurrent measure may be used as a posttest measure as well. The advertiser may use an *average* of the concurrent weekly measures as a posttest summary measure to compare against similar averages of competing firms or past averages of his own firm.

Readership surveys.   There are two research techniques based on the readership of ads. One, the *recognition technique,* is a procedure made famous by the Starch Advertisement Readership Service. The Service measures readership of ads in consumer magazines, selected business magazines, and occasional issues of selected daily newspapers. Interviewing on weekly consumer magazines begins three days after the issue appears on newsstands and continues for seven days. After establishing that the respondent has received and looked through the issue being surveyed, the interviewer asks, of every large ad in the publication, "Did you see or read any part of this ad?" A "Yes" to this question places the reader in the "Noted" classification for that ad. If the reader saw or read any part of the ad which clearly indicates the brand or advertiser, he is placed in the "Seen-Associated" category. Finally, if he read at least one half of the copy, he is also counted in the "Read-Most" category. For each issue surveyed the Starch Service computes cost ratios which allow the advertiser to compare the performance of his ad against the average of all ads in that issue. Thus, an ad with a "Read-Most" cost ratio of 125 attracted 25 percent more readers per dollar in the "Read-Most" category than the average ad in the issue being studied.

The other readership research method is referred to as *aided recall.* It, too, involves memory; and it makes greater demands on the reader than does the recognition technique. In aided recall, the interviewer shows a magazine's cover to the reader, then asks the reader to recall those ads he remembers having seen in that issue. The reader does not see the ads during the interview. The interviewer may mention brand names or advertisers' names in this issue, he may ask which the reader remembers, and of those remembered he may ask, "What did the ad look like? What did it say?" Ads are seldom remembered unless there was penetration, unless there was grasp, acceptance, and association in the reader's mind.

We classify both recognition and recall readership surveys as a posttest information source for a number of reasons. First, they are clearly gathered days or even weeks (in the case of monthly magazines) after the publication of the ads. More importantly, however, sellers of readership services urge advertisers to use the information over time. The percentages from one particular issue may be clouded by the size of that issue (more ads competing near Christmas than in midsummer), by the nature of competing editorial matter, by respondent fatigue, or by any of a number of factors. The pattern of ad readership over time, on the other hand, may provide measures of competitive advertising performance when the firm compares the performance of its ads with those of similar products in the same medium. Readership data becomes useful, then, only after some months of continuous collection and study.

Split run.   The split-run technique is useful in printed media for testing different ad approaches. We list it as a posttest technique because the responses are measured after the ads are run. But we must recognize that this is a very important *pre*test device to select ads which will be run on a nationwide scale after the results of the split-run are analyzed. Suppose a newspaper or magazine is able to print an advertiser's ad A in one half of an issue and his ad B in the other half. The ads contain an offer of information by coupon, keyed so that the advertiser knows which ad is prompting the request for information. The one half of the circulation receiving ad A do not know the existence of ad B, and the same is true of those getting copies containing ad B. The split is evenly distributed throughout the entire issue so that if 100 copies come into a certain market, 50 contain ad A and 50 contain ad B. If ad A stresses comfort and draws 200 requests but ad B, stressing attractiveness to the opposite sex draws 500 replies, the advertiser would hardly choose comfort as the benefit to promise in a large-scale campaign.

The outstanding merit of split run is the freezing of so many variables. The two ads appear in the same issue of the same publication, in the same position on the same page, on the same day, affected by the same news and weather. A number of newspapers offer the advertiser an assortment of splits in any issue for the purpose of testing and evaluating advertising approaches.

EVALUATION AND CONTROL OF PROMOTION

With as many types of sales promotion activities as there are in modern marketing, we do not propose to attempt to list common evaluation techniques or information types. The reader should, by now, have a feel for the variety of approaches used in personal selling and in advertising. We will discuss, instead, a sampling of information sources and evaluation approaches and trust that the reader will see potential application of other measures discussed under personal selling and advertising to the problems of evaluating sales promotion activities.

Pretest information

Sales promotion plans and proposals are pretested for the same reason that other elements in the promotion mix are pretested: to help improve efficiency and reduce costs. If more persuasive sales promotion techniques can be developed through pretesting, management hopes that full-scale campaigns can be made more productive.

Test mailings. The user of direct mail often tests sample pieces of campaign material on short lists, compares the response, and then selects the leading response puller. Test mailings of standard direct-mail literature can also be used to evaluate mailing lists. In conducting a test mailing, the advertiser tries to use exactly the same material he hopes to use in the full-scale campaign, and he sends it to a random sample of names from the actual mailing list he plans to use. The attempt is to create exactly the same conditions, but on a smaller scale, as will prevail when a full mailing occurs. Attention must be paid, therefore, to the day, week, and season of the sample mailing, to insure that representative conditions hold true for the test. If several ideas are to be tested, then a split-run approach is used. Every other name, or every third name, or some other interval depending upon the variations being tried, is selected from the same mailing list. The mailings are keyed (by box number or department code) and responses tallied.

Test markets. The test market, which we mentioned under personal selling and under advertising, is another technique suitable for other forms of promotion. In sales promotion, it is a most useful approach because sales promotion often depends upon all the promotional forces available to the firm. If a firm can select a control city and a test city, then before-after testing of the effectiveness of its sales promotion plans is possible. Suppose a firm wishes to test a cents-off coupon offer. Holding everything else equal in the two cities (and everything includes such factors as national ads, price, shelf positions, point-of-purchase displays), the cents-off coupons may be distributed in the test city by mail, in a newspaper ad, or however the firm plans to do so. Store audits can be arranged in both cities to check the impact on sales, and sales can be measured to assess the effect of the coupon offer. With two test cities, the firm could explore mail distribution of coupons versus coupons in newspaper ads as a means of stimulating sales. The existence of the control city provides a basis for interpreting sales. In a single test city, with no control, split-run approaches can be used to pretest premium offers or other promotional ideas

Concurrent information

The concurrent checks on sales promotion activity are equally varied. In sales contest, for example, a daily ranking may be computed, both for control and for salesman-stimulation purposes. In direct-mail promotions, the rate of returned cards or inquiries may be posted daily and compared against rates of return in prior campaigns. Numbers of entries received in consumer contests may be tallied and used as a measure of the appeal of the contest theme and promotion.

Other concurrent information collection may include a periodic accounting of the percent of cooperative advertising funds being utilized by class of store or region of the country. If one region or store type seems to be falling below planned levels, additional merchandising of ad campaigns may be in order. If the data indicate that retailers are using all their cooperative funds in the last month of a campaign, when management wishes these funds used throughout the campaign, this information may signal a need for review of cooperative contracts and plans.

In trade shows and exhibitions concurrent measures include counts of traffic past the exhibit or counts of the number of people registering at the booth for information. In dealer-stimulation campaigns a daily or weekly count of orders received may provide a measure of the impact of the promotion.

Posttest information

After the sales promotion campaign has been executed, the promotion manager will want to have information on the outcome by which he can evaluate the effort. For some campaigns the final count of some of the concurrent measures will suffice: number of inquiries, number of coupons redeemed, number of contest entries, and so on.

Cost ratios may be employed for some promotion efforts. If every consumer who entered a contest has had to enclose a box top or other proof of purchase, the actual sales can be tabulated and related to the cost of the campaign. Many sales promotion activities have longer-range goals, however, and do not lend themselves to precise cost-ratio analysis. Where the campaign has a direct-action goal, and where the action is readily measurable (coupons returned, not sales in a store 2,000 miles away), then costs and returns may be computed with some confidence.

COMPLEXITY OF EVALUATION AND CONTROL

What about *sales?* Here we have listed all these various types of information on which promotion efforts can be evaluated and yet we have not suggested that sales is a good measure for personal selling or for advertising or for sales promotion. There are, sadly, various reasons why sales is not a satisfactory measure of promotion efforts. Some of these are of the firm's own making, others are uncontrollable complications.

Controllable complications

In planning promotional strategies we have emphasized the need for a carefully coordinated promotional mix. The result, of course, is a mixed-up situation that defies precise allocation of sales results. A housewife buys a box of our brand of cake mix in a supermarket. How do we decide that this purchase was the result of a specific promotion activity? Any or all of the following could account for her selection:

1. She saw an ad for the product this morning on TV, in a magazine, in the newspaper, or all three.
2. A point-of-purchase sign attracted her attention.
3. The reusable container strikes her fancy (a package form).
4. She saw an ad for our product last week but just remembered her desire for the product on this shopping trip.
5. The store is offering our brand at a special saving, and the price attracted her purchase.
6. A demonstrator in the store gave her a sample taste of cake made with the product, so she bought some.
7. She received a contest entry blank in the mail and needs a box top.

The list, of course, could continue, but the point is obvious. There usually are many forces at work in our promotion mix, which is a part of our total marketing mix; so any attempt to isolate the contribution of any one factor is virtually hopeless. If only there were some magic yardstick to measure what each form of promotion does to sales volume! Such a measuring technique, in addition to being valid, should also be reliable, speedy in operation, quite simple, and of relatively low cost. While the search for such a technique continues, the odds on success in finding it are not too favorable. And as controllable influences of promotional techniques seem to be increasing in variety, so the problems of measurement are further compounded.

Uncontrollable complications

The measurement of promotion's effects on sales is made even more complicated when we consider the external or uncontrollable factors which may be at work. To cite a few, the housewife may have bought the cake mix because:

1. The store is out of stock of her favorite brand, our competitor's.
2. Our comptitor's quality control slipped and she found a bug in the last box of his brand, so decided to shift.
3. A friend whom she trusts recommended our brand.
4. Our competitor has raised his price, and she always buys the lowest-priced brand.
5. Our competitor's advertising offended her, so she is out to show him who's boss.

Thus the sales of our firm's products are influenced by the entire marketing mix of each of our competitors, by local economic conditions, and by all the other uncontrollable factors we discussed in Chapter 1. Because these influences are sometimes direct, sometimes indirect, the problem of measuring the contributions of our controllable promotion activities is further obscured.

Time-lag complications

A third complicating dimension is the problem of lagged response to promotion efforts. By lagged response we mean the cumulative effect of promotion efforts and the fact that a purchase in a particular time period T may have resulted from promotion efforts in period $T - 1$ or from continuous promotion in many time periods. Stated another way, evaluating promotion efforts is difficult because management tends to use time-specific measures (*this* year's ad expenditures, or *this* specific campaign's cost) while the impact of those expenditures is most often a time-continuous effect.

Images of products and brands form slowly over time. Some consumers may take months in the listing stage or screening and evaluation stage; others may be "sold" on our product but temporarily stuck in the economic frustration of not having funds available to complete the buying cycle. We have noted that these conditions call for continuity of promotion efforts, throughout the year and years. Thus the time-lag problems join the controllable and uncontrollable complications for the seller trying to use sales volume as a measure of promotion effectiveness with any precision or reliability.

Range of possible measures

If not sales as a measure, then what can be said about evaluating promotion efforts? We have discussed a variety of types of information that promotion managers use, collected at different times in the promotion cycle, using different research designs. Between the act "promotion expenditure" and the act "purchase of product," there are several steps which may serve to define a range of possible measures. We will look at the steps, then examine the types of measures appropriate at each point.

Potential exposure. If promotion is to influence buying activity, it must reach prospects. One measure, then, is the potential exposure promotion efforts have. In advertising, circulation data provide such a measure. If magazine X has 5 million readers, we may conclude that the potential exposure of a message in that magazine is 5 million, or we may estimate that three persons will see each delivered copy and estimate potential exposure at 15 million. Estimates of audience share in broadcast media, traffic counts for outdoor media, gross attendance at trade shows, number of customers in a sales territory—all are measures of potential exposure.

Exposure. Managers of promotion know that not every potential prospect will be reached. A more stringent test or measure is the number actually reached by the promotion. In personal selling, number of sales calls is such a measure. In advertising, readership studies like those of

Starch and coincidental telephone surveys for broadcast media attempt to measure actual exposure.

Comprehension. Prospects must not only get the message but must also understand it and associate it with a brand or product. In communication terminology, they must both detect and decode. The buyer must understand and appreciate the salesman's message, the firm's ad, if the message or ad is to influence his buying behavior in the desired fashion. Recall techniques which ask the reader or listener the name of the sponsor or brand and some questions about the message content are attempts to measure comprehension.

Belief. The prospective customer may fully comprehend what the promotion is trying to convey, yet not believe a word of it. He may understand the claims made for a product or service but not be convinced of their truth. A luggage manufacturer, for instance, once ran an ad which showed two full-grown elephants standing on a broad supported by one of the firm's suitcases. Many viewers had no trouble comprehending the scene; they knew that the illustration was attempting to demonstrate the strength of the product. They expressed disbelief, however, by indicating that the suitcase must be full of cement and that this was "just another advertising trick." Promotion must be believed, and the degree to which it is may serve as a measure of effectiveness.

Attitude change. The goal of much promotion is to exert a positive influence on customer attitudes toward company and brand. A measure of the direction and intensity of attitude shifts over time would be useful. Only by extensive personal interviews or use of attitude scales can this result be assessed. Many firms do this on a continuing basis and thus have a series of before-after measures with which they can determine the effect of promotion campaigns on prospects' attitudes.

We have suggested that there is a range of possible measures of promotion effectiveness as follows:

1. Promotion expenditure
   a) Potential exposure
   b) Exposure
   c) Comprehension
   d) Belief
   e) Attitude change
2. Sales

To this list, one further possibility must be mentioned: retention. A housewife may see, comprehend, believe, desire, *and forget.* Many of the recall studies, therefore, are also measuring this retention dimension. Studies of brand awareness or slogan impact are designed to test the retention customers have of the promotion message.

Now, looking back at the range of measures by which promotion efforts can be evaluated, we may conclude that the range is from the relatively easy to the extremely difficult, from inexpensive to expensive, from quickly available to time consuming. As we move down this list, we move from data available from many sources (circulation figures, audience characteristics, etc.) to data that can be provided only by personal interviewing on behalf of the firm itself. This holds true until we come to sales, which again is an internal type of information.

SUMMARY

The control process requires information on which corrective action can be based if goals are to be reached. As control is an active, continuous process, information is needed on a regular, continuing basis. As a measure of the total marketing effectiveness of the firm, sales and market share data may be helpful. There are controllable and uncontrollable complications, however, which in most cases frustrate the use of sales as a specific measure of promotion effectiveness. Other evaluation and control measures have been developed to aid the promotion manager before efforts are launched, during the campaign, and after the effort is concluded. They range from inexpensive estimates of potential customers reached to carefully controlled studies involving extensive personal interviewing before and after a promotion activity is conducted.

QUESTIONS AND PROBLEMS

17–1. Why is control more difficult for a newly established firm than for the long-established enterprise?

17–2. What might make a manufacturer suspect that he is not spending enough for marketing?

17–3. Why would an advertiser prefer a consumer diary to store audit data?

17–4. Some advertisers claim they know which ad dollar produced which sales. How can this be?

17–5. How can retailers evaluate the personal selling their clerks do?

17–6. A firm decides to spend $60,000 for a trade show booth or exhibit. What measures of success can be gathered to defend this expenditure?

17–7.   Is preoccupation with market share dangerous?

17–8.   Prepare a suggested checklist for evaluating a salesman's presentation.

17–9.   A paper company has developed a facial tissue which dissolves completely in water in 10 minutes. They have devised two marketing approaches to this product. One approach stresses the ecological advantages of the dissolving feature; the other stresses the softness and quality of the tissue with only passing mention of the feature. They wish to select only one theme for the final introduction of this product.

17–10.   For the firm in the above question, assume that the ecological theme is selected after appropriate tests. Define some suitable goals for the promotion in the first year of this new product, and suggest how the campaign might be evaluated during and at the end of the year.

INDEX

Index

*This book has been set in 10 and 9 point
Janson, leaded 3 points. Part and chapter numbers are in 10 point Helvetica. Part and chapter titles are in 18 point Helvetica Medium.
The size of the type page is 27 by 44 5/6 picas.*